Musical Truth

Mark Devlin

Musical Truth

Mark Devlin

Paperback Edition First Published in Great Britain
in 2016 by aSys Publishing

eBook Edition First Published in Great Britain
in 2016 by aSys Publishing

ISBN: 978-1-910757-48-2

aSys Publishing
http://www.asys-publishing.co.uk

Acknowledgements

My huge thanks goes out to Robbie Allen for an outstanding job on the cover design, to John Hamer and his razor-sharp eye for the proof-reading, and to Nicola Mackin for her professional guidance through the publishing process.

I would also like to give respectful nods to the work of Vigilant Citizen, Matt Sergiou of Conspiro Media, Lenon Honor, Mark Passio, Freeman Fly, Isaac Weishaupt of Illuminati Watcher and Dave McGowan (R.I.P.,) all of whom have inspired and helped me to make sense of the vast amount of information that went into this volume.

Contents

'MUSICAL TRUTH 2'
IT'S NOT OVER!

It became clear during the writing of this book that a volume two was going to be needed! To have included all of the following in this book would have delayed its release for at least another year. On the way next time, therefore, will be:

- Cymatics and The Science of Sound.

- Mind-manipulation through sound frequencies.

- 432 vs 440hz, and 528hz, the 'Love Frequency.'

- Algorithms and other scientific methods to create the 'perfect' pop song.

- Evidence of the Hidden Hand in the Electronic Dance Music scene.

- The acid house/ rave era of the late 80s; parallels to the 60s hippie scene in narcotic influences and social effects.

- Satanism and the dark occult within Heavy Metal.

FOREWORD FROM THE AUTHOR

"It is proof of a base and low mind for one to wish to think with the masses or majority, merely because the majority is the majority. Truth does not change because it is, or is not, believed by a majority of the people."

Giordano Bruno (1548-1600)

"It's the action, not the fruit of the action, that's important. You have to do the right thing. It may not be in your power, may not be in your time, that there'll be any fruit. But that doesn't mean you stop doing the right thing. You may never know what results come from your action. But if you do nothing, there will be no result."

Mahatma Gandhi (1869-1948)

"There are only two mistakes you can make on the path to truth. One is not starting, the other is not going all the way."

Mark Passio

The title for this book was chosen because it reflects my two main passions in life–music and truth. To be absolutely clear, though, I'm not claiming that everything mentioned in this volume is the absolute, undisputed truth. No-one could ever make so bold a claim. Much of it, by necessity, has to be conjecture, or an account of what other researchers have themselves claimed. Overall, though, the 'truth' bit can be taken as the observation that nothing in the entertainment industry is as it appears on its glossy surface. That much at least is a consistent truth!

What is written in this book will shock many people–particularly those I've known since before 2010, the year that I 'woke up.' This is entirely understandable given the degree to which the content goes right against the grain of everything we're raised to believe is 'normal' and to accept as truth. All I would ask is that, when confronted with information that, heard for the first time sounds ridiculous or impossible, you do not reject it out of hand on the basis that it 'doesn't sound right.' It is a natural tendency of the human psyche to throw out anything that doesn't fit in this way.

As recently as 2011, anyone claiming that UK 'national treasure' Jimmy Savile was a vile paedophile who sexually abused children on BBC premises unimpeded for almost 50 years, would have been scoffed at and written off as a wild fantasist. Yet with the passage of time and the availability of new information, we now know this to be the case. The same principle can apply to any of the information contained within this book, and an open mind that is prepared to go where the evidence takes it and, crucially, question for itself at all points, is an essential tool to get anything out of the information you're about to read.

As many other researchers in the alternative realm often say, I absolutely encourage readers *not* to just take anything that I say here at face value, but to go away and research all these points for themselves. An avoidance of corporate-owned, mainstream media outlets is going to be necessary to this process for reasons that will be obvious, and any on-line endeavours require a mindfulness of the vast amount of mis- and dis-information on the web—some of it there through the writer's well-meaning error, some posted to deliberately mis-inform and lead visitors up the garden path. Either way, a vigilant researcher with the genuine will to want truth will be synchronistically led to the information they need. An enquiring mind coupled with a strong dose of intuition will provide the results that are sought.

None of the scenarios I outline in this book are that way just because I, or anyone else, says they are. I sincerely wish most of them *weren't* that way and that I'd never had to tell this story. There are many things I'd prefer to be doing with my life than putting out information like this. But truth is truth, and it remains so eternally regardless of whether any one individual likes it, believes it or chooses to look at it.

The following is pretty much the best debunk I've seen of the classic accusation levelled against individuals who prefer to think for themselves rather than take their instructions from other sources, being labelled 'conspiracy theorists' as a convenient way of writing them—and therefore anything they say—off. It really makes the point:

"You keep asking for evidence, as if anything anyone posts on-line will qualify as such. How about looking at the world around you? Do you not see what is happening? The architects of the New World Order are anything but subtle.

"I was once sceptical, as society instructed me to be, of anything that implied that all the horrible things that happen in the world are conjured up by conspirators, as if it's perfectly natural for things like slavery, fascism, and the wholesale rape of our planet to occur. But pure logic eventually overwhelmed my programming and forced me to take a closer look at what I was being told was true.

" . . . The evidence that well-organised, well-funded, sinister organisations are implementing an Orwellian totalitarian society is so ubiquitous that one must pay no attention at all to world news to avoid being assaulted with horrors.

"The state of the world is evidence enough for me that someone is conspiring to bring these things about, and the only places I find any answers that make a lick of sense are the so called 'conspiracy' nuts, who look into these things and risk their own lives to share what they find. If you really don't know better, then I feel sorry for you; if you do and are just dutifully debunking the enemies of your masters, then you might want to consider what's going to happen to you once they completely take over and you are no longer useful to them . . ."

To get the most out of this book, I recommend reading the chapters sequentially, rather than dipping in and out at random. If nothing else, however, do not depart without reading the chapter on Predictive Programming, and the final two chapters, as this is where the most valuable information this entire story has to impart resides.

Strap yourself in, and watch the ride!

CHAPTER 1

THE ROAD TO TRUTH

The origins of an awakening.

> *"Wake from your sleep, kid,*
> *Let it settle in,*
> *We be living in the strangest times that's ever been."*
> *Alais Clay: 'Wake 'Em Up' (2013)*

> *"If you are wondering who are the designers of the terrible lie, they*
> *are those who in secret conspire to control the Earth and all of its*
> *resources. They reign by using terror, lies, murder and deceit. They*
> *have created the illusion that pain, suffering, war, death and slavery*
> *is just how things have to be. Do not be fooled by them, live freely,*
> *walk uprightly. Ashe!"*
> *Mel Bell-Grey: You're Not Invited' (2014)*

> *"You wouldn't be here if you didn't want this."*
> *Santos Bonacci*

It was always written, it seems to me, that I was to become a music man. A lifelong love of it was instilled in me from a very early age. I'd like to say this was as a result of my Dad being some Bohemian singer/ songwriter always at his guitar, or my Mum playing soul and blues records around the house. In fact, it was all down to Sunday bathtimes. Enduring memories of my childhood involve being given my bath ready for school on Monday, at the time of the weekly top ten countdown on 'Pick Of The Pops' as it was called back then, on Radio 1. (Unfortunately most of the DJs presenting it seem to have been exposed as

1

paedophiles or sex pests of one variety or another in recent years, but that's the BBC for you.)

Anyway, this routine exposed my impressionable young brain to whatever pop songs were doing the rounds over the course of several years, and was responsible for me scraping together some pennies and buying my first 7-inch single from my local Woolworths at the age of five. Given some of the appalling tosh that was around in 1975 this could have had disastrous results; ('Whispering Grass' by Windsor Davis & Don Estelle? 'The Magic Roundabout' by Jasper Carrot, 'The Ugly Duckling' by Mike Reid? 'The Trail Of The Lonesome Pine' by Laurel & Hardy?) Thankfully, my induction into a lifetime of musical consumption was far more cool. It was Queen's 'Bohemian Rhapsody' during its nine-week run in the UK number one spot at the tail end of '75.

My remaining childhood and early teen years were spent soaking up the pop music of the times, before some fine-tuning of my musical tastes at the age of 15, aided by the strong influence of a progressive-thinking school-friend, turned me on to the appeal of what was broadly termed 'black dance music.' This encompassed the soul, funk and electro styles that were prevalent in the mid-80s, along with early hip-hop, and we were pretty much the only kids in my school that showed an interest in this stuff. It just wasn't that kind of town.

Nevertheless, standing out from the crowd and not blindly doing what everybody else was doing held a certain appeal for me. Plus the music was bloody good. So a few years down the line I decided that what I really wanted was some kind of career playing and exposing all this stuff to as many people as possible. Things didn't get off to the best of starts. Social inadequacy and a crippling lack of confidence held me back from doing anything constructive for many years, and the lack of resources at my disposal based on where I lived didn't help.

But to cut a very long story short, I eventually went on to re-invent myself as a radio and club DJ, and later a music writer. The driving factor behind all of it was simply a desire to generate the same kind of passion and enthusiasm for others towards anything that I considered a great tune, and to reflect the amazing power that music has for capturing the emotions; to articulate in three or four minutes a state of mind that would be impossible to communicate adequately in any other way, and to help conjure up cherished nostalgic memories in the way that only a song which truly resonates can really do.

I'll spare readers any specific anecdotes from my DJing career. I covered plenty of those in my debut book 'Tales From The Flipside' anyway, (still available at http://www.authorhouse.co.uk/Bookstore/ BookDetail.aspx?BookId=SKU-000227787 for anyone who's interested,) published in what now feels like another lifetime long before I 'woke up.'

Suffice to say that, for many years, I played the game and felt very much a part of the machine referred to as 'the industry.' I did everything DJs were expected to do; got myself on to promotional mailing lists, helped the record companies out by playing certain tunes that had been designated promotional 'priorities,' sent off my weekly chart returns to show which records I was supporting, interviewed key artists for the radio, etc. In the early years, I rarely found myself playing tunes I wasn't personally into myself. I was active within the hip-hop, R&B and 'urban' music fields, and most of what came out of the big labels during the 1990s was credible, high-quality material which I still love. Sadly, the same can't be said of the product that emerged during the decade that followed, but the degeneration of those styles was a slow-drip effect that crept up stealthily like a mugger in an alley. In retrospect, the product of the early 2000s, though not a patch on what had preceded it, was still of masterpiece quality compared to the stupefying garbage that mainstream so-called 'R&B' and 'hip-hop' had become by 2009.

Not that I really gave much thought to it at the time. Like all my peers, I was swept along with the scene as the years progressed, and continued to play my position as a professional DJ, reflecting public tastes by giving the crowds whatever they wanted to hear, and helping to gain familiarity for new styles, sounds and production techniques as they occurred.

By 2008 though, the indicators that all was not quite as it should be in these genres—and in popular music generally—was becoming too blatant for even my wholly unawake self to ignore. I presented a 'Top 40 Urban Tunes of 2008' on the radio and remember only personally liking two of them. Something had gone wrong. Lyrics in hip-hop, once a wonderfully creative, energetic and inspiring genre, had all gone the same way, and talk of sex, champagne, gold chains, assorted high-fashion brand names and girls with big butts in the club were the only subjects that ever got referenced. The production styles had changed. Gone were the sample-based beats of the 90s, evoking wonderful mood and emotion through the use of old soul and funk records. Everything by this point had taken on a grating, electronic style and seemed to be mastered to an ear-splitting frequency range that created a feeling of imbalance and unease. There was also a tidal wave of Auto Tune, a vocal production 'style' straight from the bowels of Hell which I'll do proper justice to in a later chapter.

Either way, the glut of rappers that were now being presented as the current-day hip-hop royalty—Lil' Wayne, Drake, Nicki Minaj, Rick Ross, T-Pain, Akon, Flo Rida, Pitbull, and a severely degenerated Jay-Z and Kanye West, just didn't hold the same appeal as the likes of A Tribe Called Quest, Gang Starr, Brand Nubian, Pete Rock & CL Smooth, KRS One, De La Soul, Main Source, Naughty By Nature, Wu Tang Clan, Public Enemy, Notorious BIG, MC Lyte, Foxy Brown and Lil' Kim had a decade before. Everything felt corporate-controlled to an extent that had not been evident before, and all output seemed to be produced according to some standard blueprint or other, with individual creative expression being stifled. Above all, the music just wasn't fun any more, and no longer spoke to me in any meaningful way.

So some dis-satisfaction was already present on my part prior to being led to some revelations that were altogether more disturbing.

The paradigm shift

By 2008 I'd already come to some realisation that the world is nothing like what we've spent all of our lives being told it is by governments and the mainstream media. And if anything, this is understating the situation grossly! Although I was still 'unawake' at this point, and was blindly stumbling around in the world with no proper awareness, I'd still spent a fair bit of time in my life musing over some of the bigger questions; who or what are we? Why are we here? What is 'here' anyway? What happens when we die? You know, lightweight pub conversations like that. I'd been through a phase as an agnostic, followed what I believed to be a born-again Christian, then a long period of ardent atheism, largely as a result of frustration that my previous status hadn't come anywhere near to answering my big questions, but had instead raised a whole bunch of new ones. I'd always had a propensity towards open-minded free thinking, something enthusiastically encouraged by my Dad, who had been a prodigious reader and late-night armchair ponderer for as long as I could remember.

In 1995 I read Graham Hancock's 'Fingerprints Of the Gods', which proposed that human civilisations were far, far older than the conventional history books would have us believe, with some evidence for humanity having been seeded by off-world entities, and this was a real paradigm-shifter for me. This was the first time I'd heard about the Mayan calendar and the end of the yuga cycle that it foretold in December 2012, some 17 years ahead at my time of reading. This seemed like a doom-laden prophecy at the time, and as I read the book amidst the high-rise buildings of Manhattan, imagining all kinds of destruction that the 'end of an age' might bring, I remember making contingency plans for being at the top of a very high mountain when December 2012 came around. (I wasn't.)

The books of David Icke had come on to my radar by 2008, and there are two phrases of his which resonated big time and really summed up what I'd come to understand, and which again, were probably huge understatements. One was, 'the gulf between what's really going on in this world and what we're told is going on, is absolutely immense.' The other was, 'this world is being run by *unbelievably* sick people.' Those two phrases ring ever truer with every passing year.

Something which was very easy for me to take on board was the assertion that world events are not controlled by those we are told they are. Governments don't run countries. The truth is that there is an 'elite' class of individuals, very small in number as a percentage of the world population, who over an immense period of time, have consolidated their position as the manipulators of pretty much every aspect of daily human life. Membership of this group is mainly by genealogy, and families of this cabal obsessively interbreed with each other in order to keep their bloodlines 'pure,' such is the importance they place on their DNA. (This, of course, raises the question of their true origin, and whether or not they descend from a source that is fully human.)

This group has a deep understanding of the true nature of reality—that everything in existence is an expression of the same universal field of sound and light energy, vibrating at an infinite number of frequencies, and that when you understand this and learn how to manipulate it, it can be shaped and moulded to bring about the type of physical manifestations you desire. If you just happen to be a group with malevolent intent and hell-bent on gaining a tactical advantage over the rest of humanity by controlling and enslaving them physically, mentally and spiritually, the implications are immense, and the power that you stand to gain is monumental.

Understanding this dynamic—or even entertaining its possibility—actually makes sense of so much of the insanity, injustice and human suffering that we see in this world, and have done throughout history. Wars, engineered famines and diseases, corporate and financial slavery, all take on a different nature when viewed from this perspective.

The evidence is overwhelming that groups of families, frequently operating through various secret societies that reflect their dark occult practices, have come to hijack and infiltrate all walks of life, in all parts of the world. It is this group that has been responsible for instilling royalty, (and the question of where the 'divine right to rule' of kings may come from is a whole new subject in itself which a great many authors and researchers go into.) They've long since installed the governmental rulers of the world to enforce their will upon the respective populations. Through various covert methods they have worked on mind control and social engineering programmes, to literally 'hypnotise' humans into accepting their version of what constitutes 'normal.' They've created the world of corporations and business, and have worked to establish materialism and the idea that the more possessions you have the happier you will be in life, as the ultimate dream to pursue.

They created the illusory concept of 'money' through instilling fiat currencies, and have crafted the world's financial systems to keep humanity enslaved and restricted in the type of life they can live according to the amount of 'money' they have access to. And through recognising that, on the whole, humans have an innate and inherent tendency towards exploring their true spiritual nature, they have created and manipulated the religious systems of the world, to keep people further enslaved by the dogma of whatever religion so many adhere to by sheer virtue of the world region that they happen to be born into.

They've even provided for those who reject any kind of spiritual world view by creating the equally rigid and restrictive dogma of scientism—the idea that there are no mysteries to life, that there is no great intelligence beyond the human mind, and that anything that can't be explained by government-funded, peer-reviewed scientific 'fact'—usually by people who place assorted letters after their name—can be rejected by default as 'unscientific' bunkum. Then there's rigid atheism and denial of anything of an esoteric, non-physical nature peddled by the likes of Oxford University Professor Richard Dawkins, (whose work I deludedly followed for many years,) to make sure that every base is covered.

I fully understand how preposterous this suggestion sounds to so many when heard for the first time, because it flies in the face of everything we've spent a lifetime being conditioned to accept as 'normal'. I can understand that it becomes harder to accept the older the recipient of the information is, because embracing its validity involves admitting that you've spent an entire lifetime being duped, and that you now have to start afresh with a proverbial blank sheet of paper and recreate your entire world view from scratch. But to any rigid sceptic I would pose the following question: Looking at the way the world is today, which version of events makes the most logical sense? That it's this way because of random chance and the way things *just happen* to have evolved through human beings just not being able to get on with each other? Or that it's this way because it's been coldly manipulated to be so by an extremely powerful group of individuals obsessed with gaining power and control for themselves to the detriment of everyone else?

British hypnotherapist and writer on the subject of mind control, Neil Sanders, commented in a 2013 interview:

> *"It's not really as paranoid as it might sound to assume that, essentially, there's a status quo, and they quite like the way it is and they quite like being in charge. So it's not unreasonable to assume that powerful people have consolidated their position, and wish to maintain this position, and one of the ways that they do this is by the setting of roles and the setting of 'norms' in society."*

The Canadian researcher and writer Henry Makow observes:

> *"People who control a grossly disproportionate share of the world's wealth will take measures to consolidate their position."*

Fairly obvious when you think about it. And it was put even simpler by the late, great US comedian George Carlin.

> *"It's a big club . . . and you ain't in it."*

I was ready to accept this state of affairs as a reality, because it made sense of so many unanswered questions. But many struggle with accepting it for months or years as a result of a condition that's come to be known as cognitive dissonance. This is described as 'the mental stress or discomfort experienced by an individual who holds two or more contradictory beliefs, ideas, or values at the same time, or is confronted by new information that conflicts with existing beliefs, ideas, or values.'

Cognitive dissonance comes into play when you raise any kind of theory which conflicts with the official take on a given subject. Suggest to some that 9/11 was covertly staged by elements of the US government, and many, (although their number are diminishing by the day,) will still be quick to dismiss you as a 'conspiracy theorist,' (a phrase specifically created by the CIA in the 1960s to discredit those who were asking valid questions about the JFK assassination,) and cling desperately to the official line that 'Bin Laden did it.' Because to accept the alternative suggestion would set off a whole sequence of mental spanners-in-the-works. If the US government was somehow involved, that would mean they've been lying to us all these years. That would mean that the 'War on Terror' and the invasions of Afghanistan and Iraq launched in its wake were based knowingly on a lie, and that millions of people have died needlessly as a result of that lie. And if the US government has no problem seeing millions of innocent people killed on the basis of a lie they knowingly concocted, what does that say about the true nature of the people we look up to and who claim to represent us and have our best interests at heart? And if they lied about something as monumental as 9/11, what else could they be lying about? (The answer, by the way, would be 'pretty much everything!')

This is the type of cognitive dissonance brought about by just one event. The evidence to support the fact that 9/11 was, to a very large extent, an 'inside job' and not the work of 19 Arab hijackers armed with box cutters directed by a man living in a remote cave on a dialysis machine, as the governments and mainstream media outlets of the world would have us believe, is monumental. The fact that at least five of the 'hijackers' are still alive is one. The idea that the incriminating paper passport of one of the 'hijackers' *just happened* to survive the carnage in New York City intact, when all around steel and concrete had been pulverised to rubble is another. World Trade Center Building 7 standing intact behind BBC TV reporter Jane Standley as she announced it had collapsed a full 26 minutes before it actually did, and the BBC *just happening* to 'lose' their archive tapes of the broadcast is another. (You don't see much of Jane Standley on TV any more, do you? Funny that.) But you can take your pick from the several hundred other anomalies and discrepancies if you choose, as there's no shortage to select from, with the number of books, articles and videos now into the hundreds of thousands.

And all this from just one event. 9/11 is far from an isolated incident in terms of the big picture of what's really going on in our world, and the same anomalies with the 'official version' can be applied to pretty much every other major news event of the past several decades and beyond. While 'conspiracy theory' is a convenient catch-all term to dismiss any truthseeker who offers an alternative view to the official line, the majority of popular conspiracy 'theories' can now be demonstrated, with supporting evidence, to be conspiracy *fact*. And in the twisted, inverted reality in which we find ourselves, it's the official government story which is the real 'conspiracy theory,' laden as they always are with glaring inaccuracies and discrepancies that make no sense under the scrutiny of a truly inquisitive and unbiased mind.

This being the case, there are two stances that I generally take with those sceptics who automatically scoff and dismiss any suggestion that the world could be just a little different to what we're being told, on the basis that it can't possibly be true because it 'doesn't sound right.'

One is to ask them to use their imagination and put themselves in the place of an 'elite.' For this, they need to forget all about how they themselves would act in any given situation, and instead, take on the mind-set of a psychopath—one whose mental condition makes it impossible for them to empathise with the feelings of others, thus leaving them free of any qualms whatsoever about how their actions might cause others to suffer. Their priority is to maintain their position as a ruler and controller over the rest of the population, and this must be upheld at all costs. Imagine also that you happen to be a satanist, and immersed in dark energy that allows any act of evil to be fair game. With these tenets in place, now consider what tactics you would employ.

Would you seek to install obedient governmental leaders around the world that would do your bidding and adhere to your agenda? Would you instruct these governmental leaders to present an innocent and benevolent-sounding cover story for their actions to disguise their true nature? (Telling the public that you are invading an overseas nation to 'protect the people' while you slaughter the population and steal that nation's land and natural resources would be just one of a multitude of examples that would apply.)

Would you bring all the main media outlets—newspapers, television and radio news, prominent internet sites—under your control, and shape and mould the content to give the masses the versions of events that suit you, while completely ignoring and side-lining those subjects that you don't want the people to know about?

Would you coerce the public into eating food and adopting lifestyle habits that bring on cancer and other diseases, then deliberately suppress known natural cures and criminalise their use, instead offering pharmaceutical drugs, chemotherapy and radiotherapy, knowing that these treatments are actually responsible for killing off many of the patients even quicker and causing the very diseases they're claimed to cure, while at the same time creating an industry worth billions every year to those that run it?

Would you seek to introduce a worldwide financial system that keeps the population in perpetual economic slavery to the bankers that run it, and that keeps the people of the world needing to constantly work for the majority of their lives just to be able to afford to live?

Would you create religious systems that keep vast groups of people controlled by creating a belief that they will suffer eternal damnation and separation from their 'god' if they dare to disobey the rules and regulations set out in a particular book?

Would you seek to create a paradigm in which what's considered 'normal' or 'possible' is what suits your ongoing agenda of control, and of cutting people off from a recognition of their true spiritual nature and potential, in which anyone who deviates from these 'norms' and tries to tell others that there's another way of looking at things is immediately demonised and branded as 'crazy?'

I can say for myself that I would certainly do all of the above. Is it really too much of a stretch to imagine that this might be exactly what has happened?

Consider also, the type of public reaction that would most suit the dark controllers in such a scenario. Would it not be a widespread scoffing condemnation of any information offered regarding their true nature on the basis that it 'can't possibly be true'? Dismissing information on this basis without doing any independent research of your own whatsoever, is *exactly* the type of response they would rely on. This stance is the origin of the phrase made famous by Albert Einstein: "Condemnation without investigation is the height of ignorance."

The other stance is to ask people whether they can afford to take the chance that the above scenario might be true, given the implications for human freedom that it brings. Yes, the idea of a worldwide conspiracy spanning generations that has prevented human society from taking what would have been its natural course if left free of these manipulations *might* be a load of old bollocks. But then again it might not. And, with doubts being cast by so many researchers into the subject, and evidence presented at every turn to suggest all might not be as it seems, . . . can you afford to take the chance? Through adamantly refusing to look at the evidence, despite the free abundance of it now available through the internet, are you allowing this system of human subjugation to continue unimpeded by your tacit co-operation? It's a question I would suggest everyone owes it to both themselves and their families to ask.

There are the two classic errors of judgement that people so often make:

1. They'd never do that

(No, *you and I* would never do that. *They* do it all the time!)

2. If they did the media would tell us about it.

(Well, the alternative media has been trying to do just that for a long time now, but they're the ones so quickly brushed off as 'crackpots.' So much for the assertion that we'd know if there was a conspiracy against humanity then. As for the mainstream media, they're just another expression of the very problem we're talking about here. How could they not be when they're ultimately owned and controlled by the same organisations?)

What it boils down to is that most of us have been deliberately lied to and deceived about great truths in the world from the moment we were born. We have been taken for fools, and in the case of those who continue to blindingly accept what they're told without applying any kind of critical research for themselves, as *willing* fools, complicit in their own duping. To put it in everyday language, we've all been taken for mugs, and who appreciates being treated as a mug? Not this one. It's so bizarre that you can say to people, 'if there were a sinister, far-reaching agenda to subvert and enslave you and your family, would you want to know about it?', to which most people would answer 'yes, of course I would.' Having established this, you can then go on to point out that this is exactly what *is* happening right now, to which most of those same people would laugh, sneer and dismiss the suggestion. I guess they didn't really want to know after all, then?

Wakey, wakey

And so, what I came to understand caused me to grudgingly accept that I had to re-evaluate my entire perspective on the world and who was really controlling it, and this led to even bigger questions such as, how have they been able to do it . . . and what is the true nature of this existence in which we find ourselves in the first place? The answers to these are beyond the scope of this book, (although I'll be attempting to touch on them from time to time to put some of the other contents into a full perspective.) For me, the process of serious questioning which had begun in 2007/08, reached a peak in September 2010, and again, this was on a trip to New York City.

In the midst of my typically hectic lifestyle, I was able to take four days out that month to visit Niagara Falls, along with a quick stop in Manhattan. The hours spent travelling gave me the enforced downtime

I needed to get some quality reading done, and on the agenda was David Icke's new book 'Human Race Get Off Your Knees: The Lion Sleeps No More'. Like the earlier Hancock book, this one was a life-changer by any standards, and although I was already familiar with much of the material, there came a point where it felt as if a light bulb had gone on in my head, suddenly illuminating great truths which had been hidden just out of sight in the darkness up to that point. I later came to realise that I had undergone what so many refer to as a 'conscious awakening'. It was a raising of my personal vibratory frequency out of the depths of base consciousness, to a higher state of awareness. Once you achieve this, you start to access the part of you that goes beyond the physical body into the realms of pure source consciousness, of which we are all individual expressions.

Again, these are all terms which, I fully appreciate, will sound utterly alien and 'out there' to anyone new to the subject. But there are a great many scholars in these subject areas who can explain the concept far better than I can, and an infinite number of resources for anyone who wants to delve into it.

It became clear that my experience was far from unique, and there is something about this point in the human timeline in which those of us alive today are having our experiences, which is causing vast numbers of people to 'wake up,' remember who they are and where they have come from, and to gain a new perspective on truths which have been deliberately veiled and cloaked from the bulk of humanity for aeons.

An article I found posted on the Above Top Secret website forum (http://www.abovetopsecret.com/forum/thread715284/pg1) put it very well:

> *"Folks, whatever you may believe, I hope you understand that the people who have the most gold make the rules. If you want to connect the dots, you will not find the necessary information from the mainstream media. In order to come to grips with this incredibly profound truth, you must first be de-programmed.*
>
> *"... After maybe 100 hours of reading and listening to these serious truth researchers and learning about what is really happening you*

may be sufficiently de-programmed to both understand and accept the real truth about the evil ruling elites running our planet.

"Hopefully, when enough people know the truth, the power in this truth will establish the morality, justice, and freedom human beings should have."

An obligation to Truth

It took a while for me to mentally compute the 'awakening' process. But despite many initial doubts, the confirmations that I was on the right road were all around me, and my experiences were validated by so many other people who I became synchronistically connected with. After a while of quietly walking this new path, an instinctive feeling of responsibility to start communicating to others what I had started to learn swept over me. As so many who have undergone similar experiences have surmised, anyone coming to an understanding of great truths, takes on with it an obligation to communicate that knowledge. It's an obligation that comes from the creative force behind the universe, (which is very different from the assorted 'gods' of the man-made religions,) of which we are all individualised expressions.

And this is the stumbling block for so many. As has been frequently pointed out, one of the greatest mental prison cells that people can find themselves in is the fear of what other people might think. Some have less to lose than others in coming right out and saying what needs to be said, however, regardless of the likely response from family, friends, employers or others.

My process of awakening, then, led to me understanding how certain facets of the music industry of which I'd been a part, were an important piece in the overall jigsaw puzzle of the real control system. Going back to the earlier hypothesis of a malevolent international elite wishing to control all aspects of human life and mentality, having taken the time and trouble to shape religions, governments, the financial system, all the major worldwide corporations, the world of science, the military, and the educational and academic establishments . . . why would they possibly miss out one of the greatest opportunities for mass mind control and social manipulation that is offered by complete control of the entertainment industry—movies, television, and—my special area of interest—the corporate-controlled mainstream music industry?

They haven't, of course. And, given that communicating the truth becomes a moral obligation of anyone coming to gain an understanding of it, here's where our story begins.

Resources:

Mark Devlin's debut book 'Tales From The Flipside' at Authorhouse:

- http://www.authorhouse.co.uk/Bookstore/BookDetail
aspx?BookId=SKU-000227787

CHAPTER 2
NOTHING NEW UNDER THE SUN

The early days of the music industry machine.

> *"For, you see, the world is governed by very different personages from what is imagined by those who are not behind the scenes."*
>
> *Benjamin Disraeli, British Prime Minister, 1874-1880*

> *"By now, more and more people become aware of that this world is, to a major degree, controlled by a secret cabal we call the Illuminati, a Shadow Government if you will . . . They have already taken over a big part of world politics, business, education and religious movements. This fact is accepted by many, because the evidence is overwhelming. So why would this cabal, who wants total control and the ability to take over our minds and thinking processes, leave the film and music industries alone?"*
>
> *Wes Penre, Illuminati News article, 2008*

The dark manipulations of the music business are as old as the industry itself, and early examples of the dubious calling cards evident in the contemporary scene are equally present in its formative years. Mind-control, military 'intelligence', paedophilia and occult fascination are, it seems, nothing new.

The 'king' of rock and roll

A good starting point, then, would appear to be with the first world superstar of popular music. Elvis Presley stands as a classic example of an artist manufactured by the industry machine, and whose entire persona was carefully crafted. US President Jimmy Carter stated after

Presley's death that he had "permanently changed the face of American popular culture". This, apparently, was the plan.

Elvis' eventual wife, Priscilla, was just 14 when they met. According to Wikipedia:

> *"Elvis and Priscilla met on September 13, 1959, during a party at Elvis' home in Bad Nauheim, Germany, while he was serving in the army. Despite her being 14 years old, she made a huge impression on Elvis with her much older appearance."*

This in itself is no proof of illegal sexual activity, of course. Presley biographer Albert Goldman didn't mince his words in declaring him to be a 'paedophile' and 'pervert', however.

In her own book, 'Elvis and Me', Priscilla insists that even though she and Presley engaged in heavy petting and kissing, they always stopped before it led to intercourse, claiming they waited until their wedding night in 1967. Very restrained.

The circumstances surrounding Presley's death do not disappoint either, and rival any of the later stories involving the exits of Jim Morrison, Jimi Hendrix or Michael Jackson. Music lore has it that a heavily bloated and sick Elvis died in his bathroom at Gracelands, (on the toilet, according to most accounts,) on 16th August 1977, (which just happened to be Madonna's 19th birthday.) The cause of death was attributed to a heart attack brought on by heavy drug use and poor diet. In an early example of a musical 'conspiracy theory,' there have been several alleged sightings of Presley since 1977, amid rumours that he faked his own death to escape the public spotlight and live out his remaining years quietly.

It has to be acknowledged that much of this could be down to denial and cognitive dissonance; fans form a very personal connection to their heroes, and the idea that they have gone can be too hard for some to acknowledge.

Nevertheless, this doesn't alter the fact that there are some strange factors that require debunking before the official version of events can be comfortably accepted. Presley's demise was echoed in 'Orion,' a novel by Gail Brewer-Giorgio about a Southern-based superstar who fakes his own death, her story having been inspired by the newspaper coverage of Presley's death. Giorgio states that, shortly after her book's initial publication, she started getting calls advising that the book had become unavailable from the retail stores. In one case, there was an account of two businessmen in suits buying up all copies from a shop in Pennsylvania. Giorgio says that her distributor had told her he'd been ordered to withdraw the book by the publisher, despite her having been paid a healthy advance. (Identical problems of publisher interference were reported years later by Alan Power, author of 'The Diana Conspiracy,' alleging that M16 were behind Princess Diana's murder, acting upon the direct instructions of Prince Philip. Do you think he upset someone?)

Strangely, the same thing was experienced simultaneously by Monty Nicholson, author of the book 'The Presley Arrangement,' which investigated some of the anomalies concerning Elvis's apparent death, such as an allegedly doctored autopsy and the disappearance of photographs, medical notes and toxicology reports. This joins claims from witnesses that the body in the casket did not resemble Presley. Some attested that it appeared to have a fake glued-on hairpiece, the nose was the wrong shape, and there were beads of sweat on the face.

Maria Columbus, co-president of the oldest Elvis Presley fan club, spoke to Presley's father shortly after the death announcement.

> *"He asked us not to come out, said that he wanted us to come to Memphis a week later. He said that it was too hectic, too many people, the press was there, and that it would be more quiet and beneficial for us to talk to him a week later. So we agreed.*
>
> *"We arrived the next week, and there was a whole feeling of make-believe, not of reality. When we went to the mausoleum there was the atmosphere of a carnival. There were people selling popcorn and soft drinks, people standing in front of the mausoleum posing for pictures with the security guards. It felt like it was a game, and we didn't feel like Elvis' spirit was there. It felt like a coldness. Like a joke."*

There have also been stories of missing cheques, jewellery and a private jet, and the cashing in of only two of the three life assurance policies.

And further intrigue comes from claims that the handwriting on the death certificate matched Elvis' own, as verified by handwriting experts.

This occurred amidst revelations that Elvis had long been an undercover agent for the US intelligence services, the police departments of several cities, and the Drug Enforcement Agency. His enthusiasm for his law enforcement activities, and the difficulty of maintaining these alongside his public fame, is cited as one of the reasons for his death hoax, so that he could quietly be inducted into the Witness Protection Programme. Other more ambitious theories exist, too, such as that of the website http://elvistruth.wordpress.com/, which alleges that Elvis' newly-deceased body was taken to the secret Area 51 base in Nevada, where government scientists used cryogenics, homeopathy and a blood transfusion to re-establish his life force, then applied plastic surgery to alter his appearance!

Whatever the truth concerning Elvis' 'death'–and who can honestly claim to know for sure what that is?–it demonstrates that suspicion and scepticism over official versions of events were just as rife in decades past as they are now. As long ago as the 1960s there was widespread public doubt over what we were told about the deaths of John F Kennedy and Marilyn Monroe, and the Apollo moon landings too.

Buddy Holly, The Big Bopper, Richie Valens, Eddie Cochran and the rest

In the same way that the fortunes of the Kennedy political dynasty have been said to be cursed, an air of doom-laden misfortune also seems to surround the story of 1950s rocker Buddy Holly. It seems to extend beyond the fateful night of 3rd February 1959 when he and fellow musicians The Big Bopper and Richie Valens died in a plane crash, being synchronistically entangled with the fates of many other characters associated with the rockers. The intricate story is best told in this thorough article from the Angelfire website:

- http://www.angelfire.com/music5/archives/curseofholly.html

All known vices

The early British music industry of the 1950s and 1960s is infested with stories of paedophilia, sexual deviancy, drug abuse, extortion, and organised crime on a scale that would be right at home within the political establishment of the present day. Synchronicity rears its head in many of these stories, too, with a baffling array of links and apparent 'coincidences' between the key players.

Acknowledgement must go here to an unpublished article written by the ex-intelligence operative known as T Stokes, (and later expanded upon by British writer Chris Spivey.) This unveiled a fascinating and sinister web linking, among many others, record producers Robert Stigwood and Kit Lambert, Labour MP Tom Driberg, and the Tory peer Lord Boothby. (Hold tight because we're going to meet a fair few 'Lords' and 'Sirs' in this story!) The notorious Kray twins are present in the saga, which is steeped in the London criminal underworld, and involves blackmail, shotgun murders, the discovery of rent boy Bernard Oliver's body in a suitcase, 'suicides' and the ever-present influence of Aleister Crowley. (Much more of him later, too!)

According to a blog article on the UK's Aangirfan website, The Krays may well have been mind-control victims themselves, (twins were often favoured in early experiments conducted by Nazi doctor Josef Mengele.) They were known for their sudden moodswings from placid and urbane to violent and psychopathic, in keeping with multiple personality disorders. Aangirfan suggests they were put to use in London's criminal underworld in the 60s, and involved with the procurement of children for the same elite paedophile rings we see today. They had links to key characters in the music industry, including BBC DJs Jimmy Savile and Alan 'Fluff' Freeman, producer Joe Meek and Beatles manager Brian Epstein. The Krays were said to be 'crypto-Jews,' those of Jewish genealogy who prefer to keep this aspect of their background hidden from the public, often changing their surname to disguise their roots.

Another key figure is David 'Lord' Sutch, a pioneer of the British pirate radio scene of the 1960s, and later a parliamentary candidate, who just happened to die in mysterious circumstances in 1999, aged 58. The paedophile artist Graham Ovenden and 'Sergeant Pepper' sleeve artist Peter Blake also make appearances, as does former Bee Gee

Robin Gibb. In several cases, the males concerned turn out to have been homosexual, and/ or paedophiles, and in certain cases, Satanists.

It also has to be pointed out that, throughout the back story of the mainstream music industry, on both sides of the Atlantic, a hugely out-of-proportion number of the key players are of Jewish background. Because of the mechanisms in place to instantly demonise as 'anti-se-mitic' those who question anyone who happens to be Jewish—regardless of whether the inquiries have any foundation or not—this is a factor which is rarely discussed. But it's neither slander nor conjecture to point out the large number of Jewish individuals in the entertainment industry. It's a provable fact. Why would this be when Jewish people make up such a small proportion of British and American society in the aggregate? If such vast numbers of, say, Swedish or Portuguese people just happened to populate an industry so abundantly, against all the odds, people would surely find it strange and ask why it should be. I think the question remains equally valid when it comes to the Jewish influence. The same could also be said of the large number of homosex-uals in the business—again, way out of proportion to the ratio in society generally, (and it's not 'homophobic' to point this particular fact out, either!) Indeed, a popular quote attributed to John Lennon runs: "Only queers and Jews can get on in showbiz."

Two other factors wildly out of proportion to the average are the sheer number of sudden deaths attributed to either 'suicide' or 'acci-dental overdoses.'

A couple of T Stokes' articles containing some of the information, reside at the following domains:

- http://www.thetruthseeker.co.uk/?p=13451

- http://www.thetruthseeker.co.uk/?p=36860

Chris Spivey's much-expanded (and highy recommended) rework of the original T Stokes article is here:

- http://chrisspivey.org/sutch-as-it-is-based-on-the-unpublished-t-stokes-article-who-murdered-screaming-lord-sutch/#comment-172748

The work of T Stokes also appeared on the UK investigative blog site Aangirfan in 2012, in an article which included the following information:

> *"At a big London railway station in the spring of 1970, a plastic carrier bag was found in the regular search for bombs before the station closed for the night. The contents were an odd assortment of letters and photos, which seemed to have been taken at a kinky party attended by some well-known figures in entertainment.*

> *"One in particular showed a pop singer who masquerades under a Christian persona; dressed in women's underwear, he was pictured with young boys.*

> *"The bag was duly taken to the station office, and as a senior rail worker wrote out a report for the lost property office, two MI5 men and a special branch officer arrived and demanded the photos.*

> *"The pop singer in question had even threatened to commit suicide if the photos were released.*

> *"However MI5 passed one particular letter from the bag to the tax authorities, because it seemed to indicate that the three brothers who had a virtual monopoly over Britain's entertainment industry were short-changing the taxman.*

> *"The brothers—Bernard Delfont, and Lew and Leslie Grade (Winogradsky)—had a stranglehold over stage and screen appearances in Britain and gave preference to Jewish stars and promoters. Such were the amounts involved that fellow Jews the Kray twins were asked to launder much of the money in clubs and fixed boxing matches, gambling and other dubious enterprises."*

The Aangirfan blog articles can be found here:

* http://aangirfan.blogspot.co.uk/2012/10/jimmy-savile-kray-twins-cliff-richards.html

- http://aanirfan.blogspot.co.uk/2015/08/cliff-richard-rolf-harris-jimmy-savile.html

'White' Cliff?

A very prominent character in the early British music scene is Cliff Richard, often dubbed 'the British Elvis'.

Richard was born Harry Webb in India in 1940, reportedly of British and part-Spanish ancestry, settling in England in 1948. His recording career began ten years later with 'Move It', and his early releases saw him coupled with The Shadows as his backing band. He started out with a rebellious rock-and-roll image suited to the times, largely modelled on Elvis, before re-inventing himself as a Christian singer in the 1960s, at which point his output switched to a middle-of-the-road style, earning him a legion of middle-aged, largely female fans. He opted for a more edgy rock image in the 70s with the the single 'Devil Woman' and a handful of others, before focusing his attention on regular, profitable Christmas appearances with the likes of 'Mistletoe And Wine,' 'Saviour's Day' and 'The Millennium Prayer.' Richard made the history books by becoming the only artist to have ever scored a UK number one single in five consecutive decades, a feat that seems unlikely to ever be repeated.

Richard was appointed a Knight Bachelor by the Queen in 1995, achieving his 'Sir' status.

On 14th August 2014, Richard's £3-million penthouse home in Sunningdale, Berkshire was raided by police in his absence. Media reports claimed that this was in connection with an alleged sexual assault on a 15-year-old boy at a 'Christian' rally in Sheffield involving the US celebrity evangelist Billy Graham, and dating back to 1985. Richard subsequently returned from his vineyard home in Portugal's Algarve to be questioned by police. Although reports later emerged that the alleged victim had contacted the police well over a year before in the wake of the TV documentary exposing Savile, Richard was released without arrest or charge, insisting upon his innocence. By August of the following year, however, South Yorkshire Police advised that the number of alleged offences by Richard that they were now investigating had risen to three, both in the UK and abroad.

The BBC was publicly criticised for its apparent advance knowledge of the raid, when it already had a camera crew in place to record the arrival of police. Because of this, the search and the related questioning was said to have been 'compromised,' preventing the normal course of action in such cases from taking place. Conveniently for Sir Cliff, the BBC's 'bungle' saw him walk away scot-free. Richard announced some three months later that he planned to sue the BBC and demand damages.

Although the incident only raised further suspicion within the alternative community as to what the real story was, it seemed to have little effect on Richard's mainstream image. A consortium of fans, rallying to their hero's support, started a campaign to get his 1992 song 'I Still Believe In You' back into the Top 40. It managed a showing at number 57 for one week in late August 2014. Seemingly benefiting further from the ardent support of his fans, Richard went on to announce a world tour in 2015 to mark his 75th birthday, despite his spokesperson claiming at the time that the police incident had caused his career 'irreparable damage,' and his lawyer claiming he had suffered 'immeasurable harm.' For some inexplicable reason, Morrissey, former frontman of The Smiths, was due to tour with Cliff in 2014, a partnership that sounds about as compatible as that of Buju Banton and Liberace, but the gigs were called-off following Morrissey's unfortunate announcement that he had developed cancer. An equally unlikely pairing had come from Sir Cliff's 12-date tour of Germany alongside Boy George. The previous year, George had been imprisoned for the assault and false imprisonment of a male escort.

In his early years as a singer, Richard was closely linked to the Tory peer Lord Robert Boothby, a prominent MP from the 30s through to the 60s. ('Lords' and 'Sirs' tend to move in close circles, it would appear,) and portrayed rather unflatteringy in the 2015 Kray Twins biopic 'Legend.' Boothby kept eclectic company; he was also an associate of both Ronnie Kray and Winston Churchill, with all three reported to have been homosexual paedophiles.

Richard himself also had an association with the Kray twins, particularly Ronnie Kray, and was an associate of Jimmy Savile. Richard appeared on the first episode of 'Top Of The Pops,' hosted by Savile, in January 1964. Another long-standing friendship was with Cilla Black.

Interestingly she changed her name from Priscilla White at the start of her career. Readers can decide for themselves given the hidden nature of the entertainment industry, whether there was any symbolic relevance to trading 'white' for 'black.' Richard and Black both had BBC television shows during the 1960s and 1970s, and each would regularly guest on the other's programme. Cilla Black was also a long-standing friend of Jimmy Savile. She remained noticeably silent upon the revelations of Savile's historic paedophilia, but did rally to the defence of her old pal Cliff during his brush with the law. She said in a statement: "Cliff is a very close friend of mine and has been for a million years. I, like everyone else, was shocked to hear of these allegations and I am absolutely positive that they are without foundation." She also spoke of her 'disappointment' over Rolf Harris' conviction for indecently assaulting young girls, stating: "I've never known Rolf be any different to anyone else. I thought he was lovely." Cilla Black is one of a few who passed away during the writing of this book. With 50 years in 'showbiz,' who knows what other secrets she took to the grave with her?

Interestingly, Leslie Grade, father of the TV executive Michael Grade, was Cliff Richard's talent agent for many years. Lew Grade was the founder of ATV, one of the regional franchises of the newly-created ITV television network, on which Richard hosted an entertainment show in the early 1960s. Lew Grade was knighted in 1969.

In the wake of the house raid incident, it was reported that Cliff would be selling his Berkshire home, and would now spend all his time in the British Commonwealth island of Barbados, of which he had obtained citizenship. Tony and Cherie Blair are among the guests reported to have stayed at his home there. According to a 2006 story on the politics.co.uk website, Cliff offered to lend his home to Blair after seeing him looking "dwindled and haggard" during the Iraq war. How very Christian. The Berkshire property sale was completed in May 2015, in the same week as the announcement that the police's Operation Hydrant was investigating more than 1,400 men in the UK over claims of historic sexual abuse. Of these, 261 were said to be 'high-profile' individuals, with 76 politicians, and 43 connected to the music industry.

Elton and Aleister

Another titan of British rock with an intriguing background, and a long and successful career to match, is Reginald Dwight of Harrow, better known as 'Sir' Elton John. He is one of several artists of his era that has expressed a fascination with the occultist Aleister Crowley and ritual magick. Some of his songs, such as 'Goodbye Yellow Brick Road', are also said to have been written in 'witch language.'

The late US record industry whistleblower John Todd, who we'll encounter again later in this story, stated in a testimony:

> *"Now, much of the music is written in witch language by witches. Elton John has made the statement that he has never written a song that was not written in witch language. That is why many songs you don't understand. That is why many people who listen to them don't understand. Until they get high on drugs, and then all of a sudden the meanings start coming to them."*

This seems to be a variation on the phenomenon of 'automatic writing', where an individual makes a connection with an off-world spirit, which uses their body to channel through certain information from the spirit realm. Participants have talked of being given words and phrases so fast that they are unable to comprehend them as they come, only to write down what they receive as fast as possible. Only afterwards are they able to try and deduce any meaning from what they have written. Sometimes the writing is clear, other times it is seemingly nonsensical, but may well include cryptically encoded messages. Many rock songs in music history are said to have been written in this way. David Bowie has talked of assembling songs by cutting up pages from newspapers, then re-attaching the shreds at random and basing his lyrics on whatever phrases emerge, which sounds like an interesting variation on the phenomenon. Kurt Cobain of Nirvana and Thom Yorke of Radiohead are also said to have used the technique for some of their popular songs.

Bernie Taupin, John's co-writer, has said that "John's home is laden with trinkets and books relating to Satanism and witchcraft." Just the household for two young babies to be raised by two homosexual adult males in then. (John and his partner David Furnish adopted two baby boys named Zachary and Elijah, making for a rather unconventional domestic set up.)

In 1999, John caused controversy by performing at a charity concert with dancers dressed as boy scouts, subsequently forcing them to strip. He was joined on stage by George Michael. John Fogg, a spokesman for the Scout Association, said at the time:

> *"We think it is pretty deplorable and in bad taste in terms of denigrating our uniform and what it stands for. We are disappointed that someone of Sir Elton's standing should involve himself in something of such poor taste. It linked homosexuality with paedophilia. If Stonewall are completely for the rights of homosexual people, they have not done themselves any favours."*

The issue of paedophilia rears its head again when it comes to John's artistic and photographic preferences. As the excellent UK website The Coleman Experience reported in its 2014 article 'Elton John's Mysterious Meltdown':

> *"In a little reported incident, Elton John was stopped and searched at an airport in 2007. A paedophilic photograph was confiscated from his person. John's excuse was that the photograph was part of an art exhibition. The photo in question was amateurish and any real photographer would be able to point out the elementary technical mistakes, but John's name gives it 'status' as so called 'art.'*

> *"He is also known to collect 'artwork' by convicted sex-offender Graham Ovenden."*

And this article by Chris Spivey raises some highly pertinent questions about how John and Furnish, who married on the Winter Solstice in 2014, were so easily able to adopt two baby boys, given John's history of promiscuous sexual activity, (with album titles like 'Captain Fantastic And The Brown Dirt Cowboy' it's not like he didn't offer the odd clue,) his close association with known paedophiles, his collection of art by paedophile painters including depictions of naked children, his background in dark occultism, and his status as a notorious alcoholic and drug addict. As Spivey observes, had John and Furnish been a regular working class non-celebrity couple, does anyone believe they would have got the green light for adoption, or that the boys wouldn't have been seized by Social Services and placed into 'care?' It seems membership of the 'Sir' club is the gift that just keeps on giving.

- http://chrisspivey.org/
  something-about-the-way-you-look-tonight/

For Pete's sake

The same broad subject area crops up in the story of The Who. Guitarist Pete Townshend was famously arrested for viewing on-line child porn in 1999. As the Daily Mail reported:

> "He insisted at the time that he had simply been conducting 'research' when he paid £7 with his credit card in 1999 to access a website bearing the message 'click here for child porn'.

> "Despite his denials of harbouring depraved desires, he accepted a police caution, and was duly placed on the sex offenders' register for five years."

Later, Townshend claimed to The Times newspaper that he paid for child pornography to prove that British banks were complicit in channelling the profits from paedophile rings.

He offered a different explanation in a statement at the time of his arrest, however:

> "I have been writing my childhood autobiography for the past seven years. I believe I was sexually abused between the age of five and six-and-a-half when in the care of my maternal grandmother who was mentally ill at the time. I cannot remember clearly what happened, but my creative work tends to throw up nasty shadows—particularly in 'Tommy.'

Elsewhere in his interview with The Times newspaper, Townshend stated:

"I had experienced something creepy as a child, so you imagine, what if I was a girl of nine or ten and my uncle had raped me every week? I felt I had an understanding, and I could help."

The Who are perhaps best known for their rock opera 'Tommy,' made into a Ken Russell-directed movie in 1975. This featured the titular character, a deaf, dumb and blind kid played by Roger Daltrey, (MBE,) being sexually abused by a paedophile babysitter, 'Uncle' Ernie, played by drummer Keith Moon. Almost four decades later, it emerged that (Sir) Jimmy Savile had been sexually abusing disabled and paralysed children at Stoke Mandeville Hospital.

All that Glitters ...

Gary Glitter, meanwhile, (born Paul Gadd in Banbury, Oxfordshire,) is an artist who could be said to be way ahead of his time in getting arrested on child pornography charges as long ago as 1997. According to Wikipedia:

> *"In November 1997, Glitter was arrested after pornographic images of children were discovered on the hard drive of a Toshiba laptop that he had taken for repair to a branch of PC World at Cribbs Causeway, near Bristol.*

> *"In 1999, Glitter was sentenced to four months' imprisonment and listed as a sex offender in the UK following conviction for downloading thousands of items of child pornography.*

> *"He was also charged with having sex with an underage girl, Alison Brown, around 20 years earlier, when she was 14 years old."*

Glitter went on to reside in Cambodia, before being deported to Vietnam as a result of suspected child abuse. Wikipedia reports that:

> *"From March 2005, Glitter resided in Vũng Tàu, Vietnam. In late 2005, at age 61, Gary Glitter was arrested by Vietnamese authorities and charged with molesting two underaged girls, aged 10 and 11, at his home in Vũng*

Tàu. He initially faced possible child rape charges carrying the death penalty, but prosecutors did not find enough evidence for those charges, so Glitter was instead tried for lesser child sexual abuse charges. Early in 2006, he was convicted of committing obscene acts with minors and sentenced to three years imprisonment."

On his eventual return to the UK in 2008, after years of residing in Asia, Glitter was placed on the Sex Offenders' register for life.

Glitter's Wikipedia entry goes on to detail his alleged links with Savile and the BBC sex scandal:

"In October 2012, ITV showed the documentary 'The Other Side of Jimmy Savile' in its 'Exposure' strand. The story developed and extended over the ensuing weeks, and included an accusation against Glitter. He was alleged to have been seen having sex with a 13 or 14-year-old girl in Savile's dressing room at the BBC."

A clip from Glitter's vintage appearance on ITV's 'This Is Your Life' subsequently appeared on Youtube, and turned out to be quite revealing in retrospect. Guest Tessa Dahl relates an anecdote about her sister bringing adolescent girls in school uniform to meet Glitter, at which point he touches his neck nervously and whispers 'sssshhh!' to her. You can view the clip here:

- http://www.youtube.com/watch?v=F8OZTB03azM

And this clip of Glitter guesting on Savile's 'Clunk Click' programme on the BBC, with their arms around assorted children, speaks for itself. Right there in plain sight.

- https://www.youtube.com/watch?v=j6Hx7Q2oC5U

Either way, you know something's gone wrong with your life when your name gets adopted in your homeland as crude rhyming slang for a craphouse, ("Gary Glitter" = "shitter".)

Jimmy Jimmy

Led Zeppelin were a group that picked up the term 'devil rockers' in the 1970s, owing to their flirtation with dark occult and esoteric imagery in their record sleeves and stage shows. (See the chapter on Backmasking for some interesting detail on their flagship song 'Stairway To Heaven.') They were also keen on hard drugs and extreme sex and provided more than a little inspiration for the classic spoof rockumentary 'This Is Spinal Tap'. Guitarist Jimmy Page was happy to admit an infatuation with occultist Aleister Crowley and his works, telling Sounds Magazine in a 1978 interview: "I feel Aleister Crowley is a misunderstood genius of the 20th century." Page had a variation on Crowley's famous 'do what thou wilt shall be the whole of the law' quote inscribed into the vinyl of his group's third album 'Led Zeppelin III,' which read: 'Do what thou wilt. So mote it be'. For a time Page owned an occult bookshop and publishing house, The Equinox Booksellers and Publishers, in London's Kensington High Street. Keeping the theme of paedophilia and ritual sex magick alive, (although seemingly preferring girls to the usual choice of boys), Page embarked on a sexual affair with a 14-year-old Los Angeles groupie, Lori Maddox, known popularly as Lori Lightning.

As an article on the website stryder.de explains:

> "According to Lori, after Jimmy tried and failed several times to get together with her, Jimmy had Led Zeppelin's tour manager 'kidnap' Lori and bring her back to the Continental Hyatt, the hotel where Led Zeppelin was staying. Lori was brought to Jimmy's room, where as she described in the Led Zeppelin book 'Hammer Of The Gods': 'It was dimly lit by candles . . . and Jimmy was just sitting there in a corner, wearing this hat slouched over his eyes and holding a cane. It was really mysterious and weird. He looked just like a gangster. It was magnificent!'

> "That night, Jimmy and Lori began a torrid affair, but they had to keep their relationship a secret from the public since Lori was underage and Jimmy was at risk of being arrested."

Page was already in a relationship with another groupie, Pamela Des Barres, at the time of meeting Maddox on the group's 1972 tour. Page reportedly dumped Maddox around a year and a half later after taking up with yet another groupie, Bebe Buell, at the same time as seemingly maintaining a long relationship with French model Charlotte Martin, who had earlier dated Eric Clapton.

Page wasn't the first in line with Maddox, however. That dubious honour seems to have fallen to David Bowie, to whom she is said to have lost her virginity at the age of 13. Maddox admits to the affair in the VH1 documentary, 'Let's Spend The Night Together', (available on Youtube,) while interviewed by Pamela Des Barres, her former love rival. Maddox states that Bowie 'was very gentle with me knowing it was my first time.' Elsewhere she states that the Bowie experience pre-dated her time with Page.

If Maddox was 13 when she was deflowered by Bowie, (who, like Page, has also expressed infatuation with the works of Aleister Crowley,) this evokes an earlier unsavoury musical relationship. American rock & roller Jerry Lee Lewis married his 13-year-old cousin, Myra Gale Brown, when he was 22. It was the third of Lewis' seven marriages, and lasted 13 years. (The first was to a 17-year-old when he himself was 13, so presumably any paedophilia present here was inflicted on him.) Lewis and his management insisted that Brown was actually 15 (because it makes all the difference, right?) but the resulting controversy led to the cancellation of Lewis' British tour of 1958. He encountered similar hostility back home when his records were dropped from radio playlists, and interviews and other shows cancelled.

Lewis' scenario—though lacking much of the moral judgement that he underwent—was later echoed by Bill Wyman of the Rolling Stones, when he embarked on an affair with child model Mandy Smith in 1983, when he was 47 and she was 13. In a later interview, Smith admitted to having sex with Wyman from the age of 14. They married in 1989, divorcing two years later. (That's a surprise.) Smith had always been presented as being older than her years, but when the truth about their sexual relations emerged, Wyman says he voluntarily contacted the police, but was told they 'weren't interested' in pursuing it.

Aleister Crowley, rock star

In so many ways, Crowley was the original rock star, with ritual sex magick and mind-altering drugs ever-present in his life story. Crowley's influence on, or associations with The Beatles, The Rolling Stones, Jimmy Page and Jay-Z are well-documented. His deification by pop culture goes much further, however. The Doors' '13' album sleeve shows the band posing with a ceramic bust of Crowley, Stephen Tyler of Aerosmith has talked of practicing Crowley magick, and Frank Zappa and Sting have both been students of his works. Russell Brand has publicly quoted him, while Kanye West, taking a day off from the Baphomet designs, has worn a necklace depicting the aeon of Horus, as espoused in Crowley's teachings. 'American Idol' singer Adam Lambert, Kevin Jonas of The Jonas Brothers and singer and actress Taylor Momsen are among those to have been recently pictured sporting Crowley T-shirts. 'Brave New World' author and eugenicist Aldous Huxley was a personal friend of Crowley, as was James Bond creator Ian Fleming, and LSD guru and CIA agent Dr. Timothy Leary talked of continuing his work during the 1960s counter-culture era.

Ozzy Osbourne called Crowley "a phenomenon of his time," and recorded a song called 'Mr. Crowley.' David Bowie referred to Crowley in his song 'Quicksand' from the album 'The Man Who Sold the World.' Graham Bond claimed to be Crowley's illegitimate son and recorded albums of what have been said to be satanic rituals with his band Holy Magick. Iron Maiden's famous song 'The Number Of The Beast' is thought to be in part-reference to Crowley's self-imposed moniker. Daryl Hall of the duo Hall & Oates reportedly owns a signed and numbered copy of 'The Book Of Thoth' and has said in interview: "I was fascinated by him (Crowley) because his personality was the late-nineteenth-century equivalent of mine—a person brought up in a conventionally religious family who did everything he could to outrage the people around him as well as himself." Church of Satan priest Marilyn Manson's song 'Misery Machine' includes the line 'We're gonna ride to the Abbey of Thelema.' Perhaps the most surprising endorsement came from Barack Obama during his 2012 presidential campaign, in which a photograph showed him hugging a young boy, and wearing a T-shirt with Crowley's face on it and the slogan AC2012.

Some have suggested that the picture is a photo-shopped fake, but the general consensus among those that have examined it scientifically is that it was genuine and part of the campaign known as 'AC2012' which resides here–http://ac2012.com/

Either way, in spite of an extremely colourful and extraordinary life, Crowley died a bankrupt heroin addict in December 1947. Perhaps surprisingly in the circumstances, a BBC poll in 2002 cited Crowley as the 73rd Greatest Briton of all time, as voted for by viewers.

Resources:

(The URLs given are obviously clunky to re-type when not reading on-line. Typing the description of the article into a search engine in each case, therefore, will usually yield the required results.)

Elvis/ They Sold Their Souls For Rock N Roll" Part 1:

- https://www.youtube.com/
  watch?v=e10Wv373uKA&feature=related

Elvis/ They Sold Their Souls For Rock N Roll" Part 1:

- http://www.youtube.com/
  watch?v=MftkmYWpqKU&feature=related

Aangirfan blog: Cliff Richard, Crusaders, Military Intelligence:

- http://aanirfan.blogspot.co.uk/2015/09/cliff-richard-crusaders-military.html

CHAPTER 3

SECRETS AND LIES

Vice and depravity at the BBC and beyond.

"I would say that I am moral during the day, and even higherly (sic) moral during the evening. But of course, we won't say anything about the night-time, because that is when all real wolves like myself rise from the darkness and leap about causing chaos left and right."
Jimmy Savile (1926-2011)

'I myself was little-prepared for many of the shocking revelations which appeared as this story unfolded. I sit and write as fast as my fingers will propel this computer keyboard, but know that I will only be able to commit a portion of the findings which are being revealed in this investigation.'
Hiddenmysteries.org article

In a November 2014 article delving into the depravity of the Dolphin Square revelations, the UK Coleman Experience blog site began:

"If you thought for one minute that Britain is really as it appears to be, you're very sadly mistaken. Beneath the pomp and pageantry lies a network of paedophilic depravity so vile and despicable, it literally beggars belief.

"Don't be fooled into thinking Jimmy Savile was an isolated case either. He wasn't."

Savile and 'Auntie' Beeb

The British Broadcasting Corporation, a propaganda arm for the British Establishment, has itself been up to its neck in vice during recent times. The activities of Jimmy Savile as a serial child-rapist have been well-documented since his exposure in October 2012, a year after his death at the age of 85. The revelations came from a documentary, 'Exposure: The Other Side Of Jimmy Savile,' researched and presented by Mark Williams-Thomas, which was screened in the UK by ITV on 3rd October 2012.

Williams-Thomas was originally a consultant for the BBC's 'Newsnight' programme, which had started investigating the claims against Savile for an episode of the show. This was reported to have been shelved at the eleventh hour by BBC management, however, as it would have conflicted with the schedule of programmes the Corporation had lined up for that Christmas celebrating Savile's life, including a tribute episode of 'Jim'll Fix It' presented by a sycophantic Shane Richie, (Alfie Moon in 'Eastenders.') Despite evidence of Savile's crimes having been presented, this and other tributes still went on to be broadcast at the end of 2011.

Savile was employed by the BBC for several decades, as the host of two long-running and highly prominent TV shows, 'Top Of The Pops' and 'Jim'll Fix It', (what some relevance to that title there turned out to be given that Savile was subsequently exposed as a procurer of children to rich and famous paedophiles,) as well as for many years as a DJ on BBC Radio 1. The Savile exposure revealed how he had been sexually abusing children unimpeded for years, with some of the offences having taken place in his BBC dressing room. The suggestion that this could have gone on for so long without the knowledge of senior BBC management is inconceivable, particularly with 'celebrities' such as Esther Rantzen, Terry Wogan, (who was reported to have died from cancer on 31st January 2016,) Bill Oddie, Noel Edmonds and Paul Gambaccini having acknowledged recently that Savile being a 'kiddie fiddler' was an 'open secret' within the Corporation. For Savile's 80th birthday, Prince Charles sent him a pair of gold cufflinks engraved with the words: 'No-one will ever know what you have done for this country, Jimmy.' At Savile's funeral, prior to his crimes being made public, former boxer

Frank Bruno, (who Savile had introduced to his friend Peter Sutcliffe, aka The Yorkshire Ripper,) remarked that Savile had done 'a lot of good, special things that people don't even know' and that Savile 'helped me in a lot of ways that I can't really talk about on the television.' In June 2000, comedian Frank Skinner made what seemed to be a knowing reference to Savile's penchant for necrophilia in a live show. In a 1978 interview, Sex Pistols frontman Johnny Rotten remarked that he'd like to kill Jimmy Savile, saying: 'I bet he's into all kinds of seediness that we all know about but we're not allowed to talk about,' adding, 'I know some rumours!' The general public, it seems, were the last to know.

In addition, James Anderton, the Chief Constable of Greater Manchester Police, is reported to have warned the BBC back in 1975 that several of their performers, including Savile, had been named as using teenage boys who were being sold for sex in the Canal Street area of Manchester. Despite this, no former director of the BBC has been called on to address the subject by Operation Yewtree, the exercise in damage limitation that was hastily set up in the wake of the scandal.

Elsewhere, Savile was discovered to have abused children at the hospitals at which he 'volunteered', including disabled children in the spinal injuries unit of Stoke Mandeville hospital, and inmates at Broadmoor Psychiatric Hospital. He was also exposed as a necrophiliac, having had sex with dead bodies in the mortuary of Leeds General Infirmary where he 'volunteered' as a night porter, (a claim made by fellow Radio 1 DJ Paul Gambaccini . . . before he himself was arrested on suspicion of historical sexual offences, but later released without charge.) Apparently no-one in BBC senior management had the slightest clue. Neither did the Queen when she awarded him an OBE in 1972 and as a Knight Bachelor in 1990. I'm sure it was all just one big misunderstanding. Savile's funeral was held on 9th November (or 9/11,) but I'm sure that's just a coincidence.

Savile is said to have been obsessed with Satanic practices, and some researchers have suggested he was a black magician, and hailed from a long-running bloodline of occultists. He referred to his late mother as 'The Duchess', and it has been suggested that this was far more than a random nickname, hinting at the relevance of the bloodline from which he descended. Savile was a friend of the Yorkshire Ripper, Peter

Sutcliffe. The body of one of Sutcliffe's victims, Irene Richardson, was discovered close to Savile's home in Roundhay Park, Leeds.

In the BBC2 documentary with Louis Theroux, 'When Louis Met Jimmy,' screened in April 2000, Savile shows the audience what he claims to be the wardrobe of his late mother in Scarborough, claiming to have kept many of her garments as souvenirs of her memory. Irish researcher and author Thomas Sheridan and others have speculated that these may in fact be trinkets of some of his victims, and that his crimes may go beyond child abuse to include murder.

Elsewhere in the documentary, Theroux is seen questioning Savile about the ongoing allegations of paedophilia that had plagued him for years. The dialogue runs as follows:

> *"Louis: So, why do you say in interviews that you hate children when I've seen you with kids and you clearly enjoy their company and you have a good rapport with them?*
>
> *Jimmy: Right, obviously I don't hate 'em. That's number one.*
>
> *Louis: Yeah. So why would you say that then?*
>
> *Jimmy: Because we live in a very funny world. And it's easier for me, as a single man, to say 'I don't like children' because that puts a lot of salacious tabloid people off the hunt.*
>
> *Louis: Are you basically saying that so tabloids don't, you know, pursue this whole 'is he/ isn't he a paedophile?' line, basically?*
>
> *Jimmy: Yes, yes, yes. Oh, aye. How do they know whether I am or not? How does anybody know whether I am? Nobody knows whether I am or not."*

The 'When Louis Met Jimmy' documentary, which used to be viewable in its entirety on Youtube, now appears to have been removed. It has also disappeared from Vimeo, a message in its place reading: "Vimeo has removed or disabled access to the following material as a result of a third-party notification by BBC Worldwide claiming that this material is infringing."

Among the glut of 'celebs' who were hung out to dry by Operation Yewtree amidst accusations of sexual impropriety were BBC 'It's A Knockout' presenter Stuart Hall, comedians Freddie Starr and Jim Davidson, former BBC producer Wilfred De'ath, publicist Max Clifford, Ted Beston, known in BBC circles as 'Uncle' Ted and a one-time radio producer for Jimmy Savile and Tony Blackburn, BBC DJ Paul Gambaccini, (later vindicated,) and the former BBC2 announcer and Radio 1 DJ Chris Denning.

Many people who were abused as children turn out to exhibit the same behavioural patterns as adults. Denning has said that he was a rent boy for the rich and famous from the age of 13 to 18. His first conviction was for gross indecency and indecent assault as long ago as 1974. Prior to this, Denning had been working with Jonathan King on his UK Records label. The pair were later implicated in the Walton Hop paedophile breeding ground, along with Tam Paton, manager of the Bay City Rollers. Denning went on to do jail time for various child sex offences. In November 2014 he admitted to a total of 41 sex offence charges against young boys involving 26 victims between the years 1967 and 1987.

A further veteran Radio 1 DJ whose name has cropped up in many related instances is Alan 'Fluff' Freeman, long-time host of the BBC's 'Pick Of The Pops.' In September 2013, seven years after Freeman's death, UK newspapers ran a story of a man who claimed Freeman and Savile had raped him at a party in a London flat, (in the same block in which Freeman himself lived,) when he was a schoolboy. The Daily Mirror's version of events stated:

> *"Speaking out for the first time since being interviewed by detectives, he claimed Freeman and Savile 'showed me no pity and arrogantly thought they could get away with anything.'*

> *"'Fluff" Freeman—famous in the 1960s for his catchphrases 'Greetings, pop pickers' and 'not 'arf'—is the latest on a growing list of stars named in the massive sex crimes investigation.*

> *"It raises further concerns about a paedophile network that flourished at the heart of the BBC.*

"The victim, happily married for 20 years, claims his horrific ordeal came in 1964–the year Savile and Freeman were founder presenters of 'Top Of The Pops'."

Former Radio 1 DJ Dave Lee Travis, (real name David Griffin), was convicted of two sexual offences in 2014, but unusually, these concerned the groping of adult women's breasts, rather than involving young boys. Although morally wrong, this was hardly in the same league as the other grotesque offences Yewtree was supposed to be investigating, and Travis seems to have been used as a convenient scapegoat to satisfy the public appetite for 'something to be done,' deflecting scrutiny from the *real* key players involved.

Down with the King

Radio 1 and BBC presenter, (is it me, or is there a pattern emerging here?) Jonathan King was exposed as a serial paedophile with a preference for young boys long before the Savile scandal, getting convicted and sentenced to seven years in jail in 2001. Wikipedia reports that:

> *"The investigation led to King's prosecution, which, for 'case management' purposes, was split between three trials at the Old Bailey. King denied the charges but, in September 2001, he was found guilty, in the first of the trials, of four offences of indecent assault, one of buggery and one of attempted buggery against five boys aged 14 and 15 during the 1980s. Two months later, he was sentenced to 7 years' imprisonment for those offences.*

> *"In sentencing him, Judge David Paget, QC, said 'You used your fame and success to attract adolescent and impressionable boys. You then abused the trust they and their parents placed in you.' Shortly before he was sentenced, King was acquitted in the second trial. The prosecution had offered no further evidence after the alleged victim admitted during the trial that he was 'probably 16' at the time of the alleged offences; the prosecution had been unable to prove that the sex was non-consensual. The prosecution then dropped the charges in the third trial."*

According to a July 2014 article on The Coleman Experience website:

> *"Documents presented in Operation Arundel's court case against DJ Jonathan King, were that he invited back boys from the Walton Hop club, and would also drive round in his Rolls Royce outside schools enticing boys into the car to help him with a pop quiz. He had a secret 'fantasy room', a large rectangular suite in his Bayswater mansion bedecked in lush black leather sofas, large swastika flags hung ceremoniously from ceiling to floor.*
>
> *"Although Jewish, he had commissioned elaborate faked photo blow-ups of himself in SS uniform, shaking hands with Hitler. He also screened 16mm projections of Nazi films which seemed to excite him.*
>
> *"Boys were told if they mentioned to anyone what had happened, the police would be told they had taken drugs and they would be in serious trouble. So the boys in the main kept quiet. One report shown to me said these DJs were regular visitors to the twelve London care homes, and boys taken out were known as 'the sweety boys' as they always came back with sweets.*
>
> *"Margaret Hodge (Oppenheimer) was the children's minister who was accused of hiding up the child abuse scandal. She was alleged to be close friends with Tony Blair, Peter Mandelson and Jonathan King."*

King has consistently behaved as if he feels he has done nothing wrong. He has refused to apologise to his victims and their families, instead stating in 2012: "The only apology I have is to say that I was good at seduction. I was good at making myself seem attractive when I wasn't very attractive at all."

Interestingly, record industry svengali and TV mogul (and freemason) Simon Cowell put up £50,000 of King's £150,000 bail money when he was first jailed. The Mail Online reported in 2004 that Cowell's publicist Max Clifford was angered at Cowell's actions, saying he subsequently 'set him straight about what kind of man King is' . . . before Clifford himself was sentenced to eight years imprisonment in 2014 after being found guilty of eight charges of indecent assault against girls and young women.

The BBC hit the headlines for all the wrong reasons again in 2014, meanwhile, when the publicly disgraced Jonathan King was wheeled out to give comments to a BBC2 documentary about the rock group Genesis. King is credited with 'discovering' the band while they were still pupils at Charterhouse public school in Surrey, which he himself attended. Apparently no-one else would do and the BBC considered King's inclusion more important than the insult that would be caused by giving airtime to a child-rapist in a programme funded by public licence payers, despite having already been embroiled in paedophile scandal for two years following the Savile revelations. A cynic could be forgiven for concluding that they were smugly and knowingly taking the piss. And King was in the headlines yet again in September 2015 when he was arrested on suspicion of yet more historical sex offences linked to the Walton Hop.

Peel away the layers

It seems even the hero of the alternative scene, John Peel, (real name John Ravenscroft), whose anti-establishment image flew in the face of the conventional side of 'Auntie' Beeb, was not immune to the odd temptation in the spirit of the times, or the sickness that seems to have afflicted the Corporation. Maybe Peel was more of a BBC man than his carefully crafted rebel image led us to believe. He did, after all, come from a public school background, the *de facto* Establishment breeding ground, and joined the VIP club by getting awarded an OBE in 1998.

Before joining the original line-up of Radio 1, and going on to enjoy a long BBC career which lasted all the way up his death in 2004, Peel worked at a Texas radio station in the early 60s. In later interviews, he recalled some of the perks of that particular period as involving many girls, some as young as 13, queuing up outside his studio to offer him sexual favours.

"Well, of course, I didn't ask for ID,' Peel has said in interview. "All they wanted me to do was to abuse them sexually, which of course I was only too happy to do.

"It was the glamour of the job... but frustratingly, American girls of that period—as they do now, actually—had this strange notion of virginity as a tangible thing which you surrendered to your husband on your wedding night. So they would do anything but shag you. They'd give you a blowjob before they'd shag you."

One of the girls who queued up outside his studio was Shirley Anne Milburn. Peel went on to marry her in 1965 when he was 26 and she was 15. They moved to London, but divorced in 1973. Shortly afterwards Shirley returned to the US where she committed suicide.

Peel wrote a column for the music magazine 'Sounds' through the 1970s, in which he often joked of how he preferred fans when they were dressed in schoolgirl outfits. For one series of pictures illustrating the column, Peel posed dressed as a St. Trinians-style schoolgirl himself, complete with stockings and suspenders.

Peel also ran a 'Schoolgirl Of The Year' competition on Radio 1.

Meanwhile, a glance at the Wikipedia biography of Ed 'Stewpot' Stewart, famous for his stints on Radio 1, Radio 2 and hosting 'Crackerjack' on BBC1, reveals that: "Stewart met his wife when she was 13 and he was 34. They married four years later."

'The spirit of the times'

Some may look at these 'crimes' and consider them mild when compared with some of the other horrors now being uncovered, such as Satanic ritual abuse against children. Such encounters are often written off as merely in keeping with 'the spirit of the times,' when 'everyone was at it,' and attempts are made to justify the situation by pointing out that the girls were willing participants and were 'throwing themselves' at the celebs concerned. What's a red-blooded male to do?

But whichever way you cut it, sex with underage girls is still paedophilia, (with Dave Lee Travis getting jail-time for the lesser crime of adult fondling to keep things in perspective,) and it would be a difficult task to find too many fathers of teenage girls who are absolutely fine with the idea of their daughter being lured to bed by a grown man as a perk of his 'celebrity' status. Viewing things from this perspective, I find, always acts as a good moral compass for judging a situation.

In 2012, The UK Daily Mail carried the story of a 15-year-old schoolgirl, Claire McAlpine, who had been a dancer on BBC1's 'Top Of The Pops' show. She had been discovered dead by her mother in 1971, apparently the result of a suicidal overdose. Claire had left behind a diary for her parents, in which she had written accounts of how she had been sexually abused by a string of BBC presenters and celebrities. The celebrities in question were never publicly identified, though it has emerged that Jimmy Savile, (surprise, surprise, as Cilla Black would have said,) was quizzed by detectives over whether he knew her, which naturally, he denied. One of Claire's friends, Jenni Bale, later stated that Savile was one of the DJs who had abused Claire, but that he had 'bluffed his way out of it,' Claire was written off as a troubled fantasist, with the coroner ruling that she had taken her own life in anticipation of not being able to fulfil her dreams to become a pop star.

As The Mail reported in its 2012 article:

> "The allegations made—and casually dismissed both within and out-side the BBC—by Claire McAlpine all those years ago can point only to one dreadful conclusion: that far from being alone, the preda-tory behaviour displayed by Jimmy Savile, national icon and char-ity fundraiser, was common among many big showbusiness names of the time.

> "Indeed, all this week accusations have been appearing in national newspapers about various well-known DJs. How many famous men are sitting at home now terrified that the truth is about to come out?

> "They may not have been paedophiles, (although we know of at least two, namely Jonathan King and former Radio 1 DJ Chris Denning, who were,) but they were part of the same culture of permissive-ness that allowed the moral boundary surrounding under-age sex to become blurred.

> "Might this be the real reason for the code of omerta that seems to have prevented many of those who must have known about Jimmy Savile's predilection for young girls from speaking out?"

Stories such as these are the true, bitter legacy of celebrities taking advantage of their status to get their sexual kicks. The fact that 'everyone was doing it' only makes it worse. There were no lack of visual clues as to the zeitgeist of that era either, it seems. Original copies of Alice Cooper's 1972 album 'School's Out' were sold with a pair of panties wrapped around the sleeve, (and available in four different colours to increase collectability.) The debut album from Blind Faith, meanwhile, appeared around the same time with a topless, adolescent girl on the cover.

Sharks in Dolphin Square

The Mail article went on to give accounts of another former victim of child rape, who named a former celebrity DJ as having abused her, along with a former associate of another DJ who made similar claims. The article did not reveal their identities, though it was hinted that one of them worked for London's Capital Radio. What it did say was that one of the DJs in question allegedly tried to rape a girl at a party in Dolphin Square, in Pimlico, London, in the 1980s. Dolphin Square has been hitting the headlines for all the wrong reasons in recent months. Flats and apartments there are owned or rented by prominent MPs, and many have been implicated in accusations of child rape on-site.

Scotland Yard confirmed in 2014 that they had launched a murder investigation connected to allegations of child sex abuse dating back to the 1970s and 1980s, involving three paedophile MPs and centred around flats in Dolphin Square.

One former Capital Radio DJ who was publicly named and arrested for historic sex offences was Neil Fox, who had also been a judge on 'Pop Idol' alongside Simon Cowell. Fox was charged in 2015 with nine sex offences against six people, of whom three were said to be under the age of 16. (Purely as a matter of curiosity, 'Fox' translates into '666' using Pythagorean numerology, and this is not the last time we'll be encountering that particular number!)

Two Little Boys (and the rest)

Rolf Harris' conviction as a child-rapist was wholly shocking for many, given his kindly public persona. New relevance was placed on a sketch filmed for the 1980s BBC2 comedy 'Not The Nine O Clock News' but never broadcast, when it recently emerged on Youtube. It shows several children being abducted from a town centre and herded into a BBC lorry. As the lorry drives off, the words 'Rolf's On Saturday OK' can be seen on the side.

You can watch the video here:

- http://www.westerndailypress.co.uk/Rolf-Harris-1980-s-comedy-sketch-showing-children/story-21343123-detail/story.html

A similar story surfaced in the wake of Cilla Black's death in August 2015, when The Sun 'newspaper' revealed that a sketch from comedienne Tracey Ullman's upcoming BBC comedy show had been 'put aside.' It was said to feature Ullman portraying Black visiting a number of showbiz homes . . . only to realise that they'd all been, as The Sun puts it, "done for Jimmy Savile-type offences." Hiding the truth in plain sight once again.

Jill Dando and the Establishment ring

There is strong evidence to suggest that BBC journalist Jill Dando was in the process of investigating institutionalised paedophile rings within the British Establishment when she was shot in the head at point blank range on her London doorstep in 1999.

These revelations became so widespread within the alternative media that even corporate mainstream newspapers were forced to report on the story in July 2014 to avoid being seen to be out of touch or deliberately avoiding the issue. A friend and retired co-worker of Dando's stated:

> *"I don't recall the names of all the stars now and don't want to implicate anyone, but Jill said they were surprisingly big names. I think she was quite shocked when told about images of children and that*

information on how to join this horrible paedophile ring was freely available.

"Jill said others had complained to her about sexual matters and that some female workmates also claimed they had been groped or assaulted. Nothing had been done and there seemed to be a policy of turning a blind eye."

Barry George, the man originally charged with the Dando murder in a useful diversion to satisfy the general public that 'something was being done,' was later revealed to have been framed when he was acquitted in 2008 after serving seven years in jail. His claims for wrongful imprisonment were rejected.

The plot goes further yet, in another interconnected labyrinth involving, among others, the BBC's Nick Ross, Esther Rantzen, Royal gynaecologist (and former fiancé of Jill Dando) Alan Farthing, Childline founder Sarah Caplin, and many others, as detailed in the following two 2013 articles from the UK Coleman Experience and Aangirfan blog sites:

- http://thecolemanexperience.wordpress.com/2013/06/03/ the-curious-case-of-nick-ross-vip-child-abuse-filthy-comments-operation-yewtree-crimestoppers-and-the-death-of-jill-dando/

- http://aangirfan.blogspot.com/2013/07/il-principe.html

And in this Coleman Experience piece, which speculates on whether the deaths of the former BBC celebrities Kristian Digby, Natasha Collins, Mark Speight, Kevin Greening, Rik Mayall and Mike Smith could have been connected to knowledge of a high-ranking paedophile network:

- http://thecolemanexperience.wordpress.com/2014/10/25/ mysterious-deaths-at-the-bbc/

Natasha Collins, the girlfriend of BBC children's entertainer Mark Speight, was found dead in a bathtub in 2008. Death by Bathtub seems to be a common theme in the passing away of celebrities, and this is not the last time we will encounter it in this book. Speight is reported to have sunk into a deep depression after being arrested on suspicion of murder and of supplying her with Class A drugs, though he was not charged. Speight's body was discovered hanging from a disused part of Paddington train station in London three months later.

Greening is said to have died of a heart attack a day before his 45th birthday after taking large quantities of cocaine, ecstasy and GHB. His boyfriend, Sean Griffin, was arrested in connection with his death, but charges were not subsequently pursued by the police. Given the large number of unpleasant deaths of so many of its employees, the BBC sure could be said to be one 'unlucky' organisation.

And just to keep it all in perspective, not forgetting this blog article which lists many of the current and former BBC employees, (but by no means all of them,) who have been convicted and charged with various crimes, (and whose salaries are paid for by public money extorted with threats of violence via the BBC TV licence scheme, lest we forget.)

- http://scrapthelicence.weebly.com/bbc-criminals.html

Cheggers drops a bomb

The comments about the BBC being under Jewish control brought to mind the remarkable cameo of a bloated, latter-day Keith Chegwin on Ricky Gervais' 'Extras' comedy, screened on BBC2 in 2006. Chegwin is seen back in a BBC studio, the joke being that he's long past his glory years of presenting 'Swap Shop' and 'Cheggers Plays Pop' and is now all washed up. Getting nostalgic he says: "14 years at the BBC . . . still run by Jews and queers, is it?" It seems all the more incredible with every passing year that Gervais got the green light to include this line in his show. Particularly as Chegwin follows it up with: "Gay!' I forgot! Not allowed to say 'queer' nowadays, are you? Suggests something 'abnormal'. What could be more 'normal' than shoving your cock up a bloke's arse?" This particular clip of Extras is another item which used to be available on Youtube but now seems to have 'disappeared.'

As blatant as it gets

The more you delve into the truth behind the sick, diseased nature of the British Establishment, the more you come to realise that they love placing clues to their activities in plain sight, knowing that they will go right over the heads of all but those open-minded and vigilant enough to go where the truth leads them. Perhaps none of us should have been too surprised at the sickening child sex abuse now known to have taken place within the British Broadcasting Corporation, given the statue that stands outside its iconic Broadcasting House building in London. Named 'Ariel and Prospero' after Shakespeare's 'The Tempest,' it depicts an adult male in ecstasy as a naked male child writhes against his crotch. The 'work' was sculpted by Eric Gill, a known paedophile whose activities have been reported by the BBC itself. Despite the revelations, and the ongoing Savile scandal, the statue remains in place.

Which all goes to make a sick joke of the BBC's 'Children In Need' appeal. This annual money grab seems like a dark mocking of the nation's gullibility. Here is an organisation which covered up paedophilia on a monumental scale, which then has the nerve to tug at the heartstrings of the public and claim to care about the plight of children, with Sir (what else?) Terry Wogan wheeled out as the cuddly, friendly face of 'Auntie' Beeb. Just how much of the millions raised goes to any constructive, practical use in alleviating child suffering is anybody's guess, since recent enquiries into many leading charities have revealed that the bulk of money raised goes towards paying executive salaries and on 'admin' costs. The BBC-supported 'Comic Relief' found scandal when it was revealed in 2013 that some of the money raised, far from going to help people in need in Africa, had been invested in tobacco and arms companies. The findings were even reported on an episode of 'Panorama' broadcast by BBC1 itself. Lenny Henry, the friendly face of 'Comic Relief' for many years, was made a Knight Bachelor in the Queen's Birthday Honours in 2015.

In light of this book's imminent chapter on the one-eyed symbolism peddled by A-list celebrities, isn't it interesting that the mascot for the BBC's 'Children In Need', Pudsey Bear, *just happens* to have one of his eyes covered up by a bandage, and in earlier years, appeared inside a pyramid? The official mascots for the 2012 London Olympics, Wenlock and Mandeville (man-devil?), were two entities who *just happened* to have one eye. But I'm sure it's all just coincidence.

Black is white, white is black

It seems grotesque in retrospect that convicted paedophiles Jimmy Savile, Gary Glitter and Rolf Harris all appeared on 'Children In Need' appeals clutching Pudsey Bear and imploring the public to part with their cash. History has shown that many of the real 'children in need' ended up in that status *because* of the sexual deviants the BBC has employed. The nerve of such an organisation in moralising to the public and manipulating a guilty response is deplorable. But it becomes clear that this is how the various expressions of the Establishment operate. In Satanic ideology, meanings are back-to-front, which is why upside-down crosses and inverted pentagrams are among their favoured symbols. It's reflected in speech, too. When a politician tells the public he won't under any circumstances be raising taxes or sending the country to war, you can take it that the opposite is what is really meant. (There's also a playout of this ideology in the phenomenon of backwards speech recordings, as we'll discover in a later chapter.) So 'Children In Need', as some have suggested, could be taken as covertly meaning 'in need of children.'

The control system also likes to mock us by revealing their true motives right there in plain sight, arrogantly secure in the knowledge that the vast majority will have no idea what's really going on, and will blindly go along with the surface narrative they're given. Most people, with a warm, feel-good image of dear old Terry Wogan on screen with a cute bear with a bandaged eye, evoking an emotional response and piquing at their guilt, will go right along with the coercion to give whatever they can, without thinking to question where the money will end up. Few would believe that such cynical duplicity is possible, which is why so many had great trouble believing the revelations about Rolf Harris' child abuse given his amiable public image. Even Jimmy Savile hid behind his cover story of 'doing a lot of good work for charity,' much of it ensuring he got to hang around large numbers of kids. This is a standard trick used by the control system to disarm the general public, by instilling a glossy veneer so reassuring that it breeds an absolute disbelief that any wrongdoing could be taking place. Of course, *we* could never do anything so outrageously deceptive. But *they* play by different rules of morality and do it all the time. Things have been operating this way, on so many levels, for a very long time. Have we had enough yet?

The Savile scandal should have spelled the end of the BBC, or at the very least, led to a nation so collectively outraged by what had been going on right under their noses, that they refused, en masse, to continue paying the licence fee that funds the BBC's activities. Somewhere in a parallel universe stands a country of aware, morally motivated people where exactly that has happened. But not, sadly, in this one.

Either way, Rolf Harris' 'Two Little Boys,' Gary Glitter's 'I'm The Leader Of The Gang (I Am),' Cliff Richard's 'The Young Ones' and Jonathan King's 'Let It All Hang Out,' are four songs you needn't expect to hear again on the radio any time soon.

Please, Sir

There's no doubt that this section only scratches the surface of the sick, filthy, sordid nature of what really goes on beneath the surface glitz of the entertainment industry, and that alternative stories will be legion. People often express bewilderment at how one industry can spawn such depraved behaviour, immoral lifestyles and negative outcomes. In fact, it's not much different from another level of The Establishment—that of politics. This is an area infested with the same type of activity when you really get down to it—much as the mainstream media may try to downplay it—and politicians are selected for prominent positions in much the same way that Hollywood actors, TV personalities and music artists are.

In the wake of the Savile scandal, media attention—both alternative and mainstream—turned towards the notorious Elm Guest House in South West London. It was kept by Mary Moss, herself a child abuse victim, and formerly with the National Association Of Young People In Care. Elm Guest House was revealed to have been the setting for an ongoing series of depraved orgies through the decades, where famous politicians, business chiefs and well-known entertainers would engage in sex with children that had been procured from various 'care' homes and plied with drugs and alcohol. The guest list that Mary Moss kept makes for very interesting reading.

The fact that the British government has been populated by such a high number of child-rapists, sexual deviants, perverts and Satanists through the decades, defies the laws of probability. The Savile scandal, which would never have been public knowledge had the 'elites' had their way, lifted the lid on a huge swathe of parliamentary paedos that have been protected from public scrutiny for decades. In most cases, they've not only been given important positions, but they've been knighted in the process. By 2015, even the mainstream press was reporting on the fact that former British Prime Minister Sir (anyone surprised?) Edward Heath had been a child-rapist and part of a parliamentary paedophile ring, and had taken young boys from 'care' homes out on the yacht he used to sail to Jersey. They were never seen again. Heath reportedly worked in league with Savile, who was a 'friend.' These revelations should have filled the general British public with absolute outrage and led to demands for questions to be answered. Like everything else, predictably, the story faded from the headlines after a couple of days and the nation carried on going about its business. Wherever the moral line in the sand is in this nation, clearly it's a long way from being reached yet.

It has to be acknowledged that the amount of public figures exposed as paedophiles who just happen to be 'Sirs' is staggering, and it defies all possibility that the Queen could not have known about their activities, particularly as the M15 security services are supposed to thoroughly vet the backgrounds of anyone that the royal family comes into close contact with. The fact that Jimmy Savile, a serial child-rapist, necrophiliac and Satanist, remained a close personal friend of the royals for decades, speaks volumes about how effective and relevant this supposed method of vetting really is, not to mention the type of company that the 'Windsors' (Saxe-Coburg-Gothas) choose to keep.

Conversely, an observer could be justified in theorising that the bestowing of a knighthood is in fact a reward for services rendered. Either way, given the violent and bloody history of the British Empire, and what it has stood for through the centuries—invading foreign lands, slaughtering the indigenous populations, (more often than not people with black and brown skin,) and plundering their natural resources—I find it hard to understand why anyone would want to be associated with it by way of letters after their name. It suggests pride at the Empire's murderous activities, which seems a very strange thing for any morally decent person to want, no matter how much a knighthood might stoke the ego. Recently, DJs have started getting them, too. Reggae supremo David Rodigan and soulful veteran Norman Jay are now 'Sirs', while Soul II Soul's Jazzie B is an OBE, and BBC Radio 1 veterans Pete Tong and Annie Nightingale are now MBEs. Pete might want to think about re-wording the text at the top of his Twitter page, by the way, where he refers to himself as 'the pied piper of dance,' given that The Pied Piper, who in the story kidnapped all of a town's children, has also been a nickname for R Kelly, Russell Brand and Jimmy Savile!

My respect goes out to those conscientious individuals who have declined knighthoods. Among them are poet Benjamin Zephaniah who stated in 2010: "I get angry when I hear the word 'empire'; it reminds me of slavery, it reminds me of thousands of years of brutality, it reminds me of how my foremothers were raped and my forefathers brutalised." Another knighthood decliner is British hip-hop dance supremo Jonzi D, who remarked: "I am diametrically opposed to the idea of empire. Man, I'm a 'Star Wars' fan—empire is bad." I recorded an interview with Jonzi in which he went further into his reasoning, which can be listened to here:

- https://soundcloud.com/mark-devlin/
  mbes-to-b-boys-mark-devlin

Resources:

Sir Cliff Richard 2014 arrest:

- http://www.itv.com/news/story/2014-08-23/
  cliff-richard-not-charged-or-arrested-after-police-interview/

- http://www.mirror.co.uk/news/world-news/
  cliff-richard-planning-new-life-4296739

Sir Cliff Richard plans to sue the BBC:

- http://www.dailymail.co.uk/news/article-2845650/Sir-Cliff-
  Richard-vows-sue-BBC-demands-damages-TV-news-crew-
  filmed-abuse-inquiry-police-raiding-home.html

Led Zeppelin's underage groupies:

- http://www.independent.co.uk/arts-entertainment/music/
  features/led-zeppelin-there-was-a-whole-lotta-love-on-
  tour-763446.html

Lori Maddox's affair with Jimmy Page:

- http://www.stryder.de/rest/Groupie_Central_Lori_%20
  Maddox.html

VH1 documentary 'Let's Spend The Night Together':

- http://www.youtube.com/watch?v=SnViqstGsYs

VH1 documentary on groupies, including interview with Lori Maddox
re Jimmy Page and David Bowie:

- https://www.youtube.com/watch?v=SnViqstGsYs

Was Elvis Presley a paedophile?:

- http://www.nkornitankwa.com/
  were-these-6-incredibly-talented-men-pedophiles/

Jill Dando investigating alleged paedophile ring at the BBC:

- http://www.express.co.uk/news/uk/490169/
  Dando-alarm-paedophile-ring-BBC

The BBC paedophile ring:

- http://thecolemanexperience.wordpress.com/2014/04/03/ the-bbc-and-the-paedophile-ring/

Jonathan King and the Walton Hop paedophile ring:

- http://www.youtube.com/watch?v=PGAUWw6s6r4

Tony Blair, BBC, Britain's missing children and the VIP paedophile connection:

- http://thecolemanexperience.wordpress.com/2014/07/19/ tony-blair-britains-missing-children-and-the-vip-paedophile-connection/

The Who's Who of Satanic Child Abuse, by Chris Spivey:

- http://chrisspivey.org/the-whos-who-of-Satanic-child-abuse/

Elton John's mysterious meltdown, by The Coleman Experience:

- http://thecolemanexperience.wordpress.com/2014/08/02/ elton-johns-mysterious-meltdown/

Pete Townshend interview with The Times:

- http://www.telegraph.co.uk/culture/music/music-news/9572773/Pete-Townshend-I-paid-for-child-porn-to-prove-British-banks-were-channelling-sex-ring-cash.html

Wikipedia: Jimmy Savile: After His Death:

- http://en.wikipedia.org/wiki/Jimmy_Savile#After_his_death

Jimmy Savile, The Kray Twins, Cliff Richard, by Aangirfan:

- http://aangirfan.blogspot.co.uk/2012/10/jimmy-savile-kray-twins-cliff-richards.html

Gary Glitter on 'This Is Your Life':

- http://www.youtube.com/watch?v=F8OZTB03azM

Jimmy Savile and Gary Glitter in their element:

- https://www.youtube.com/watch?v=j6Hx7Q2oC5U

Mysterious deaths at the BBC:

- http://thecolemanexperience.wordpress.com/2014/10/25/
  mysterious-deaths-at-the-bbc/

Man tells of agony at the hands of BBC paedo ring involving DJ Alan Freeman and evil pal Jimmy Savile:

- http://www.mirror.co.uk/news/uk-news/
  man-tells-agony-hands-bbc-2292125

Daily Mail: Special report: A 15-year-old who killed herself after leaving a diary naming DJs as abusers. Disturbing questions about John Peel. So how many stars WERE involved?:

- http://www.dailymail.co.uk/news/article-2213621/
  Claire-McAlpine-A-15-year-old-killed-leaving-diary-
  naming-DJs-abusers-Disturbing-questions-John-Peel-So-starts-
  WERE-involved.html

The curious case of Nick Ross, VIP child-abuse, filthy comments, Operation Yewtree, Crimestoppers and the death of Jill Dando:

- http://thecolemanexperience.wordpress.com/2013/06/03/
  the-curious-case-of-nick-ross-vip-child-abuse-filthy-comments-
  operation-yewtree-crimestoppers-and-the-death-of-jill-dando/

The Coleman Experience: The curious case of Jill Dando, Mark Williams-Thomas, Britain's VIP paedophile ring and the missing murder theory:

- https://thecolemanexperience.wordpress.com/2015/04/05/the-
  curious-case-of-jill-dando-mark-williams-thomas-britains-vip-
  paedophile-ring-and-the-missing-murder-theory/

Paedophiles, the BBC and way beyond:

- http://aangirfan.blogspot.co.uk/2013/07/il-principe.html

VIP paedophile ring at Dolphin Square:

- http://thecolemanexperience.wordpress.com/2014/11/16/ murderous-vip-paedophile-ring-at-dolphin-square/

Scrap The TV Licence: BBC Dodgy Employees:

- http://scrapthelicence.weebly.com/bbc-criminals.html

Crimewatch TV expert groomed boys for sex:

- http://www.mirror.co.uk/news/uk-news/ crimewatch-tv-expert-groomed-boys-564996

CHAPTER 4

LIVING IS EASY WITH EYES CLOSED

Scratching the surface of the Beatles.

> *"There are only 100 people in the world who really understand what our music is about'*
>
> *John Lennon in 'Rolling Stone' magazine upon the release of 'Magical Mystery Tour', 1967*

Given the many manipulations of the industry that it's now possible to understand, nobody should be too surprised to find evidence of the Hidden Hand in arguably the most popular and influential pop group of all time. Sure enough, a thorough delving into the story of The Beatles does not disappoint—even if some sober discernment is needed to identify likely truths from the ever-present glut of misinformation in circulation, whether by deliberate diversion, or well-meaning mistake.

It's been widely claimed that The Beatles were the creation of The Tavistock Institute of Human Relations, the British organisation concerned with mass mind control and social engineering techniques. Its headquarters in London's Tavistock Square was the site of the fourth bomb that went off during 7/7 in 2005. A slogan for a film ad on the side of the wrecked bus just happened to read: "Outright terror . . . bold and brilliant." Tavistock's public cover story is that it's a 'British charity concerned with group behaviour and organisational behaviour,' but the truth about its activities and influence is likely to be rather different. Baron Jacob Rothschild is described officially as a 'philanthropist,' after all, as is David Rockefeller, showing that publicly-acceptable cover stories are a wonderful thing.

The Beatles/ Tavistock theory seems to have become viral after originating from Dr. John Coleman, who, like T. Stokes, was a former

British intelligence officer turned whistle-blower. The account appeared in his book 'The Conspirators' Hierarchy: The Committee Of 300,' and is linked to the allegation that the majority of The Beatles' lyrics were actually written by Theodor W. Adorno, a representative of The Frankfurt School, a German organisation similar in nature to the Tavistock Institute. Adorno appears to have been a professor of philosophy who wrote music, but the claim of his involvement with The Beatles came originally from Coleman. He stated in an interview:

"Theodor W. Adorno was well-known to Tavistock. He was known as 'the Karl Marx of music.' Adorno called his sound 'corrosive' and 'unacceptable,' and it was based on a 12-atonal system, consisting of heavy, repetitive sounds. He started writing all his songs using this system. Adorno believed the bourgeoisie wanted music that didn't bother them or make them think. Tavistock wanted to pass on these new musical experiences to new audiences, affecting the masses. So 'uncomfortable' music was born."

Coleman also claimed that The Beatles' music was later used to normalise recreational drug usage among young people, creating an entirely new and irreversible social dynamic within the course of a few years.

Many have viewed The Beatles' music, image and cultural legacy in new light in the spirit of these times. The suggestion that they were a project of unseen forces, rather than four working class lads from Liverpool who just happen to have found success through hard work and some catchy songs, seems distinctly probable. It's also been pointed out that The Beatles' monumental success in America, off the back of their fabled February 1964 appearance on 'The Ed Sullivan Show,' occurred only weeks after the assassination of President Kennedy which had so traumatised that nation. The Beatles served as a hip and uplifting distraction to the sinister aftermath of that event.

Despite this, however, substantiating Coleman's claim is difficult. Many fans have pointed out that the notion of a dusty old professor writing lyrics as hip and poignant as those of The Beatles is absurd—particularly ones such as 'Penny Lane' and 'Strawberry Fields' which supposedly drew on John Lennon's personal childhood memories.

Although Coleman is often apparently 'debunked,' a wide variety of researchers and Beatles scholars tend to find the idea that the group were a Tavistock project entirely plausible. And claims that The Beatles' against-all-odds success story involves more than meets the eye, do not go away through simply dismissing Coleman's account.

A done deal?

In 2008, lifelong Beatles fan-turned-author Joseph Niezgoda released his book 'The Lennon Prophecy: A New Examination Of The Death Clues Of The Beatles.' Like many US authors, Niezgoda makes no secret of the fact that he is a Christian patriot, and his religious views tend to colour his findings. He does make some intriguing contentions, however.

The crux of Niezgoda's theory is that dark occult clues and symbols were placed throughout The Beatles' material, but rather than hinting at the premature death of Paul McCartney, (we'll get to that!), they all relate to a kind of demonic curse that followed John Lennon. The reason for this, Niezgoda states, is that Lennon entered into a contract with 'The Devil' in the early days of the group, in which he was promised 20 years of fame and fortune on an unprecedented scale. Lennon's fee was a heavy one, involving him effectively giving over his soul, while 'The Devil's end of the deal speaks for itself.

This deal was reportedly made in 1960, and there is a point in December of that year where the phenomenon of teenage fans screaming hysterically and trying to mob the stage can first be seen—an unseen spectacle in Britain up to that point. This would seemingly have been sometime between 10th December, when The Beatles returned uneventfully from a lacklustre stint performing in Germany, and the 27th, the date of a far more successful turn at Liverpool's Litherland Town Hall.

Certainly, this article by Dave Persails detailing the early incarnations of the group, and the changes in name and personnel before their breakthrough, begs the intriguing question of just what it was that magically gelled to propel the Beatles to overnight success after years of struggling amateurism—http://abbeyrd.best.vwh.net/named.htm. Indeed, Robert Whitaker, the photographer behind the infamous 'butcher' cover of the 'Yesterday And Today' album, remarked: "All over the world I'd watched people worshipping like idols, like gods, four Beatles. To me they were just stock standard normal people. But this emotion that fans poured on them made me wonder where Christianity was heading."

These last days of 1960, goes the story, were the starting point of the fame and fortune deal. Bearing in mind it was only to last for 20 years, however, it would have expired in December 1980, the month when Lennon was murdered outside the Dakota building in Manhattan.

According to an uncredited article on the blog site No-One Has To Die Tomorrow:

"The Beatles' ascension to the top rung of the Rock & Roll pantheon, displacing Elvis Presley and American rock legends who had a lock on the reins of Rock & Roll, was rigged and engineered into place by the British Crown and British Military Intelligence.

"For instance, in August 1963, at their first major television appearance at the London Palladium, the newspaper reported that police had to hold back '1,000 squealing teenagers,' but the story was fabricated. The newspaper photo actually tightly cropped three screaming teenagers and claimed it was a thousand. One reporter who was there later said there were less than eight girls present. There was no 'riot' by frenzied teenage girls.

"Similarly, 'Beatlemania' hysteria was manufactured at JFK Airport in February of 1964 when the Beatles arrived in the USA to perform for 'The Ed Sullivan Show.' Busloads of girls from a Bronx school were paid by Beatles promoters to scream hysterically when the Beatles got off the plane and went into the terminal.

"It was a manufactured publicity stunt, but it paid off in priming the pump for the 'Ed Sullivan Show' appearances, which did create a frenzied attitude among many American teenagers, set the stage for a looser rein on moral boundaries, and opened the door for kids from 'decent,' middle-class families to start using drugs, which is precisely what British Intelligence, Tavistock, and the CIA had in mind all along."

Lennon's assassination appeared to have been foreshadowed by film footage shot in early December 1969, which later appeared in the BBC documentary 'John Lennon: 24 Hours.' Lennon is with Yoko Ono, going through letters sent in by fans. He reads out one from someone saying they'd been using a Ouija board and received a message that someone will try to assassinate him, writing: 'The spirit that gave me this information was Brian Epstein'.

Almost exactly 11 years later the prophecy became true.

Winged Beatles

The very naming of The Beatles is an aspect that has intrigued researchers into the group's more occultic aspects. 'Beatles' is taken to be a simple pun, in reference to their status as a 'beat' group. In its earliest incarnation as a late 50s skiffle band, Lennon first called his ensemble The Black Jacks, before it morphed into The Quarry Men, then further monikers such as Johnny and the Moondogs, The Nerk Twins, (for just two days,) The Beatals, The Silver Beetles, The Silver Beats and The Silver Beatles, before eventually surviving as The Beatles. Original member Stuart Sutcliffe is supposed to have come up with the 'Beatles' idea as a play on Buddy Holly's Crickets. (Sutcliffe died of a reported brain aneurysm in 1962 at the age of just 21. A common internet rumour refers to Sutcliffe's sister Pauline claiming that John Lennon had a homosexual affair with her brother, that he later beat him up out of confused guilt, and that Lennon's blows to the head led to Sutcliffe's eventual fate. However, Pauline denied ever making these comments in 2003 as she unveiled a collection of her brother's personal items to be sold at auction.)

When writing an article for his friend Bill Harry's 'Mersey Beat' magazine in 1961, in the days before The Beatles had found Ringo, Brian Epstein or George Martin, Lennon stated: 'Many people ask what are The Beatles? Why Beatles? Ugh, Beatles, how did the name arrive? So we will tell you. It came in a vision. A man appeared on a flaming pie and said unto them: 'From this day on you are Beatles with an A'. 'Thank you, Mister Man,' they said, thanking him.' ('Flaming Pie' cropped up as the title of Paul McCartney's tenth studio album decades later in 1997.)

The alternative consensus, however, appears to be that the group's name is derived from the horned scarab beetle, a religious symbol of Ancient Egyptian culture. These insects were revered as symbols of regeneration and creation, conveying ideas of transformation, renewal, and resurrection. Furthermore, their habit of making balls of dung and rolling them, were considered a symbol of the sun god Ra rolling the sun across the sky every day. Synchronistically, these particular beetles have wings, with Paul McCartney choosing 'Wings' as the name of his later group. Intriguingly, "The Winged Beetle' was the title of a collection of poems by Aleister Crowley. Heard of him anywhere?

Hearts on their sleeves

Any advanced study into the hidden nature of the corporate industry machine reveals a heavy reliance on symbolism, steeped in occult, esoteric and mystical practices, and designed to have an unknowing effect on the subconscious mind of the viewer. When it comes to The Beatles, students of this phenomenon have had a field day with the group's album covers, and it would take a very heavy dose of world-weary cynicism to deny that something—whatever the interpretation—is designed to be communicated by some of the key images.

An early album sleeve, Parlophone's 'With The Beatles', has the four pictured in black-and-white with one half of their faces shaded, the other illuminated, evoking the eye of Horus/ all-seeing eye/ illumination symbology we will encounter elsewhere. The 'Hard Day's Night' sleeve similarly features half of The Beatles' faces, this time cut off below the nose, with one eye slightly shaded in each case. On a rare Dutch version of 'Help,' the band are paraded in front of a giant version of the Shell petroleum company logo. Except the Shell logo has always been a cleverly-disguised representation of the rays of the rising sun. Sun symbolism crops up throughout Beatles imagery and in the lyrics to a great many of their songs. The more common version of 'Help' has the members striking 'grade sign' poses straight out of Crowley's AA occult secret society. Similarly, there are telling hand signs from Lennon and McCartney on the sleeve to 'Yellow Submarine,' (a slang term for both a cannabis joint and a mild pharmaceutical stimulant capsule.) The 'Beatles' '65' sleeve has the band posing under umbrellas, which is interesting bearing in mind Lenon Honor's interpretation of Rihanna's 'Umbrella' song and video that appears in the later chapter on video symbolism.

The meanings hidden in the 'Sergeant Pepper' sleeve could cover an entire book in themselves, and we'll get on to that one later, along with the similarly ambiguous and endlessly-analysed 'Abbey Road.' Only one other sleeve has received anywhere near as much analysis and opining in recent years, and this is the infamous 'butcher' cover for the June 1966, (6/66?) compilation release 'The Beatles: Yesterday And Today.'

The image, surely shocking by anyone's standards, has the four smiling Beatles dressed in butchers' smocks, with raw meat draped all over them, along with naked toy baby dolls. The dolls are mutilated, with heads and arms missing. Lennon is pointing downwards with one of his fingers. The image was one of nine known to have been taken during a photographic session directed by the aforementioned Robert Whitaker. The unused images, all grisly, differ widely from the one chosen. In one, Lennon alone smiles, covered in meat, displaying teeth and eyes on his hands. Another has McCartney alone, gazing upwards while clutching mutilated dolls and meat, (an interesting stance for one of the world's most famous vegetarians,) with what looks like an umbilical cord dangling from his wrist. The four are seen smiling as Lennon puts a pair of sunglasses on a doll's decapitated head. Two pictures similar to the final choice have the Beatles looking sullen and forlorn, rather than smiling. In another, all have their eyes closed, seeming to be asleep or in a trance.

Decades later, the raw meat look would be resurrected by Lady Gaga and her notorious 'meat dress,' which caused similar shock and controversy.

The meaning of the meat

Unsurprisingly, there have been multiple interpretations of the sleeve. Among the most popular, (put forward by Joseph Niezgoda among many others,) is the unsettling suggestion that the group were subliminally communicating the practice of infanticide, the ritual sacrifice of babies and young children by the elite ruling class. Certainly, there has been endless evidence provided by researchers and whistleblowers to show that this sick and horrific practice is one routinely employed by the dark occult priest class who ultimately control human activity.

The idea is that The Beatles, presumably at the behest of their controllers, were providing a representation of this, either as a well-meaning indicator of what goes on, or as a way of mocking their fans, in the sure knowledge that all but a handful would be completely ignorant of the true meaning. A glance at the full photoshoot reveals four men who appear far from in confident control of the situation they find themselves in, looking more like manipulated stooges following every stage of their instructions. In fact, the uniformity of the Beatles, with all four members looking, dressing, talking and acting in the same way throughout their formative years, smacks of a quartet of puppeteered dupes, rather than four fiercely creative and self-driven individuals making statements of their own independent choosing.

There is another, far more innocent-sounding interpretation of the 'butcher' cover, however, which seems to have become equally prevalent. This version was described to me in an e-mail from Bruce Reid, a filmmaker currently involved in a project called 'The King And The Queen's Men,' examining the cultural impact of The Beatles and Elvis Presley:

> *"When The Beatles made their splash in the US, the record label, (Capitol,) that distributed their music came up with a brilliant idea. Capitol completely altered albums, or came up with completely different albums that never existed outside the US and Canada. 'The Beatles' 2nd Album', 'Something New', 'Beatles' 65', 'Beatles VI' and 'Yesterday And Today' are examples of these type of albums.*

> *"Until the release of 'Sergeant Pepper' none of the British albums lined up with the US versions. When 'Yesterday And Today' was released, it was two months before 'Revolver.' What they decided to do was remove three songs from the unreleased 'Revolver' and place them on 'Y&T.' The songs were 'And Your Bird Can Sing.' 'I'm Only Sleeping,' and 'Dr. Robert.' The Beatles were tired of their artistic works being butchered, which resulted in the picture being sent to Capitol as a message to quit butchering their albums in order to make a quick buck. Somehow, it was determined by Capitol that this was*

supposed to be used as the official cover. That was Capitol's mistake, not The Beatles'."

This makes for an interesting case. But if this was indeed the motivation behind the cover, it occurs to me that the statement could have been made with just the smocks and the raw meat. Why the need for the mutilated babies too?

However, Bruce Reid adds:

> *"I truly believe that someone in The Beatles' camp, (George Martin, Brian Epstein or Sir Lew Grade—probably Lew Grade,) was involved with The Tavistock Institute that, unbeknownst to the Beatles, were involved with their tremendously quick rise to the top. I feel that when they discovered they were too far in to get out, they decided to let the fans know what was going on. I've heard that one of the reasons John Lennon was assassinated, was that he was going on a world tour in 1981 and that he was going to expose Tavistock for what they were."*

Both Robert Whitaker and Paul McCartney have claimed credit for the photoshoot idea. Some fans have suggested that McCartney was the most conscientious of The Beatles regarding what they came to realise they were a part of. According to a 2002 interview in the music magazine 'Mojo,' former Capitol president Alan W. Livingston stated that it was McCartney who pushed strongly for the photo's inclusion as some kind of comment on the Vietnam War, rather than a comment on infanticide. Whitaker's apparent version is that he wanted to push the envelope by creating something genuinely avant-garde, simply for its shock value. He is said to have been trying to recreate the work of the German surrealist Hans Bellmer.

A fascinating array of information on hidden aspects of The Beatles residing just beneath the surface, (or sometimes, right upon it,) comes from the following blog site, meanwhile. As ever, readers must decide for themselves whether all the claims and contentions have merit. At the very least, it provides for many hours of deep pondering and musing for those who like to embrace all the possibilities of a situation:

- http://pinballking.blogspot.co.uk/2010/07/whats-wrong-with-beatles-alot.html

It all serves to further muddy the waters when it comes to the truth behind The Beatles. The only thing that remains undeniable, whatever the finer detail, is that there was always far, far more to the group than the carefully cultivated image of four fun, wholesome lads that was presented to the general public.

And that's before you even get into the whole area of 'PID.' Hold tight—now we're really heading into the Belly of the Beast!

Resources:

The Beatles–Illuminati Mind Controllers:

- http://www.henrymakow.com/beatles_were_mind_control.html

The Beatles created by the Tavistock Institute. Interview with Dr. John Coleman:

- http://www.henrymakow.com/beatles_were_mind_control.html

Plastic Macca blog: Disinfo that Theodor Adorno wrote Beatles' music abounds:

- http://plasticmacca.blogspot.co.uk/2013/06/disinfo-that-theodore-adorno-wrote.html

The Beatles: What's In A Name? by Dave Persails:

- http://abbeyrd.best.vwh.net/named.htm

What's Wrong With The Beatles? A Lot. The occult Symbols Of the Beatles:

- http://pinballking.blogspot.co.uk/2010/07/whats-wrong-with-beatles-alot.html

Stuart Sutcliffe's sister denies Lennon claim:

http://news.bbc.co.uk/1/hi/entertainment/3092533.stm

The Beatles: Social Agitators:

- http://noonehastodietomorrow.nwotradingcards.com/occult/media/3268-3268

Bruce Reid's movie project regarding the influence of Elvis and The Beatles, 'The King and the Queen's Men.':

- www.elvisbeatlesmovie.com

Did Brian Epstein's Ghost Predict John Lennon's Assassination?:

- http://dangerousminds.net/comments/epsteins_ghost_predict_lennons_assassination_bbc_documentary

Mind Control: Sharon Tate, Charles Manson, The Beatles & Hollywood's Satanic Spell:

- http://youtu.be/Hhr-wPVvNOw?list=RDa_C4UZh2nHk

Evil Beatles:

- http://stargods.org/stargods.org/BeatlesEvil.html

CHAPTER 5

PAUL IS DEAD ... ISN'T HE?

Did the real Paul McCartney die in 1966?

> *"Sometimes people hold a core belief that is very strong. When they are presented with evidence that works against that belief, the new evidence cannot be accepted. It would create a feeling that is extremely uncomfortable called 'cognitive dissonance.' And because it is so important to protect the core belief, they will rationalize, ignore and even deny anything that doesn't fit in with that core belief."*
>
> *Frantz Fanon, philosopher and writer (1925-1961)*

> *"There are two ways to be fooled. One is to believe what isn't true; the other is to refuse to believe what is true."*
>
> *Søren Kierkegaard (1813-1855)*

When it comes to 'conspiracy theories,' the music industry has its very own favourite to rival JFK, the Apollo moon landings or 9/11. Over the years the idea has come to be known as 'Paul Is Dead,' or 'PID,' and it refers to the surprisingly widespread suggestion that the real James Paul McCartney died sometime in 1966 and was replaced by an impostor who has been taking his place ever since.

Anyone hearing this idea for the first time is likely to react the same way as I initially did; scoffing condemnation towards a patently ridiculous idea.

As with almost every other subject, however, some delving beneath the 'official' version of events reveals some plausible alternatives that anyone with an open mind and a capacity for critical thought might like to spend a little time mulling over. And so it is with PID. Although *sounding* worthy of instant dismissal, some proper investigation at least takes it beyond the realms of the outright impossible. You don't gain the right to dismiss a subject as 'ridiculous' until you've at least looked at the evidence and given it a chance. And cynics are invited to debunk and explain a huge array of discrepancies before retiring into smug certainty on this one, or to nominate any alternative 'ridiculous' claim at random that involves so many potent synchronicities. It surprises me the amount of 'truth' and 'conspiracy' researchers who won't go near the fine detail of this one purely because it doesn't 'sound right.'

This chapter, therefore, is a thorough chronicle of the widespread claims of a McCartney replacement. As with all things, readers must make up their own minds based on the information available.

Accident? . . .

There seem to be two widely circulated versions of the PID myth. In one, McCartney, 24 at the time, is said to have got into a heated argument with the other Beatles during a recording session, (at around 5am supposedly,) and stormed off in his convertible sports car. An Aston Martin, by all accounts. He is then said to have been involved in a freak accident, (some accounts suggest this was somewhere on the M1, others that it occurred in London,) where he was near-decapitated and killed instantly. In this version of the story, news quickly reached the remaining three and their management who panicked, anticipating mass suicides among Beatles fans if the news got out, and worked alongside British 'intelligence' services to quickly replace Paul with a double so that the public would be none the wiser and the group could continue as before. (I'd initially scoffed at the idea of any announcement of Paul's death being the cause of mass suicides among fans. Then I saw the headlines after Zayn Malik left One Direction in 2015, with accounts of young females taking to self-mutilation in their despair and counselling helplines being set-up to aid fans through their grief, so I stand corrected on that one. Still, the idea of MI6 being concerned about young Beatles fans committing suicide seems implausible given that this particular agency is not exactly famed for the great value it places on human life.)

According to some accounts, this happened on 9th November 1966–so an early showing for 9/11, as that date is expressed in the UK format, merged with a couple of sixes for good measure. This was a Wednesday, and the lyric 'Wednesday morning papers didn't come' in the later song 'Lady Madonna' is taken by some to be a lyrical clue as to the cover-up and press blackout that was hastily arranged by the forces that controlled the Beatles. As an aside, 9th November 1966 is also said to be the date that John Lennon first met Yoko Ono, having been introduced by Paul McCartney. This event is taken by many Beatles fans to spell the beginning of the end for the group, so the date could carry some symbolic 'death' relevance in that sense. And by way of additional curiosity, Mary Kelly, the final victim of Jack The Ripper, is reported to have been murdered on 9th November 1888–9/11/88.

Others, however, assume the date to have been the US-style rendering of 9/11, suggesting it occurred on 11th September 1966. (This is another date loaded with Beatles-related 9/11 synchronicity. John Lennon appeared on 'The Dick Cavett Show' on US TV on 11th September 1971 to premier the film for his song 'Imagine', and the recording date for the song 'Glass Onion' on 'The White Album' is given as 11th September 1968.) I was greatly impressed to see the respected US researcher Jim Fetzer cover the McCartney deception in great detail in a series of essays he brought together for his 2015 book 'And I Suppose We Didn't Go To The Moon Either.' Fetzer points out that the 11th September date is the more likely one for McCartney's death, since Beatles manager Brian Epstein announced the following month that the group would no longer be performing live, citing the unconvincing reason they could no longer hear themselves play above the screams from the audience. Why would Epstein have needed to make this diversionary statement in October if Paul didn't die until the following month, Fetzer asks?

An alternative spin on the story of McCartney's demise suggests he stopped to pick up a female hitchhiker he saw in the rain. Supposedly her name was Rita, as in the song 'Lovely Rita'. Once Rita realised who the driver was, she excitedly tried to hug him, causing the crash, though it's difficult to understand how this story could have got out if true, since no-one other than 'Rita' would have known it happened. This smacks of the over-embellishment of a myth.

There are two other possible motives for the Beatles' controllers to have worked so desperately to find an instant replacement if you go for this version of the story. One is straight corporate greed; the group had become such money-spinners for everyone in their camp, that there was much at stake if it were all to come to an abrupt, unplanned end. The other is that, more important than the Beatles' financial potential, was the original reason for their engineered creation—as a Tavistock Institute-spawned exercise in brainwashing and social engineering for an entire generation of young people that had not yet achieved all of its goals.

This version of events certainly seems far-fetched, because it relies on the Beatles team being able to find someone within days who looked and sounded enough like the original McCartney, had sufficient musical ability to be able to impersonate him convincingly, and had nothing in his diary for the next 50-plus years. That's the trouble with household name-impersonating doubles. There's never one around when you need them.

... or 'accident'?

It's the second variation of the PID legend that carries more plausibility in my book. In this version, McCartney's demise was no tragic accident, but was an impeccably-planned affair, with enough time to identify and fully train a double to take his place, and to apply whatever cosmetic tweaking was needed to his appearance. It's an equally big ask of whoever could have taken his place to give up their own identity for the rest of their life, but this version at least offers a substantial preparatory period. The offing of the real Paul would either have been some form of ritual sacrifice favoured by the dark controllers of the entertainment industry, (there's more on this whole subject in later chapters,) or a damage-limitation exercise assuming McCartney had become troublesome and unco-operative with the agenda he was expected to be fulfilling. Some believe that McCartney was unhappy about the radical change in the Beatles' music that was scheduled for the latter half of the 60s, tying in with the psychedelic era and LSD, and that he had become a liability to these plans. The real Paul is also rumoured to have taken a healthy interest in the details surrounding the recent JFK assassination, and to have started questioning the official story. He is known to have offered to create the music score to the JFK-related movie 'Rush To Judgement.'

The suggestion that the method of execution may actually have been an *arranged* car accident is, of course, a possibility. Memories of the death of Princess Diana will come flooding back to many, but few will be aware that this exact same method of assassination—by applying a blinding light to a car as it passed through a tunnel—was being planned by British 'intelligence' services for Serbian leader Slobodan Milosevic during the Balkan War, as revealed by former M16 employee Richard Tomlinson during the inquest into Diana's death. It seems a good idea can always be recycled.

The only remaining option is that the real McCartney wasn't killed but, for whatever reason, 'disappeared' into a life of obscurity, but this to me seems like the most improbable of the possibilities.

Arguably the leading proponent of the PID theory is Tina Foster, proprietor of the website plasticmacca.blogspot.com, ('Macca' has long been McCartney's public nickname in the UK.) I interviewed her for one of my 'Good Vibrations' podcasts on the date of James Paul McCartney's 72nd birthday in 2014, where she ran through the whole story and many of the key clues. You can listen to it here—https://soundcloud.com/mark-devlin/good-vibrations-podcast-vol-42.

She postulates that the replacement of McCartney took place not in November, but in late August 1966. This would have been shortly after the Beatles' concert in Seattle on the 25th, and before a press conference in Los Angeles on the 28th. (The following day marked their concert in Candlestick Park, San Francisco, their last live performance with the exception of the Abbey Road rooftop jam in 1969.) The LA press event is taken by many to be the first public appearance of 'Faul' (faux Paul,) as the alleged impostor has come to be known.

I included a section on the PID theory in a talk I gave in Liverpool a couple of years back. In the interval, a guy came up to me and said, 'you do realise all the Beatles were replaced and not just McCartney, don't you?' I'd certainly heard the idea that Lennon was replaced, but not the whole group. The guy said he once presented this in a public talk in the Beatles' home city, and had narrowly escaped getting chased down the street and lynched for blasphemy. While I know that doubles have been widely used for public figures—particularly politicians and world leaders—my brain just can't deal with more than one Beatle at a time. And this would of course mean that the 'John Lennon' who put out such profound music throughout the 1970s and who was apparently assassinated in December 1980, wasn't really him at all, but a double!

For the record, though, Tina Foster is open to the idea of Lennon being replaced, as well as McCartney, and details her observations on the subject here:

- http://plasticmacca.blogspot.co.uk/2014/10/imagine-john-fennon.html

Well, no-one ever made the claim that this conspiracy game is straightforward.

Methods to the madness

Before we examine some of the many clues that have been put forward by fans over the decades—and there are reckoned to be at least 400—it's worth bearing in mind a couple of factors. As I hope the rest of this book shows, the entertainment industry, just like the world in general, is nothing like we've spent most of our lives thinking it is. The same forces are at work throughout, and the uncomfortable truth is that they are steeped in Satanism, Luciferianism and other dark occult practices. The evidence to support this is so widespread that I don't know what more to say to anyone who still doesn't accept it.

In this context, their rituals have always been of supreme importance, as has Kabbalistic numerology. They are equally obsessed with symbolism, and have demonstrated their need to cryptically encode their intentions and their past deeds into works of popular culture. This, in their sick, twisted mindset, allows them to escape the proper karmic consequence for their evils, because, as they see it, they gave the public the opportunity to know what they have done, and to therefore object. When no objection is voiced, (how could it be when the information is so ambiguous?) they take this as the tacit approval of the masses, and a green light to keep pressing on. This is a complicated concept related to a deep understanding of Natural Law, and I'll go into this further in the final section of the book and in the chapter on Predictive Programming. I would suggest that their logic in assuming they can cheat the moral laws of the universe in this way suggests supreme ego-driven arrogance, and a deeply flawed understanding of how everything works, bringing with it some very heavy payback. Either way, this all stands as a point of reference to bear in mind before diving fully down the PID rabbit hole.

The makings of a myth

There are claims that some vigilant Beatles fans noticed anomalies with McCartney straight away in 1966. There was also an incident in January 1967 which resurrected the death rumour, when his Mini was involved in a road smash, (on the M1 again.) It turned out, however, that McCartney was not in the car at the time, and that it was being driven by a Moroccan student named Mohammed Hadjij.

Here, the story is taken up by an article on thebeatlesbible.com website:

> "Hadjij was an assistant to London art gallery owner Robert Fraser. The pair turned up at McCartney's house on the evening of 7th January, and were later joined by Mick Jagger, Keith Richards, Brian Jones and antiques dealer Christopher Gibbs. The party decided to head to Jagger's home in Hertfordshire, before moving on to Redlands, Richards' Sussex mansion (and scene of his later drugs bust). McCartney travelled with Jagger in the latter's Mini Cooper, while Hadjij drove in McCartney's Mini.

> "The two cars became separated during the journey. Hadjij crashed McCartney's Mini and was hospitalised with injuries. The heavily customised car was highly recognisable, so rumours began circulating that McCartney had been killed in the incident. The following month a paragraph appeared in the February 1967 edition of the 'Beatles Book Monthly' magazine, headed 'False Rumour':

> "Stories about the Beatles are always flying around Fleet Street. The 7th January was very icy, with dangerous conditions on the M1 motorway, linking London with the Midlands, and towards the end of the day, a rumour swept London that Paul McCartney had been killed in a car crash on the M1. But, of course, there was absolutely no truth in it at all, as the Beatles' Press Officer found out when he telephoned Paul's St. John's Wood home and was answered by Paul

himself who had been at home all day with his black Mini Cooper safely locked up in the garage."

So much for that one then.

It wasn't until 1969 that the replacement theory gained mainstream prominence. The first known print reference came from an article penned by Tim Harper that appeared in the 17th September edition of 'The Times-Delphic', the newspaper of the Drake University in Des Moines, Iowa. Harper claimed later that his article was written for entertainment purposes only, and that he'd got the information from a fellow student named Dartanyan Brown, who in turn, claimed he'd heard the story from a musician in California.

This article seems to have led to the now-legendary phone call to DJ Russ Gibb's show on Detroit radio station WKNR-FM on 12th October 1969. The caller, identifying himself as 'Tom,' told Gibb that McCartney was dead and that the Beatles had placed a clue in the track 'Revolution No. 9.' He urged Gibb to play the record backwards, which he somehow achieved, and the repeated phrase 'number nine, number nine, number nine', was heard as 'turn me on, dead man.' PID's mythical status was born. The day before Gibb's show, the Beatles' press officer Derek Taylor had responded to the rumour, stating: "Recently we've been getting a flood of inquiries asking about reports that Paul is dead. We've been getting questions like that for years, of course, but in the past few weeks we've been getting them at the office and home night and day. I'm even getting telephone calls from disc jockeys and others in the United States."

Two days after the Gibb programme, however, an article entitled 'McCartney Dead; New Evidence Brought to Light' was published by 'The Michigan Daily.' It was a satirical review of the 'Abbey Road' album credited to University of Michigan student Fred LaBour. He confessed that he had invented many of the clues that he had cited as pointing to McCartney's death. Despite this, however, the myth failed to go away, and LaBour's admission seems to have only fuelled a huge appetite among Beatles fans to scour their record collection for further clues.

The Macca mission

The 1969 rumour had gained such prominence that a mission had begun in the press to try and track 'McCartney' down. He had not been seen in public for some time—perhaps wisely if he was the replacement, as there would have been renewed scrutiny of his appearance, height, accent, etc. By way of an 'official' confirmation that all was well, 'Life' magazine commissioned a journalist to travel to McCartney's Scottish farm on Mull Of Kintyre, where they reported him to be alive and well, living with wife Linda and their children, and contemplating his forthcoming solo career with the Beatles now all but finished. In the edition of the magazine dated 7th November 1969, in an article headed 'The Case Of The 'Missing' Beatle—Paul Is Still With Us,' McCartney is quoted as saying: "Rumours of my death have been greatly exaggerated," paraphrasing Mark Twain. "However," he continued, "if I was dead, I'm sure I'd be the last to know." He added: "Perhaps the rumour started because I haven't been much in the press lately. I have done enough press for a lifetime, and I don't have anything to say these days. I am happy to be with my family and I will work when I work." BBC Radio 4 also sent their reporter Chris Drake on the same mission, and 'Rolling Stone' magazine published an article assuring that McCartney was still alive.

This particular edition of the magazine didn't quite put the theories to rest as effectively as some would have liked, when it was discovered that if you hold the front page up to the light, some bleed-through from a car advertisement on the other side can be seen. This has the visual effect of cutting Paul's head in half, with the speeding car emerging through the middle of his body.

Follow the white rabbit

There are literally hundreds of lyrical and sonic clues that are said to have been found in Beatles music, and visual hints on record sleeves to support PID. And for every single claim of a valid 'clue' there are stories to rubbish it as 'disinformation.' Entering into the PID rabbit hole is guaranteed to take up days or weeks of any researcher's time in trying to assimilate and validate all the information. It certainly piqued my interest to that degree. It would be impractical to list every single clue that's been identified here–that's a whole book in itself, and there is an unending supply of websites, forums and Youtube videos for readers wanting to study the full set. I'll just summarise a few of the most frequently-cited ones here.

- The previously-referenced avant-garde track 'Revolution No. 9' from 'The White Album' is generally taken to be the Beatles' most obscure recording, much of it consisting of effects and noise. When played in reverse, besides the 'turn me on, dead man' message, many claim to hear other clues such as the sound of a fiery car crash and someone screaming "let me out."

- The rest of 1968's 'The White Album' was thoroughly searched for clues by fans. A major one was supposedly found in a back-masked message at the end of 'I'm So Tired.' As the music fades at the end, John Lennon can be heard speaking incomprehensibly. When this is played in reverse, some hear the words 'Paul is dead man, miss him, miss him, miss him.'

- Meaning has been placed on a couple of lines from 'I Am The Walrus', a bizarre track by any standards. The line 'man you've been a naughty boy, you let your face grow long' certainly has some compatibility with the observation that the pre-'66 McCartney's face appeared rounder than in post-'66. Just before it is the reference to 'stupid bloody Tuesday'. Fans claim that McCartney was last seen alive on a Tuesday, (though 11th September and 9th November '66 were a Sunday and a Wednesday respectively, which blows that particular theory out.) The 'eggman' lyric is supposed to be a reference to Humpty Dumpty, who cracked his head open, as did Paul according to the legend.

- 'I Am The Walrus' was inspired by occultist author Lewis Carroll and the poem 'Jabberwocky.' An excerpt from this reads: 'She puzzled over this for some time, but at last a bright thought struck her. 'Why, it's a looking-glass book, of course! And if I hold it up to a glass, the words will all go the right way again.'

This, according to researchers, adds further validity to reversing Beatles recordings to find hidden messages. Paul is said to have occasionally used the alias 'Ian Iachimoe', which sounds like 'Paul McCartney' being said in reverse.

The 'Walrus' phrase has other dubious connotations, meanwhile. Crazed psychopaths, it seems, are not without a warped sense of irony when it comes to naming their operations. The music writer Alex Constantine in his book 'The Covert War Against Rock,' reveals that Project Walrus was a below-the-radar CIA-controlled black op, involving surveillance, psychological operations and assassinations. John Lennon's murder, and the subsequent defacing and 'disappearing' of his journals and other materials, are all said to have occurred at the hands of 'Walrus,' staffed by some of the people who were closest to Lennon, including Beatles chauffeur and author of 'The Last Days of John Lennon: A Personal Memoir,' Fred Seaman.

- In the song 'Glass Onion,' Lennon sings: 'Looking through a glass onion. I told you about the walrus and me, man. You know that we're close as can be, man. Well, there's another clue for you all: the walrus was Paul." Some have said this is a reference to a Nordic belief that the walrus is a sign of death, whilst a 'glass onion' is said to be a nickname for the transparent corner knob of a coffin.

- The song 'Nowhere Man' is supposed to be a maudlin reference to Paul's corpse state: 'He's a real nowhere man, sitting in his nowhere land, making all his nowhere plans for nobody.'

- Meaning has been placed on the lyric: 'You were in a car crash and you lost your hair' from the song 'Don't Pass Me By' as being a reference to the mythical accident. A similar reference is said to come from the words: "He hit a light pole. We better get him to see a surgeon. So, anyhow, he went to see a dentist instead, gave him a pair of teeth that weren't any good at all. My wings are broken and so is my hair," as part of the jumbled noise of 'Revolution No. 9'. This could certainly be seen as tying in with the findings of two Italian forensic experts, (who we'll meet in a while), who observed that the dental palates of the pre-1966 Paul and those of Faul appear completely different, but that the latter could have undergone surgery to make one tooth look crooked to more closely emulate his predecessor.

- The lyric in 'Hello Goodbye' from 1967, 'You say goodbye, I say hello' is taken by some to mean Faul is saying goodbye to the real McCartney, and introducing himself as the new one.

- Some claim the phrase 'it was a fake moustache,' referring to attempts to conceal Faul's recent plastic surgery, can be heard when the chorus to 'Sgt. Pepper's Lonely Hearts Club Band' is played backwards.

- The phrase 'Ma Ma Ma McCartney, he's dead', dead, dead, dead, dead' is said to be encoded backwards in 'Hey Jude'.

- John Lennon's song 'How Do You Sleep,' an acknowledged bitter swipe at McCartney, contains the lyric: 'Them freaks was right when they said you was dead, the one mistake you made was in your head.' Some feel this is a reference to the obvious differences in appearance between the pre- and post-replacement McCartneys. A further lyric goes: 'A pretty face may last a year or two, but pretty soon they'll see what you can do.'

- There are claims of a backwards message contained in the song 'Magical Mystery Tour,' where the words 'Will Paul be back as Superman?' can be heard.

- On page 13 of the 'Magical Mystery Tour' album insert, there is a photo of McCartney playing bass in his socks with a pair of bloody shoes next to him, insinuating that there should be someone else standing in the spot.

- On 1970's 'Let It Be' album sleeve, Paul is the only Beatle pictured with a blood-red background added. Originally the photos were in black and white.

- John Lennon can supposedly be heard faintly muttering 'I buried Paul' at the end of 'Strawberry Fields Forever.' Lennon has addressed this particular one in interviews, claiming he was in fact saying 'cranberry sauce' or 'I'm very bored.'

- McCartney admitted to planting hidden clues and messages in his album 'Memory Almost Full.' Lennon has also admitted the Beatles were always placing clues in their records: 'All our messages were subliminal.'

Cracking the code

The idea that secret messages could be cryptically encoded in the first place is by no means far-fetched. An excerpt from the www.baconsocietyinc.org website, charting the activities of the enigmatic Sir (what else?) Francis Bacon, (who many attest was the real William Shakespeare,) states:

> *"Many Baconians of the esoteric persuasion hold that Bacon and his fellow occultists encoded secret messages or cryptograms into printed books, using both text and image. Bacon himself is believed by some to have told an outlandish secret history through such cryptogrammic methods."*

Anyone who's read Dan Brown's novels, or seen the films starring Tom Hanks, will doubtless recall that the hero, Harvard symbologist Robert Langdon, spends his adventures deciphering ancient esoteric codes to solve mysteries. It's the same dynamic at work. Dan Brown would appear to be highly in-the-know as to what goes on, and it's no coincidence that his books started to appear in an era when, fuelled by the internet, public interest in matters of the occult, symbology, and the existence of powerful secret societies has never been stronger.

Given that those who ultimately pull the strings of the entertainment industry are steeped in the same mystery school traditions that have been in place for centuries, it takes no wild stretch of the imagination to assume that tried and tested tactics from ages past might still be put to use in contemporary times.

Anomalies abound

James Paul McCartney was left-handed. In a 1963 interview, he said: "The only thing I couldn't cure myself of was being left-handed. I do everything with my left hand, and no matter how I try I can't change the habit. I just seem to do everything back-to-front. I used to even write backwards. Every time the schoolmasters would look at my handwriting they would throw swinging fits." From mid-1966 onward, fans started noticing that 'Paul' was using his right hand for key tasks—holding bottles of beer and cups of tea, smoking, and most notably, holding and playing his guitar. Adherents to the PID theory have observed that, however much you might be able to alter the appearance of an impostor, and even train them musically and vocally, you can never turn a right-handed person left-handed, or vice-versa.

Many PID adherents have also pointed to what they consider to be the strange reaction of McCartney to news of the death of John Lennon in 1980. In footage widely available on Youtube, Paul appears nonchalant, chewing gum and writing off the sudden murder of the old friend with whom he had written musical history as 'a drag.'

This would certainly tie in with claims that Lennon and the McCartney replacement were never able to get along. Sceptics, meanwhile, have claimed that McCartney's seemingly flippant reaction could have been down to shock and the impact of the situation having not yet sunken in. Readers must make up their own minds. You can view the reaction here: https://www.youtube.com/watch?v=xf30KfAUK5k

This brings in a possible motive for Lennon's assassination according to some, who have speculated on whether, no longer able to live with the terrible secret, he was about to spill the beans on the McCartney deception and had to be swiftly silenced. (That's if you don't go for the theory that he's still alive!) There has been similar speculation regarding the frenzied knife attack on George Harrison by an intruder in his home in 1999 which he survived, only to die of lung cancer two years later.

What the drummer knew

In a May 2011 interview with the UK's 'Daily Mail,' Ringo Starr stated twice that he was 'the last remaining Beatle.' His exact comments were reported as follows:

> *"I think it's people on the outside who perceive Paul as thinking he's the only one left. Actually, it's me. I am the last remaining Beatle.*
>
> *"You all know that the only person round this table who can go is me. I was in the biggest Rock & Roll band in the history of music. I am the last remaining Beatle."*

Starr did, however, precede these comments by referring to McCartney as follows:

"We are good friends. We don't live in each-other's pockets, but if we're in the same country, we get together. He's singing and playing on my latest album and I played on several of his. We're just pals. We're the only two who've experienced all this who are still here."

The Mail states that "deadpan is (Ringo's) default setting." It's impossible to know if comments such as this just slip out, as an involuntary rendering of the truth, or if they're all part of the Beatles' mischievous sense of humour, knowing that they will further empower the PID rumours and thus the bank balances of those from the Beatles camp who are still alive, as new generations of fans arm themselves with copies of their music to search for further clues.

What Ringo Knew took on new life in early March 2015, meanwhile, when what purported to be a new interview with the drummer went viral on-line. It was said to have been given to a publication known as 'The Hollywood Inquirer,' and claimed that Ringo had decided to break his silence on the McCartney deception after almost 50 years. He went on to basically reinforce the story of McCartney dying in a tragic accident on 9th November 1966 and an impostor by the name of William Shears Campbell being swiftly groomed as his replacement.

This was followed a couple of days later by an alleged response from 'McCartney', completely refuting Ringo's claims, as reported on the site World News Daily Report. 'McCartney' is quoted as saying: "I know that Ringo is growing senile and losing his mind, but he doesn't need to invent such idiotic stories to attract attention . . . I've seen Ringo do and say many stupid things in my life, but this is one of the worst! If he's so badly in need of media coverage, he could just invent crap about himself without implicating me in his delirium."

World News Daily Report, it turns out, is a well-known spoof site that specialises in satire. Its 'About Us' section states: "World News Daily Report is an American Jewish Zionist newspaper based in Tel Aviv . . . Our News Team is composed of award winning Christian, Muslim and Jewish journalists, retired Mossad agents and veterans of the Israeli Armed Forces." Similarly, there's the small matter of 'The Hollywood Inquirer' not actually existing.

While there's an amusing side to this rendering of the subject, stories such as these also serve to reinforce the apparent absurdity of it in the minds of many. It follows that any researchers seriously proposing the idea are then treated with the same scorn and ridicule, regardless of what validity the evidence they put forward may have. You have to question, therefore, whether or not there is a deliberate element of disinformation in such 'spoofs' appearing.

Pepper bombs

Acres of meaning and interpretation have been applied to the iconic 'Sgt. Pepper's Lonely Hearts Club Band,' the first Beatles studio album since the alleged replacement. The sleeve design is credited to 'Sir' (count 'em) Peter Blake, known as 'the Godfather of pop-art' and a tutor and close friend of the paedophile artist Graham Ovenden, who was sentenced to two years' imprisonment in 2013 at the age of 70 for sexual offences against children. Besides Blake, McCartney, (the fake one, if you go for the theory,) is said to have had a strong influence on its composition, along with his friend Robert Fraser. Fraser was, in turn, linked to the satanist film-maker and mentor to the Rolling Stones, Kenneth Anger. Anger had introduced both the Stones and the Beatles to the works of Aleister Crowley, and in particular, the OTO occult secret society which has proven a fascination for many a rock star through the decades. Reportedly, it was only McCartney for whom it all had any real appeal. Fraser and McCartney intended the 'Sgt. Pepper' sleeve to be a kind of treasure map full of clues that could be deciphered by those in the know, but which would go over the heads of the 'profane' masses.

(Incidentally, although the 'Sgt. Pepper' track 'Lucy In The Sky With Diamonds' has long been taken to be a barely-concealed reference to LSD, which the Beatles' psychedelic period was being used to help embed into youth culture, there is an alternative interpretation to its meaning. 'Lucy' can be taken to be a depiction of 'Lucifer,' an entity revered by the OTO and other occult mystery schools, and the 'Diamonds' reference is highly reminiscent of the 'Roc' sign of Jay-Z and co. that we'll encounter in a later chapter—really an ancient symbol used by the OTO and other Crowley-related secret societies.)

A depiction of Crowley himself famously appears in the top-left of the album sleeve. Some have claimed that the opening line to the album, 'it was 20 years ago today,' was a kind of veiled tribute to Crowley, who died in 1947. That was in December, however, whereas the album was released in June '67, so technically it was 'nineteen and a half years ago today.' Crowley is far from alone in terms of questionable choices of 'heroes,' however. The blogger Pinball King in his article titled 'What's Wrong With the Beatles?', lists some of the others depicted, as follows:

"Other 'heroes' include four Indian gurus (occult mysticism,) Carl Jung (occult psychology,) Edgar Allan Poe (alcoholic horror mystic,) Aldous Huxley (globalist, eugenicist, LSD promoter,) William S. Burroughs (homosexual junkie murderer,) Karl Marx (satanic father of communism according to 'Marx and Satan' by Richard Wurmbrand,) Oscar Wilde (homosexual writer,) George Bernard Shaw (racist eugenicist,) Lewis Carroll (paedophile,) Marlene Dietrich (decadent lesbian singer,) James Joyce (alcoholic writer,) Lenny Bruce (junkie comedian,) H.G. Wells (eugenicist occultist writer,) Terry Southern (obscene writer,) Sigmund Freud (neurotic father of psychoanalysis,) a doll of six-year-old Shirley Temple with a shirt that says 'Welcome The Rolling Stones' with blood-stained gloves (implied paedophilia,) and a legionnaire from the Order of the Buffalo (behind the standing Shirley Temple.)

"There is also a doll of the Hindu goddess Lakshmi pointing 'as above, so below', a hookah (drug bong,) a purple velvet snake (serpent/ Satan/ phallic,) Snow White (from occultist Walt Disney,) a Mexican Tree of Life (usually depicting the serpent Satan offering Adam and Eve forbidden knowledge in the Garden of Eden,) and a Saturn trophy (sun/ Satan) near the 'L' (90-degree square.)

"Note Ringo's flat hat ('Here come ol' flat-top',) resembling that of 15th-century occultist Heinrich Cornelius Agrippa, and George's secret society bicorn hat.

And later:

"The Beatles also wanted to include their 'hero' Adolf Hitler on the cover of 'Sgt. Pepper,' but were not permitted by EMI. Hitler waits forlornly in the wings, to the right. If you think this was just John's grim humour, then here's a quote from Paul: 'I had the idea that instead of Hell's Angels, they put up pictures of Hitler and the latest Nazi signs and leather and that. We went into it just like that. Just us doing a good show."

Researchers and fans claim to have uncovered many other visual clues in the sleeve:

- On the right-hand side of the front cover is a figure with a child seated in its lap, with the caption 'welcome The Rolling Stones, good guys' on her T-shirt, and with what looks like a bloodstained driving glove. The child, (said to be Shirley Temple,) is holding a white sports car in one hand.

- The focal point of the front cover is the word 'Beatles' spelled out in flowers on a grave. There are wax dummies of George, Ringo and Paul in their early days looking at the grave, whereas John is looking away. Amid the grave are yellow flowers shaped like a guitar. This has been taken to mean that 'Sgt. Pepper,' the first album since the alleged replacement, signifies that the old Beatles are dead and gone, never to return.

- Paul is markedly taller than the other Beatles on the front cover. On the reverse, his back is turned to the camera, perhaps signifying that he does not fit in.

- A hand is held up behind Paul's head on the front cover which, in some religions, is seen as a mystical depiction of death. A hand raised behind Paul's head is a recurring clue in many photos of the band.

- On the back cover, Paul is wearing an arm patch with what appear to be the letters 'OPD,' which is police jargon in Britain for 'Officially Pronounced Dead.' This one is frequently debunked, however, as actually reading 'OPP,' standing for Ontario Provincial Police. Paul was apparently given the patch while on tour in Canada.

- In a real mindblower, it's been pointed out that if you hold a mirror horizontally across the words 'lonely hearts' on the front cover's bass drum, with the reflective part of the mirror pointing away, the letters in both the mirror and the album collectively spell out '1 ONE 1 X= HE/DIE.' The "/", resembling an upward arrow, points at Paul. This phrase has been claimed to be marking out the date of the alleged death. The 1 and ONE make 11, whereas I and X equals 9 in Roman numerals. Together these form 11/9, (or 9/11 in reverse.)

- The blogger known as Horselover Phat, meanwhile, as part of his truly fascinating and impeccably-researched article, applies Crowley's 'law of reversal' to the front sleeve image, demonstrating that even more symbolism crops up when you create a full mirror image. I thoroughly recommend a delve into this article for all who want to truly absorb themselves in the Sgt. Pepper magic(k)–http://subliminalsynchrosphere.blogspot.co.uk/2014/02/oto-hip-hop-hollywood-and-msm-masonic.html

- The official story behind the lyric 'he blew his mind out in a car, he didn't notice that the lights had changed' in the track 'A Day In The Life,' is that it refers to the socialite and heir to the

Guinness empire Tara Browne, who died aged 21 in the same way that Paul is supposed to have done, in a car crash, on 18th December 1966. There are reports that this occurred after an LSD session with McCartney, and that Browne was travelling in excess of 100mph. According to the Wikipedia account of his death: "He failed to see a traffic light and proceeded through the junction of Redcliffe Square and Redcliffe Gardens, colliding with a parked lorry. He died of his injuries the following day."

Many have questioned this account, however, by pointing out a few discrepancies. Among them are the observation that it's impossible to get anywhere near a speed of 100mph in highly built-up Central London. Photos of his crashed car show only minor damage, too, which is certainly not compatible with a fatal crash at that speed. This has led to claims of foul play in Browne's death from some quarters. It may have been the origin of Lennon's further line in 'A Day In The Life:' 'Well, I just had to laugh. I saw the photograph.'

The cryptic crossing

The other album whose sleeve design has been pored over and studied to the point of obsession is 'Abbey Road.' It's this album's iconic image of the band walking over the zebra crossing which seemingly inspired the call to Russ Gibb's radio show, springboarding the world of PID into the mainstream.

Significance has been placed on the group members apparently depicting a funeral procession. John, dressed in white, is supposed to represent a priest, Ringo in black is said to be a pallbearer, with George, in denim, as a gravedigger. Paul, in a scruffy suit, is out of step with the others, and is barefoot. It has been pointed out that corpses are traditionally buried barefoot in several European countries. Left-handed Paul is holding a cigarette in his right hand. A VW Beetle car parked in the road displays the licence plate '28IF', and fans have said this means McCartney would have been 28 if he'd lived. This one doesn't quite work though. 'Abbey Road' was released in 1969, at which point McCartney, born in June '42, would only have been 27.

On the back of the sleeve the words 'the Beatles' are spray-painted on a brick wall, but with a crack running through the name, signifying for some that the original four have been split. This ties in with many other suggested clues pertaining to three Beatles, rather than four. Among those unearthed have been the family coat-of-arms of key Beatles producer George Martin. This features three beetle insects in the crest. It has been noted that, with six legs each, the three could be taken as a depiction of 6/6/6. The scarab to the left of the crest appears to have a Kabbalah 'Tree of Life' pattern. (The Guinness Family's coat of arms, meanwhile, features a raised hand very similar to the one that appears behind Paul on the 'Sgt. Pepper' sleeve!)

The science for a switch

For the more scientifically-minded who don't go for the concepts of cryptic symbolism and the occult, and prefer cold, hard, verifiable fact, there's no shortage of this available when it comes to forensic evidence to support the idea of a switch.

Even a cursory glance at certain photos of McCartney prior to and after 1966 show some anomalies. His face is much rounder and fatter in earlier pictures, but is much longer with a more pronounced jawline after '66. The eyes seem to have changed colour. Then there's the issue of Paul's height. In early pictures of the band, McCartney is roughly the same height as John Lennon and George Harrison, all approximately 5'11". Post-1966, however, McCartney towers over Lennon in pictures, not least in the sleeve photos for the 'Sgt. Pepper' album.

In August 2009, the Italian magazine 'Wired' ran an article focusing on the findings of two Italian forensic experts, Francesco Gavazzeni and Gabriella Carlesi. The pair had set out to finally put an end to the persistent PID theories by proving that no replacement had taken place, but ended up concluding the exact opposite in the face of the evidence. They conducted a biometrical analysis of Paul pre- and post-1966, and reported discrepancies in the facial features that could not be accounted for by error or plastic surgery. There's a thorough breakdown of the conclusions here–http://hugequestions.com/Eric/TFC/FromOthers/Paul-McCartney-Italian.html

Among the key findings, the Italians decided that the front curvature of the jaw between photos is different, there is evidence of imperfect cosmetic surgery around the area of the eyes, the line separating Faul's lips is much wider, which perhaps accounts for his growing of a moustache to hide it, the ear shape differs widely, (something which cannot be modified by surgery,) and the teeth are different, with Faul's crooked tooth suggesting dental surgery to simulate the real Paul's. (Faul apparently displays a chipped tooth, however, consistent with the real Paul chipping his in a motorcycle accident in late 1965.)

An article on the hugequestions.com website observed:

> *"Therefore, if the conspiracy theories are false, ie, if the Paul McCartney that we see today with a large palate is the original Paul McCartney with a small palate—then Paul went through some very serious dental surgeries, and he would have suffered for a long time, and it would have had an effect on his voice.*

> *"The more logical conclusion is that the Paul McCartney of today is a substitute, and that Faul went through a much simpler dental operation to make one of his teeth crooked."*

An intriguing incident occurred in January 1980 when McCartney arrived for a tour in Japan, and ended up being imprisoned for nine days when a customs officer found marijuana in his luggage. There are claims that McCartney's fingerprints were taken, but did not match those already held on record, (he had previously toured Japan in early 1966), and that this was the real reason for his incarceration before some useful intervention from higher up secured his release.

Then there was a paternity case involving a German woman named Bettina Krischbin, who emerged in 2007 to allege that she was his illegitimate daughter. The claim was that during the Beatles' early days of playing in Hamburg, McCartney had an affair with her mother, and that Bettina was the result.

McCartney has always denied being the woman's father and when the blood test proved negative in 1984, a Berlin court dismissed her claim. However, this story took a freak twist when Bettina claimed that McCartney cheated the blood tests by sending a stand-in. Adding fuel to the fire, she also stated: "The signature in the old documents is false. We have found the signature is from a right-handed person, but Paul is left-handed."

She told 'Bild Zeitung' magazine that McCartney, estimated to be worth almost £1 billion, gave her mother 30,000 deutsch marks in 1966, followed by 200DM a month for years. "Why would he do that if he supposedly isn't the father?," she asked. Erika Hübers said she supported her daughter's wish for a new paternity test and recognition as McCartney's daughter. "I think we have a good chance now," she said, "because he lied to the court—provided it with false evidence."

Just William?

Of course, having digested all of the cryptic and scientific information, we're left with a highly reasonable and vital question which still requires answering. If the real Paul McCartney is dead . . . who the hell is it that's been passing himself off as Macca for the past fifty years? And furthermore, why would anyone undertake such a monumental commitment and outrageous deception, knowing they could never return to their former identity for as long as they go on living?

Certainly, a lifetime of fame, fortune and untold wealth would be of appeal to many, as the glut of 'talent' shows on TV constantly reminds us. In this context, the idea of taking the place of an already-established superstar and enjoying the associated riches without having to climb the ladder yourself, could be of great egoic appeal. It's also worth bearing in mind that when it comes to occult secret societies, members are known to swear oaths of allegiance that last their entire lifetime, promising to never divulge secrets upon pain of death, and with very high rewards offered as an incentive.

(Incidentally, Faul's veganism at face value appears to be entirely at odds with the idea of an unscrupulous charlatan happy to spend the rest of his days impersonating a beloved dead celebrity. But it could also be viewed as an ingenious element to the deception. Benevolent-sounding cover stories often mask far more nefarious activities. Some have even questioned the true nature of the Linda McCartney range of soya-based vegetarian foods, given that the health risks associated with a soy diet are now under much scrutiny.)

The name that crops-up more than any other as a possible candidate for Faul is William Shepherd 'Shears' Campbell, who is supposed to have been the winner of a Paul McCartney lookalike competition set by the Beatles' official magazine in the 1960s. Campbell was apparently from Edinburgh. Adherents to the story think that Campbell became of great interest when the plan was being hatched to dispose of McCartney, and he was somehow co-opted into the scheme.

Tina Foster and others have speculated that the line 'so may I introduce to you, the one and only Billy Shears' is a hint that the 'new' McCartney was being unveiled on that album. To add further intrigue, included in the video 'Paul Is Dead: The Shocking Clues Collection Video' available on Youtube, there is an out-take of George Harrison saying 'hello, William' as 'McCartney' enters a room. Additionally, in the movie 'Give My Regards To Broad Street', a character says 'do you know William?', as McCartney walks in. Fans have also pointed to the McCartney-penned track 'I Will' as being intended to mean 'I, Will'!

Still others, meanwhile, surmise that 'William' and 'Billy Shears' are both sly references to William Shakespeare, another character whose true identity has come in for much speculation. There are strong suggestions that Shakespeare was actually a fictional composite character whose works were actually written by the Royal courtier and occultist Sir Francis Bacon. Other accounts have Shakespeare down as being the close associate to Queen Elizabeth 1, Sir (naturally) John Dee, (whose codename of '007' was the inspiration for Ian Fleming's James Bond centuries later.) Shakespeare's works are loaded with the same codes, ciphers and clues for those in the know, as the Beatles' post-1966 works are said to be.

In other apparent clues, it was reported that the original title of the 'Abbey Road' LP was to be 'Billy's Left Boot,' and in the live concert DVD 'The Space Within Us,' there is allegedly a sign saying 'Bill' next to a shot of McCartney. Some have also suggested that the character of Bungalow Bill from the track 'The Continuing Story Of . . . ' on 'The White Album' may have been a mocking reference to William Campbell/ Shears and his 'bungling' slip-ups in keeping up the pretence.

There have been other claims that early representations of the replaced McCartney were none other than Denny Laine of The Moody Blues, meanwhile, and that the Beatles song 'Penny Lane', with its lyrics 'Penny Lane is in my ears and in my eyes' is another clue, with 'Penny' really being 'Denny.' But complication surrounding this one arises from the fact that 'McCartney' later founded the group Wings with Laine, and both appeared publicly together for years, so I'm not entirely sure how that one works.

In his essay entitled 'Replacing Paul: The Who, How & The Why,' James A Larson presents some other possible candidates for the *doppelganger*, albeit in a seemingly tongue-in-cheek style. These include Keith Allison, the winner of a 1965 McCartney lookalike contest, Dino Danelli, member of the 60s US rock group The Rascals, British singer Ian Whitcomb, and a character by the name of Phil Ackrill, who he claims is an alias for Vivian Stanshall, a member of the Bonzo Dog Doo-Dah Band, and the voice introducing the instruments at the end of Mike Oldfield's 'Tubular Bells.' Vivian/ Phil is reported to have died in March 1995.

It has been claimed that Faul is actually five years older than the original Paul, meaning he would have been born in 1937, and that part of the surgery process, and the initial growing of a moustache, was to disguise his looking older than his bandmates. Larson's essay asks whether the song 'When I'm 64,' with its lyric, 'will you still need me . . . when I'm 64?', could have represented the Faul character wondering whether his deception will have been discovered by then, or will still need to be kept up. If he was indeed born in 1937, he would have been 64 in . . . 2001. That infamous year again.

If there were ever any danger whatsoever of the waters becoming remotely clear in the world of PID, the American author and researcher Thomas E. Uharriet was there to ensure they became sufficiently murky again with 'The Memoirs Of Billy Shears.' This epic tome, presented in the form of fictional memoirs written by the replacement, offers the unique view that the genuine James Paul McCartney was actually a willing participant in his own sacrifice, and that he was fully aware of the character that would take on his identity for the rest of his days. There have also been claims that Uharriet wrote the book in league with Faul, as a way of the latter finally getting his story off his chest, but with it all dressed up as 'fiction' so plausible deniability could be claimed whenever required. With 66 chapters, (nice touch,) somehow the printers saw to it that the book stretched to exactly 666 pages, and produced it with an acrostic code in place; the first letter in every other line combines to spell secret messages which are revealed in the sister book 'Billy Shears Acrostical Decoding.' The book was also released on

9th September 2009, so 09/09/09, (or 06/06/06 upside-down if you prefer,) and this date just happened to be the same one on which Apple in the US released the back catalogue of Beatles albums in new digitally-remastered CD form. For any brains that aren't already fried by all the other clues, symbols and theories, this one will surely complete the process.

So it's goodnight from me, and it's goodnight from Him

'McCartney' seems to have found some amusement from the rumour over the years, having made occasional references to it. He parodied PID with his 1993 album 'Paul Is Live.' The sleeve design was based on the infamous Abbey Road image. The '28IF' on the car number plate had been switched to '51IS.'

At other times, meanwhile, (and bearing in mind we have almost 50 years' worth of interviews to draw on here,) McCartney has uttered some highly cryptic comments which, whether by design or accident, have only served as ammunition for the PID crowd's arguments. Or maybe it's down to the favourite manipulator's tactic of placing the truth right there in plain sight? His many ambiguous one-liners and soundbites have included:

"I'm not him. I'm some guy in a fictitious band."

"There are two Paul McCartneys."

"In a way, I think of Paul McCartney as 'him.' I do wake up some mornings and think, Jesus Christ, am I really that guy that is in the same body as I'm inhabiting?"

"I've learnt to compartmentalise. There's me and there's famous him. I don't want to sound schizophrenic, but probably I'm two people."

"I've always had this thing of him and me; He goes on stage, He's famous, and then me; I'm just some kid from Liverpool. Occasionally

I stop and think, I am Paul McCartney! Feckin' hell, that is a total freak-out!"

"I look in the mirror and just think, I, in this shell, am the guy I've read so much about. I don't know whether it's a schizo thing. I'm very proud of him, but you know, I don't imagine I am him, 'cause otherwise it would just blow my head off."

"So I thought, being Paul McCartney, the whole bit is really, you know, too much to live up to. The advantages, I like to think they outweigh the disadvantages."

"Why do the rumours come about? Because Paul McCartney's dead, of course."

"I dreamed it, didn't believe it was mine really. I didn't even write it really, in a way." (Talking about the song 'Yesterday.')

"We were kind of experimenting with anything. I'd written the title song, and I put it to the guys that, what we should do, we could make this record now under another persona. Kind of like hiding behind a pseudonym." (Talking about the identity of the character Sgt. Pepper.)

Curiously, McCartney appeared on 'The David Letterman Show' at the Ed Sullivan Theatre in New York, on 15th July 2009, the exact date that Italy's 'Wired' magazine published the findings of the two forensic experts. The pair joked about the replacement rumours, with McCartney quipping that he makes 'a very good double.'

To add to the ambiguity, Paul/ Faul guested on 'The Tonight Show With Jimmy Fallon' in late 2014, on which Fallon told him he does 'the best Paul McCartney impersonation.'

And this article from the Plastic Macca site documents a modern-day McCartney in interview stating he had 'a couple' of jobs in factories before the Beatles, which conflicts with what a young McCartney used to say. Are his homework studies failing? He also seems to get confused about his age:

- http://plasticmacca.blogspot.co.uk/2010/01/oops-things-faul-says-sometimes.html

To the power of six

There does seem to be a lot of occult significance placed on the year 1966. Something about the sixes seems to appeal to the elite priest class. '66 provided the backdrop for the alleged McCartney replacement, and was the year that the Beatles' music changed from innocent rhythm and blues-based pop songs, to the experimental sonics of the psychedelic age. John Lennon's first wife, Cynthia, said of the era in her book 'A Twist Of Lennon': "The years 1966-67 were tremendous years of mental and physical change for the Beatles." Cynthia died during the writing of this book in April 2015, so another original voice that would surely have carried knowledge of any replacement, was lost forever. Another candidate would be Beatles associate and Liverpool contemporary Cilla Black.

1966 was also the year that Anton LaVey founded The Church Of Satan. This was a 'front' organisation that acted as a recruitment arm for higher-up degrees of Satanism, and which has counted many 'celebrities' among its members, including Sammy Davis Jr., Jayne Mansfield, Liberace, Soft Cell frontman Marc Almond, and more recently, Marilyn Manson who became a fully inducted priest appointed by LaVey himself. It's also interesting to note that 1966 has significance to Roman Polanski's 'Rosemary's Baby,' a darkly fascinating movie based on the Ira Levin novel that contains many barely-hidden truths about how Satanism and the entertainment business are intrinsically linked. The film was released in 1968, but the narrative is set two years earlier in '66. This is described by the lead satanist character as 'year one' and marks the birth of the Antichrist. 'Rosemary's Baby' was set in the Dakota Building near New York City's Central Park, which just happens to be where Lennon had an apartment for many years, and outside which he was shot dead in December 1980. LaVey himself described 'Rosemary's Baby' as 'the best paid commercial for Satanism since the Inquisition.'

(Incidentally, as with the McCartney rumour, Jayne Mansfield is said to have been virtually decapitated when she was involved in a car accident in 1967 with boyfriend Sam Brody. Some accounts have claimed that LaVey had put a curse on Brody, and took it particularly bad when Mansfield was killed as well.)

Further ritual significance to 1966 comes from the fact that construction of the World Trade Center towers in Manhattan began in that year. They would stand for 35 years before the events of September 11th 2001, and there is widespread conjecture among 9/11 researchers that they were built with the specific purpose of being brought down decades later. Numerical symbolism is present throughout, (lots of 11s and a fair dose of our old mate Aleister Crowley's doctrines too.) Finally, '66 was the year that principal production took place on Stanley Kubrick and Arthur C. Clarke's enigmatic masterpiece '2001: A Space Odyssey', even though, like 'Rosemary's Baby', it didn't get its commercial release until 1968. It's intriguing that this story postulates something of world-changing significance happening 35 years later in 2001, particularly as Kubrick and Clarke were both rumoured to be 'insiders'—if not high-ranking members of the cabal, then privy to certain hidden knowledge. In England, the movie had such a profound effect on a young David Jones, (another Crowley-ite,) that he chose David Bowie as his artist identity for the rest of his career, after the '2001' lead character David Bowman, and his debut single, 'Space Oddity,' was a dark homage to the film.

And for anyone still salivating for more relevance to '66,' according to the American researcher Freeman Fly, who specialises in showing how the occult and esoterica is weaved into popular culture, 66 is 'the number of the abyss.' In Kabbalistic magic, it equates to The Qliphoth, said to represent negative aspects of, or separation from divinity. America's fabled Route 66 highway is said to have been the continent's first military route from East to West for the purposes of transporting gold.

A tale of two lovers

McCartney is said to have lived at girlfriend Jane Asher's home for a while. He started seeing her in 1963 and they announced their engagement on Christmas Day, 1967, by which point he was also going out with Linda who was shortly to become his first wife. The Beatlesbible. com website states:

> *"The engagement didn't last, however. It was called off when she returned from working in Bristol to find McCartney in bed with another woman. They attempted to continue the relationship, but on 20th July, Asher announced to the BBC that the relationship was over.*
>
> *"McCartney had continued to sleep with other women throughout their relationship, considering it permissible as they weren't married. In addition to his infidelities, Asher had found McCartney had changed since his experiences with LSD, and her commitment to her career meant they were often heading in different directions.*
>
> *"Since their split Asher has consistently refused to publicly discuss her relationship with McCartney."*

If the replacement story is indeed true, this would mean Asher dated both the original and the 'new' Paul. The terroronthetube.co.uk website surmises:

> *"Jane had to be seen going out with the new 'Paul.' But once Faul married Linda Eastman, she was out of the picture and might have needed a warning never to talk about what she knew. Her father's death would have achieved that, and to this day, she will never talk about this matter."*

Jane's father, Richard, was a leading neurologist who reportedly worked with Scotland Yard studying the effects of LSD. McCartney is said to have written many of his key songs at Asher's house, including 'Paperback Writer' and 'Yesterday.' Richard Asher died in 1969, having apparently committed suicide after suffering a bout of depression. His son Peter was one half of the duo Peter And Gordon, for whom McCartney penned hit songs including 'A World Without Love' and 'Nobody I Know.'

The terroronthetube.co.uk article goes on to address Paul's first wife, Linda, portraying her as something of an opportunist who saw a chance to blackmail her way into being a famous pop star in her own right.

> *"The US photographer Linda Eastman homed in on the new 'Paul' and they married very quickly. The story is that she said to him she knew of his identity change, and had it on photographic record, but she would stay mum if he married her and made her a star. Faul realised that this was exactly what he needed! Here was a sexy female with whom he could talk about all the weird stuff he had been through, and she'd keep his secrets and be part of his new band Wings and help to build up his confidence. And her Jewish lawyer father could be exactly what he needed in tricky times. He in fact acted for Faul as the Beatles broke up."*

Just like the Beatles' famous manager, Brian, Linda's real family name was Epstein. Her father changed his name from Leopold Vail Epstein to Lee Eastman to sound less Russian/ Jewish and more American. She grew up in Scarsdale, Westchester County, New York.

Linda died in 1998 after a battle with cancer. Of course, it's impossible for anyone outside of the small circle of people who were personally involved to know the truth behind her death, but inevitably, it led to speculation that it might have been some sort of engineered offing, given that it's relatively easy to induce cancers. It has been suggested that she was disposed of to prevent her knowledge of the truth about the McCartney switch from ever coming out.

Readers might like to consider this possibility in tandem with the infamous interview comments given by Heather Mills, Paul's second wife.

The Heather enigma

For many PID proponents, Heather is the real smoking gun. Though they don't prove the theory in itself, her words and behaviour sure take some explaining.

Mills is a former high-class prostitute and soft porn model, and it's often pointed out that those attracted to these professions aren't necessarily the most trustworthy. Indeed, Mills would appear to be a habitual liar. There are discrepancies over her account of her childhood sexual abuse, (which seems to be an ever-present spectre in stories related to the entertainment industry.) As her Wikipedia entry puts it:

> *"Mills later wrote that she was kidnapped and sexually assaulted by a swimming pool attendant when she was eight years old, but her next-door neighbour, Margaret Ambler, who was sexually abused by the swimming pool attendant, alleged that Mills' story was 'nothing what she made it out to be.' that Mills was never a victim, and that the pool attendant did not commit suicide, as Mills had written."*

And later, with regard to her relationship with Alfie Karmal:

> *"After returning to London, Mills asked Karmal to marry her. Karmal said yes, but on one condition: "I told her I couldn't marry her until she did something about her compulsive lying, and she agreed to see a psychiatrist for eight weeks. She admitted she had a problem and said it was because she'd been forced to lie as a child by her father."*

And:

> *"Mills has been accused by several newspapers of having embellished her life story. Journalist namesake Heather Mills, then at 'The Observer,' accused Mills of impersonating her for over a year in the late 1990s, showing people cuttings of articles the journalist had written, which helped Mills secure a job presenting 'The General' TV show."*

Despite her track record in attention-seeking, however, in the key TV interviews in question, Mills seems genuinely distressed, and declines to be specific about what she's referring to, presumably out of fear of the consequences.

Her 2008 US TV interview with Billy Bush on the show 'Access Hollywood' is the one that has come in for the most scrutiny. This occurred in the midst of her break-up from McCartney prior to their divorce settlement. Evidently addressing McCartney, she says to the camera:

"You know why I've left you. Protect me, and I will say nothing."

Quizzed by Bush, she goes on to say:

"Something so awful happened. Someone I've loved for a long time I found out had betrayed me immensely. And I don't mean infidelity or anything like that. Like, beyond belief. I have to protect myself.

"People don't want to know what the truth is, because they could never, ever handle it. They'd be too devastated."

Bush asks: "Knowing what you know now about Paul, would you have married him in the first place?" Mills replies: "Never."

Given that she makes it clear she's not talking about infidelity, what other kind of revelation about a beloved celebrity could be considered this devastating that the public could never, ever handle it if the truth emerged?

In a separate interview for a morning television show for the UK's ITV channel, Mills added to the intrigue by saying to the camera:

"I have a box of evidence that's going to a certain person should any-thing happen to me. So if you top me off, it's still going to go to that certain person and the truth will come out. There is so much fear from a certain party of the truth coming out that lots of things have been put out and done, so the police came round and said, 'you have had serious death threats from an underground movement.'"

Mills added to the intrigue in an interview for the BBC where she was asked if she feared for her life. She replied: "Yes I do, yes I do." Asked if she meant that "Paul McCartney does not protect you and your child?", she replied: "I'm afraid not." (McCartney and Mills had a daughter together, Beatrice, born in 2003.)

Mills was subsequently demonised by the mainstream media, particularly in the UK, where she was generally portrayed as unstable, neurotic and hysterical. The corporate media is skilled in tactics to influence mass public opinion on particular individuals, and given his massive clout as, by this time, a Knight in the British Establishment, it's not unreasonable to assume that 'McCartney'—or those he associates with—could have held considerable sway over editorial decisions made by the BBC, ITV and the like.

Boxes of tricks

Heather's reference to her 'box of evidence' brings to mind another story from the Beatles camp. Alongside Neil Aspinall, Mal Evans was a long-time assistant and roadie for the group, and was travelling with McCartney in Kenya in late 1966. Some researchers who opt for the 11th September 1966 date of death have speculated that Faul's visit in November was for the purpose of undergoing plastic surgery, away from the public glare of the UK, and in a country then still under British colonial control. According to some accounts, girlfriend Jane Asher also went along on the 'holiday' between 6th and 19th November, via France and Spain. Evans would appear to have been a particularly trusted confidante of the Beatles, and if full knowledge of Paul's replacement were to have been to only a select few, he would presumably have been among them. He is reported to have been the only Beatles-related person present at the marriage of Paul and Linda in 1969. Beatles lore has it that the 'Sgt. Pepper' album idea was hatched between McCartney and Evans during the Kenya trip. Mal Evans' Wikipedia entry describes events as follows:

> *"They spent their final night in Nairobi at a YMCA, before they returned to London. The Beatles, according to McCartney, needed a new name, so on the flight back to England, Evans and McCartney*

played with words to see if they could come up with something new. Evans innocently asked McCartney what the letters 'S' and 'P' stood for on the pots on their meal trays, and McCartney explained that it was for salt and pepper, which led to the 'Sgt. Pepper's Lonely Hearts Club Band' name."

Evans was all set to publish his memoirs from the Beatles years in a book to be entitled 'Living the Beatles' Legend.' He was due to deliver this to his publishers, Grosset & Dunlap, on 12th January 1976. A week earlier, on 5th January, he'd reportedly told John Hoernie, the book's co-writer, to ensure it got published at all cost in the event of anything happening to him. Within hours, an apparently doped up and erratic Evans had been shot dead by the LAPD in an altercation, and the suitcase containing the manuscript reportedly 'disappeared.' Only one page is said to have remained, page 146. According to an essay by British writer Nick Kollerstrom, this page detailed Evans' uneasiness with being charged by Beatles manager Brian Epstein to sack Paul's loyal butler George Kelly, and get him removed from his London home before 'Paul' returned from his Kenya visit. It also chronicled a meeting of the Beatles' inner circle where Paul outlined his plans for 'Sgt. Pepper.' Evans then teasingly writes, (assuming the page is genuine,) 'it was like we had known him forever.'

Epstein himself famously 'committed suicide' in 1967, and some have inevitably questioned whether this was a hit by the 'intelligence' services to eliminate any chance of him ever revealing what he had been a part of.

More questions than answers

A comment on the Beatlesbible.com website under the article 'The Paul Is Dead Myth,' from a user by the name of 'Seeker,' sums up an embracing of the PID theory well:

"People do not understand just how crucial the Beatles were to the economy of Britain at the time. If you understand that then you can start to see how, if Paul died, the truth would not necessarily have come out.

"The Beatles were also far more 'managed' than people thought and think. They were a real group who honed their skills during countless nights in Hamburg, but there seems little doubt that George Martin had a lot to do with their song writing.

"I am not sure the Theo Adorno theory is credible, but I have always wondered how Michael Jackson got to buy the Beatles back catalogue when McCartney had far more money than him and far more clout in the industry by virtue of his status. And the fact he wrote those songs either by himself or with Lennon, and with more than a little help from George Martin to begin with.

"I was a sceptic until I started reading various articles and watching various clips on Youtube. I am old enough to remember the Beatles in the few years before their break-up, and I remember even then thinking how Paul had changed in the space of a few short years. We're not talking about the changes that usually happen in people's physical features when they are in their late thirties and after. His face changed in the space of a couple of years when he was in his twenties.

" . . . Now that writers have the background information about Tavistock, (the actual facts and not some bright ideas,) and how it was definitely about social engineering, now that we know Jane Asher's father kept company with doctors who abused hypnotherapy to perform deep sleep hypnotherapy on unsuspecting victims and killed himself, now that we know of the Beatles' links with those closely connected with Manson etc., we know there is more than meets the eye to all of this.

"Truthteller though John Lennon was, he did lie, and all his dismissal of song lyrics as just playing with words or with fans does not ring with the truth. Clearly there are references that are not there to mock the fans or the world."

Truth, lies and audio tape

In 2010, a hoax 'mockumentary' entitled 'Paul McCartney Really is Dead: The Last Testament of George Harrison' appeared. The tongue-in-cheek story claims that, in the Summer of 2005, a package arrived at the Hollywood offices of London-based Highway 61 Entertainment, containing two audio mini-cassettes. These were said to be labelled 'The Last Testament of George Harrison,' and purported to contain Harrison's voice, spilling the beans about the car crash which killed McCartney, and the M15 conspiracy to replace him with a double. There were slight problems with verification given that Harrison himself had inconveniently died in 2001.

The hoax was in pretty poor taste. The tapes are dated 30th December 1999, the date of Harrison's attack in which he was savagely stabbed by an intruder at his Oxfordshire home. Recording his memoirs whilst in a critical condition in hospital is not likely to have been at the forefront of his mind. And in the section where 'Harrison' describes the remaining Beatles being taken by an MI5 agent to view the body of McCartney, the head was said to have been mangled with two teeth protruding outwards, causing the agent to observe, 'he kinda looks like a walrus, doesn't he?' and John to respond, 'No! I'm the walrus! *I'm* the walrus!" The girl known as 'Rita' who, in one version of the story caused the car crash, is said to have been targeted by MI5 years later and lost a leg in a hit and run. You guessed it . . . she cropped up later under the new identity of Heather Mills, and tried to blackmail Faul. Given that this story has Mills already as an adult in 1966, she would have been at least 60 years old when she made her famous TV interviews in 2007, (and clearly wasn't.) Furthermore, the MI5 agent's name is given as 'Moxwell,' presumably as in 'mocks well,' which the documentary sure does. The narrative is full of glaring inaccuracies, and the laughingly unconvincing attempt at a Liverpool accent fails to hit the funny spot—all dropped h's, and sounding more like a Brummie than a Scouser.

Like the Ringo Starr spoof in 2015, the 'Testament' farce did damage to the credibility of genuine researchers into the McCartney enigma, and, aside from being a self-indulgent piece of fun, it's worth bearing in mind that this may have been the intention of the creators all along—to taint any Beatles-related conspiracy with an air of implausibility, so that all will be dismissed as 'ridiculous' in one fell swoop.

Keep it in the family

There is another aspect of the story that requires some explanation before it can be fully accepted. (Who ever claimed anything in the world of PID is clear-cut?) A small circle of individuals keeping quiet about a replacement is one thing. But there's then the question of the real James Paul McCartney's family. If he did indeed die–whether taken out or the victim of a tragic accident–there's no way an impostor could have fooled Paul's own parents and sibling, (brother Mike McGear, a member of the 60s group The Scaffold of 'Lily The Pink' fame.) The fact that none of them have ever spoken publicly about any foul play means they would have to have been involved in the deception.

Upon first suggestion then, the idea that they would have co-operated with the lie sounds preposterous. But, however unfeasible, possibilities do exist. Multi-million pound pay-offs have been known to buy silence, and threats, intimidation and mind control techniques have also been highly efficient in keeping people in line, as have oaths of allegiance sworn to secret societies.

It's certainly on record that Paul never attended the funeral of his father when he died in 1976. This was two days before the start of a Wings European tour, with Paul apparently choosing to play the gigs rather than pay his last respects.

Many PID researchers have pointed to the behaviour and liaisons of the modern-day McCartney as further evidence of their claim. Even some Beatles fans who reject the claims of a McCartney replacement are prepared to acknowledge that *something* has happened to him, and that he's a very different character to the cheeky cherub-faced chap of the early 1960s. McCartney's acceptance of a Knighthood from The Queen has led to a seemingly close friendship with the royals. Could this have been a reward given knowingly for services rendered? If the replacement really did take place, it would have involved complicity among the very upper levels of the British Establishment to ensure the story never got out. McCartney can barely contain his glee at fraternising with the monarch in many photos of them together. (Incidentally, it was revealed by the mainstream press in 2013, after gaining access to documents through Freedom of Information laws, that George Harrison was offered an OBE in the Queen's New Year's Honours of 2000, but had turned it down, apparently considering anything less than the full Knighthood his bandmate McCartney had received to be an insult. Harrison was dead less than two years later.)

Additionally, photographs show that he has become fond of flashing up the 'Baphomet' hand sign that we'll examine in a forthcoming chapter, at many of his live performances of recent years. As many have pointed out, there seems to be a moral corruption that accompanies recruitment to the upper levels of entertainment's VIP Club, and McCartney's seemingly willing induction into it is very much at odds with his innocent past. There's a certain poetic relevance to Paul/Faul appearing on record with Kanye West on the track 'Only One' in 2015, and again with Kanye and Rihanna on 'Four Five Seconds.' One generation of artificiality and manipulation meets another. Even if his appearance did highlight the cultural ignorance of young people in America when many of them Tweeted comments like, 'who's this new Paul McCartney cat?' That's what I like about Kanye, man; always willing to give a platform to new up-and-coming names!' It may well be that the McCartney replacement was only ever supposed to play the role for the few years until the Beatles' final break-up, then fade away into a private life of obscurity, but that he so got the taste for musical fame and fortune that his ego got the better of him, and motivated him to go on putting out his own music for decades afterwards.

'McCartney's' carefully cultivated family-friendly image took a battering in 2003 when American illusionist David Blaine was in London to perform an endurance stunt, suspending himself in a glass box over the Thames for 44 days. McCartney decided to pay a late-night visit. According to the book 'Fab: An Intimate Life of Paul McCartney' by Howard Sounes, Paul's publicist Geoff Baker beckoned a photographer, Kevin Wheal, to go and take his picture. An enthusiastic Wheal reportedly ran towards McCartney, incurring some hostility. McCartney, who appeared drunk, is said to have pushed Wheal away and said, "listen mate, I've come to see this stupid cunt. You're not going to take a picture of me tonight. Fuck off! I'm a pedestrian on a private visit." Alerted to his presence, a member of the public then came up and asked if they could shake McCartney's hand, to which they received the reply "fuck off." McCartney is then said to have fired Baker and ordered his driver to take him home.

Prior to 2015, Paul had already made some comments about the famous Lennon-McCartney song writing tag, suggesting that it should be alternated so that his own name appeared first 50 per cent of the time. In July 2015 he took things further and angered many John Lennon and Beatles fans in the process, in an interview given to the UK's 'Telegraph.' McCartney complained that Lennon's assassination had made him a martyr. The article quotes him as saying:

> *"When John got shot, aside from the pure horror of it, the lingering thing was, 'OK, well, now John's a martyr. A JFK.' I started to get frustrated because people started to say, 'Well, he was the Beatles.' And me, George and Ringo would go, 'Er, hang on. It's only a year ago we were all equal-ish.'*

> *"John was the witty one, sure. John did a lot of great work. And post-Beatles he did more great work. But he also did a lot of not-great work. Now the fact that he's martyred has elevated him to a James Dean, and beyond.*

> *"So whilst I didn't mind that—I agreed with it—I understood that now there was going to be revisionism. It was going to be: John was the one. I mean, if you just pull out all his great stuff and then stack it up against my not-so-great stuff, it's an easy case to make."*

Stories such as this leaking out at the same time as spoofs like the Ringo one, do make me wonder whether they're paving the way for some kind of disclosure regarding the whole Paul Is Dead subject area. Truth does sometimes take years, decades, even centuries to reveal itself. But it always gets there in the end.

Denial runs deep

It's worth bearing in mind that, for most people alive in the world today, their entire perception of who 'Paul McCartney' is and what he looks like, has been formed since 1966. The number who have vivid recollections of witnessing the pre-'66 Paul are dwindling with every passing year. What if enough time has amassed for an impostor to have been so thoroughly integrated into the public's consciousness, that he is now unquestioningly accepted? As terroronthetube.co.uk puts it:

"The world has greatly forgotten what the real Paul McCartney looked like; that cute, round-faced cherubic look, the heart and soul of the original Beatles, adored by his fans around the world, so successful has been the 'morphing' of the new lad."

The suggestion of the McCartney replacement does tend to be met with scorn and derision from those old enough to remember the Beatles and their impact on the 1960s. This generation often maintains that the switch couldn't possibly have taken place. In many ways this is understandable. There is a lot invested in personal nostalgia, and to have these memories challenged in a way that would force you to re-evaluate the entire experience is too difficult for many to face. Acceptance of a hoax also involves admitting that you were duped, along with the rest of the population on whom the deception was foisted, and it seems many prefer not to acknowledge that they're capable of being fooled in such a way. I recently asked an old boss of mine, who was a young musician himself in the 1960s, what he thought of the idea that the music of that decade could have been a cynical exercise in social engineering. His response, 'I prefer the 60s as I remember them, thanks', will be a common stance among members of that generation.

The McCartney replacement—if it did take place—was very much a product of its time, where a reliance on largely black-and-white printed photographs was the only chance any researcher really had of highlighting any discrepancies. And anyone who thought they might be on to something only had newsletters, fanzines and the occasional radio phone-in through which to communicate their suspicions. Such an audacious plan could never work in today's internet era, where vigilant 'webheads' would be all over any anomalies between photos and video footage in seconds, and with a Youtube video and blog essay posted to the world by the end of the day.

I can't prove that a McCartney replacement really did take place, and the number of people who could is limited only to those who had a first-hand involvement in the events of those times. The rest of us are left to speculate based on the evidence that is available to us, along with whatever logic and intuition we individually bring to the table. Maybe the full revelations will emerge only after the passing of Paul/ Faul, just as the truth about Jimmy Savile did. Maybe lifetime oaths of allegiance really do work like that.

Stranger things have happened. As we'll see.

Resources:

The Paul Is Dead Myth: the Beatles Bible:

- http://www.beatlesbible.com/features/paul-is-dead/

'Paul Is Dead' on Wikipedia:

- http://en.wikipedia.org/wiki/Paul_is_dead

Was Paul McCartney 'Replaced' by a 'Double' in 1966?–Andrew Johnson:

- http://plasticmacca.blogspot.co.uk/2013/04/was-paul-mccartney-replaced-by-double.html

Undeniable Proof that Paul McCartney was replaced with a Look-Alike: Part 4 section 2: The Imposter's Height:

- http://digilander.libero.it/jamespaul/fc42.html

The Curious Case of Faul McCartney and the Beatles 1966:

- https://www.youtube.com/watch?v=Z-FFRpBKeiU

Disseminating the Paul Is Dead rumour:

- http://hoaxes.org/archive/permalink/paul_is_dead

Paul Is Dead–For those who do not believe in Paul's replacing double:

- https://www.youtube.com/watch?v=KjUs2Uhxj68

Paul Is Dead: The Shocking Clues Collection Video:

- https://www.youtube.com/all_comments?v=XskhB7g-t78

'Paul likes to think he's the only remaining Beatle': Ringo Starr interview with The Daily Mail, 2011:

- http://www.dailymail.co.uk/home/moslive/article-1388489/The-Beatles-Ringo-Starr-Paul-McCartney-likes-think-hes-remaining-Beatle.html

A Double-Identity Beatle? Terror On The Tube:

- http://terroronthetube.co.uk/related-articles/a-double-identity-beatle/

Beatles interview database:

- http://www.beatlesinterviews.org/db63.html

Full analysis of 'Revolution No. 9' by Ian Hammond:

- http://beatlesnumber9.com/1number9.html

Forensic science proves Paul was replaced:

- http://www.whale.to/b/mccartney_h.html

Horselover Phat's Subliminal Synchrosphere Blog: OTO, Hip Hop, Hollywood and MSM 'Masonic Mystery Religion' Mind Control:

- http://subliminalsynchrosphere.blogspot.co.uk/2014/02/oto-hip-hop-hollywood-and-msm-masonic.html

Mark Devlin's Good Vibrations podcast interview with Tina Foster of the Plastic Macca blog site:

- https://soundcloud.com/mark-devlin/good-vibrations-podcast-vol-42

Paul Is Dead: The Rotten Apple 63 (including footage of Heather Mills' interview with Billy Bush on Access Hollywood):

- https://www.youtube.com/watch?v=dCQtP4AjVg8

Plastic Macca: Was Heather Mills threatened into silence?:

- http://plasticmacca.blogspot.co.uk/2009/09/what-does-heather-mills-know.html

Plastic Macca: Funny Faul Flubs:

- http://plasticmacca.blogspot.co.uk/2010/01/oops-things-faul-says-sometimes.html

Paul is Dead: New evidence based on computer enhanced forensic techniques:

- http://hugequestions.com/Eric/TFC/FromOthers/Paul-McCartney-Italian.html

Project Walrus And The Murder Of John Lennon:

- http://wariscrime.com/new/ project-walrus-and-the-murder-of-john-lennon/

The Last Testament Of George Harrison:

- https://www.youtube.com/watch?v=8oApfDhOT24

George Harrison Turned Down OBE, Wanted to be Knighted Instead:

- http://www.newsmax.com/TheWire/ george-harrison-obe-knighted/2013/12/24/id/543593/

Plastic Macca blog: Imagine: John Fennon:

- http://plasticmacca.blogspot.co.uk/2014/10/imagine-john-fennon.html

Thomas E. Uharriet: The Memoirs Of Billy Shears on Amazon:

- http://www.amazon.co.uk/ Memoirs-Billy-Shears-Thomas-Uharriet/dp/1475145888

Diana inquest: MI6 'plotted tunnel murder':

- http://www.telegraph.co.uk/news/uknews/1578498/Diana-inquest-MI6-plotted-tunnel-murder.html

CHAPTER 6

ROLLING IN THE DEEP

Dark occult aspects of The Rolling Stones.

"There are black magicians who think we are acting as unknown agents of Lucifer, and others who think we are Lucifer."
Keith Richards

The rivalry between the Beatles and the Rolling Stones in the 1960s–largely accentuated by their respective promotional teams–is the stuff of legend, and has been endlessly evoked in subsequent musical rivalries, notably between Blur and Oasis during the 'britpop' era of the mid-90s. Certainly, a glance at record sales and chart positions achieved by the two groups, provides instant confirmation that they were the two leading collectives in the early rock era. However much the Beatles' latter career was characterised by occultic activity and symbolism, however, the Rolling Stones were not to be outdone and, if anything, walked all over their Northern rivals when it came to dark, Satanic overtones, and the ever-present shadow of death.

While the Beatles–in their early days at least–were marketed as a kind of wholesome, clean-cut group singing catchy, innocent songs that young fans could listen to with their grans, from the start, the Rolling Stones were portrayed as a much rougher, more dangerous outfit. Andrew Loog Oldham started out as the Beatles' early publicist, but defected to the Stones in 1963, and straight away worked on hyping their loutish image. It's Loog Oldham who's credited with inventing the quote 'would you let your daughter marry a Rolling Stone?' and similar provocative headlines in the press of the time. Loog Oldham's father was a British Air Force pilot who was shot down and killed before his son was even born in yet another of an endless glut of connections between the music industry and the military/ "intelligence" services.

Loog Oldham was of Jewish parentage—another ever-present credential in the music industry's back-story. He also worked for a time as the publicist for reported paedophile and satanist record producer Joe Meek. A full house.

Part of Loog Oldham's plan to shape the rebellious image of the Stones involved pictures taken by his Jewish photographer friend Gered Mancowitz, the son of the screenwriter Wolf Mancowitz. Following Loog Oldham's defection to the Stones, the Beatles became managed by the Jewish Brian Epstein. Meanwhile, when Loog Oldham's tenure with the Stones came to an end in that magical year of 1966, management was turned over to a Jewish, (just a coincidence, nothing to worry about) New York accountant named Allen Klein.

Something in the air

From the start, the vibe at the Rolling Stones live shows had a very distinctive air, attracting unruly audiences, and their gigs became known as hotbeds of brewing angst and discontent. One such example was a gig at The Empress Ballroom in Blackpool in 1964. The violence that erupted when Keith Richards had an altercation with an aggressive member of the audience led to the group being banned by the town council for the next 45 years.

These types of experiences were only the prelude to a far darker live performance, however, which has gone down in the annals of rock history alongside The Who's ill-fated gig in Cincinatti and Pearl Jam's fatal appearance at Denmark's Roskilde Festival for all the wrong reasons. This was the Altamont Free Festival held at a racetrack in California in December 1969, where a black, 18-year-old Stones audience member named Meredith Hunter was stabbed and beaten to death in front of the stage as the group performed.

Fellow British DJ, writer and researcher Matt Sergiou, who runs the brilliant and endlessly fascinating Conspiro Media blog site, has published a mindblowingly comprehensive overview of the Stones' darker side. Here, in an abridged version of the heavily-detailed article on the site, he takes up the story of Altamont:

"(Meredith Hunter) had got locked into an altercation with members of the Hells Angels, the notorious motorcycle club which, it's said, was hired to take care of security, although this has been denied by some who were closely involved with the gig. The reputed photographer Ethan Russell, who's shot album covers for the Beatles and The Who during his lengthy career, was with the Stones at Altamont. He wasn't impressed with what he saw from the start. For him, the location of the venue 'was a dull, lifeless landscape. There was no hint of green, not a tree, not a blade of grass. When we arrived there was no palpable feeling of joy or even happiness. It slowly dawned on me that this concert might not turn out to be what I expected . . . '

". . . Fellow Altamont performer Grace Slick, who was a singer with the Jefferson Airplane at the time, is also said to have picked up on the 'strange' vibrations that day, recalling that 'the vibes were bad. Something was very peculiar, not particularly bad, just real peculiar. I had expected the loving vibes of Woodstock but that wasn't coming at me. This was a whole different thing.' The magazine 'Rolling Stone', in a special Altamont issue published shortly after the event, reported that 'a chick toward the front of the stage" on the opening day of the festival 'was telling her old man: 'It's weird. They consulted the astrologers before setting the dates for Woodstock, but they couldn't have consulted an astrologer about today. Anyone can see that with the moon in Scorpio, today's an awful day to do this concert. There's a strong possibility of violence and chaos and any astrologer could have told them so . . . '

"The Stones took to the stage the following morning at around 4am. Mick Taylor is quoted as describing the scene before him as 'completely barbaric, like there was so much violence there it completely took the enjoyment out of it for me . . . it was impossible . . . to enjoy the music, or anything, because most of the violence was going on right in front of the stage, right in front of our eyes, and like I've never seen anything like it before. I just couldn't believe it. The Hells Angels had a lot to do with it . . . '

"The Stones' performance at Altamont, and the horrors which unfolded before them as they played, are featured in the documentary, 'Gimme Shelter,' which picks up on their set some two songs in when they launch into 'Sympathy for the Devil,' but not before Jagger addresses the crowd in a soft, almost effeminate manner, asking them to 'just be cool down the front there and don't push around. Just keep still, keep together ...'

"A few seconds later, the opening beats of the number 'Under My Thumb' begin. Jagger calmly asks the crowd to 'sit down just keep cool and let's just relax, let's just get into a groove, come on, we can get it together. Sit down.' As the song ends though, we see a wide, empty space forming in the audience again. There's trouble, and there's Meredith Hunter at the edge of the rapidly receding crowd, recognisable by his bright green jacket and trousers. A Hells Angel comes lunging at him, making stabbing-like motions into the 18-year-old before pushing him out of shot into the darkness.

"Bill Wyman was recently quoted as saying, "'Mick Taylor and I were the ones nearest to it. We saw the crowd open up and the guy chase the other guy right in front of us. We both saw the commotion when the guy got stabbed. We saw the whole thing, and my heart skipped a beat.' In the documentary, we see people tending to a stretcher. There's a bloodstained sleeve hanging out from underneath a blanket that's been strapped into it, and it's the same shade of green as worn by Meredith Hunter. We can't see him. The face has been covered. We can also hear a voice say, 'we pronounced him dead at six o'clock.'

Albert Maysles, director of the documentary 'Gimme Shelter', has confirmed that one of the camera operators at Altamont just happened to be a young aspiring director named George Lucas. Purely as a matter of curiosity, the name Lucas is said to mean 'bright', 'shining' or 'luminous', and is connected to the name Lucifer, meaning 'the light bearer.' Mick Jagger gave the name Lucas to his third son, born in 1999.

It was a devastating event for the Stones' mainstream public image, though it only served to reinforce their credentials within rock music's darker circles.

The Devil goes mainstream

'Sympathy For The Devil' itself is arguably the Stones' most notorious track. It remains on frequent radio rotation around the world, bringing demonic connotations into the general public's consciousness. Wikipedia claims it to be:

"An homage to Satan, written in the first-person narrative from the point of view of Lucifer, who recounts the atrocities committed throughout the history of humanity in his name."

This reinforces the idea, central to modern Christian teaching, that 'Lucifer' and 'Satan' are both names for a singular entity known as 'The Devil' who stands as the antithesis to the God of creation. This is an over-simplification of the occult teachings of ancient civilisations. Within the circles of esoterica and black magic(k), 'Satan' is represented by the Planet Saturn, in recognition of the dark influence it is said to have had over human affairs for aeons. It's no coincidence that the spellings are so similar. 'Lucifer,' meanwhile, is a symbolic rendering of Venus, commonly known as The Morning Star.

Either way, 'Sympathy' has Mick Jagger assuming the person of 'The Devil,' and gloating over the death, misery and human suffering he has brought through the ages, citing Jesus' trial at the hands of Pilate, the bloody Russian Revolution, and the murder of the Kennedys among his achievements. (Reportedly, Senator Robert Kennedy was assassinated during the time that Jagger was writing the song, so the lyric 'I shouted out, who killed Kennedy' was swiftly pluralised to 'the Kennedys.') The song, originally titled 'The Devil Is My Name,' appeared on the album 'Beggars Banquet,' and is credited to Jagger/ Richards, although Jagger is acknowledged as having penned the lyrics single-handedly. In interviews, he has said that he was inspired by a book given to him by his girlfriend Marianne Faithfull, (in turn recommended to her by film-maker Kenneth Anger,) 'The Master And Margarita' by Russian author Mikhail Bulgakov, which concerns The Devil paying a visit to the Soviet Union. 'Sympathy' inspired the title of a 'producer's edit' of a 1968 film by Jean-Luc Godard. The film was originally titled 'One Plus One' and is a depiction of the late 60s US counter-culture scene.

Its footage features the Stones in the process of recording 'Sympathy' in the studio.

It was inevitable that the song would gain the group a reputation among Christian groups as 'devil worshippers,' given that John Lennon's earlier comment that 'we're more popular than Jesus now' had caused such a stir. The Stones acted shocked at the reactions—at least for the purposes of interviews. Jagger stated: "When people started taking us as devil worshippers, I thought it was a really odd thing, because it was only one song, after all. It wasn't like it was a whole album, with lots of occult signs on the back. People seemed to embrace the image so readily, and it has carried all the way over into heavy metal bands today."

Keith Richards observed:

> "Before, we were just innocent kids out for a good time. They're saying, 'they're evil, they're evil.' Oh, I'm evil, really? So that makes you start thinking about evil... What is evil? Half of it, I don't know how much people think of Mick as The Devil or as just a good rock performer or what? There are black magicians who think we are acting as unknown agents of Lucifer and others who think we are Lucifer."

These comments seem naive or carefully contrived when put into the context of the rest of the Stones' career, because 'Sympathy' is far from alone in representing the group's dabblings into diabolical realms. An earlier eyebrow-raiser had been the album 'Their Satanic Majesties Request,' released in December 1967. According to the Stones' official website, the title was a play on the wording found in a British passport of the time: 'Her Britannic Majesty's Secretary of State requests and requires...' The Stones version will no doubt provide particular intrigue to anyone who has researched the true nature of the British monarch and her family, and some aspects of their background that somehow never seem to get covered by the BBC's 'Royal correspondent' Jennie Bond and her like! In countries such as South Africa and The Philippines the album had to be retitled 'The Stones Are Rolling', due to controversy over the word 'Satanic'.

The album was notable for the distinct similarities between the sleeve design and that of the Beatles' Peter Blake-designed 'Sgt. Pepper' album which had appeared six months earlier. It utilises lenticular printing, giving the image the feel of 3D depth. According to legend, the original cover was to feature an image of a naked Jagger being crucified, before it was rejected for being in 'bad taste.' (That's a surprise, eh?) The image that got used, designed by acclaimed rock photographer Michael Cooper, depicts the band members in various garb, much of it similar to that on 'Sgt. Pepper.' Jagger stands out in the centre, dressed as a black magician, complete with pointed wizard's hat adorned with a crescent moon. A blood-red Planet Saturn (Satan) hovers ominously overhead, along with a quarter of a 'supermoon' in the top-right corner. On the back cover is a painting by Tony Meevilwiffen depicting the four elements of Earth, Water, Fire and Air.

'Their Satanic Majesties' stands as the Stones' sole outing into the experimental and psychedelic style of the times, the rest of their pantheon remaining grounded in Rock and Rhythm & Blues territory. The group themselves were less than happy with the outcome, with Jagger commenting: "There's a lot of rubbish on 'Satanic Majesties.' Just too much time on our hands, too many drugs, no producer to tell us, 'Enough already, thank you very much, now can we just get on with this song?" Beatles John Lennon and Paul McCartney reportedly contributed uncredited backing vocals on the songs 'Sing This All Together' and 'We Love You,' which is an interesting state of affairs considering their respective groups were marketed as 'rivals'.

Keeping up with The Jones's

When it comes to black magic(k) and other dark occult activity, it's founding Stones member Brian Jones, (who always bore more than a passing resemblance to British sex-comedy actor Robin Askwith,) whose name crops up time after time. Even the name of his first pre-Stones band, Thunder Odin's Big Secret, with its nod to the Norse god from whose name the word Wednesday is derived, has other-worldly overtones.

Matt Sergiou again takes up the story:

"German singer Nico met the band in 1965. Of Brian Jones, she reportedly told a writer, 'do you know Brian was a witch?' We were interested in these things and he was very deep about it.' According to the book 'Nico, the Life and Lies of an Icon' by Richard Witts, 'she said on another occasion that Jones was keen on the occult but he was like a little boy with a magic set. It was really an excuse for him to be nasty and sexy. He read books by an old English man, (Aleister Crowley) who was The Devil.'

"Rock author Mick Wall states that well-renowned Aleister Crowley devotee Jimmy Page was a regular visitor to Brian's and Anita's London flat when he was a member of The Yardbirds, and that the Rolling Stone 'was into paganism, Zen, Moroccan tapestries . . . and drugs.' Anita (Pallenburg) was an aspiring film-star and model, into magick, sex, hanging out with rock stars . . . and drugs. A small-time crook as a teenager, not only was Brian a gifted and successful musician, he was up for anything. He and Anita would hold séances at the flat using a ouija board; or they would pile in the car and drive off to look for UFOs in the dead of night."

Elsewhere, the Conspiro Media article makes mention of Brian's alleged 'Witch's Tit':

"Kenneth Anger is widely quoted as saying, 'the occult unit within the Stones was Keith, Anita and Brian. I believe that Anita is, for want of a better word, a witch . . . ' Indeed, Pallenburg has reportedly declared, 'yes, I did have an interest in witchcraft, in Buddhism, in the black magicians that my friend Kenneth Anger, the film-maker, introduced me to. The world of the occult fascinated me . . . ' Of Jones, it's claimed that Anger said, 'you see, Brian was a witch too. I'm convinced. He showed me his Witch's Tit. He had a supernumerary tit in a very sexy place on his inner thigh. He stated, 'in another time they would have burned me.' He was very happy about that.' Of course, Jones wasn't wrong to assume that his purported third nipple might've led to persecution in a long bygone age. At the height of the witch-hunts in Europe in the 17th century, it was said supernatural entities which appeared in animal form fed off these marks on

the body. Known as 'familiars,' these spirits were supposedly assigned by The Devil to act as the servants of witches; to aid them in their magick and protect them from attack."

Jones' background throws up yet another link to the government and military 'intelligence' services, (Michael Franti observed wonderfully on the track 'Television: The Drug of the Nation' that 'military intelligence' is actually an oxymoron.) The fact that so many prominent musicians have family connections to these establishments, almost invariably through their fathers, surely goes beyond the realms of 'coincidence.' If the fathers of countless rock stars just happened to share jobs as, say, carpenters, traffic wardens or bakers, this would surely be considered strange. In his book 'Your Thoughts Are Not Your Own, Volume 2', British writer Neil Sanders lists just some of the famous music-makers whose parents have come from military, secret service, or government department backgrounds. These include: Kris Kristofferson, John Denver, the band America, Ciara, Lionel Richie, Christina Aguilera, Michael Stipe, Emmylou Harris, Ann and Nancy Wilson of Heart, Marilyn Manson, Trey Songz, Pete Doherty, Englebert Humperdink, Elton John and Bob Marley. There will be many others, not least the huge array of US and Canadian artists detailed in the next chapter on Laurel Canyon. Meanwhile, the list of artists who themselves have served in the military is just as extensive, including, but by no means limited to: Elvis Presley, Johnny Cash, John Coltrane, John Fogerty, Billy Cobham, Lou Rawls, Jerry Reed, Woody Guthrie, BB King, Henry Mancini, Charlie Rich, Tony Bennett, Grover Washington Jr., Jim Croce, Bill Wyman, Artimus Pyle of Lynyrd Skynyrd, Rick James, Shaggy, Ice T, Turbo B of Snap, MC Tee of Mantronix, James Blunt, Rihanna, Canibus, Fred Durst and Maynard Keenan. A notable one is Stewart Copeland, the drummer with The Police. His father was Miles Copeland, a high-ranking London-based CIA officer from the time of its mutation from The Office of Strategic Services, and in his retirement, creator of the 'Game Of Nations' board game. 'The Police' becomes an interesting choice of band name within this context, as do lyrics like 'every step you take, I'll be watching you!'

In Brian Jones' case, he was born Lewis Brian Hopkins Jones in Cheltenham in 1942 to a well-off musical family. They originated from

Wales, but had moved to Cheltenham to further his father's career as an aeronautical engineer. Cheltenham, as well as being a favoured retirement town for military top brass and government officials, has a rich history as a seat of British government 'intelligence' services. In 1951, it became home to the newly-founded General Communications Headquarters (GCHQ,) a prominent government spying post, and the equivalent to America's NSA, whose nefarious activities were recently exposed by the 'whistleblower' Edward Snowden.

According to an excellent on-line article titled 'Rolling Through The Intelligence Community' on the anolen.com website, the young Brian Jones gained a notorious reputation around Cheltenham for impregnating young girls, then absolving himself of any responsibility towards mother or child. He reportedly fathered six illegitimate children in this manner, becoming something of an embarrassment to his father, and to the defence industry for which he worked. At the same time, Jones was showing considerable talent as a blues musician. Before long, he'd been recruited to play in a collective known as Blues Incorporated in London, headed by the charismatic Alexis Korner, then dubbed 'the father of British blues.' Korner's father was Austrian-Jewish, while his mother was Turkish-Greek. They had moved to London in 1940. It was here that Jones was introduced to a young Mick Jagger and Keith Richards. Korner had for some reason recruited the pair, despite them having no previous musical experience. Charlie Watts and Ian Stewart, later to become the Stones' drummer and guitarist, were also a part of the Blues Incorporated collective. Korner is credited with having spring-boarded the careers of many other prominent music-makers, including Rod Stewart, John Mayall and Jimmy Page, and pretty much founding the groups Led Zeppelin and Cream. Korner went on to enjoy a successful television career with the newly-launched ITV, (headed by the Jewish Grade brothers,) and later joining BBC Radio One as a presenter.

Elsewhere in the fascinating anolen.com article, which you can find here: http://anolen.com/tag/up-and-down-with-the-rolling-stones/ the writer speculates on there being an organised link between the British music scene of the mid–to late-1960s, and that which emerged out of LA's Laurel Canyon district in the same timeframe, all connected by the British and US government, military and "intelligence" services.

The suggestion of many researchers is that, like the Beatles, the Rolling Stones were a creation of some arm of the British government/ 'intelligence' services—possibly The Tavistock Institute—and that, like their Northern counterparts, they also constituted a massive exercise in shaping the social attitudes of a generation. Mind-altering drugs were never far from the picture. Neither were the suspicions of 'plants' and 'handlers' within their inner circle. Brian Jones was the original in-band boyfriend of Anita Pallenberg, before she later became attached to Keith Richards. Little is known about exactly how she came to be integrated into the Stones' fraternity, leading some to speculate that she could have been some kind of 'insider.' It was Pallenberg who is said to have introduced Jones to LSD, to which he quickly became addicted, and which led to a rapid downward spiral all the way to his untimely death. The sexual antics in the Stones camp have led to much theorising that the group was run as a kind of mind-controlled cult. Members of such groups are typically cut off from family members and their former friends, and encouraged to fraternise only with fellow members. This is certainly a phenomenon seen throughout the music industry. Once they cross a certain threshold, many artists have spoken of only having 'industry friends,' and of having all ties with their previous life severed.

The other Stones girlfriend, Marianne Faithfull, also comes from a military family background. Her father was reportedly a British spy in wartime Berlin, while her half-Jewish mother was a cabaret dancer in Germany. Does anyone else see any patterns forming here?

The mysterious death of Brian Jones

By the time of his sudden death at the age of 27, (remember that number!), Jones' career with the Stones was all but finished. As the rest of the band planned an ambitious tour of the US in the Spring of 1969, Jones had effectively been kicked out of the group he had formed. He was said to have been badly affected by years of drink and heavy drug abuse, had become unpredictable, aggressive, unfit and bloated, and had holed himself up as something of a recluse at his 16th century farmhouse, Cotchford Farm, in East Sussex. (This just happened to be the former home of Winnie The Pooh creator and alleged paedophile AA Milne.)

Ever the party guy, however, Jones never lost his enthusiasm to entertain, and hosted small parties for friends during a period where his house was undergoing renovation. At around midnight on the night of 2nd/ 3rd July 1969, at the tail end of one such gathering, Jones' lifeless body was discovered in the outdoor swimming pool of his house.

The official verdict was 'death by misadventure,' the implication being that a heavily drunk and drugged-up Jones had accidentally drowned after deciding to take a lone, late-night swim. The coroner's report made a point of noting that his liver and heart were unnaturally enlarged due to drug and alcohol abuse.

The suspicion that Jones was actually murdered has persisted in rock music lore ever since, and the candidate frequently cited as his killer is a man by the name of Frank Thorogood. A builder, he was part of the construction team working on Jones' property shortly before his demise, also seemingly acting as Jones' unofficial minder and supplier of drugs. It's said that, years later, Thorogood confessed to the killing to Rolling Stones driver Tom Keylock. This story became the subject of the 2005 movie 'Stoned,' with Leo Gregory playing the part of Jones, and Paddy Considine portraying Thorogood.

By 2009, an investigative journalist named Scott Jones claimed to have traced many of the people who had been at Jones' house the night he died, and as a result, Sussex Police agreed to open the first review into the death since 1969. Soon afterwards, however, they announced they would not be re-opening the case, stating: "this has been thoroughly reviewed by Sussex Police's Crime Policy and Review Branch, but there is no new evidence to suggest that the coroner's original verdict of 'death by misadventure' was incorrect." In an article published in 'The Mail On Sunday' in 2008, Scott Jones alleged that Frank Thorogood had killed Jones following a fight, and the police at the time had covered up the cause of death. Jones had allegedly sacked Thorogood from the building project earlier in the day, having been dissatisfied with his work.

One of the small group gathered at Jones' house was Janet Lawson, girlfriend of Stones assistant Tom Keylock. In his 2008 article, Scott Jones relates what Lawson had told him about that fateful night, shortly before she died from cancer:

"Frank was not doing the building work properly. Jan told me: 'Brian had sacked him that day. There was something in the air. Frank was acting strangely, throwing his weight around a bit. In the early evening Frank, Anna, Brian and myself had dinner—steak and kidney pie.'

"After eating, the group returned to the garden where Jones and Thorogood larked about in the pool. Later, when Jones was in the pool by himself, he asked Janet to find his asthma inhaler. 'I went to look for it by the pool, in the music room, the reception room and then the kitchen. Frank came in in a lather. His hands were shaking. He was in a terrible state. I thought the worst almost straight away and went to the pool to check.

"When I saw Brian on the bottom of the pool and was calling for help, Frank initially did nothing. I shouted for Frank again as I ran towards the house, and he burst out before I reached it, ran to the pool and instantly dived in. But I had not said where Brian was. I thought, 'how did he know Brian was at the bottom of the pool?'

"I ran back to the house and tried to call 999 but Anna was on the phone and would not get off it.

"But in her original statement, Janet did not mention the tension between Jones and Thorogood, or the fact that she feared the worst as soon as she saw Thorogood coming in from the pool. Nor did she reveal how Thorogood initially ignored her cries for help or that he dived into the pool without her telling him that was where Jones was. Did she think Thorogood had killed Jones?

'Yes. I went into the house to look for Brian's inhaler. Frank jumped back in the pool, did something to Brian and by the time I came back, Brian was lying peacefully on the bottom of the pool with not a ripple in the water.'

"... Jan believed that Thorogood had not intended to kill Jones but the guitarist's death was probably the result of horseplay that had got out of hand."

According to another researcher, Trevor Hobley, one of Jones' neighbours had seen a large bonfire burning on Jones' property a few hours after his body had been found, in which Jones' clothes and some documents were being burned. An American author and former editor of 'Rolling Stone' magazine, meanwhile, Robert Greenfield, has claimed that Tom Keylock, Janet Lawson's boyfriend, was assigned to cover up Jones' death at the hands of Thorogood. His claim came as the result of conversations with Keith Richards, with whom he lived in the South of France in 1971. Richards was apparently convinced that Thorogood had been Jones' killer.

Thorogood himself died in 1993. The story, however, did not die with him. In 2013, Thorogood's daughter, Jan Bell, spoke to the UK's 'Daily Mail' to claim that her father had told her of a vicious row between Jones and other members of the Stones on the day of his death. She had related this story as part of her report to Sussex Police, she said, but the police had decided to take no action on it. Thorogood's claim was that Mick Jagger and Keith Richards had visited the farmhouse to ask Jones to agree to a financial settlement for giving over the name of the Rolling Stones. A row reportedly broke out when Jones refused. According to Thorogood, Richards then drew a knife on Jones in anger. Thorogood is said to have calmed everyone down, after which Jagger and Richards left the property.

Just before things start to become too clear-cut and transparent, however—because that would never do in the world of rock music deaths, would it?—a different slant is put on the Jones affair by respected US music author Alex Constantine in his book 'The Covert War Against Rock.' Constantine claims that, by the time of his death, Jones had been on a rehabilitative path and had been clean of drink and drugs for some weeks, making a nonsense of the coroner's report findings. The book's chapter on Jones places a different emphasis on the construction crew at the house of which Thorogood had been a part:

"A hostile clique, a very odd construction crew hired to restore Brian's home, originally AA Milne's cottage, muscled their way into his private life at Cotchford Farm. Brian's friend Nicholas Fitzgerald ran into the rhythm guitarist and founder of the Stones at a pub before he was found at the bottom of his swimming pool. Jones was in a snit

over 'a bunch hanging out at the farm.' For a lark, they'd hidden his motorcycle. When on the phone, the line would sometimes suddenly go dead. 'Then when I get the engineers in, they say there's nothing wrong. They're always leaping up to answer the phone and then they tell me it was a wrong number. I just can't trust anybody. I know you think I'm paranoid. Maybe I am, but not about this. I know they're up to something.'

"Bassist Bill Wyman found the crew 'a horrible group of people,' and it was largely due to their intimidations that Jones decayed "physically, mentally and musically."

Fitzgerald offers a further account of having arrived at Jones' house on the night of the death:

"Nick Fitzgerald now acknowledges that he arrived at the Jones estate shortly after the drowning, walked past the Summer house behind the mansion and 'saw the full glare of the lights over the pool and in the windows of the house. We had a clear view of the pool.' Fitzgerald approached to find three men dressed in sweaters and blue jeans, probably workmen, but the spotlights 'blotted out their features and made their faces look like white blobs. At the very moment I became aware of them, the middle one dropped to his knees, reached into the water and pushed down on the top of a head that looked white.' Two others, a man and a woman, watched passively. 'The kneeling man was pushing down on the head,' Fitzgerald told Hotchner, 'keeping it under. The man to the right of the kneeling man said something. It sounded like a command.' One of the men leaped into the pool and 'landed on the back of the struggling swimmer.' A third man was 'commanded' into the pool to hold Jones down.

"From the bushes near Fitzgerald, a 'burly man wearing glasses' rushed him. The man pushed Richard Cadbury, a companion, out of the way and grabbed Fitzgerald by the shoulder. He stuck a fist in Fitzgerald's face. 'Get the hell out of here, Fitzgerald,' the man spat, 'or you'll be next.'

"He meant it,' Fitzgerald reported decades after the fact. He had never seen the Cockney before, yet somehow the brute knew his name. Shaking, he stumbled to his car and Richard floored it away from the murder scene. They were too terrified to go to the police. 'Brian was dead. I couldn't rectify that and I might be putting my own life in danger. So I let it pass. But that scene hasn't passed from my mind, and even to this day it troubles me very much."

Apparently, Jones had never held out hope of making it much beyond the age at which he died. Keith Richards has reportedly said: "There are some people who you know aren't going to get old. Brian and I agreed that he, Brian, wouldn't live very long... I remember saying, 'you'll never make 30, man,' and he said, 'I know.'

Charlie Watts and Bill Wyman were the only Stones members who attended Jones' funeral, at a cemetery back in Cheltenham. Two days afterwards, the group played their historic open-air gig in London's Hyde Park, where new guitarist Mick Taylor was unveiled. The show was said to be dedicated to Jones' memory, with Jagger reading excerpts of the Percy Shelley poem 'Adonais.'

Enter the Acid Man

A saga which further cemented the Stones' reputation as the bad boys of 60s rock was the notorious drugs busts of 1967, first at Keith Richards' Sussex house Redlands in February of that year, then at Brian Jones' London flat on the very day that Jagger and Richards were standing trial for the earlier offence on 10th May. A photograph of a handcuffed Jagger and art dealer Robert Fraser hiding their faces as they're driven away in a police van the following month has become one of the most iconic of the era. A more telling one that will be of interest to numerologists emerged from Brian Jones' court case, when he was photographed driving away in a car with the personalised registration plate DD 666.

Some examination of the finer details, however, offers the suggestion that the February bust was a long-planned event manipulated into place by certain parties outside of the Stones' close circle, and with the ever-present element of British and American security service collusion. A key piece of evidence is the convenient emergence—and prompt disappearance–of a highly ambiguous figure by the name of David Schneiderman, (among various other pseudonyms.)

Conspiro Media takes up the story:

> *"In his memoirs, Keith makes note of the police raid on Brian's London residence which occurred 'almost on the hour' that he and Mick were standing before magistrates. The 'stitch-up,' as he describes it, 'was orchestrated and synchronised with rare precision. But due to some small glitch of stage management, the Press actually arrived, television crews included, a few minutes before the police knocked on Brian's door with their warrant."*

The suggestion, reinforced by Tony Sanchez in his book 'Up And Down With the Rolling Stones,' is that certain parties within the British Establishment had decided that the Rolling Stones' influence on the youthful generation had in some way gone 'off-script,' and that the group needed to be reminded of who was ultimately calling the shots. Enter David Schneiderman.

> *"One of the most intriguing aspects of the raid is the cloud of suspicion that hangs over the enigmatic David Schneiderman, who Keith and Marianne believe was sent to discredit The Stones. Of particular interest is his attaché case which was supposedly full of drugs and which police allegedly failed to search, even though it sat on a table in full view of them at Redlands that night.*

> *"Marianne also questions the timing of Schneiderman's unexpected arrival in the UK, which just so happened to coincide with Mick Jagger's legal moves against the 'News of the World.' . . . "They must have flown him in for this bust. He appeared very fast; right after the writ had been issued he showed up at Robert Fraser's flat. Robert called up and said: 'We've got this guy here, David Schneiderman, a Yank, just got in from California and he's brought this great Acid with him from the States. It's called White Lightning or something fabulous like that and he wants to lay some on us, man.' So I said, 'how f*****g great! Wait, Robert, I've got a fantastic idea, why don't we all go down to Redlands for the weekend? I'll call Keith right now*

and set it up.' And right after all this, Schneiderman vanished into thin air, (whisked out of the country I should think)."

It was many years later in the 1980s, that a television producer and failed actor by the name of David Jove was found to be none other than Schneiderman/ Synderman operating under a new guise. This story was related by Philip Norman, author of the book 'The Stones,' based on accounts given to him by Maggie Abbott, a British film agent who had befriended 'David Jove' in LA. In an article for 'The Mail OnLine,' Norman states:

> *". . . In January 1967, according to the account he gave Maggie Abbott, Snyderman was a failed TV actor, drifting around Europe in the American hippie throng with Swinging London as his final destination. At Heathrow Airport he was caught with drugs in his luggage and expected to be thrown into jail and instantly deported. Instead, British Customs handed him over to some 'heavy people' who hinted they belonged to MI5 and told him there was 'a way out' of his predicament. This was to infiltrate the Rolling Stones, supply Mick Jagger and Keith Richards with drugs, and then get them busted. According to Snyderman, MI5 were operating on behalf of an FBI offshoot known as COINTELPRO (Counter Intelligence Program,) set up by the FBI's director J. Edgar Hoover in the 1920s to "protect national security and maintain the existing social and political order."*

Scneiderman / Jove, was said to have been yet another devotee of the occult works of Aleister Crowley, coincidentally.

Meanwhile, despite the British Establishment's apparent moral stance against the recreational use of narcotics, the 1967 bust didn't appear to have done Mick Jagger any lasting damage when he was awarded a knighthood in the Queen's Birthday Honours list in June 2002. She's clearly a highly liberal and forgiving individual.

Where's Charlie?

Like Aleister Crowley, the murderous cult leader Charles Manson is a name that crops up all over the place in the story of rock music's pivotal years, synchronistically woven into the fabric of the era. Manson's reputation as a crazed satanic psychopath has overshadowed his status as a reasonably accomplished musician in his own right. Capitalising on his notoriety following his murder conviction, various artists have recorded songs written by him, including Guns N' Roses, White Zombie and Marilyn Manson, (whose artist name is a hybrid of Marilyn Monroe and Charles Manson.)

The suggestion that the infamous Tate/ LaBianca murders at the hands of Manson's 'family' were influenced by the Beatles' track 'Helter Skelter' has long been a part of rock music lore. The story goes that Manson believed in an imminent apocalyptic race war between whites and blacks which he had dubbed 'Helter Skelter.' This war would be won by militant blacks, he surmised, leaving only a few white survivors—himself and his 'family'—who would hide out in an underground city below California's Death Valley, before re-emerging to conquer the blacks who, he believed, would be incapable of ruling themselves. It's said that he had interpreted subliminal messages to this effect hidden in music from the Beatles' 'White Album', as well as from the Book of Revelation in The Bible.

'Helter Skelter' later became the title of the 1974 book written by Vincent Bugliosi, who was the prosecuting attorney in Manson's Los Angeles trial. Bugliosi got Manson charged for the murders despite him not having been present at the scene, by arguing that he still bore responsibility for orchestrating them.

Some researchers, however, have claimed that the Manson/ Beatles connection is one that has been hyped out of proportion by certain parties keen to deflect attention from Manson's far closer association with another group. The Beach Boys, similar to the Rolling Stones, were marketed as something of a rival act to the Beatles in the mid-60s. Manson's reputation as a dangerous killer does not sit comfortably with the Beach Boys' clean and wholesome all-American image. The facts, though, tell a different story.

Manson reportedly struck up a friendship, leading to a musical working relationship, with founding Beach Boy Dennis Wilson in 1968. Wikipedia relates the story as follows:

> *"The events that would culminate in the murders were set in motion in late Spring 1968, when, (by some accounts,) Dennis Wilson of the Beach Boys picked up two hitchhiking Manson women, Patricia Krenwinkel and Ella Jo Bailey, and brought them to his Pacific Palisades house for a few hours. Returning home in the early hours of the following morning from a night recording session, Wilson was greeted in the driveway of his own residence by Manson, who emerged from the house. Uncomfortable, Wilson asked the stranger whether he intended to hurt him. Assuring him he had no such intent, Manson began kissing Wilson's feet.*

> *"Inside the house, Wilson discovered 12 strangers, mostly women. Over the next few months, as their number doubled, the Family members who had made themselves part of Wilson's Sunset Boulevard household, cost him approximately $100,000. This included a large medical bill for treatment of their gonorrhoea and $21,000 for the accidental destruction of his uninsured car, which they borrowed. Wilson would sing and talk with Manson, whose women were treated as servants to them both.*

> *"Wilson paid for studio time to record songs written and performed by Manson, and he introduced Manson to acquaintances of his with roles in the entertainment business. These included Gregg Jakobson, Terry Melcher, and Rudi Altobelli, (the last of whom owned a house he would soon rent to actress Sharon Tate and her husband, director Roman Polanski). Jakobson, who was impressed by 'the whole Charlie Manson package' of artist/ lifestylist/ philosopher, also paid to record Manson material."*

Manson is said to have recorded at the home studio of Dennis Wilson's brother, Brian, but the recordings have never been made public. On their 1969 album '20/20,' the Beach Boys released a song written by Manson, originally titled 'Cease To Exist,' but changed to 'Never Learn

Not To Love'. Dennis Wilson is said to have distanced himself from Manson as word of his volatile nature spread, and he ended up simply moving out of his own house and leaving Manson there.

And so—bear with me—the assorted Manson connections gradually come back round to links with the Rolling Stones, all via a sinister organisation known as The Process Church. Matt Sergiou's reporting in Conspiro Media's Stones retrospective can't be bettered in telling the story:

> *"After brief sexual dalliances with Brian Jones and Keith Richards, the young beauty, (Marianne Faithfull,) eventually left her husband and began a four-year relationship with Mick Jagger in 1966. She too was fascinated by the occult and was briefly involved with the Process Church of the Final Judgement, a religious group founded in London in the early 1960s by former Scientologists, Mary and Robert DeGrimston.*

> *"In his book, 'Turn Off Your Mind: The Mystic Sixties and The Dark Side of the Age of Aquarius,' Gary Lachman quotes Faithfull as saying of The Process: 'I was attracted to them at first, mostly because they took me seriously when nobody else did. They were very admiring of me—they must have recognised that I have got magic powers.'*

> *"... He adds: 'in Haight-Ashbury, (the DeGrimstons) visited the offices of the 'San Francisco Oracle,' hoping to bring the underground newspaper over to the cause. 'The Oracle' was too busy hyping the coming Age of Aquarius to give Satan much time.*

> *"... They paid a visit to the Black Pope, Anton LaVey, head of the Church of Satan, but he had no use for them either. They set up a church at 407 Cole Street. Their neighbour at 636 Cole was someone who would cause them a lot of grief in a year or so. His name was Charles Manson, soon to become head of 'The Family,' responsible for the gruesome Tate/ LaBianca murders in August of 1969."*

Just as the notorious Kray twins pop up in the interconnected stories of the 1960s British pop industry, so another infamous serial killer remains intertwined in the American version. David Berkowitz, who was convicted of six murders in the 'Son Of Sam' killings in New York in 1976-77, made a series of allegations to investigative reporter Maury Terry from his jail cell, which Terry documented in his book 'The Ultimate Evil'. At the time of his capture, Berkowitz claimed he was acting alone, and on the instruction of a demon which communicated with him through his neighbour's dog, (as immortalised in the 1999 Spike Lee-directed movie 'Summer Of Sam.') Berkowitz later amended his confession, however, stating that he was a member of a satanic cult, and that the shootings were ritual slaughters. Berkowitz implicated the Process Church in this regard, also stating that the organisation was implicated in the 'Manson murders.'

Conspiro Media continues with Terry's account of his Berkowitz interviews:

> "The Process was very sophisticated and dedicated,' Berkowitz told me. 'They had their hands in a lot of things, including drugs and that disgusting child pornography. They also provided kids for sex to some wealthy people, and I did see some of those people at parties.' Michael Tsarion suggests Manson carried out the 1969 murders on behalf of The Process. He says: "all these families living on Cielo Drive were deeply involved—not only in drugs, but in child pornography—that's the Tate family, the LaBianca family, and the Polanski family, and even Sharon Tate. They were all involved in paedophilia and child pornography. And The Process hit them for internal reasons."

The amazing synchronistic quirks that eventually tie together so many key names, places and cultural events to the Rolling Stones, (and similarly the Beatles)—however tenuously—are so abundant that it seems to go beyond the realms of human planning. It starts to feel far more likely that unknown forces within the universe are bringing everything together in these strange, interconnected ways. It's a process which has been dubbed 'synchro-mysticism.'

Look back at Anger

No account of the Rolling Stones' involvement with the dark occult is complete without examining their association with the independent avant-garde film-maker and practising satanist Kenneth Anger. Born Kenneth Anglemeyer in California in 1927, he began making films at the age of ten, and has produced more than 40, his speciality being short montages of striking images lasting just a few minutes. His themes merged homo-eroticism with occult and esoteric imagery. Like so many of his rock star peers, Anger has expressed a fascination with the works of Aleister Crowley, and has been a follower of his Thelema religion. There have been many claims that he was also an asset of the CIA, involved with the drugs aspect of the nefarious MK-Ultra programme.

Crowley is said to have channelled a set of instructions and principles from a 'guardian angel' he called Aiwass in 1904, and these formed 'The Book Of The Law,' which was the central basis for Thelema. This is the Greek word for 'will,' and Crowley described the art of 'magick,' (his preferred spelling was with the extra k,) as 'the art of causing change to occur in accordance with will.'

In the 1920s, Crowley established The Abbey Of Thelema in a farmhouse in Cefalu, Sicily, where he reportedly practised ritual and sex magick, until he was deported by Mussolini. This period saw him labelled in the mainstream press as 'the wickedest man in the world.'

In 1955, Anger and his friend, the renowned sexologist Alfred Kinsey, travelled to the now-derelict Abbey of Thelema. The pair had gone to film a short documentary titled 'Thelema Abbey.' Anger and Kinsey restored many of the erotic wall paintings which had since been whitewashed over. Their arrival was less-than-enthusiastically greeted by Sicilian locals, who had strongly resented Crowley's presence there.

Anger moved to London during its 'Swinging Sixties' heyday, apparently attracted to the homeland of his hero, Crowley. He mixed with the aristocrats, artists and rock stars who populated the city's society scene, and was reportedly introduced to the Rolling Stones by art dealer Robert Fraser, sometimes known by the nickname 'Groovy Bob.' At the invitation of Jimmy Page, who owned the place from 1971 to 1991, he spent some time staying at Boleskine House, Crowley's former residence on Loch Ness, Scotland, reportedly to help Page exorcise the ghost of a headless man.

In a 2013 radio interview with Miles Johnson, former mind control victim-turned whistle-blower Max Spiers had some comments to add regarding Crowley's infamous home:

> *"Crowley opened a door to another dimension at Boleskine House. He was trying to summon Baal in a six-month ritual . . . He collapsed a broken man at the end and couldn't finish it and just left the house. He went back to London and had a big fight with McGregor Mathis . . . They were the two leaders of the Golden Dawn at the time. They had a massive feud, they fought for two or three years, and Mathis was left a broken man too."*

(Boleskine is said to have been situated where it was due to the lack of direct sunlight that hits that particular region of the Lochside valley. Its latitude and longitude is also of importance in the energy grid system.)

Anger's working association with the Rolling Stones first came from his 11-minute film 'Invocation Of My Demon Brother', released in 1969. It is said to be loosely based on Crowley's 1929 novel 'Moonchild.' Anger himself stars in the movie, as does his friend Anton LaVey, founder of the Church Of Satan. (There have been suggestions, however, that Anger himself was the real power behind the Church and that the role of LaVey, a former circus lion tamer, was merely as a charismatic celebrity-style frontman.) Jagger provided what's loosely described as the 'soundtrack' on his new Moog synthesiser, in reality a series of bleak, soulless instrumental stabs.

Anger began collating footage back in 1966, (when else??) for what was intended to be a film called 'Lucifer Rising', this time an interpretation of Crowley's poem 'Hymn To Lucifer'. Anger assembled the film at The Russian Embassy, a house in the Haight-Ashbury district of San Francisco which he was renting, and the film was intended to draw on the hippie/ counter-culture movement of the area which was then in full swing. 'Invocation' consisted largely of footage intended for 'Lucifer Rising' which had been binned but later retrieved. The footage that wasn't retained is said to have been stolen by a young musician and aspiring actor and poet named Bobby Beausoleil, ('beautiful sun' in French,) with whom Anger was rumoured to be having a gay affair. Anger's affectionate nickname for Beausoleil was reportedly 'Lucifer.' Beausoleil had been a one-time guitarist with the Laurel Canyon group Love. He would go on to achieve notoriety as a disciple of Charles Manson's 'family,' getting life imprisonment for the torture and murder of music teacher Gary Hinman. Beausoleil paid Hinman a visit, along with Manson disciples, Susie Atkins and Mary Brunner, to reportedly call in a debt owed to Manson, and ended up stabbing him to death.

'Lucifer Rising' eventually got completed in 1972, with Anger filming new scenes, but didn't attain a full cinema release until 1980. Anger had decided to steer its theme away from the San Francisco hippie scene, instead focusing on the incoming astrological Age of Aquarius. Rolling Stones girlfriend Marianne Faithfull was cast as the goddess Lilith, appearing in a strikingly memorable scene filmed in front of The Sphinx in Egypt. Fellow film-maker and close friend of Anger, Donald Cammell, appeared as the Egyptian deity Osiris. Jimmy Page, by this point with the highly successful Led Zeppelin, was hired to produce the film's soundtrack. Page also appears briefly, credited as 'Man Holding The Stella Of Revelation.' Anger and Page had a public falling-out before the film's 1980 release, however, and soundtrack duties were given to the murderer Bobby Beausoleil who composed the music from his prison cell. By this point, Anger had retracted his earlier claims that Beausoleil had stolen the film footage from him. Page's version of the soundtrack was released in 2012.

Donald Cammell went on to direct the cult classic 'Performance', in which Mick Jagger starred as the stereotypical reclusive rock star alongside James Fox's London gangster. Jagger also recorded the film's soundtrack. In turn, Cammell's father, Charles, was said to have been a close friend of Aleister Crowley. (It's never too long before 'the Great Beast' himself pops up like the proverbial bad penny in rock music history!) Reportedly, Crowley used to draw up 400-page horoscopes for the Cammell children, who he lived close to.

As well as inducting the Stones and their girlfriends into the world of Crowley and the dark occult, Anger also generated a strong interest from Paul McCartney, (the real one, presumably!) who occasionally hung out with the Stones. McCartney had, in turn, been led to Anger through a mutual acquaintance, Robert Fraser. These revelations came from 'Spanish' Tony Sanchez, in his book 'Up And Down With the Rolling Stones'. Sanchez was a long-time assistant and 'runner' for the Stones, as well as being a gang member and drug dealer, with both Keith Richards and John Lennon among his reported clients. Fraser is also said to have introduced Yoko Ono to McCartney, and later John Lennon. Diehard Beatles fans would doubtless concur that he therefore has a lot to answer for. Prior to his art career, Fraser served in The Kings' African Rifles colonial military regiment in East Africa, where his sergeant was none other than Idi Amin, later the murderous dictator of Uganda. There have even been claims that Fraser and Amin had a homosexual affair.

The links just keep on coming.

Anger himself had been initiated into the OTO, or Ordo Templi Orientis, ('Order Of The Temple Of The East,') a secret society once helmed by Crowley, with some very deep connections with the music industry through the ages, and of which, much more in a later chapter.

And finally...

The sudden death that has surrounded the Rolling Stones came knocking one more time in 2014 when Mick Jagger's 49-year-old girlfriend, L'Wren Scott, was found slumped on the floor of her New York apartment having apparently been hung from a doorknob by a black scarf. Despite being wealthy and successful, the absence of a note and of any strange behaviour before her death, and her holding a dinner party for friends just the night before, the coroner's report was quick to write her death off simply as 'suicide.'

Resources:

Conspiro Media's three-part Rolling Stones retrospective, Part 1:

- https://conspiromedia.wordpress.com/2013/03/20/last-years-mass-media-fuelled-celebrations-to-mark-the-50th-anniversary-of-the-rolling-stones-first-ever-gig-have-long-since-ended-one-year-on-conspiro-media-turns-up-late-to-the-party-with/

Conspiro Media's three-part Rolling Stones retrospective, Part 2:

- https://conspiromedia.wordpress.com/2014/07/16/the-three-part-conspiromedia-rolling-stones-retrospective-continues-this-sprawling-second-instalment-delves-into-their-public-and-not-so-public-dabblings-in-the-occult-and-also-re/?relatedposts_hit=1&relatedposts_origin=1181&relatedposts_position=0

The Rolling Stones 'Sympathy For The Devil' lyrics:

- http://www.azlyrics.com/lyrics/rollingstones/sympathyforthedevil.html

'Their Satanic Majesties Request' album on Wikipedia:

- http://en.wikipedia.org/wiki/Their_Satanic_Majesties_Request

Anolen blog: Rolling Through The Intelligence Community: Up And Down With the Rolling Stones:

- http://anolen.com/tag/up-and-down-with-the-rolling-stones/

Wikipedia: Kenneth Anger's 'Lucifer Rising':

- http://en.wikipedia.org/wiki/Lucifer_Rising_(film)

Anolen blog: The Other Loch Ness Monster:

- http://anolen.com/2014/12/26/the-other-loch-ness-monster/

Aangirfan blog: Mick Jagger, Satanism & The CIA:

- http://aangirfan.blogspot.ca/2014/03/mick-jagger-satanism-and-cia.html

Esquire: Kenneth Anger: Where The Bodies Are Buried:

- http://www.esquire.co.uk/culture/features/5483/kenneth-anger/

Daily Mail: Has the riddle of Rolling Stone Brian Jones's death been solved at last?:

- http://www.dailymail.co.uk/tvshowbiz/article-1090439/Has-riddle-Rolling-Stone-Brian-Joness-death-solved-last.html

Daily Mail: How the Acid King confessed he DID set up Rolling Stones drug bust for MI5 and FBI:

- http://www.dailymail.co.uk/news/article-1323236/The-Acid-King-confesses-Rolling-Stones-drug-bust-set-MI5-FBI.html

L'Wren Scott, noted fashion designer, Mick Jagger's girlfriend, found dead:

- http://edition.cnn.com/2014/03/17/showbiz/celebrity-news-gossip/lwren-scott-designer-obit/

CHAPTER 7

ADVENTURES IN PSYCHEDELIA

Military-intelligence connections in the LSD era.

"No matter how paranoid or conspiracy-minded you are, what the government is actually doing is far worse than you can imagine."
William Blum, formerly of the US State Department

As even the official version of events concedes, the decade of the 1960s was one of huge social change and was marked by many significant events, the ripples from which have been felt by the world's population ever since. Regardless of whether anyone accepts the approved accounts, or more alternative viewpoints, the Apollo 11 (faked!) moon landing, the Bay of Pigs invasion, the Vietnam War, the civil rights movements and the assassinations of John and Robert Kennedy, Martin Luther King and Malcolm X characterise the 60s as a world-changing decade like none before. The arrival of the contraceptive pill and the resulting sexual emancipation also had their part to play in reshaping social norms.

There is another aspect of the decade's second half which has arguably had as much cultural impact as any of the above. This is the emergence of LSD, contemporary with what has come to be known as the 'hippie' movement, and the music which provided the soundtrack for the transition. The youth-aimed sounds of 1965 and after–much of which came to be known by the newly-created moniker of 'folk rock'–were markedly different to what had been produced in the five years previous. Although some may choose to put this down the organic progression that occurs naturally in any art-form as time marches on, there are others who will claim this mutation was less by accident than by design.

There is some disagreement over the correct application of the term 'hippie,' particularly among the generation that has vivid recollections of the 60s. Alternative labels for the scene in question are 'counter-culture' and 'anti-establishment.' Either way—on the surface at least—the artists that permeated this period were taken to be youths of a rebellious spirit who had grown tired of the hypocrisy and corruption of 'The Establishment,' and the austere values of their parents' post-war generation. Their age group now had its own foreign war, in Vietnam, and there was much opposition to it. Simultaneously, the recreational use of LSD, cannabis, psilocybin mushrooms and other substances to attain altered states of consciousness, had been ushered in. The phrases 'make love, not war' and 'turn on, tune in, drop out' became the cultural soundbites of the era.

From Haight to the Canyon

Rock music lore has it that the cultural movement of these times was centred around the 'free love' city of San Francisco, and particularly, its Haight-Ashbury district. As Wikipedia puts it:

> *"The earlier bohemians of the beat movement had congregated around San Francisco's North Beach neighbourhood from the late 1950s. Many who could not find accommodation there turned to the quaint, relatively cheap and under-populated Haight-Ashbury. The Summer of Love (1967,) the 1960s era as a whole, and much of modern American counter-culture have been synonymous with San Francisco and the Haight-Ashbury neighbourhood ever since."*

> *"During the 'Summer of Love,' psychedelic rock music was entering the mainstream, receiving more and more commercial radio airplay. The Scott Mackenzie song "San Francisco (Be Sure to Wear Flowers in Your Hair,)' written by John Phillips of The Mamas & the Papas, became a hit single in 1967. The Monterey Pop Festival in June further cemented the status of psychedelic music as a part of mainstream culture and elevated local Haight bands such as the Grateful Dead, Big Brother and the Holding Company and Jefferson Airplane to national stardom."*

In 2008, however, a rock music journalist by the name of Dave McGowan began a series of web-based articles making an alternative claim for the birthplace of the counter-culture movement. This was a little-known district of his native Los Angeles known as Laurel Canyon. McGowan pointed out that a vastly larger array of artists who characterised those years emerged out of this small region in the Hollywood hills, starting in 1964-65, a good two years before the Haight-Ashbury explosion. Their number includes, but is far from limited to; the Doors, the Mamas & The Papas, the Byrds, Frank Zappa & The Mothers Of Invention, Captain Beefheart, the Monkees, Steppenwolf, Alice Cooper, Arthur Lee & Love, The Eagles, John Mayall, Carole King, Crosby, Stills, Nash & Young, Buffalo Springfield, Joan Baez, Judy Collins, Jackson Browne, James Taylor and Joni Mitchell. Even a pre-Lindsey Buckingham Fleetwood Mac based themselves there, as did the Beach Boys. Many of these artists did not hail from LA at all, but had been drawn, magnet-like, from all corners of the US, Canada and even Britain. What could have been the attraction of a neighbourhood that had no previous musical heritage whatsoever?

McGowan wasn't the first researcher to highlight the Canyon's musical heritage. He revealed that his own interest was sparked after reading a copy of Michael Walker's 2007 book 'Laurel Canyon: The Inside Story of Rock-And-Roll's Legendary Neighbourhood' while on holiday. What McGowan found so interesting, following some further delving, was that this community of rebellious musicians seems to have grown up out of the Canyon almost overnight, and the influence that they went on to wield on youth culture was almost unbelievable, given the tiny district of just a few streets from which it all happened.

His findings constituted his 2008 web series entitled 'Inside The LC: The Strange But Mostly True Story of Laurel Canyon,' and the resulting book, 'Weird Scenes Inside The Canyon,' published in 2014. As McGowan told me in the Good Vibrations podcast interview I recorded with him:

"It happened very, very quickly. You think of an organic, grass roots movement, and you think of these struggling artists playing coffee houses, and maybe getting on college radio, and slowly working their way up to some sort of mainstream acceptance. And this didn't happen

like that. I mean, these people arrived in town and within weeks they had fully-formed bands and brand new instruments and recording contracts and studio space. So all these people, really just in the space of two years, just simultaneously congregated on Laurel Canyon. LA did not have any kind of vibrant music scene before Laurel Canyon. The music industry pretty much moved here because that's where the artists were, rather than the other way around."

Coming to realise the true scale of impact that Canyon residents had had, he felt inspired to do some digging into the backgrounds of these artists. What he found was highly revealing, and may well provide the answer to the earlier question. Almost without exception, he discovered, the fathers of the music-makers came from backgrounds in either the US military, the CIA, various 'intelligence' (their words) and security services, or some other department of the US government. One of the key characters was one Admiral George Stephen Morrison.

"You don't find a stranger juxtaposition between father and son than with Jim Morrison and his father. Jim Morrison was actually one of the most unlikely rock stars. His dad—which had never been reported before it first appeared in my web series in 2008—was actually the navy Admiral that was in charge of the fleet of ships involved in the notorious Tonkin Gulf incident. And this was the incident that led America directly into a very prolonged and bloody ground war in South East Asia! This was what provided the justification to send in ground troops and turn it into a complete bloodbath. And it's been all but officially acknowledged that the incident is likely to never have happened. The ships never actually came under attack. It was a classic false flag orchestrated directly by Jim Morrison's dad! And almost simultaneously, we had him emerging out of Laurel Canyon as this fully-formed icon of the anti-war crowd."

Admiral Morrison died at the tail end of the very year McGowan published his findings into the strange links between Laurel Canyon and the US military. After LC's heyday, Jim Morrison went on to attain dubious fame as a member of the fabled '27 Club'—one of an absurdly high number of prominent musicians who *just happened* to meet an untimely end at the age of 27. (That's if you don't accept the claims of him faking his own death with US secret service assistance–more of that in a later chapter!) A popular quote attributed to Jim Morrison reads: 'The most loving parents and relatives commit murder with smiles on their faces. They force us to destroy the person we really are; a subtler kind of murder', which takes on a chilling resonance in light of the information above.

Crucially, McGowan added:

> *"The neighbourhood just happened to house a covert military intelligence facility, which was the first thing that raised alarm bells with me when I read Michael Walker's book."*

This was The Lookout Mountain Air Force Station, founded in 1947, the same year as the CIA, which secretly produced motion pictures and still photographs for the United States Department of Defense and the Atomic Energy Commission, and was involved in the US government's nuclear testing programme. Walt Disney, Marilyn Monroe and Ronald Reagan are said to have worked there covertly. The base was decommissioned in 1968 during Laurel Canyon's musical heyday. It was later converted into a private residence and was bought in January 2015 by the Hollywood actor Jared Leto.

As McGowan continued:

> *"Frank Zappa's another interesting one. His dad was a chemical warfare engineer, initially assigned to the Edgewood Arsenal, which was not only the long-time homebase of US chemical warfare research, but has been implicated repeatedly in various unclassified documents as a hotbed of MK-Ultra research. Frank Zappa was actually born at the Edgewood Arsenal! The family lived in housing right there on the base. Zappa was born, raised and educated there for the first seven years of his life, which is a pretty curious background for a rock star to have!*
>
> *"Then, on top of that, his wife, whose maiden name is Gail Sloatman, was also from a naval intelligence family. Her dad came from a long line of career naval officers. And she actually knew Jim Morrison*

from 20 years earlier. They knew each other as kids and actually attended a naval kindergarten together when they were five years old! So here you have another strange 'coincidence.' 20 years later he emerges as this larger-than-life rock star, and she as the wife of another larger-than-life rock star, all connected through military intelligence circles. What are the odds that that just happened by chance?"

The father of Mamas & Papas' star John Phillips was also a career marine corps officer, McGowan added, and his mother, sister and first wife were all career employees of the defence department at The Pentagon. Furthermore, John Phillips' first wife, Susie Adams, was a direct descendent of John Adams, America's second president. Even Phillips himself went to West Point and was being prepped for a military career.

Further revelations about Phillips, meanwhile, came from his daughter Mackenzie. Phillips named her after his good friend Scott McKenzie, for whom he wrote the hippie anthem 'San Francisco (Be Sure To wear Some Flowers In Your Hair)'. She claimed in her 2009 book 'High On Arrival', that on the eve of her 1979 wedding she had sex with her father. "He was full of love," she wrote, "and he was sick with drugs. I woke up that night from a blackout to find myself having sex with my own father." Mackenzie appeared on the 'Oprah Winfrey Show' in September 2009 and embellished the story by adding that her father also injected her with heroin and cocaine, a process known as 'speedballing.' She claimed her incestuous relationship ended when she became pregnant, but did not know who had fathered the child. Her father paid for her to have an abortion. John Phillips is said to have been closely involved in a satanic network involving four characters we have already met—cult leader Charles Manson, 'Rosemary's Baby' director Roman Polanski, murderer and one-time guitarist with the band Love, Bobby Beausoleil, and satanist film-maker Kenneth Anger.

In July 1980, by which point he was chronically addicted to heroin, Phillips was arrested and charged with running a large-scale drugs wholesaling operation. He had apparently been funding his habit by trading books of stolen prescriptions for bottles of pharmaceutical drugs at a Manhattan pharmacy, then trading those with his drug dealers for cocaine. Phillips narrowly escaped a possible 45-year prison term. He died in 2001, aged 65, of reported heart failure.

Meanwhile, similar military backgrounds can be uncovered with David Crosby, Graham Nash, Stephen Stills, and virtually all the other key players from the LC crowd, said McGowan. Gram Parsons' stepdad, who raised him after his own father supposedly committed suicide, (though there are suspicions he was murdered,) turns out to have been closely involved in training Cuban expatriot groups in Florida to overthrow the Castro regime, with the obvious suggestions of a CIA background that such a link brings. Parsons just missed becoming a member of the fabled '27 Club.' His birthday was just seven weeks away when his body was discovered in a motel room near the Joshua Tree National Monument in San Bernardino County, California, having apparently overdosed on morphine and alcohol. (D'you know, I think I've come across that scenario before somewhere.)

These revelations call into question just how organic and grass-roots the growth of the hippie movement may have been after all. Conversely, they present the very distinct possibility that the entire scene may have been an exercise in social engineering, cynically concocted by various Establishment think-tanks and their military-intelligence offshoots. The offspring of families employed in the programme would have been charged with spearheading it, either out of family loyalty or by some method of coercion, and with giving it a credible public face that the kids would willingly buy into. It's a suggestion that has horrified many original-generation hippies, who consider it sacrilege that their cherished memories of this time could be subverted in such a way. The evidence, however, speaks for itself and takes some explaining away.

Some grudging acceptance, along with some insight into the way that social conditioning covertly works away at affecting the human mind, came from the user known as 'choose2know' in the comments section of a blog article entitled 'What Happened To The Music?' She writes, insightfully:

> *"Patrick, I enjoyed your article as I'd read Dave McGowan's exposé several years ago and had seen the Youtube videos that were once available. It was all certainly an eye-opener for me, and yet his allegations did not seem foolish or over the top. I was coming of age in the 60s era and the music impacted me more than any other single thing in the culture. I was educated, well-read, and I had an integral*

Christian background, yet I was completely taken over by the promise of enlightenment to be found in rebellion. I'd almost prefer to believe that I'd been manipulated by some Power Elite than to acknowledge that I'd fallen for some vapid cultural shift that negatively impacted my life for many years.

"Sex, drugs and rock and roll was a choice that many of us made, stupidly thinking that within the self-destructive behaviour lay some freedom, some meaning that our parents couldn't fathom. Obviously they just weren't cool enough. I still listen up when I hear a Jim Morrison song, Hendrix wailing, or Janis Joplin singing her pain out. Neil Young was in a class by himself and seemed to be some mystic who had answers to all the questions. This music accompanied my life. It was the backbeat to failed relationships, getting high, and it provided me with the notion that I 'got it,' that I was in on some secret.

"And the regrets still keep me awake some nights. I threw away an opportunity for a first-class education. I said no to the good men and followed the bad boys to the clubs where they were doling out their imitations of my musical 'gods.' I wonder how many of my generation failed to achieve what they could have because they too were seduced by this empty trap? Some may think I'm being too harsh because, after all, aren't the 60s the 'good ol' days' now? Yes, the civil rights and feminism seemed to gain ground, and you can bet I burned my bra and married the first draft dodger/ musician I could convince myself I loved. Well, my false idols began to die of drug overdoses, of suicide, and I woke up to the fact that they didn't have any answers for me at all. I reclaimed my life and rectified as many mistakes as possible.

"Then the 80s arrived and I saw my own adolescent children being manipulated in the same ways, just by different faces and a different beat. I saw it and I fought it, but the system took them in too, into negativity and darkness. Television made it cool to be promiscuous, and the term 'friends with benefits' was part of their college education. Absolutely I believe that none of this was by coincidence or mere synchronicity."

And a viewer comment left below one of my Youtube talk videos on the subject concurred:

> *"What the 'hippie' movement did was discredit the voice of the youth by the Establishment that was sending them to die in Vietnam. All their parents saw was a bunch of dropout stoners that didn't 'love' their parents, country or God. They were at worst demonic, at best freeloading sex-addicted bums. And all the while their children thought they were 'expanding' their minds, loving their fellow human beings and doing what's right. They were tricked, lied to and manipulated by a power greater than they were able to understand."*

Further links between the record industry and the military intelligence complex, meanwhile, come from Thorn EMI in Britain and RCA in America, two of the biggest music corporations of decades past, having divisions steeped in military research and development and weapons systems. As a matter of curiosity, Cliff Richard's father was a one-time employee of Thorn Electrical Industries. Cliff began recording for the EMI record label in the 1970s prior to its merging with Thorn in 1979.

Tragically, as this book was being finished in late 2015, the news came that Dave McGowan had passed away aged just 55, apparently as the result of cancer. He had died on 22nd November, the anniversary of the Kennedy assassination, and a highly symbolic date for a renowned conspiracy researcher to depart this realm. He left behind a body of work that remains invaluable, and the key to understanding so much about the bigger picture.

Acid reign

As will be apparent throughout this book, the idea that certain conveniently-timed events can be written off as 'coincidence' when the resulting outcome just happens to suit the agenda of the world's controlling forces so well, goes well beyond the realms of credibility. And so it is with the emergence of LSD into the public domain, completely contemporaneously with the unfolding of the Vietnam War, and the changing identity of rock music.

The iconic figure involved in the rapid arrival of Lysergic Acid Diethylamide, is the psychologist and hallucinogenic researcher Timothy Leary, who was attached for a time to Harvard University, before getting expelled following extensive experimentation with mind-altering drugs. Leary's credentials go a little further, however. Many had suspected that he was working on behalf of the CIA, and this appears to have been borne out in a few cryptic comments he made in his later years. At one point, referring to his Harvard tenure, he reportedly admitted that: "some powerful people in Washington have sponsored all this drug research." In Leary's autobiography 'Flashbacks,' published in 1983, he credits CIA executive Cord Meyer with: "helping me to understand my political cultural role more clearly." Leary is said to have had an affair with Cord Meyer's wife, Mary, who was also intimately associated with President John F. Kennedy. According to Leary, Mary had sought him out for the purpose of learning how to conduct LSD sessions with Kennedy. In October 1964, Mary Meyer was found with a bullet in the back of her head and another in her heart after going for a walk along a canal in Georgetown, Washington DC.

In 1954, Leary is reported to have been director of clinical research and psychology at the Kaiser Foundation Hospital in Oakland, California. Part of his work involved devising a personality test which he called 'The Leary,' which was used by the CIA to assess prospective employees.

Reading between the lines it seems Leary was not in the direct employ of the CIA, but was rather utilised as a dupe. The controllers have long enjoyed the well-worn strategy of engaging people who believe wholeheartedly in an individual cause, and subverting that cause to suit their own, wider agenda. These individuals remain largely unaware of how their passion is being exploited for more nefarious means. The CIA had already run experiments to study the effects on human behaviour of LSD during the 1950s. Leary would appear to have been just the candidate, given his track record, to be co-opted into the Agency's plans to roll out mind control experimentation through drugs on a much larger scale in the following decade. Another character, contemporary to Leary and an active name in the 'counter-culture' era, was Jerry Garcia of The Grateful Dead, a key group from the Haight-Ashbury scene, who is often reported to have been an undercover spy for the CIA.

Incidentally, in 'The Playboy Interviews with John Lennon & Yoko Ono,' by David Sheff and G. Barry Golson, John Lennon is quoted as saying: "We must always remember to thank the CIA and the army for LSD, by the way. That's what people forget."

Like the Laurel Canyon story, Leary's CIA links call into serious question the conventional idea that he was a solo maverick, the self-styled 'Acid Guru,' who was operating to his own personal agenda, connecting with a youthful generation and taking them on a wonderful journey of new discoveries. Viewed from the perspective of 50 years of hindsight, it becomes far more likely that the LSD era was another cynically calculated plot, running concurrent with other social engineering methods in place at that most volatile of times.

Further intrigue comes from a seemingly religious aspect to Leary's activities, very much tapping into the emerging New Age movement of spirituality that was being ushered in during the 1960s. According to many accounts, this 'movement' was a creation of dark occult establishments such as the Church Of Satan as a form of 'controlled opposition' rather than something that evolved organically. There was also much talk of the upcoming zodiacal Age Of Aquarius, as immortalised in the popular musical of the time 'Hair'. Nobody seems to be able to give a definitive date as to when the earth moved, or will move, from Pisces into this new astrological age, the estimates remaining hundreds of years apart. Wikipedia observes:

> *"The approximate 2,160 years for each age corresponds to the average time it takes for the vernal equinox to move from one constellation of the zodiac into the next. According to different astrologers' calculations, approximated dates for entering the Age of Aquarius range from 1447 AD, (Terry MacKinnell,) to 3597, (John Addey.) Astrologers do not agree on when the Aquarian age will start or even if it has already started."*

Leary described himself as 'a pagan,' and had sought to establish his own 'religion' just prior to the acid era in 1966, (where have I come across that year before?) which he called The League for Spiritual Discovery—LSD for short.

The aim of the LSD influx would appear to be to have been the creation of a whole generation of young people who might otherwise have been galvanised into the type of political activism that had occurred earlier in the decade–particularly in defiance of the unfolding Vietnam War–instead being sedated into a state of chemically-induced passivity, content in the spirit of the times, to 'drop out.' At the same time, this caused ever greater alienation between this generation of human lab-rats and that of their parents, kick-starting a long-term plan to break up family units and create generational rifts in society, rendering each group more rife for further methods of control and manipulation.

If the plan was indeed for this era to have a long-term and extremely far-reaching effect on all aspects of Western culture and fashion, few would disagree that the experiment could be considered a great success. Wikipedia comments:

> "Hippie fashions and values had a major effect on culture, influencing popular music, television, film, literature, and the arts. Since the 1960s, many aspects of hippie culture have been assimilated by mainstream society. The religious and cultural diversity espoused by the hippies has gained widespread acceptance, and Eastern philosophy and spiritual concepts have reached a larger audience. The hippie legacy can be observed in contemporary culture in myriad forms, including health food, music festivals, contemporary sexual mores, and even the cyberspace revolution."

Tribal gatherings

LSD had become an important backdrop to the Haight-Ashbury 'hippie' scene in San Francisco by the time of the legendary 'Summer Of Love' in 1967. It is said to have arrived there as part of a CIA project, (with input from British 'intelligence' services,) connected to the notorious MK-Ultra mind control project, (of which much, much more in a later chapter!), with this aspect of it being handled by a character named Ken Kesey. In popular culture, Kesey is best known as author of the 'One Flew Over The Cuckoo's Nest' novel of 1962, a story of experimentation in a psychiatric ward which was made into a well-received film starring Jack Nicholson in 1975. Kesey's extra-curricular activities, besides being a convicted drug dealer, a stated CIA asset, and a former MK-Ultra test subject himself, involved running what was referred to as his 'Merry Pranksters.' This was a commune which travelled around in a tour bus, freely distributing LSD tablets and Koolaid laced with LSD, in key locations in California. The after-effects were then observed and studied.

It also figured majorly at the fabled Monterey International Pop Festival in California in June 1967, where up to 90,000 young people are estimated to have congregated over three days. In his book 'Aquarius Rising', author Robert Santelli documents the open use of hallucinogens at the event:

> *"LSD was in abundance at Monterey. Tabs of 'Monterey Purple' were literally given to anyone wishing to experiment a little. The police made no arrests, and set a precedent for future outdoor concerts, as there was a larger scheme in operation tied into the MK-Ultra project."*

Sure enough, similar scenes were witnessed at the equally legendary Woodstock concert in New York State two years later in August 1969. Interestingly, the original funding for Woodstock, the brainchild of Artie Kornfeld of Capitol Records, came from John Roberts, the heir to a large Pennsylvania-based pharmaceutical company, along with two business partners. (It was another pharmaceutical company, Sandoz Laboratories of Switzerland, which is credited with having first synthesised LSD.) Roberts was later accused of using his company for the mass drugging of the attendees, which appears to have been the plan.

Either way, by the time of Woodstock, the original 'vibe' of the hippie era had all but fizzled out, not helped by the horrors of the Manson murders over in California just a few days before the event. The Beatles were all but over too. Much of the consciousness and ideals of the counter-culture era, no matter how genuine or manipulated it may all have been, made an exit along with the decade as the 1970s dawned.

Resources:

Inside The LC: The Strange but Mostly True Story of Laurel Canyon and the Birth of the Hippie Generation:

- http://www.davesweb.cnchost.com/nwsltr93.html

Was Timothy Leary a CIA agent?:

- http://www.whenthenewsstops.org/2011/04/was-timothy-leary-cia-agent-was-jfk.html

Timothy Leary's liberation, and the CIA's experiments! LSD's amazing, psychedelic history:

- http://www.salon.com/2013/12/14/timothy_learys_liberation_and_the_cias_experiments_lsds_amazing_psychedelic_history/

Timothy Leary: The Daylight Test:

- http://thedaylighttest.com/category/timothy-leary/

Ken Kesey: The Electric Kool-Aid Acid Test:

- http://en.wikipedia.org/wiki/The_Electric_Kool-Aid_Acid_Test

Memory Hole blog: What Happened To The Music?:

- http://memoryholeblog.com/2015/04/29/what-happened-to-the-music/

How the CIA and Military Control the Music Industry:

- http://www.illuminati-news.com/00357.html

CHAPTER 8

SIGNS OF THE TIMES

Occult symbolism in pop videos.

> *"Symbols rule the world, not words nor laws"*
> *Confucius (551-479 BC)*

> *"If a picture is worth a thousand words, then a symbol is worth a thousand pictures'"*
> *Jay Weidner*

> *"In the music industry we have seen the rampant increase of rappers and pop stars using what have been termed 'Illuminati symbols' and gestures such as the one-eye symbolism, 666 gestures and making pyramids with their hands, as if they know something we don't know. Perhaps they're just puppets of the Illuminati and just do what they're told. Or perhaps they have sold their souls, figuratively or even literally for fame and fortune, and are now 'in the know?'"*
> *Wayne Bush on The Higherside Chats podcast, June 2015*

Hidden in plain sight

Call me old-fashioned, (I get called much worse,) but like many who grew up during the 1980s, I do tend to hold a nostalgic affection for the pop videos of that decade, and they have tended to colour my view of what a music promo should entail. Memories of Midge Ure evoking 'The Third Man' in Ultravox's atmospheric 'Vienna', The Human League's mock film set on 'Don't You Want Me,' Duran Duran cavorting on a Caribbean yacht in 'Rio' and Frankie Goes To Hollywood pitting world leaders Reagan and Chernenko in a wrestling ring in 'Two

Tribes' have stayed with me. (As well as anything involving Samantha Fox . . . but that's for slightly different reasons.) The likes of Madonna gyrating on a gondola in 'Like A Virgin' and Michael Jackson's zombie-fest in 'Thriller' may take on a more morally questionable tone put into their fuller context, but even they were innocent by comparison to music video content in the 2000s.

Of course, 1980s pop videos were pretentious and overblown, and the visuals bore little relevance to the lyrics which were often ambiguous themselves anyway. But on reflection, it was more about what you *didn't* get from videos in decades past. Particularly when it comes to dark occult symbolism, Satanic icons, and trauma-based mind control triggers. Things are a little different now.

Blink and you miss it

In my early days of grudgingly accepting that all was not quite as I'd thought in the mainstream music industry, one of the first elements I got put on to was the analysis of contemporary music videos that was done by the researcher calling himself Vigilant Citizen. On his monumentally popular website www.vigilantcitizen.com, VC reveals himself to be a young Canadian researcher who has studied symbolism and the occult, as well as the MK-Ultra and Monarch and Beta Programming facets of trauma-based mind control. (This subject area gets covered in-depth soon.) In the late 2000s, the VC site started posting detailed articles taking apart the symbols and occultic imagery that was routinely appearing in music videos. In all cases, the symbols involved were unannounced, appeared in and out of shot very rapidly, and bore absolutely no relation to the lyrical content of the song.

An early example was the video to Rihanna's 2007 hit 'Umbrella,' which featured Jay-Z, and was a number one hit in the US, the UK and several other countries. It turns out that the song was originally written for Britney Spears, but was given to Rihanna when her label rejected it, such is the interchangeable nature of corporate A-list artists. The video was directed by veteran industry player Chris Applebaum and, conveniently, won Video of the Year at the 2007 MTV Video Music Awards.

VC's analysis of the lyrical theme of 'Umbrella' was based wholly on the work of the wonderful US researcher Lenon Honor, whose work all resides at www.lenonhonor.com. Lenon had deduced that, far from portraying Rihanna's appreciation of her lover keeping her safe and secure in their relationship, its underlying meaning concerns demonic possession and dark energetic manifestations. As VC writes:

> *"In a nutshell, the song talks about a storm that's about to take place, and Rihanna offers her loved one protection under her umbrella. In this song, 'You can stand under my umbrella' can have a sexual connotation, but it mostly means 'You can be under my protection'. When you are under something's protection, this something has more power than you regarding your own security. You depend on it. It has control over you."*

He goes on to explain that Rihanna herself portrays two roles throughout the video. In some shots she is seen in a virginal white dress, symbolising the innocent 'good girl' archetype. In others, she appears in black complete with clawed fingernails, symbolising a dark entity that is trying to take her over. The album from which the track is taken is called 'Good Girl Gone Bad.' One of the song's lyrics is: 'You're part of my entity, here for infinity.'

For no apparent reason, the video features split-second images of Rihanna inside a pyramid, and striking a very curious anatomical pose, (which gets further analysis in this book's chapter on demonic possession.) Some of these strange aspects rang some early alarm bells for me, as they did for Lenon and a number of other researchers. One was Freeman Fly. Another was Mark Dice, whose pride at being a 'Christian patriot' does tend to colour the tone of his Youtube videos, along with his references to the likes of Ke$ha and Miley Cyrus as 'satanic sluts' making him unpalatable for some. Either way, he still makes some astute observations, and his work, I would suggest, is worth a look.

'Umbrella' is very far from an isolated case. Further examples of videos providing an A-Z of dark occult imagery are everywhere. Katy Perry's 'Dark Horse' is replete with ancient Egyptian symbolism, with Perry playing the role of a Pharaoh who uses black magic to destroy men and acquire their belongings. Plenty of human-animal hybrids and snakes in attendance, and a giant floating pyramid resembling a UFO. Standard.

Azealia Banks' 'Yung Rapunxel' sees an owl flying out of her head before she rides a bull and swallows a miniature Beats By Dre-branded audio speaker. Esoteric and Masonic symbols depicting duality and astro-theology lie all around. As they so often do.

Jessie J provides a rare example of a British artist displaying all the trauma-based mind control hallmarks usually reserved for American artists. In her 'Price Tag' video she sports Mickey Mouse ears and appears as a marionette having her strings pulled, as well as posing inside a doll's house.

Kanye West's unsettling 'Power' meanwhile, takes the dubious art form to a new level, consisting of just one stationary composite image of occult symbols, the camera panning out as the song progresses to reveal ever more detail, ending just as Kanye is about to be beheaded by two swords.

Whatever excuses the deniers may come up with–'they're just fashion statements,' 'they're just a way to look cool,' etc–I'd love to hear their reasoning behind why depictions of demonic entities have been placed into recent videos by three prominent artists.

In Lil' Wayne's video for 'Love Me,' for a split-second Wayne is seen depicted as a type of devil, with horns, a bizarrely tattooed forehead and maniacal grin, and standing next to a girl with a Monarch butterfly obscuring one of her eyes. This occurs at the point in the lyrics where Wayne states "these hoes love me like Satan, maaan." (Quite why the hoes love Satan in the first place isn't explained, but apparently it's a given that they do.)

A horrific demon-like entity appears, again for a split-second, in the video for Robin Thicke's 'Get Her Back.' And a similar being makes a cameo a little after three minutes into Beyonce's 'XO,' generating a horrified reaction from Beyonce's female companion, while B herself smiles knowingly. In these cases, the images bear no relation to the lyrics being heard at the time.

What possible reason could there be for the inclusion of such imagery if all in the music business is good and well?

Some readers may recall the stir created by Madonna's video for 'Like A Prayer' in 1989 when she was depicted kneeling at the statue of a black Jesus, suggesting imminent fellatio. This was clearly calculated controversy for the sake of marketing, and seems almost innocent when compared with the dark, sinister overtones being placed into music videos now. Sceptics still claim that the Satanic stuff is being put in for no other reason than to get the artists talked about, and thus increase sales for the corporations. But anyone who has even a rudimentary understanding of the priest class that controls human activity, and the ancient symbols they use as their calling cards, will be able to see another dynamic at work. These symbols are being used for a very dark method of mind control, with aspects of Predictive Programming at play too. There's far more on that particular subject later in the book as well.

As VC and many other researchers were starting to observe, the same icons were cropping up time and time again in the videos of the most prominent stars of the time—Beyonce, Jay-Z, Katy Perry, Kanye West, Lil' Wayne, Britney Spears and others—besides recurring offerings from Rihanna and Lady Gaga. Among the most common were depictions of pyramids, all-seeing-eyes, pentagrams, crosses, (inverted or otherwise,) Monarch butterflies, dolls, broken mirrors, unicorns and rainbows. A classic example of these images on full display came from Ke$ha's video for the charming song 'Die Young,' (which advances the view that life is harsh and ultimately pointless, so we may as well all party wildly, and accept that we're going to die young—really great stuff considering the target market for Ke$ha and artists of her ilk is girls aged around 8 upwards.) The 'Die Young' video features an upside-down cross, a pentagram of the type often depicted in satanic rituals, and a pyramid with an all-seeing eye super-imposed, all in the space of a few seconds.

A nice, alternative message to the one peddled by 'Die Young' came from Raquel Castro in 2015 with her song 'Young & Dumb,' which pretty much tells you everything you need to know. A promo shot for the song shows her obscuring one eye with a flower.

'Eye' symbolism is an aspect of the agenda that has transcended the videos, to the point that virtually every prominent music-maker of the past decade has been photographed highlighting or obscuring one of their eyes. There are various methods to achieve this; the eye can be encircled, one eye can be obscured by a hand, or the hair, or the brim of a hat. There was a style of photography which became very fashionable a few years ago, whereby just one half of a celeb's face would be shown in a promotional picture, the other half being out of frame. I never understood why this was 'cool' or had become so widespread, but now it all makes sense.

Either way, the idea is to draw the viewer's attention to one eye. As with all symbols, this is interpreted in different ways according to who's doing the interpreting. It's often assumed that this pays homage to the 'all-seeing eye' depicted in freemasonic imagery, and on the pyramid on the US dollar bill. This, in turn, is taken as a representation of the Eye of Horus of Egyptian mythology. A common view is that both of these symbols reflect the pineal gland that lies at the centre of the human brain, often referred to as 'the third eye,' which gives access to higher levels of consciousness when activated, and acts as a portal to other realms of existence.

A further interpretation, however, is that limiting a person's vision to just one eye, rather than tapping into the balanced unity of both, is evoking a human's base consciousness, the absolute lowest form of self-awareness making it just possible for the person to operate mechanically in this physical domain, but completely cut off from any higher spiritual capacities. Certainly, the type of music that now accompanies the artists employing this symbol seems in-keeping with that overall concept. For me, the jury is still out on two prominent artists whose wearing of an eye patch was always an iconic part of their image—90s singer Gabrielle, and 80s hip-hop pioneer Slick Rick. In Rick's case, a promo shot exists of him sporting his patch whilst concealing his arm in his jacket, in a Napoleon-esque Masonic stance. Was he being employed as a very early example of calling-card symbolism in that particular genre?

Whatever the case, a surprising number of your favourite pop stars feel the need to make this gesture when in the public eye, (no pun intended.)

Thematic throwbacks

I think anyone vaguely alert to what's going on around them would be well within their rights to ask what these motifs have to do with pop songs aimed at young people and played daily on mainstream TV outlets. It's a far cry from The Specials crammed into a car in 'Ghost Town' or Dexy's Midnight Runners romping in dungarees, isn't it?

Despite the apparent innocence of previous decades, however, there is the odd exception, giving an indication that The Hidden Hand has been making its presence felt for far longer than just the past few years.

Duran Duran's 'Union Of The Snake' promo from 1983 offers some very interesting visual imagery. At the time it would have been seen as a normal part of the self-important pretentiousness that Duran videos typically carried. But viewed in the context of what we've now come to know about the true nature of the world, it takes on rather more sinister connotations.

It begins with the group driving a jeep at night through a remote desert landscape, (the Area 51 region of Nevada, possibly?) Slinking around on the sand dunes are bizarre, lizard-like creatures. Simon Le Bon gets distracted by a pretty female bellhop, who beckons him over to a strange elevator which descends below the desert surface. It emerges into an underground candlelit temple that could be a depiction of the DUMBs (Deep Underground Military Bases) which are known to exist in the US, Australia and other countries. More lizard beings are around, and the base is full of children who appear to be kept captive, many of them in white robes. A character is seen juggling wearing a black and white chequered top, similar to the pattern found on the floor of masonic temples, as well as being a known trigger in trauma-based mind control. The title of the song itself takes on an intriguing air, of course, and a curious added touch is the depiction of a single eye on the record sleeve image.

(Another veiled allusion to Area 51, incidentally, comes from the 1971 James Bond film 'Diamonds Are Forever.' In one scene, Bond tails a scientist in a camper van as he drives out of Las Vegas into the Nevada desert. Entering what looks like a secret military base, the van goes into a lift and descends several storeys underground into a covert research facility. We later see what appears to be a mock-up of the Apollo moon landings on a film set—possibly a sly nod to the 'conspiracy theory,' still fresh at the time, that NASA faked the real moon landings in 1969?)

From the same year, meanwhile, comes a very popular offering lifted from Michael Jackson's 'Thriller' album. The aforementioned Lenon Honor put out a comprehensive analysis of the video for 'Beat It' a few years ago. On the face of it, the song appears to be all about warfare between two rival street gangs, with the title taken to mean 'scram,' or 'get out of here if you know what's good for you.' Lenon's highly plausible breakdown, however, reveals much about how depictions that are so obvious to the conscious mind once pointed out, can otherwise go completely un-noticed to all but the subliminal mind, which stores and reacts to information without the discerning awareness of the viewer.

The most telling aspect comes in the latter part of the video where the rival gang members meet in a warehouse. As they go through their carefully choreographed dance routines, it becomes clear that Jackson and the other dancers are simulating masturbation with their hand gestures, suddenly bringing a whole new meaning to the term 'beat it.' Closer inspection reveals the openly gay mannerisms and garbs of the gang leaders, along with a scene where Michael is seen apparently sporting an erection in his bedroom as he anticipates the showdown that lies ahead. The video, Lenon Honor concludes, is a celebration of male homosexuality rituals and group masturbation. This ties in with the agreed view of many observers that one of the entertainment industry's social engineering objectives is to promote homosexuality and the destruction of the traditional family unit, through slyly implanting ideas into the public psyche. You can view the video for yourself and assess his findings here–http://www.YouTube.com/watch?v=oRdxUFDoQe0 Some of the reasons as to why the controllers would go to such lengths to promote such ideas will become clearer as this book progresses.

For those who wish to see

As the observations of VC and others came across my radar, it coincided with my new understanding of who, or what, has really been pulling the strings of human affairs for aeons, and I was able to put the two together to gain a view on what was really being communicated here. It became clear that the elite forces controlling the world, who many refer to as the Illuminati, utilise a variety of symbols and cyphers to announce and highlight their activities. The Illuminati nametag actually refers to The Bavarian Illuminati, a secret-society established in Germany on the esoterically significant date of 1st May 1776, and in close conjunction with the Rothschild banking family who were still based in Germany at the time. Official lore, (along with some useful disinformation peddled by the author Dan Brown through his book

'Angels And Demons',) dictates that 'the Illuminati' has long since dissolved and is now defunct, although many researchers would disagree. Either way, 'the Illuminati' has come to be adopted as a convenient catch-all phrase for the secret-society dark occultists who continue to run the show, so for the sake of convenience, I will use it from time to time when referring to the control network.

There always seems to be more than one reason why the Illuminati reveal themselves in their various different ways—a main purpose with several subsidiary reasons attached—all of which serve their agenda in some way. So the question of why the forces that control the entertainment industry would choose to announce their presence and their full ownership of the artists concerned, has a few possible answers. One is that the manipulators like to place their calling cards in full view—albeit subliminally. Part of the reason, it has been suggested, is that this offers a method of covert communication between members, so that a dark occultist spotting one of their 'own' symbols in a music video can understand that this is the work of like-minded individuals sharing the same mindset.

(You also have to wonder, given the large number of alert individuals who are now up on the use of occult symbolism thanks to the research opportunities afforded by the internet, whether there's actually an element of the manipulators taunting and mocking those that are on to them. As if to say, 'we know *you* lot can see what we're doing, but you try communicating that to the rest of the brainwashed population and see where it gets you. Let us know how it works out for ya!')

A stronger suggestion, however, is that these images are in place to have a hypnotic effect on the subconscious mind of the viewing public, which in the case of most pop music videos, comprises children, teenagers and young adults. Conventional science tells us that the human brain absorbs several million pieces of information from any of the five senses, every second. Because the conscious mind doesn't have the capacity to fully process that colossal amount of data, however, it works to filter out the bulk of it so that only what are considered the important elements are retained in the conscious memory. This dynamic is seen at work among motorists, who often realise that they've driven several miles without being able to recall any detail of the journey. It's referred to as 'automatic pilot' mode, and it's the same process. The brain has been recognising all the information, and if an accident were about to occur, the driver would have reacted instantly. But otherwise, much of the received data is considered unimportant, so no memory of it gets retained.

It's a different matter with the subconscious, or subliminal mind, (meaning below the threshold of conscious perception.) In this realm, perceived images, phrases and sensations can lie dormant in their multitudes. Most of them will have no reason to be recalled into the conscious mind, so sit there harmlessly, but some can be brought into recognition by triggers–by being experienced again, or by having memories of them evoked. Those that don't get taken through can still have an effect on the behaviour or perceptions of the individual, without them having any awareness of it.

A third reason often cited for the placement of favourite signs in music videos, goes back to the recognition that everything in existence is universal energy, vibrating at an infinite range of frequencies. Because humans are gifted with consciousness, scholars and researchers in this field concur, and because the energy field of which we are all a part is basically fluid and malleable, we are able to shape and mould our reality and determine certain results, purely by our thoughts and intent. This is a great truth which has been understood by gurus, sages and mystics throughout human history, but which has been systematically kept from the bulk of humanity, because the last thing that those controlling the show with selfish intent want, is for their subjects to understand the true power that this reality grants them. This truth has been purposely obscured by the man-made religions of the world, too, by conditioning humans to believe that the only true power in the universe lies with some named god entity to whom us insignificant mortals must all cower in subservience, rather than teaching that we are all, in fact, individuated aspects of the one source consciousness.

It's from the recognition that we have the power to create the kind of reality we wish to experience by focussing our attention on it, (if done correctly and with an appropriate level of conscious intent,) that the well-worn phrase 'energy flows where attention goes' originates. The idea is that by focussing conscious attention on an idea or a scenario–particularly when a large group of people are all pooling their conscious intent together on a desired result–a situation can be brought into reality through being empowered in this way. This is the origin of the well-known terms 'be careful what you wish for,' and 'speak of the devil and the devil will appear.'

So what many suggest is that, by placing into music videos symbols and images that represent the Illuminati power structure, the structure itself can be empowered and strengthened by the collective energy coming from the vast numbers of people making a connection with them—albeit on a subconscious level. On reflection, this struck me as a pretty good reasoning as to why pyramids, eyes, pentagrams and many other esoteric symbols were popping up between scenes of Britney Spears or Lady Gaga singing some vacuous pop song.

And they're far from the only tactics being used.

Resources:

Waking Times: The Music Industry Exposed—Misuse and Abuse of Esoteric Symbols:

- http://www.wakingtimes.com/2014/12/02/music-industry-exposed-misuse-abuse-esoteric-symbols/

Rihanna's 'Umbrella' video:

- http://www.YouTube.com/watch?v=_iQRXuAo6Eg

Rihanna's 'Umbrella' video examined by Vigilant Citizen:

- http://vigilantcitizen.com/musicbusiness/occult-and-prophetic-messages-in-rihannas-umbrella/

Kanye West's 'Power' video:

- http://www.YouTube.com/watch?v=L53gjP-TtGE

Lady Gaga's 'Alejandro' video:

- https://www.YouTube.com/watch?v=niqrrmev4mA

Katy Perry's 'Dark Horse' video:

- http://www.YouTube.com/watch?v=0KSOMA3QBU0

Lil Wayne's 'Love Me' video:

- http://www.YouTube.com/watch?v=KY44zvhWhp4

Robin Thicke's 'Get Her Back' video:

- https://www.YouTube.com/watch?v=bz_EqawkmTg

Beyonce's 'XO' video:

- https://www.YouTube.com/watch?v=3xUfCUFPL-8

Duran Duran's 'Union Of The Snake' video:

- http://www.YouTube.com/watch?v=n6p5Q6_JBes

Michael Jackson's 'Beat It' video:

- http://www.YouTube.com/watch?v=oRdxUFDoQe0

Lenon Honor video on subliminal messages and mind control:

- http://www.YouTube.com/watch?v=By6yDL7LGgY

Freeman Fly's website:

- www.freemantv.com

Freeman Fly on Youtube:

- www.YouTube.com/user/Freemantv

Mark Dice's website:

- www.markdice.com

Mark Dice on Youtube:

- www.YouTube.com/user/MarkDice

Lady Gaga 'stole' the identity of Lina Morgana:

- http://starcasm.net/archives/64492

- http://www.henrymakow.com/lina_morgana_leftby_richard_
  ev.html#sthash.yNQqJElY.dpuf

Rihanna's 'Rock 101' video analysed by Marshall Hammond:

- http://marshallhammond.hubpages.com/hub/
  Esoteric-Media-Rihannas-Rock-Star-101

CHAPTER 9

A SHOW OF HANDS

The secret language for those who who know.

'A man always has two reasons for doing anything: a good reason and the real reason.'

Banking magnate J. P. Morgan (1837-1913)

Symbolism is the language of the subliminal mind, and if the symbols in videos don't work their magic, the hand signals being flashed by many of the artists concerned just might.

Anyone paying attention to how music's A-listers behave in public will have noticed an array of hand signals on frequent display. It's merely a question of whether they've been consciously acknowledged, or absorbed at a subliminal level.

Getting the horn

At first glance, many appear completely innocent. The best example is the sign said to have been created by the American activist and campaigner Helen Keller. She devised a system of hand signing for the deaf, of which one of the most prominent is the signal to convey the phrase 'I love you.' To achieve this, the middle fingers of one hand are bent down, while the two outer fingers and thumb remain extended. The fingers are said to represent a capital 'I', 'L' and 'U.' The symbol has long since been adopted into mainstream use, and people can be seen flashing it frequently, and apparently innocently.

The key is in the thumb, because when the thumb is brought in to hold down the two bent fingers, it takes on a different connotation. This is now the 'horned hand,' known in occult circles as 'il mano cornutto,' and is an ancient method of signalling said by many to be a depiction of the androgynous goat-headed entity known as Baphomet, originally a pagan deity, but later adopted and corrupted by Satanists as a symbol of their twisted ideals.

Writer Matt Sergiou of Conspiro Media elaborated further on the origins of the Baphomet icon in a 2014 article on his site:

> *"When the Knights Templar were arrested, tortured and interrogated by King Philip IV of France in the 14th century at the time of the Roman Catholic Inquistion, some of them confessed that they had participated in the worship of a 'heathen' idol, usually consisting of a severed head and known as, Baphomet. In the mid-1800s, the French occultist, magician, and freemason, Eliphas Levi drew a picture of an androgynous figure with a goat's head, dubbed the 'Baphomet of Mendes,' a name which harks back to themes explored and recorded by Greek historian Herodotus thousands of years earlier in 'The History—Book II.' He wrote of Djedet, an ancient Egyptian city known in Greek as Mendes, and in its native language as Banebdjed, in honour of the ram deity of the same name. Herodotus described how this Mendesian God was represented with the head, legs, and fleece of a goat. He also stated that in Egyptian, the goat and Pan are both called Mendes.*
>
> *"Levi's illustration, which combined elements from The Devil in Tarot cards, lives on, most notably through organisations such as the Church of Satan, which has adopted and adapted the iconic image as its official logo."*

So we have a internationally-recognised symbol for 'I love you' just one thumb away from a calling card for mystery religion magick.

Some researchers have suggested that this apparent contradiction isn't too surprising when you delve into the background of Helen Keller, who was reportedly an occultist and student of Madame Helena Blavatsky's Theosophy practice. The suggestion is that the sign was placed into public usage after being deliberately designed to be similar to the Horned Hand. Naturally, the two signs and their meanings have been much misconstrued—particularly as Keller's version is supposed to be shown with the palm facing outwards, and the 'Satanic' version with the palm kept facing the user. It does seem very convenient, however, that a method of symbolic communication between Satanists can be written off with the innocent cover story that it means 'I love you' if ever it's called into question.

It certainly gets around. Virtually all of the world's major leaders have been photographed flashing it at public events, George W Bush, Barack Obama, Hillary Clinton and Mahmoud Ahmadinejad among them. The symbol, (with thumb tucked in,) was a favourite of Anton LaVey, the founder of the Church Of Satan, and the question of whether it was intended to evoke Baphomet or was LaVey's way of telling his followers 'I love you' is probably answered by the nature of the organisation he headed.

It's equally prolific in the music world, however. John Lennon famously throws up the sign on the front cover of The Beatles' 'Yellow Submarine', with fingers facing the camera on one hand, and turned away on the other to make sure he covers all possible meanings. Eminem and Azealia Banks are among the artists that have depicted themselves with 'devil horns' in recent times, with Justin Bieber, Rihanna, a latter-day Paul McCartney, (or should that be 'Paul McCartney'?) and an assortment of heavy metal artists among other users. Disco Mix Club founder and former Radio Luxembourg DJ Tony Prince was photographed sporting the sign at the funeral of his friend Jimmy Savile, (On 9th November 2011 as a matter of interest–9/11/11,) shortly before Savile was publicly revealed to have been a serial child rapist, Satanist and necrophiliac. (Prince said at the time: "If there's a Heaven, he'll be laughing now if he's got time." The laughing bit, yes. The Heaven bit, I beg to differ.)

All the sixes

Those quick to write off this sign as innocent confusion between two conflicting meanings have a further debunking task, meanwhile. There's another hand sign that's proven very popular within the music world. This one involves the thumb and second finger of one or both hands touching to create a circle, leaving the remaining three fingers outstretched. The perfectly acceptable explanation is that it simply means 'OK' or 'everything is fine,' and we see it in public use all the time. In many cases, the intent behind it is doubtless entirely innocent. It does, however, carry another connotation.

Within Satanic societies, the arrangement of thumb and first and second fingers is seen as a depiction of the figure 6, with the three extended fingers indicating 'to the power of three', thus 666. In itself–just as with any other number or symbol–666 remains completely neutral, with neither negative nor positive connotations. That changes when it becomes charged with the energetic intent of the individuals putting it to use, however. 666 has long been adopted by Satanists and imbued with the negative intent for which they stand. Within these circles, it is said to be a representation of base consciousness within which the majority of humans are manipulated into being kept. 666 is also heavily linked to the influence of Saturn. When the corresponding symbols are put on public display, therefore, and attract the focus of those that view them, an energetic connection is being established, completely unbeknown to most. Just as the Baphomet 'horned hand' is markedly similar to 'I love you' as an instant way of protesting its innocence, so the '666' can be written off as simply 'OK' when an explanation is required. Three sixes can be seen cleverly hidden in the Italic logo of the Disney corporation, itself a deeply Satanic organisation hiding behind a respectable front. Walt Disney himself was a 33rd degree freemason and reportedly a Satanist. The sixes also appear in the crossed fingers logo of the UK's National Lottery, disguised as single quote marks in the Vodafone logo, and in countless other corporate designs, including many of the advertisements for Dr Dre's Beats By Dre headphones with what purport to be 'b's for 'beats' actually representing 6s.

We get two symbols for the price of one with 'Yellow Submarine' again. Next to Lennon's 'mano cornutto' is 'Paul McCartney' creating a '6.' In an alternative promo shot for the album, meanwhile, 'McCartney' holds two sixes up to both eyes. A very young Michael Jackson was pictured in a promotional shot doing the sign.

Contemporary artists seem just as keen on this one, meanwhile. Beyonce put both her hands into 'sixes' as the camera focused on her at the 2013 Grammy Awards. Jay-Z, Drake, Justin Bieber and Jessie J have all felt the need to show it. And our old friends the world leaders (puppets) just happen to like this one too, with the Bushes, Obama, Bill Clinton, Benjamin Netanyahu and Tony Blair having all been pictured with it. As have Jimmy Savile, Rolf Harris and Cliff Richard. But I'm sure that's all just one big coincidence and nothing to worry about.

As is the fact that this symbol's popularity is not limited to the 20th and 21st centuries. There are many ancient depictions of the pagan god Shiva offering both this sign, and the 'horned hand' one.

Throwing up the Rocs

When it comes to hip-hop, (or what passes for it in the 2010s,) there's another symbol that will be familiar to any committed followers of the genre. It's one that has come to be associated with Jay-Z, and become known as 'the Roc sign.' This one involves creating a triangle, or pyramid shape, by placing the thumbs and first fingers of each hand together. The symbol is placed in front of the face so that the left eye can be viewed through the triangle. All-seeing-eye/ third eye symbolism meets Illuminati pyramid symbolism in one easy go. Jay-Z's own explanation is that it represents the 'rags to riches' aspect of the hip-hop game; it's the 'Roc, or 'rock,' a diamond symbolising his making it out of the ghetto to attain fame and fortune against all the odds. The 'Roc' reference comes from the name of the record label that Jay-Z founded with fellow entrepreneurs Damon Dash and Kareem 'Biggs' Burke—Roc A Fella Records.

If no other aspect of Jay-Z's career path strikes as anyone as suspect, this choice of moniker should at least raise an eyebrow. It was named after the Jewish Rockefeller family which relocated to the United States from Germany in the 18th century, changing their name from 'Rockenfelder' to sound more all-American. It was JD Rockefeller, the industrialist, oil tycoon and banker, who put the family's name into the public domain during the early 1900s. The Rockefellers, along with German-Jewish contemporaries the Rothschilds, are constantly cited as one of the most prominent interbreeding Illuminati bloodline families. Lurking beneath their public face as 'philanthropists,' their activities are said to have involved eugenics, mind control experiments, the funding of the Nazi party, drug running, whiskey bootlegging, the hijacking and reshaping of the educational and medical establishments in the US, the formation of the US Federal Reserve, the deliberate suppression and outlawing of natural cures for cancer and, many claim, a direct involvement in the events of September 11th 2001. Just the folk to name a business empire after, right kids? The sentiment appeared to be shared by Nas in the lyrics of his infamous 'diss' track against Jay-Z, 'Ether.'

In recent years the Roc A Fella tag has been phased out, replaced with Roc Nation as a catch-all name for Jay-Z's various corporate ventures. Just how grass roots its formation was in the first place remains questionable given that Jay-Z stands as the most blatant example of a fully controlled corporate stooge in the modern music business, his every look, move and sound carefully cultivated in line with a far-reaching agenda. Jay-Z went from years spent as a drug dealer and struggling rapper, to the biggest artist in the game upon the release of his debut album 'Reasonable Doubt' in 1996, this seemingly miraculous overnight success having been replicated by many rappers in the intervening years.

In a 2009 interview, (which has since been deleted from Youtube and elsewhere on the web,) Jay-Z gave the following account of having 'invented' the 'Roc' sign:

> *"Well, like I said, we had lofty goals early on. We thought we was gonna put out an album by this group called Christión, and we thought it was gonna go diamond. We thought it was gonna sell 10 million records. So we was doin' this as laughing, like, 'we gonna sell 10 million records. Diamond.' And then it stuck. We kept doin' it. Then we started doin' it at shows."*

Despite his protestations, (and Beyonce's subservient flashing of the symbol at public events, interpreted as being 'in homage' to her husband's business,) the 'Roc' sign, it turns out, is no new thing, and far from a Jay-Z creation. It is known in mystery school traditions as the Triangle of Manifestation.

As with duality, (light and dark, night and day, good and evil, male and female, etc), the concept of the trinity occurs throughout creation. It is the representation of mind, body and spirit, or the unity of thoughts, actions and emotions, which, when aligned in balanced unity, lead to the manifestation of desired situations. This concept is symbolised in Christianity as 'the father, the son and the holy ghost,' and finds its way into countless myths of the ancient world, such as Isis, Osiris and Horus of the Egyptian tradition, and Semiramis, Nimrod and Tammuz of ancient Babylon.

The website www.themystica.com describes the purpose of the Triangle of Manifestation as follows:

> *"This is a phase that indicates the principle of magical manifestation. This basic principle is rooted in the number of three. It is a meta-physical belief that in order to manifest something, three components must come together. These components are time, space, and energy. The functioning of the components is such that if a time and a space are selected into which energy is directed, a manifestation will occur.*

> *"A convenient method of directing the energy is through a triangle formed with both hands by placing the tips of the index fingers together while placing both thumbs together with all other fingers extended. This symbolic hand gesture may be employed in a ritual, chanting, or charging an object."*

So what could Jay-Z and his cohorts be trying to manifest in this way? And why the need for concealing the truth behind a highly unconvincing cover story?

Like the horned hand, the Triangle was used by Anton LaVey in the rituals of the Church of Satan. It also appears as one of the grade signs of the OTO, or Ordo Templi Orientis, the occult school of ritual magick headed for a time by Aleister Crowley, and to which many musicians have belonged. In this context, the 'Roc' sign is said to symbolise 'fire' or 'The Goddess Thoum-aesh-neith.' The same sign is also a symbol of the Levites, one of the original twelve tribes of Israel. And Jay-Z was far from the first in the music industry to use it. Among many others, there exists a picture of original Beatles member Stuart Sutcliffe striking the 'Roc' sign way back in 1962.

Given the nature of the power structure that created the entertainment industry, and its obsession with dark occultism, it's safe to assume there is more going on than meets the eye with this sign, particularly when the instruction goes out at one of Jay-Z's concerts for the crowd to 'throw up your Rocs'. Tens of thousands of people all pooling their attention into a symbol simultaneously is going to have a significant effect on the energetic field around them.

Live and direct

It's large-scale live events that offer another way for the entertainment industry to trawl the life energy of the masses using symbology. Such events have the benefit of establishing a direct energetic link with the audience. Most are also televised or recorded for later broadcast, bringing a whole new, and even greater viewer base on which to have the same effect. In recent years, the live performances of the most controlled music makers have been getting far darker and more occultic in nature, causing even those who have no knowledge or interest in esoteric subjects to comment on some of the more blatant aspects.

One of the most extreme was Madonna's half-time performance at the 2013 Super Bowl. The massive attendance aside, this event garners one of the biggest TV audiences in the world, so any musician performing is guaranteed one of the greatest opportunities for simultaneous mass mind control in the history of humanity. Madonna has long been referred to as 'the Grand Priestess' of the music industry, meaning that having faithfully served the hand that feeds her for thirty years, she's now been elevated to a senior position whereby she oversees more recently recruited artists in a ritualistic fashion. Many have suggested that this is what her famous kiss with Britney Spears and Christina Aguilera at the 2003 MTV Video Music awards was all about. In the 2013 Super Bowl, she appeared in the regalia of the ancient Sumerian goddess known as Inanna-Ishtar. Evocations of sun symbolism are seen, including the winged solar disk favoured by groups including the Freemasons and Rosicrucians, and there's plenty more ancient Egyptian themology. Subservient to her in this performance are fellow artists LMFAO, MIA, Nicki Minaj and CeeLo Green, all of whom appear to undergoing some kind of induction.

A week before the event, in interview with CNN broadcaster (and CIA asset) Anderson Cooper, Madonna alluded to the esoteric nature of her upcoming show:

"The Super Bowl is kind of like the Holy of Holies in America. I'll come at halfway of the 'church experience' and I'm gonna have to deliver a sermon. It'll have to be very impactful."

Madonna has openly admitted to her affiliation with Kabbalah, the school of Jewish mysticism, making her choice of wording with 'the Holy of Holies' very interesting. This was the name of the most sacred place in Solomon's Temple, access to which was only granted to the High Priest.

Interpretations of exactly what the symbols and icons are intended to evoke vary from researcher to researcher, and you quickly come to realise that the world of occulted knowledge is far from clear-cut and easy to navigate. Certainly, many of the hand signals we now see celebrities routinely use seem to have their roots in the Indian system of 'mudras,' described by Wikipedia as: "a spiritual gesture and an energetic seal of authenticity employed in the iconography and spiritual practice of Indian religions." The point is that subliminal communication is clearly going on, whatever the meaning, and consumers might like to ask themselves what relevance any of this has to what is supposed to be simply fun and leisurely entertainment, for the most part aimed at children and young adults. Why is it there at all?

Vigilant Citizen summed up the 2013 performance as follows:

"When taken individually, the symbols described above can be simply considered as 'cool-looking,' and most Super Bowl viewers did not give them much attention. The packing of all these signs and symbols into one comprehensive 13-minute performance cannot, however, be dismissed as 'random images.' Quite to the contrary, the combination of all of these symbols form a whole, and define with great depth the underlying philosophy and agenda of those in power—the Illuminati."

Anyone still proclaiming that this was all about Madonna 'expressing herself' and simply being 'artistic' is in a very heavy state of denial about what's really going on in this world, I would suggest.

A further ritual written off as a 'wardrobe malfunction' was the exposing of Janet Jackson's nipple during her performance with Justin Timberlake at the 2004 Super Bowl show. The cover story is that this was an unscripted accident. The 'scandal' dominated international headlines for days, and whenever any seemingly trivial matter takes precedence over war, famine, corruption and natural disasters, it's a safe bet that there's some ritualistic significance to it that the powers that be are keen to get out.

For an 'accident' it was rather convenient that Janet's nipple *just happened* to not be bare, but instead adorned with a 'shield' depicting the rays of the sun. Never miss an opportunity to get some solar cult symbolism into the public psyche in that all-important split-second, right?

(It's also interesting to note that Spears, Aguilera and Timberlake were all child stars that emerged simultaneously out of the Mickey Mouse Club of the aforementioned Disney Corporation, and all *just happened* to go on to become massive pop stars at the same time. More of that later.)

For those wanting to really immerse themselves in ritualistic occult imagery, meanwhile, no better example presents itself than the opening and closing ceremonies of the 2012 London Olympics. It's all there–phoenixes, pyramids, Glastonbury Tor, 'Satanic' mills, a cauldron, a giant baby, a rendition of William Blake's 'Jerusalem,' the theme from 'The Exorcist' movie, and 'revolutionary' Russell Brand, (right on, brother!) seemingly portraying the Child Catcher character from Ian Fleming's 'Chitty Chitty Bang Bang,' among demonic-looking figures cloaked in black overlooking ranks of children cowering in hospital beds, all occurring weeks before BBC 'entertainer' Jimmy Savile was exposed posthumously as a serial paedophile that had abused children in hospital wards. Lovely family-friendly stuff.

Fleming, incidentally, the creator of James Bond, was himself attached to military 'intelligence' during World War 2, and was a personal associate of Aleister Crowley in his latter years, and according to some, his handler. Fleming is said to have based the character of Le Chiffre, the first of Bond's adversaries in the novel 'Casino Royale,' upon Crowley. Backgrounds in military 'intelligence' and mystery religion magick–also the case with Fleming contemporaries Dennis Wheatley and Roald Dahl–are never far from the surface in these particular stories.

Resources:

The Rockefeller bloodline:

- http://www.theforbiddenknowledge.com/hardtruth/the_rockefeller_bloodline.htm

The Rockefellers at www.thetruthseeker.com:

- http://www.thetruthseeker.co.uk/?cat=47

Grade signs of the OTO:

- http://www.theorteekstasis.org/oto/pdf/signs.pdf

Ordo Templi Orientis at Wikipedia:

- http://en.wikipedia.org/wiki/Ordo_Templi_Orientis

Vigilant citizen on Madonna at the 2013 US Superbowl Half Time Show:

- http://vigilantcitizen.com/musicbusiness/madonnas-superbowl-halftime-show-a-celebration-of-the-grand-priestess-of-the-music-industry/

Vigilant Citizen on the opening and closing ceremonies of the 2012 London Olympics:

- http://vigilantcitizen.com/vigilantreport/the-occult-symbolism-of-the-2012-olympics-opening-and-closing-ceremonies/

Vigilant Citizen on Jay-Z's occult connections:

- http://vigilantcitizen.com/musicbusiness/jay-zs-run-this-town-and-the-occult-connexions/

Freeman of www.freemantv.com, on Madonna's 2013 US Superbowl Half Time show and others:

- http://freemantv.com/occult-symbolism-of-madonna-at-superbowl-halftime/

CHAPTER 10

BACKWARDS–IT'S THE NEW FORWARDS

In a world of inversion, are true motives hidden in reverse?

'Let the adept . . . listen to phonograph records reversed . . . '
Aleister Crowley (1875-1947) from the book 'Magick'

It became clear a while back that I'm not really one for supernatural experiences. That's not to say I don't accept the existence of alternative realms beyond this 'physical' world. On the contrary, an understanding of the true nature of reality and the infinite possibilities of universal consciousness have been fundamental to the process of pulling the different strands of this book together. But I seem to have made the choice before I got here to live a life that's very much rooted in the 'real' world, and to knuckle down to what needs to be done within it, rather than undergoing some of the fascinating spiritual experiences that we hear about from others. I've shown myself to be non-hypnotisable, and my curious attempts at a past-life regression merely resulted in me trawling the depths of my memory and imagination, it seems to me in retrospect, rather than awakening any genuine memories of previous lives.

But despite my lack of other-worldly experiences, there are two unexplained events that I can point to as personal evidence that this world is not all that it would seem. One involves a Satanic ritual in Prague which I detail elsewhere in the book. The one I'll recount here is an anecdote that's featured quite heavily in my public talks, and which leads us nicely into the area of backmasking, or subliminal messages hidden backwards in sound recordings.

A 3am wake-up

I'd heard whisperings of this phenomenon, apparently favoured by heavy metal bands in the 70s and 80s, during my schooldays. In late 1990, it was the subject of a feature on Channel 4's 'The Word', a programme which revelled in its reputation for controversy. The piece in question concerned Madonna's single 'Justify My Love' which had just been released. It was already raising eyebrows through its sexually explicit video and orgasmic moanings, but 'The Word' added to this by claiming that, when played backwards, a certain section of the song's lyrics emerge as sounding distinctly like 'hear us, love us, Satan.'

I've no idea who first discovers these things or in what circumstances, but apparently someone had. At this time, I was at the end of my first year working as a general dogsbody at Fox FM, my local commercial radio station in Oxford. Youthfully naive and hungry to make it in the business, I'd been spending all my waking hours as part of the Fox furniture, doing everything from making tea for the journalists, to archiving old news stories, to playing out pre-recorded shows live on air. Significantly, this was still in the era of quarter-inch reel-to-reel broadcast tape, in the last years before computers. Having access to such equipment, when I first heard about the Madonna record, I immediately saw the opportunity to try the theory out for myself.

At around 3 in the morning one weekend, a time when I could often be found hanging out in the studios rather than displaying any kind of social life or sleeping, I recorded the track on to a reel of tape, flipped it around, and fed it back on to the machine's spools ready to play in reverse. As I did, it became apparent which section of the track the TV show had referred to, as the chilling words 'hear us, love us, Satan' appeared to come from the tape, and were made all the more chilling by the distorted, non-humanesque quality of the sonics, and the fact that that the only other human in the building was the on-air DJ in the next studio.

Shocked by what I thought I'd just heard, and wanting an ally in the experience, I shot next door and told the DJ there was something he just had to come in and hear. I rewound the tape to the appropriate point, pressed Play and . . . nothing happened. Silence. The tape was completely blank, the recording never to be heard again. I have no explanation for what went on there, but it certainly sent a chill down my spine and I've never been able to listen to 'Justify My Love' in the same way since.

I recounted this story at a talk in Birmingham recently, and during the break an audience member came up to me and said, 'you do realise that FOX in English Gematria equates to the numbers 666, don't you?,' which I thought added a nice twist to the anecdote. I've also been reminded that 3am is known as 'the witching hour' when black magic is thought to have its most potent effects.

Over 20 years after the Fox incident, meanwhile, I was fascinated to come across a comment on a chat site called Feel Numb, ('useful useless info,') from a user by the name of Raul. He stated: "I used to be a DJ and remember playing 'Justify My Love' by Madonna on the turntables. Every time she sings the line 'justify my love' in the chorus, all you have to do is spin it backwards and you can clearly hear the words 'I love Satan.' I will never forget the feeling I had when I first spun this song backwards. Freaked me out!"

Raul, I know what you mean, mate.

Researching the song further, I came across an explanation of the remix that was apparently done by Madonna in conjunction with Lenny Kravitz. This was known as 'The Beast Within Mix,' and replaced the verses with passages from the Book of Revelation. The song first garnered media attention in early 1991 when the Simon Wiesenthal Centre accused it of containing 'anti-Semitic' lyrics, specifically the one that goes "those who say they are Jews but are not. They are a synagogue of Satan."

Far more truth to that lyric than might at first be apparent, I would suggest, in the context of some of the stuff covered elsewhere in the book. Either way, it reinforces that there's something special about that particular Madonna song. Perhaps it shouldn't come as too much of a shock, either, given Madonna's long-standing status as an artist who's shown signs of being subservient to her corporate masters since her breakthrough. Madonna's stands as an example of the long career that awaits when you sign a contract with the music industry machine—but one that's always on their terms with no option to say no to whatever direction they might choose to steer you in some way down the line.

Back engineering

There are three general schools of opinion when it comes to subliminal backmasking. One is that it's a cynical ploy deliberately applied by mischievous music-makers to generate attention and controversy. The second is that it represents a genuine communication of some message or thought which may have been conveyed at a sub-conscious level by the creator of the recording, albeit unwittingly. The third is that it's all a load of bollocks and that if you listen hard enough, you'll hear anything you want to hear. Sceptics will cite 'phonetic reversal,' the effect of a word unintentionally sounding like another when reversed.

It doesn't follow that every single backmasked recording has to fall into only one of these categories, of course. All three options remain feasible depending on the recording in question. The second possibility is the one where my curiosity lies, and on this front, I was interested to come across the phenomenon of reverse-speech therapy. This is the idea that thoughts or intents that are present in an individual's subconscious, but which aren't apparent to the conscious mind, can embed themselves into that individual's speech patterns in reverse form. This means the messages cannot be recognised by the alert, conscious mind, but can be absorbed subtly by the subconscious mind of the listener, allowing them to intuit the true thoughts of the person speaking the words. The subconscious mind does not need to have words and phrases presented in a linear, front-to-back fashion because, in their base state, all words are sound vibration, decoded into recognisable form by the ear and the brain. It's the vibrational patterns of the words that are picked up on.

The science of reverse-speech therapy appears to have pioneered by David J Oates in Australia. The story goes that in 1983, he accidentally dropped a tape player into a toilet, and it would only play in reverse from that point on. This led to him stumbling upon the hidden messages that can be encoded into speech, and only properly understood in reverse. Oates went on to write five books on the subject, as well as publishing a magazine called 'Backtalk,' lecturing on the subject, and running training courses in how to become a practitioner. He now lives in Australia and remains one of its leading proponents. Oates announced in September 2015 that he was starting work on a comprehensive documentary on reverse speech, expected to be released the following year.

Another advocate is the clinician and speech analyst Jon Kelly of www.yourinnervoice.com. Like Oates, Kelly remains a strong advocate of reverse-speech being a genuine psychological method of getting to the root of a person's true thoughts and emotions, and devising appropriate therapy. In his sessions, he gets subjects to speak at length on any subject of their choosing and records the results. Then begins the discipline of trawling through the recording in reverse, listening for revealing words and phrases. In his interview with Red Ice Radio's Lana Lokteff in 2013, Kelly included recorded examples from some of his therapy sessions. A woman recalling the tragedy of her little brother being killed by a car when she let go of his hand at a roadside, produced the phrase 'better hold on to him' when reversed. The phrase 'hurry, life is only a lesson' emerged from a small businesswoman reflecting on what her future might hold. Kelly goes on to reveal how this method led to him discovering highly confidential aspects of the US's 'shock and awe' programme used in the second Gulf War a full two years before it happened. As he explained: "The truth will always reveal itself eventually . . . and this is one venue via which it can be done. But you have to become an active listener. The messages are encrypted, so you have to get involved in decrypting first before you can receive that information."

You can hear his interview with Lana Lokteff on this link–http://www.redicecreations.com/radio3fourteen/2013/R314-131220.php

There's more on the phenomenon at this site too–http://reverse-speech.com/

Interestingly, Regan, the character in 'The Exorcist' movie, (based on the true story of a 1949 exorcism in Georgetown University Hospital, Washington DC,) utters words and phrases in reverse when under the possession of a demonic entity. These can only be consciously deciphered when a tape recording of them is played backwards.

Given that this method is said to involve individuals communicating hidden messages only fully audible in reverse, therefore, is it too much of a stretch to imagine it might have been at use in popular music recordings through the decades too? The science of it is certainly amusing to me as a hip-hop DJ who has spent more hours than I care to remember cleaning up explicit phrases in rap tracks to deem them appropriate for radio play. Although there are now more subtle ways of muting out offending words, all radio edits some years back used to reverse words like 'fuck', 'shit' and 'nigga,' to transform them into the inoffensive 'cuff', 'ish' and 'uggin.' If the idea of the subconscious mind accepting phrases in reverse holds true, 'clean' radio edits serve little purpose other than to provide an aesthetically pleasing veneer of apparent respectability!

This theory gained some extra notoriety when claims emerged a short while after Barack Obama's 2008 presidential victory, that one of his famous speeches takes on a different nature when the reversal treatment is applied. Each time his famously vacuous 'yes we can' slogan is spoken, in reverse form it becomes 'thank you Satan,' according to many independent researchers. As with all things, each listener must make up their own minds, but I know what it sounds like to me. And when you come to realise that the worldwide cabal that places all world 'leaders' in place is obsessed with the dark occult, the idea that something could be going on here doesn't sound too preposterous.

This could well be by design—if you want to communicate a particular idea in reverse form, it's not that difficult to work out what you need to say in regular form to achieve the effect—or it could be an example of an involuntary communication, as a reflection of the dark energy in which Obama and his like are immersed. Also, Obama is an acknowledged master at NLP, or Neuro Linguistic Programming, the science of using carefully-chosen words and phrases, delivered in certain pitches and tones, to generate a desired emotional response in a listener. We hear politicians and television news presenters doing this all the time, and in the UK, the cosy-sounding continuity announcer on BBC1 uses the technique nightly. This being the case, Obama rarely utters a phrase that hasn't been very carefully considered . . . even if someone else has written it and he's merely delivering it faithfully from the Autocue.

Either way, here's a video breaking down the effect:

- https://www.youtube.com/watch?v=C8g2nCxAVrk

And here it is in briefer soundbite form:

- https://www.youtube.com/watch?v=LS53I-k_T4o

There is also a video making the case for another phrase of Obama's—this time the repeated words 'let me express' uttered during his presidential acceptance speech–coming out as 'serve Satan' when the same reverse effect is applied. Catch that one here:

- https://www.youtube.com/watch?v=V-TMKUea87E

Either way, this event certainly hit home with Canibus, a rapper whose tricky wordplay deems most of what he says incoherent, but who occasionally astounds with amazingly hard-hitting lyrics. On the title track to his ninth album, 'Melatonin Magik', he says:

"Watch who you followin', watch who you praisin'

'Yes we can' backwards is 'thank you, Satan."

Heavy vibes

Backmasking entered the public consciousness in a big way in 1990, in a US civil action case involving the British heavy metal group Judas Priest. The case alleged that two youths, 20-year-old James Vance and 18-year-old Raymond Bellknap, shot themselves as a direct result of hearing a subliminal message hidden in the song 'Better By You, Better Than Me' from Judas Priest's 1978 album 'Stained Class'. The parents and their legal teams claimed that the song contains the phrase 'do it, do it' when played in reverse, and that the youths had interpreted this as an instruction to kill themselves in a suicide pact. (Interestingly, Mark Chapman, John Lennon's alleged killer, reported hearing voices in his head saying 'do it, do it, do it' shortly before he is said to have pulled the trigger.) The youths went to a church in Sparks, Nevada with a 12-gauge shotgun to carry out the deed. Bellknap died instantly after shooting himself from under the chin. Vance then shot himself but survived, only to die later in 1988 from related complications.

The suit was dismissed in August 1990, when the judge ruled that the alleged message was the result of a mix-up of background lyrics. It was also pointed out that the youths had been drinking and smoking marijuana in the hours leading to their death, hinting at this as the real contributing factor. The trial was covered in the 1991 documentary 'Dream Deceivers: The Story Behind James Vance Vs. Judas Priest'.

Predictably, the Christian community of the US has been highly critical of subliminal messaging techniques in music, claiming it to be, in their simplistic view of things, the 'work of the devil.' The state governments of Arkansas and California were successful in passing legislation to this effect. The California bill boldly stated that it stood for preventing recordings 'that can manipulate our behaviour without our knowledge or consent and turn us into disciples of the Antichrist.' The 1983 Arkansas bill, meanwhile, recommended that records with backmasking include the words: 'Warning: This record contains backward masking which may be perceptible at a subliminal level when the record is played forward.' This bill was subsequently thrown out by none other than State Governor Bill Clinton.

Whether there was validity to the claim or not, the case was instrumental in getting the mainstream public familiar with the suggestion that backmasking in music does go on. The satirist Weird Al Yancovic, whose pop parodies have included 'Eat It' and 'Like A Surgeon', got in on the backmasking act when he encoded a gibberish-sounding message on his track 'I Remember Larry'. When played in reverse it comes out as, 'wow, you must have an awful lot of free time on your hands.' He had another go on 'Nature Trail To Hell' which contains the phrase 'Satan eats cheese whiz.'

A similar spoof treatment came from Pink Floyd on the track 'Empty Spaces' from the album 'The Wall.' When an apparently nonsense sequence is played backwards, listeners hear:

> *"Hello, Luka ... congratulations. You have just discovered the secret message. Please send your answer to Old Pink, care of the Funny Farm, Chalfont ... Roger! Carolyn's on the phone! Okay."*

Two paths you can go by

The Beatles were well-known for dabbing in backmasking, as mentioned in the earlier chapter. Perhaps the most famous illustration of the practice, though, comes from one of the most celebrated rock tracks in history, Led Zeppelin's perpetually enigmatic 'Stairway To Heaven' from their un-named fourth album in 1971. It was vocalist Robert Plant who penned the lyrics to 'Stairway,' recounting in a later interview:

"Suddenly my hand was writing out the words . . . " Guitarist Jimmy Page has also talked of 'channelling' his songs; pulling lyrics and concepts out of the ether as if they're coming from some unknown source. Plenty of other artists, including David Bowie and Elton John, have talked of using the same process.

Surprisingly, Led Zeppelin's Wikipedia page addresses the accusation of 'Stairway' containing a backward Satanic message. This occurs during the middle section in the lyrics, "If there's a bustle in your hedgerow, don't be alarmed now. It's just a spring clean for the May Queen. Yes, there are two paths you can go by, but in the long run, there's still time to change the road you're on." When played backwards, this is said to come out as:

> *"Oh here's to my sweet Satan,*
>
> *The one whose little path would make me sad, whose power is Satan,*
>
> *He will give those with him 666,*
>
> *There was a little tool shed where he made us suffer, sad Satan."*

The website www.remnantradio.org, in its section titled 'Rock Music and Witchcraft,' elaborated further, stating:

> *"The song also used a process known as 'backward masking,' which is accomplished when a phrase is recorded on tape, played backwards, then recorded again on the master tape. One segment which says: 'Yes there are two paths you can go by, but in the long run, there's still time to change the road you're on. And it makes me wonder . . . ' played in reverse, says: 'There's no escaping it, oh, it's my sweet Satan, the one whose path makes me sad, whose power is Satan.' Other parts of the song, when played in reverse, say: 'I live for Satan,' 'The Lord turns me off,' 'Here is to my sweet Satan,' 'There's power in Satan,' and 'Take the 666.'"*

This aspect of the song was first brought to light on a 1982 US TV programme on the Christian Trinity Broadcasting Network. Even more surprisingly, Led Zep's Wikipedia page actually contains audio snippets of this section of the song in both forward and reverse formats, allowing listeners to judge the matter for themselves.

Unsurprisingly, the band themselves have always refuted the claims. Swan Song Records, Zeppelin's own label, issued the blunt statement: 'Our turntables only play in one direction–forwards.' In a 1983 interview with 'Musician' magazine, Robert Plant stated: "To me it's very sad, because 'Stairway to Heaven' was written with every best intention, and as far as reversing tapes and putting messages on the end, that's not my idea of making music."

(Led Zep removed any ambiguity when it came to the lyrics for their later song 'Houses Of The Holy', however, which included the lyrics: "From the houses of the holy, we can watch the white doves go, from the door comes Satan's daughter, and it only goes to show. You know." And: "Let the music be your master. Will you heed the master's call? Oh . . . Satan and man.")

It's interesting to note that one of the famous quotes of Aleister Crowley, a character who, like the invincible Blofeld in the James Bond movies, has a habit of popping up spontaneously through these stories, was: 'Let him train himself to think backwards.' This doctrine was known as The Law Of Reversal. An extract from Crowley's book 'Magick' reads:

"Let the adept . . . train himself to think backwards by external means, as set forth here following.

a.   Let him learn to write backwards . . .

b.   Let him learn to walk backwards . . .

c.   Let him . . . listen to phonograph records reversed . . .

d.   Let him practise speaking backwards . . .

e.   Let him learn to read backwards . . ."

It's said that in many Satanic churches the congregation will recite 'The Lord's Prayer', but start with 'Amen' and say 'Nema' and then progress in reverse.

The same concept of inversion was portrayed when the Nazis took the ancient symbol of life, the sun, power and good luck that it twisted into its Swastika, imbuing it with its own malevolent intent as it did, and totally subverting its original meaning. We live in an upside-down world full of contradictions where, when world leaders publicly announce one thing, it's in the exact reverse of what they say that the truth lies. So when Barack Obama announces that 'America stands for peace, freedom and justice', it kinda speaks for itself. Just the same as when David Cameron announces that there'll be no new taxes.

Given the Satanic practices which are inherently linked to the corporate music industry then, and bearing in mind the claims of Jon Kelly and others that backwards messages give away the true intentions of those uttering them, perhaps it's not too outrageous to assume that there could be some validity to backmasking after all?

Resources:

Ten famous cases of backmasking:

- http://listverse.com/2011/08/28/
  top-10-famous-cases-of-backmasking/

Wikipedia entry on the phenomenon of backmasking (including Led Zeppelin 'Stairway To Heaven' soundbites):

- http://en.wikipedia.org/wiki/Backmasking

David J Oates' website:

- http://davidoates.com

Jon Kelly's website:

- www.yourinnervoice.com

CHAPTER 11

ALL IN THE MIND

MK-Ultra and its evil mind-control cousins.

> *"The more we do to you, the less you seem to think we're doing it"*
>
> *Nazi doctor Josef Mengele*

> *"In the technetronic (sic) society, the trend seems to be toward effectively exploiting the latest communication techniques to manipulate emotions and control reason. Human beings become increasingly manipulated and malleable."*
>
> *Zbigniew Brzezinski in 'Between Two Ages: America's Role In The Technetronic Era' (1970)*

Clockwork oranges

When Britney Spears shaved off her hair in a salon in February 2007 before attacking a car with an umbrella, the public reaction was the same as it always is when a celeb 'goes a bit crazy.' Comments seen on-line and heard around the water cooler go along the lines of: 'What is it with these celebrities? They have fame and fortune and all the money in the world, and they just go off the rails. Why do they all act that way?'

There's a very good reason why so many famous people act in erratic, unpredictable and just plain bizarre ways, and it has nothing to do with the money and fame going to their heads. The reason is one that will shock to the core anyone hearing it for the first time, and probably bring about instant dismissal on the grounds that 'it can't possibly be true.' The evidence, however, tells a different story. Welcome to the dark and very ugly world of trauma-based mind-control.

The manipulation of the human mind by force is something that has been practiced for aeons. As an article on Monarch Programming on the Vigilant Citizen website explains:

> *"Throughout the course of history, several accounts have been recorded describing rituals and practices resembling mind-control. One of the earliest writings giving reference to the use of occultism to manipulate the mind can be found in the Egyptian 'Book of the Dead'. It is a compilation of rituals, heavily studied by today's secret societies, which describes methods of torture and intimidation, (to create trauma,) the use of potions (drugs,) and the casting of spells (hypnotism,) ultimately resulting in the total enslavement of the initiate. Other events ascribed to black magic, sorcery and demon possession, (where the victim is animated by an outside force,) are also ancestors of Monarch Programming."*

One of the most widely-documented methods of mind-control, with a reputation so notorious that many members of the public have heard of it, is known as MK-Ultra. This was a covert operation spawned by the CIA at the time of its mutation from the Office of Strategic Services at the end of the Second World War, and it involved a number of prominent scientists from Nazi Germany. Rather than facing trial for crimes against humanity as they should have done, many were covertly smuggled into the US to be put to work in laboratories continuing the work that had reportedly been done in the concentration camps. The codename for the project was Operation Paperclip. Whether these Nazis were blackmailed into co-operation with the threat of imprisonment or execution if they refused, or whether they were co-opted on more friendly terms, remains open to debate. Either way, the US Establishment was very interested in exploiting many of the techniques that they had perfected.

So, along with rocket scientists like Wernher von Braun who were put to work on a space programme that became NASA, notorious psychopaths such as Dr. Josef Mengele were recruited to start moulding and rewiring the minds of selected Americans like never before. The MK-Ultra programme took its name from the phrase *mind kontrolle* as an homage to its German roots, and its far-reaching experiments ran through the 1950s and beyond. Inevitably, some leakage of its secrets got out, and by the 1970s, many Americans had heard rumours of the programme and some of what it entailed. A CIA memo from 1952 which was leaked years later and made publicly available stated: 'The aim is controlling an individual to the point where he will do our bidding against his will, and even against such fundamental laws of nature as self-preservation.' The same methods of experimentation were known by various names in the early days, such as Operation Bluebird and Operation Artichoke. Another aspect of MK-Ultra involved experimentation with mind-altering drugs on a mass scale, which was what the controlled explosion of LSD on to the hippie/ counter-culture scene of the late 1960s was all about.

This led to a public admission by then-CIA director Richard Helms in 1973 that it had been running a mind-control programme in the two decades previous, but the Agency claimed it had now been terminated. In what was presumably a public relations exercise, on 3rd August 1977, the 95th US Congress opened hearings into the reported abuses concerning MK-Ultra. It was alleged that most of the records pertaining to previous experiments had by that point been destroyed. As evidence has shown, however, this was not the case and the hearings were merely an exercise in damage-limitation to placate the public. The Agency had now been forced into guarding its activities much more carefully.

One purpose of the MK-Ultra technique was to create assassins, for deployment in situations useful to the US government, and who would remain undetectable until their programming was activated. This theme has been the basis of many mainstream movies over the decades. The best example is the Bourne trilogy starring Matt Damon as an asset of a top secret CIA black operation known as 'Treadstone.' He spends the movies trying to recall why he possesses certain mental and physical skills that he can remember nothing about, and why his former employers are now trying to kill him and cover up all evidence of the programme of which he was a part. As with so many Hollywood movies, I would suggest there's a great deal of truth to what at first appears to be a wildly far-fetched plot. One of the very reasons for placing these depictions into works of popular culture is so that anyone seeking to claim that this subject is very real, can be scoffingly dismissed as delusional with lines like 'I think you've been watching too many movies mate. Maybe you should get out more!' (Doubtless followed by 'lol' if the comment is delivered on-line.)

Two of the best examples of individuals strongly suspected to be MK-Ultra programmed assassins are Sirhan Sirhan, said to have shot Senator Robert Kennedy in 1968, and Mark David Chapman, credited with having shot John Lennon, (though more on this in a later chapter!) I can't help thinking there's something devastatingly symbolic about Sirhan being Palestinian and being framed for murder by a network heavily connected to the Zionist regime of Israel, the US and elsewhere. Both are still serving endless jail terms for their 'crimes', with appeals for parole being consistently overturned, and both have maintained that they have no memory of what they are said to have done. There are also strong suggestions that JFK 'murderer' Lee Harvey Oswald was under the same influence before he was conveniently disposed of by club owner, mobster and CIA asset Jack Ruby, (real name Jacob Ruben-stein.) Few now swallow the official line that Oswald acted as a lone assassin in killing JFK. But researchers into the RFK and Lennon murders have suggested that both Sirhan and Chapman were also 'patsies,' programmed to provide the distraction of *appearing* to shoot their targets, whereas in fact the fatal bullets were fired from elsewhere. In this scenario the public gets a ready-made scapegoat to satisfy their appetite for justice, and a mind-controlled patsy rots away in jail for the rest of their days while the real killers slip back into the shadows. There are reports of a woman in a distinctive polka-dot dress appearing then vanishing at the scene of the RFK murder, leading many to surmise that this may have been a kind of mind-control trigger for Sirhan.

In Sirhan's case, he's said to have developed an uncanny ability to tell the time accurate to within a minute, without any access to a clock–a possible side-effect of his programming having opened up an extra-sensory ability in his mind?

In 2011, British illusionist Derren Brown presented a TV programme entitled 'The Assassin' on the UK's Channel 4 as part of a series called 'The Experiments.' It investigated the phenomenon of MK-Ultra-style mind-control techniques, with Brown revealing that this was a very real scheme at the hands of the CIA. Brown attempted to demonstrate how the programming could be achieved, citing Sirhan Sirhan as a case in point. For this, he hypnotised a member of the public, and coerced him into 'shooting' a celebrity, which turned out to be British 'comedian' (it says here) Stephen Fry. The subject fired what he fully believed to be a loaded gun, (but which was a replica firing blanks,) at a complicit Fry as he spoke on a public stage. Afterwards, he claimed no memory of what he had done. Given that Brown's shows normally take a disparaging tone towards anything vaguely conspiratorial, it was truly incredible to see the subject of mind-controlled assassins supported with credible evidence on peak-time mainstream TV, and it remains baffling how this was approved by senior management. (Brown also denies a belief in anything supernatural, and is a strong vocal supporter of Richard Dawkins and his atheistic world view. Given that Brown can clearly read peoples' minds and apparently predict or 'see' the future, I feel there could be more to his understanding of the true nature of reality than he's letting on. Maybe that's the kind of public statement you have to routinely make in order to retain a contract with a mainstream television outlet like Channel 4?)

A movie depiction of such MK-Ultra techniques was 'The Manchurian Candidate,' released in 1962 starring Laurence Harvey and Frank Sinatra, (and subject of an inferior remake–aren't they always?–in 2004 starring Denzel Washington and Liev Schreiber.) Harvey plays a US soldier returning from action in the Korean War but who, it turns out, had first been captured by the enemy and taken to a facility in Manchuria in Communist China, where he and others had been programmed to become enemy assassins. His mind-controlled alter-ego is triggered whenever he sees the Queen of Diamonds playing card.

The subject also cropped up in a 1977 Don Siegel-directed movie entitled 'Telefon' starring Charles Bronson and Lee Remick. The plot, based on a book by Walter Wager, involves the Soviet Union placing a number of deep-cover 'sleeper' agents in key positions all over the US. The film reveals that the agents have undergone brainwashing and are entirely unaware of their sabotage missions, until their programme is activated by hearing a code phrase from a poem, followed by their given name, delivered via a telephone call. The agents then commit suicide after completing their mission.

MK-Ultra actually appears by name in the Richard Donner-directed 1997 movie 'Conspiracy Theory.' This stars Mel Gibson as the titular character, a taxi driver called Jerry Fletcher who doubles as one of those batshit-crazy conspiracy theorists that the mainstream loves to mock so much, (you know, because there couldn't *possibly* be powerful people colluding to control everyone else in a world so full of fairness, peace and justice such as this, could there?) Gibson's character is made wide-eyed and neurotic, casting him in a very different light to his sex-symbol image from the 'Lethal Weapon' films. Jerry shares his concerns with a lawyer played by Julia Roberts. Soon his wild ramblings appear to have foundation as he's kidnapped and tortured by a CIA scientist played by Patrick Stewart, who later reveals to Roberts the existence of the programme known as MK-Ultra, and that Gibson had been an early experimental subject. The movie's narrative claims that the programme was terminated in 1973. Stewart states that "MK-Ultra was science, sanctioned by the government. But it all ended the moment John Hinckley shot Ronald Reagan. That wasn't us . . . but the technology had been stolen."

The propaganda that this movie successfully achieved was demonstrated to me shortly after I 'woke up' and started posting conspiracy-related articles on Facebook. A long-time DJ associate of mine suggested to me that I'd lost the plot, adding 'have you actually *seen* Mel Gibson in 'Conspiracy Theory?')

Movies such as this, made in full knowledge of the effect they will have, do no favours to those genuinely attempting to expose hidden truths about this world. It's notable that Jerry's apparently incoherent ramblings to his passengers at the start of the film all concern subjects that are provably genuine, rather than any 'theory'–fluoride being added to water supplies to make people docile, the existence of US militia groups and 'black' helicopters, manipulated earthquakes, the fact that George HW Bush was a 33rd degree freemason, the agenda to microchip the population, the existence of The New World Order. The fact that these subjects are addressed in a work of fiction, by a character presented as mentally compromised, serves to discredit their validity in the minds of those who take everything Hollywood and the television industry gives them at face value, and who can't be bothered to do any independent research of their own.

There are also allusions to mind-control in Stanley Kubrick's 'A Clockwork Orange'. Kubrick was an insider who carried a great deal of knowledge about the elite secret societies and their workings, and encoded aspects of it into all his movies from 1962's 'Lolita' (which depicted elite paedophilia,) onward. In 'A Clockwork Orange,' Malcolm McDowell's violent sociopathic character is sedated into a barely functioning automaton by a series of mind-control and psychological experiments. Kubrick's screenplay was based on the novel by Anthony Burgess who is said to have worked covertly for British 'intelligence' services, with a special interest in the area of mind-control. Reportedly, Mick Jagger was originally considered for the McDowell role.

It's not just as government-sanctioned assassins that CIA mind-control techniques have been rolled out in the decades since World War 2, however. They also have a very firm place in the entertainment industry—in Hollywood movies, in the worlds of television, fashion and sport, and of course, in music.

Mind games

Trauma-based mind-control depends on a deep understanding of the workings of the human psyche, and how to manipulate it. Robbing someone of their own mind through the application of terrifying trauma is one of the sickest, most depraved things one human being can do to another, and it beggars belief that humanity can have been degraded to these depths. Regrettably it has, as a wealth of fact-based evidence shows, and however tempting it may be to turn away from this whole area on the grounds that it's just too horrific or 'negative' to contemplate, that type of reaction will only serve to ensure its continuation, and the suffering of ever more victims. Those who remain in ignorance and those who refuse to look at it are giving the controllers *exactly* the type of reaction they want and need. Only by seeking to expose these activities, and gaining an understanding of what goes on and why, does human decency stand any chance of seeing these horrors brought to an end.

As well as the application of mind-altering drugs, it works—as the title suggests—by exposing the subject to extreme levels of trauma. This can involve physical torture, rape, the application of electroshock and sensory deprivation, and exposure to horrific sights, such as the witnessing of an animal, child or adult being murdered. The original German scientists had discovered that the human mind finds such terror so utterly overwhelming, that it resorts to a kind of firewalling function to block it out. The mind does this by fracturing, or 'shattering' into multiple compartments, creating a kind of honeycomb effect. By splitting itself into these different compartments, the conscious mind is able to block out the ability to acknowledge the trauma which it has found so unsettling. The process is referred to as 'dissociating' from reality, and the victims as suffering from 'dissociative identity disorder' (DID.)

The perpetrators had then discovered that each of these compartments of the mind could be individually programmed, and given their own personality and set of false memories, entirely independent of the others. Each compartment is referred to as an 'alter,' (because its perception of reality has been altered.) In a successfully-programmed subject, there is a 'front alter,' which is the everyday personality that other people engage with, and which is taken to be the individual's true character. Beyond the front alter, however, lie all the others. Each can be brought out to temporarily replace the front alter by whatever has been programmed to be the trigger. This can be a key word or phrase, a piece of music, or a colour or visual pattern. Each alter remains unaware of the existence of the others. When each alter is sent back into the deep recesses of the subconscious mind and the front alter is brought forward to replace it, the memories and characteristics go with them. Another phrase for people exhibiting these symptoms is Multiple Personality Disorder.

The Irish author and researcher Thomas Sheridan expanded on the effects of mind-control experiments in an interview with Lou Collins on People's Internet Radio in October 2014:

> *"The MK-Ultra programme was initially discovered by the Nazis in World War 2. People that they had in labour camps used to develop alternate personalities, so they could actually do the most horrific things on behalf of the SS. Dr. Josef Mengele discovered this, and that's why he was so interested in twins, because he was trying to develop dissociation in the twin, to see if he could switch the personalities from one into the other.*
>
> *"What they discovered under the MK-Ultra programme in Canada—and they did it there so that Americans could be taken up*

there and experimented on outside the remit of the US Constitution and the Bill of Rights . . . some of the stories that came out of there were quite horrible. There was one of a woman who had post-natal depression and she was locked in a room, and they just played a tape 24 hours a day while she was on drugs, that just said 'kill yourself, kill yourself, kill yourself' over and over. And what they discovered was, when the human brain is put into this extreme trauma, dissociation happens. And what that basically means is a partition of the human brain is created where the trauma doesn't exist, and they go permanently into that in order to block out the trauma. Then they discovered that if they needed the subject to do something, like kill someone for instance, they could use that trigger word or phrase, such as the 'kill yourself', and it would throw them right back into that state of derangement that they were experiencing."

One of the leading authorities on the application of trauma-based mind-control is the American author, researcher and counsellor Fritz Springmeier. His key works have been the books 'Bloodlines of the Illuminati' and 'The Illuminati Formula Used to Create an Undetectable Total mind-controlled Slave', written in conjunction with Monarch Programming survivor Cisco Wheeler. Springmeier works with deprogramming and rehabilitating former mind-controlled slaves. In 2003, he was jailed for his alleged involvement in an armed bank robbery, eventually getting released in March 2011. *Just happening* to get charged and jailed for a crime right at the time you've started to expose great secrets about the Establishment does tend to offer some validation that you might just be on to something, I would suggest. Either that or it's just another of those wild coincidences that seem to occur so regularly.

Springmeier's work has exposed how MK-Ultra derivatives have been used to programme women as submissive sex slaves for the rich and powerful. This technique is known as Beta Programming, with Marilyn Monroe as its icon. Marilyn was the original archetypal sex kitten, which is why so many celebrities from Madonna to Anna Nicole Smith are seen emulating her image. (Comments that always used to accompany Madonna in her early career along the lines of: 'she's so in control, she so knows what she wants' seem laughable in the context of what we're now able to know concerning mind-controlled artists, since she is almost certainly a prototype example.) A common symbol of Beta Programming is leopard-print, or other feline designs. This claim was backed up by Cathy O'Brien in her famous book 'Trance-Formation of America,' in which she talks about being used as a mind-controlled sex slave for George HW Bush, Dick Cheney, Jimmy Carter, Ronald Reagan, Gerald Ford and Hillary Clinton, among others.

Springmeier has also done much to show how many of the house-hold-name celebrities that we see and hear every day—mainly those in the US—will have undergone mind-control. He related some aspects of this in my 'Good Vibrations' podcast interview with him in 2013:

> *"The people in charge of things want to make sure that anyone in the public eye, who is an icon, is controlled so that they don't spill the beans about the controllers and what's going on, or say something that they wouldn't want said. So your movie stars, your iconic big rock stars, these big musicians, they're victims of the mind-control. But not only that, they're perpetrators too. They'll have a dual role. Basically, the UK and the USA are mind-control labs.*
>
> *"The easiest way to say it is, if someone is famous and is in the lime-light, they have gotten there because the World Order put them there. Some of them don't even have talent. I mean, Paris Hilton in my opinion is neither pretty nor talented! She's obviously an Illuminati programmed multiple. So if somebody gets up there like that, it's a fairly safe assumption that they're a programmed multiple."*

It may surprise many to know that British researcher and author David Icke, although not the obvious go-to choice on the subject, is very well-informed on the manipulations of the music industry and the use of mind-controlled artists within it. As he related to me when I inter-viewed him for my very first 'Good Vibrations' in late 2011:

> *"It's very clear that major music artists, and famous actors and actresses in Hollywood, are a part of this whole mind-control opera-tion. It's so widespread. One of the reasons they do this is, this control system is itself controlled by a force, a mentality, that is terrified of things it cannot call. It talks in its own writings about how maverick*

people are its biggest enemy, because maverick people, they're flowing with life, they're ad-libbing life. They don't know what they're doing next, never mind anyone else. And this mentality of the control system cannot cope with that.

"To use an analogy, it could not watch a football match in anything but a shaking, traumatic state unless, before the kick-off, it controlled both sides and the referee and therefore knew what the score was going to be before the game started. And they use mind-controlled people a lot for that reason. There are no mavericks in there because they haven't got control of their own mind. So they're entirely predictable."

This would explain why there are now virtually no truly maverick artists—at least signed to any of the major corporations—who make any kind of individual artistic statements through their music. We've seen their like in the past—and it's doubtless a mere coincidence that the most politically and socially outspoken of them *just happen* to have died before their time—but where are the John Lennons, Bob Marleys and Marvin Gayes of today's scene? Populating the industry with mind-controlled stooges who remain 'on script' is a surefire way of making sure any mass social engineering agenda doesn't get derailed and continues to go to plan.

The website Vigilant Citizen has, in recent years, published many excellent articles detailing the symbolism that depicts mind-control, now being routinely placed in the videos of A-list music artists. Exactly the same symbols can be seen in advertisements, in movies and TV shows, and at major public events such as the Grammys, the MTV Awards and the Super Bowl half-time show, taking things way beyond the realms of 'coincidence.' It has become abundantly clear that the forces controlling the entertainment industry, as part of their dark religion, feel the need to encode what they're doing into works of popular culture in the form of signs and symbols which can be readily absorbed by the subconscious mind.

The meaning of these archetypal symbols stays below the threshold of the conscious mind, meaning that what they convey is never properly computed. But they continue to work away having a subliminal effect. The reason they feel the need to let us know what's going on—albeit in this underhand and devious manner–is all to do with the universal concepts of consent and free will. This is a very far-reaching subject area which we'll get into in the next chapter, and which I would urge all readers to take a look at in order to understand the full picture. But for now, suffice to say that it's very important for the manipulators to reveal their methods. What they're also doing is conducting a form of magic which requires the participation of both the practitioner and a watching audience, in order to be fully effective.

Crashing symbols

There is a division of MK-Ultra known as Monarch Programming which deals specifically with trauma-based methods. This appears to be the one that most affected celebrities have been subject to and is named after the Monarch butterfly, which has very distinct orange colouring. One explanation for this is that the dissociative mental states brought about by the programming causes a kind of metamorphosis similar to that of a larva turning into a butterfly in the chrysalis. Fritz Springmeier goes further in his observations:

> "The concept is that the Monarch butterfly was one of the first scientific examples of how knowledge is passed from one generation to another. The Monarch will pass on to the next generation directions for where to fly, and this would happen during a shift. This was very important for the programmers because they need the children they programme to dissociate, and they discovered the ability to become a multiple personality is something that's passed from one generation to another. Which is why they have to keep this trauma-based mind-control within dissociative bloodlines. And the Illuminati have been traumatising their own kids for thousands of years. But in modern times, the programme has been broadened out to regular members of the population."

A further explanation for the naming came from Ron Patton in the book 'Project Monarch':

"When a person is undergoing trauma induced by electroshock, a feeling of light-headedness is evidenced; as if one is floating or fluttering like a butterfly. There is also a symbolic representation pertaining to the transformation or metamorphosis of this beautiful insect: from a caterpillar to a cocoon, (dormancy, inactivity), to a butterfly, (new creation,) which will return to its point of origin. Such is the migratory pattern that makes this species unique."

As Vigilant Citizen has pointed out, Monarch Programming has a number of symbols attached to it. It is evoked by many images relating to childhood. The majority of mind-control victims undergo trauma from a very early age while their natural personality is still being shaped. These symbols are said to represent the innocence and purity of childhood which is shattered when children are traumatised. Dolls and teddy bears with severed limbs, such as a broken arm, or a missing eye, (remember the BBC's Pudsey Bear?!) are also key icons in this regard, symbolising the helplessness child victims feel when being abused–often by their own fathers. Unfathomably sick, huh? Shattered mirrors are often featured, representing the shattered components of the mind. Rainbows, and the colour pink are very much associated with this method, too.

The US researcher Freeman expanded on the significance of the teddy bear motif in an article for his freemantv.com site:

"The Teddy Bear is used in mind-control as a symbol of your helplessness. A drugged-out, one-eyed teddy bear is beyond the concept of the message given to children by Satanic Ritual Abusers when they defile their most treasured possession. This lovable stuffed bear is turned into a constant reminder of the molestation the child has suffered. If it can happen to Teddy . . . "

All of these icons have been showing up with incredible regularity in the music videos of leading US pop artists, in most cases, having absolutely nothing to do with the subject matter of the song. Among the artists whose names crop up the most are Lady Gaga, Katy Perry, Britney Spears, Ke$ha, Rihanna, Miley Cyrus, The Black Eyed Peas and Kanye West. Exactly the same imagery also appears in videos from prominent artists in the 'J-pop' and 'K-pop' scenes of Japan and Korea, showing that this truly is a international agenda, with the entertainment industries of countries all over the world having their strings pulled by the same dark masters.

There are very few examples of British artists being presented in this way, but one exception is Jessie J. The video to her breakthrough single 'Price Tag' starts straight off with the image of a teddy bear with a missing eye and a severed arm. It goes on to depict Jessie as an ornamental ballerina doll, inside a toy doll's house, as a puppet on a string, clutching a one-eyed broken doll, and with a fractured leg complete with animal print. It couldn't be more blatant if it beat you savagely around the head with a baseball bat with the words 'mind-control' on it. Jessie studied at The BRIT School for Performing Arts and Technology in Croydon, which has spawned a massive array of successful British pop artists. 'Price Tag' elevated her from obscurity to international stardom virtually overnight. It just happened to have been co-written and produced by one 'Dr. Luke.' More on this individual later in the chapter.

These are only a handful of a great many examples which are all broken down in detail at http://vigilantcitizen.com/category/musicbusiness/

Interestingly, there are occasional depictions of these same images from previous decades too. Rock lore has it that Pink Floyd's original singer Syd Barrett went insane after years of erratic behaviour, supposedly as a result of LSD and other substance abuse in his youth. His father was a prominent pathologist and he was said to have been related to the celebrated English physician Elizabeth Garrett Anderson. It may be relevant to note that Barrett's father was connected to Cambridge University, an institution which, along with the Tavistock Institute, is said to be used for mind-control and social engineering experimentation. On the compilation album 'An Introduction To Syd Barrett,' he's pictured wearing a mask, kneeling in front of a mirror which he's touching, and flanked by a couple of teddy bears.

On the cover of the album 'Brilliant Corners' by jazz musician Thelonious Monk, meanwhile, there are five clones of Monk all pictured together, as if in a kaleidoscopic mirror image. Could this be hinting at multiple personality disorder? An interesting aside about Monk is that, against all the odds, he was involved in a long-term relationship to an heiress of the Rothschild banking dynasty, Pannonica Rothschild, known socially as 'Nica.'

In some cases, it may well be that artists are having their fame exploited as vehicles for disseminating mind-control symbolism without necessarily being victims of the practice themselves. Evidence of programming is certainly easier to spot in certain artists than in others.

Gaga by name...

Lady Gaga's persona is of course entirely manufactured. I can recall first being told about her towards the end of 2007 when someone said, 'she's going to be the next big thing.' How it could it be known that she was going to be the next big thing if artists and songs get to the top purely by merit of how good they are, and how much the public chooses to support them? They don't. Artists are pre-selected and groomed by the industry, and placed at the top of the game as required. In the same way that presidents and prime ministers aren't elected, they're *selected*, so it is with A-list artists. It's not by merit of their artistic talent that musicians rise to the top—certainly not in the 2010s anyway—but by a measure of how willing they are to be completely manipulated and puppeteered by The Hidden Hand. Public opinion is irrelevant since most consumers sadly follow whatever puppets they're given and are told are 'the next big thing' without exercising any kind of discernment on their part.

It appears that the Lady Gaga personality was in fact stolen from another artist named Lina Morgana, and 'given' to Stefani Germanotta through which to re-invent herself. Some multiple personality over-tones start to emerge here. (The Gaga identity itself is said to have been inspired by Queen's hit song 'Radio Gaga,' of which Germanotta was apparently a fan, but given the infestation of mind-control in the music industry, the 'gaga' bit could be seen to carry a different connotation.)

Lina Morgana was a fast-rising teen pop star, with whom a young Stefani Germanotta collaborated in New York City as a dancer, song-writer and backing singer. The relationship came to a sudden end in October 2008, when Morgana fell to her death from a Staten Island hotel room window in what was reported as yet another 'suicide.'

A few weeks later, Lady Gaga suddenly burst on to the pop scene as 'the next big thing,' with the distinctive image, sound, songs and persona all intact. Immediately, however, there were accusations that Germanotta had effectively 'stolen' not only the personality, but also the soul of her former collaborator, not least from Morgana's mother Yana, who told the NY Post:

> "I'm doing this because I want to keep her spirit alive. Lady Gaga is holding Lina's soul, and I want her soul to be free. Every other word she says is from Lina. She talks about having a dark and tragic life, but she had everything she wanted in the world. She went to (the same) high school as Nicky Hilton, her parents were rich. But Lina did have a tough life, and she often talked about her tragic life."

The journalist Richard Evans observed:

> "Lina's professionally-shot portfolio shows she was corrupt as hell anyway. It was just a case of which witch would be Satan's favourite. Her association with Gaga was during Stefani's 'experimental' phase—lots of orgies and drugs. Stefani became Gaga and her career took off one month after Morgana's death."

Morgana's death seems to be evoked in the video for Gaga's 'Paparazzi.' In it, Gaga is seen being thrown off a balcony, from where she tumbles in a spiral fashion until she hits the ground. The camera then pans in on a life-size manikin in her place with its limbs all twisted—another strong symbol of a mind-control victim.

As if to publicly announce that she was fully down with the industry's sick, Satanic rituals, Gaga's perfume range, 'Fame,' was revealed to contain fragrance notes of blood and semen among its ingredients. The blood traces were said to be based on Gaga's own to create, as she put it, 'a sense of having me on your skin.' The liquid is black whilst in the bottle, but turns invisible upon being sprayed. The symbolism speaks volumes as to the dark occult priest class that she serves.

Nicki and Roman

Another text-book example would be Nicki Minaj, whose entire persona gives so many in-your-face indications of programming that it's difficult to know where to start. Let's make the starting point the fact that she openly slips in and out of multiple personalities in public, and makes no attempt to hide it. During interviews, she will often start speaking in a different voice and accent. Listeners find this a source of great amusement, having no idea of what is likely going on just below the surface. One of her favourite alter-egos is the 'British girl,' where she will begin speaking in a London society accent. The interesting thing is that Minaj is not the only US celeb to slip into 'British girl' mode. Mariah Carey has frequently used the same accent in interviews, as has Britney Spears. Britney even went so far as to record the hook to her number one single 'Scream And Shout' in the very same British accent. Fans worldwide commented on how cute and funny she sounded, not realising that 'Scream And Shout' is an extremely dark song that mocks the world of mind-controlled slaves. The refrain 'I'm gonna scream and shout and let it all out' is taken to be a reference to the mental anguish a victim experiences, and the fact that when they feel the need to scream and shout and let it all out, there's unlikely to be anyone around to either hear or believe them. Also featured on the song is Black Eyed Peas frontman Will.I.Am, pictured at one point in the video with a Monarch butterfly, suggesting he too is a programmed multiple. Given that three very prominent artists all randomly slip into the same accent and persona, is it possible that 'the British girl' is a standard alter in the case of programmed females?

Minaj is also notable for having regularly slipped into an identity she refers to as 'Roman Zolanski,' obviously in reference to the paedophile film director Roman Polanski. She claims her Zolanski is an orange-haired homosexual male. She makes no secret of hiding the fact that she has 'become' Roman in her interviews–again, usually a great source of amusement for both the interviewer and the audience who are absolutely clueless as to what they're really a part of. (Interestingly, Roman is also the name of the chief Satanist played by Sidney Blackmer in Polanski's movie 'Rosemary's Baby.')

In an interview with MTV prior to the release of her second album, 'Pink Friday: Roman Reloaded,' Minaj warned the audience to get ready for the Roman Zolanski character:

"If you're not familiar with Roman, then you will be familiar with him very soon. He's the boy that lives inside of me. He's a lunatic and he's gay, and he'll be on the new album a lot."

The Zolanski character is the inspiration for the song 'Roman's Revenge' from Minaj's debut album 'Pink Friday'.

It features a charming, heartwarming cameo from Eminem, who, when he's not calling women 'sluts' and 'bitches' and threatening to kill them, talks about tying Minaj up and pissing on her while he videotapes it.

The same alter-ego is featured on 'Roman Holiday,' the opening track from Minaj's second album and described by reviews as containing 'deranged yodelling.' As well as taking on the Zolanski persona, adopting what sounds to be a Polish accent, Minaj also 'becomes' his mother Martha in a section of the song, effecting a cartoon cockney accent. I can't help but be reminded of the Norman Bates character in Hitchcock's 'Psycho' 'becoming' his murderous mother by this.

In a subsequent interview with 'Rap-Up' magazine, Minaj even addresses the question of the Roman character being exorcised from her, as if he has come to possess her:

"I had this vision for him to be sort of exorcised—or actually he never gets exorcised—but people around him tell him he's not good enough because he's not normal, he's not blending in with the average Joe. And so his mother is scared and the people around him are afraid because they've never seen anything like him. He wanted to show that not only is he amazing and he's sure of himself and confident, but he's never gonna change, he's never gonna be exorcised. Even when they throw the holy water on him, he still rises above."

Certainly, Minaj's performance of 'Roman Holiday' at the 54th Grammy Awards had strong religious overtones, including a confession and mock exorcism of Roman, and caused inevitable controversy among America's Catholic groups. She entered wearing flowing blood-red robes, (a colour representing Saturn,) accompanied by a character dressed as a Pope. It makes Madonna's 'Like A Prayer' look like a harmless nursery rhyme.

The whole Roman alter is reminiscent of one of Lady Gaga's aliases known as Jo Calderone, where she dresses in a suit and claims herself to be a gay male–another shared programming technique? She started her performance at the 2011 MTV Video Music Awards with a bizarre monologue in the character of 'Calderone.' Large-scale events such as the MTV Awards, the VMA Awards, the Grammys and the Super Bowl Half Time Show are mass rituals used to trawl the life energy of the viewing public via their attention. For this reason they're frequently used to put depictions of mind-control and occult possession right there on public display.

Another of Nicki Minaj's identities is 'Barbie Doll,' and indeed, she has often appeared depicting herself as a human doll, complete with pink hair. Her debut album was called 'Pink Friday.' Dolls and the colour pink are symbolic of Monarch Programming. She's often referred to as 'Barbie,' and her female fans are known collectively as her 'Barbz,' (with her male fans known, unbelievably, as 'Kenz'!)

In 2012, Minaj appeared in a video for the song 'Out Of My Mind' alongside 'rapper' (it says here) BoB. Is the song title ringing any alarm bells at all? In the video, Minaj appears in what looks like the cell of a mental institution in a straight-jacket. Scrawled on the walls are various symbols, including an all-seeing eye inside a pyramid, a depiction of a UFO, and phrases like 'they are us' and 'they see.' Some lyrics from the 'song' include:

"I'm out of my fucking mind, G-G-golly, oh my,

I was doing fine, once upon a time,

'Til my brain left and it didn't say bye,

Don't look at me wrong; I'm out of my mind."

Some incisive reflections on the family background of Nicki Minaj, (real name Onika Maraj,) came from an article on the MK Culture blog site in 2011:

> *"Nicki Minaj was born in Saint James, (a suburb of Trinidad and Tobago's capital city Port of Spain.) Around the age of five she moved to Queens, New York with her parents. According to Minaj, her father had an ongoing drug and alcohol problem and was abusive to her mother. This fact is the first alarming sign in Nicki Minaj's personal life. Children of Project MK-Ultra and Project Monarch often come from abusive households with parents who are on drugs and suffer from alcoholism. The children are sold at a young age and remain slaves for the remainder of their lives. Suspected MK victims Rihanna and Chris Brown also come from abusive households.*
>
> *"Nicki has revealed in several interviews that the abusive nature of her upbringing forced her to create alter-egos to escape her troubles. She has stated that her first identity was named 'Cookie' and it 'stayed with her for a while.' Her next identity was 'Barbie.' Barbie and dolls are programming tools for Monarch victims who are often programmed with doll personalities."*

This is a key point. People often ask how it is that the industry machine can get so many artists on-board with the agenda with such apparent ease. It is indeed the case that some mind-control and SRA (Satanic ritual abuse) victims are plucked from 'care' homes as children from abusive family backgrounds. In other cases, meanwhile, the parents are fully complicit in their childrens' involvement in mind-control experiments. Frequently, the families come from a military background. The control system does seem to feel it has a green light to treat those who sign up for a career in the military or 'intelligence' services as their fully-owned property, and military personnel are often the first in line for psychological and biological experiments and testing. Similarly, the children of military officers often seem to be given over, whether voluntarily or by coercion, to be used in various programmes.

Outside of military circles, meanwhile, there are examples of overbearing parents offering up their offspring to the entertainment industry, perhaps having been promised massive material gain. Joseph Jackson, father of Michael and the rest of the Jackson stars, and Mathew Knowles, father of Beyonce and Solange, are two such fathers that spring to mind. While there's no fact-based proof that Michael and Beyonce are victims of programming, there are suspicious indicators everywhere. A video emerged on Youtube in late 2014, for instance, showing Beyonce in the audience of a sporting game with Jay-Z, rocking from side to side and seemingly in some sort of trance state completely oblivious to her surroundings. Jay-Z doesn't seem to notice or care. Catch that one here–http://www.wedr.com/videos/news/99jamz-exclusivevideo-whats-going-on-with-beyonce/vCz2R3/

Another viral video from the same year saw CNN presenter Anderson Cooper, (who also happens to be the son of socialite and heiress Gloria Vanderbilt and a stated CIA asset,) mocking fellow presenter Al Roker who, midway through a live TV link, completely freezes in an apparent trance state. This happens at the precise moment one of his co-presenters says 'leave room for the Holy Ghost,' leading to the idea that this may have been a trigger phrase. That video is right here–http://www.YouTube.com/watch?v=4jjIDWfWuPE

Given the benefits of hindsight and the availability of new information, it's amazing what you completely missed in years gone by. Another article on the MK Culture blogspot site details the video to Kylie Minogue's interestingly-titled 'Shocked,' breaking down much of the imagery which appears to relate to Monarch Programming. The article mentions that subjecting victims to a dizzying spinning sensation is a standard tactic both before and after a session of abuse. In 'Shocked,' Kylie is seen in a revolving door. It also puts an interesting slant on her 'Spinning Around' song. Like many female singers, Kylie has often been portrayed in sex kitten mode, complete with animal print. You can read that article here–http://mkculture.blogspot.co.uk/2009/02/mkd-km.html

Revelation of the Method

The question of just *why* the controllers feel the need to drop these subtle symbolic hints of the presence of trauma-based mind-control is one that has puzzled many a researcher. We'll get far more into these areas in the following chapter. Fritz Springmeier offered some astute interpretation in his 2013 'Good Vibrations' interview, meanwhile:

> *"There's a reference in scripture where Satan has to come before God to ask permission to mess with Job's life. So people who are religious will often say that God insists that evil broadcasts what it's going to do. You don't just have a free ticket to go ahead and do evil, but you have to tell. It's called Revelation of the Method.*

> *"I've always thought that one reason why they do Revelation Of The Method is that it's very intimidating to the slaves. Imagine if you were a mind-controlled slave and your handler or programmer could come to you and say, 'you think you're going to get free of us? Look, we're doing this right in front of everybody, and nobody's coming to help you.' That must be very intimidating to someone who is trapped in this. Or maybe part of it is just that a psychopathic sadistic personality gets enormous pleasure out of announcing what they're going to do."*

Which Britney?

All of which brings us right back round to Britney Spears and her strange behaviour of 2007, (the same year that she released an album entitled 'Blackout.') There is much evidence to suggest that Britney is a trauma-based victim exhibiting the usual different personalities, not least the fact that she emerged as one of the 'mouseketeers' of The Mickey Mouse Club. This was a television creation of the Disney Corporation which showcased an array of child performers from 1955 to 1996. Britney appeared in the same year as Christina Aguilera and Justin Timberlake, before all three went on to become massive pop stars and public figures simultaneously. In all cases, their initial images were wholesome, pure and all-American, getting gradually raunchier and more sexual as time passed. The same dynamic can be seen with fellow Disney star Miley Cyrus in her transformation from squeaky clean Hannah Montana into the sluttish debauchery that now characterises her stage shows–from straddling giant wrecking balls in videos, to performing a refrain of Khia's strip club anthem 'My Neck My Back' at a stage show attended by pre-teen girls. You know the one, it goes 'my neck, my back, eat my pussy and my crack.' Yeah, girl power!

Disney is in fact a deeply Satanic organisation. There have been claims that the trauma-based abuse of children occurs in underground bases beneath popular Disney attractions like Walt Disney World in Florida, while dazzled crowds wander around obliviously above. There are multiple videos on Youtube showing how Disney's cartoons through the ages have used Satanic and highly sexual symbols targeted directly at the subliminal minds of children, and a quick internet search using the words 'Satanic disney' will throw up many of them. The truth of what's being conveyed in Disney films couldn't be further from the apparently clean and innocent surface narrative–another example of how the Satanic mindset twists and perverts original meanings to its own end. It's all part of an over-arching plan to sexualise children at ever-earlier ages, and to debase and degrade the purity and innocence of childhood. At the same time the agenda works to destroy the archetype of the traditional family unit; ever noticed how many of the central characters' mothers die in Disney movies?

Further evidence to suggest that Britney suffers from Multiple Personality Disorder, comes from a 'Prime Time' TV interview she gave with Diane Sawyer in 2003. When asked about the tough year she'd just endured, Britney seems to switch personalities and apparently interact with an unseen person, or entity. She turns quickly to the side and says 'oh, weird,' followed by, 'hello ... umm ... oh my goodness ... hello ... eww! Strong Britney,' before apparently snapping back into her 'front alter' and becoming tearful and overwhelmed.

You can see the video here. When armed with an understanding of how trauma techniques work on the human mind, it makes for very disturbing viewing: http://www.YouTube.com/watch?v=DMpguv7st7s

On occasion, the mind-control programming breaks down, and Britney's head shaving antics give an indication that this is what was really going on. Freeman addressed this event in an article on his freemantv.com site:

"Survivors report that when victims of mind-control approach 30 years old, their brain attempts to break the amnesiac barriers and reintegrate itself. First, she dyed her hair dark brown. She then

walked into Esther's Hair Salon and demanded to have her head shaved. The owner told Britney that she would not shave her head and Britney took the shears and did it herself. When Arizona Wilder told David Icke of her escape from the Mothers of Darkness she said that she had dyed her hair brown to be removed as the ritual goddess of the order. When this wasn't enough to keep her out of the rituals, she then shaved her head.

"When Britney was asked why she did it, she replied that she was tired of people touching her and she didn't want them plugging things into her. She had been in and out of 'rehab' before the salon incident. After she shaved her head, she checked into Promises clinic in Malibu where she terrified staff by scrawling 666 onto her bald head, screaming she was the Anti-Christ and then attempting to hang herself with a bed sheet."

This raises a good point. Are the 'rehab clinics' that we hear of so many celebs attending really mind-control labs? You can read the rest of Freeman's article on the dark occult and mind-control overtones of Britney Spears and many other artists here: http://freemantv.com/celebrities-under-mind-control-release-the-stars-weird-stuff/

Can you handle it?

Just as with the later incident involving singer Ke$ha and her producer/ manager Dr. Luke, the issue of pop stars and their mind-control handlers appeared to break the surface into the mainstream realm in 2008–albeit in a way that that only those with some prior knowledge of the subject would have been able to properly interpret.

Sam Lutfi, who for a time was Britney Spears' personal manager, brought a lawsuit against Britney's mother, citing breach of contract, libel and defamation. Britney's mother, Lynne Spears, had blamed Lutfi for her daughter's famous breakdown which incorporated the head-shaving incident. The breakdown saw Britney losing custody of her two children to dancer Kevin 'K-Fed' Federline. Lutfi denied the claims, writing on his Twitter account that he was 'falsely accused of doing horrible things by horrible people.'

Lutfi's lawsuit was thrown out, and Britney's family obtained a restraining order against him, alongside her ex-boyfriend Adnan Ghalib and attorney Jon Eardley. The order forbade all three from contacting Britney or coming within 250 yards of her, her property or family members.

As Vigilant Citizen observed in 2012:

> *"Proof is piling up that Britney Spears is a victim of mind-control at the hands of unscrupulous handlers. While mass media points their finger at specific 'controlling' individuals, it is increasingly obvious that she is the product of a system that totally suppressed her free will and personal freedom. What makes Britney's case different from others is that the apparent feud between her past and present handlers is causing some otherwise 'censored' information to leak out about how pop stars are completely owned and handled by people behind the scenes. If people are led to believe that Spears' case is special, well, it is more common than most would believe."*

Possibly the most intriguing aspect of the whole matter, however, was the phrasing used by the probate judge overseeing the conservatorship. Despite Lutfi filing papers at Los Angeles County Superior Court requesting that Britney herself be made available as a witness, the probate judge ruled that she could not appear on the grounds that being exposed to the discussions could cause her 'irreparable harm and immediate danger.' Britney's own family made the claim that she was 'mentally incapable' of testifying.

Anyone not directly involved in the event is left to speculate, of course, but is this curious piece of terminology not compatible with a mind-control subject being sheltered from memories that could trigger an unwanted deviation from their programming–particularly when this had already happened in the not-too-distant past?

Britney's father Jamie was awarded conservatorship in 2008, giving him full control over her personal and business affairs. A conservatorship is normally awarded when someone develops dementia, a brain injury, or is otherwise deemed mentally unfit to handle their own business. What could have caused such dissociation from reality in the case of Britney Spears, I wonder? The conservatorship was meant to be temporary, but Britney's family argued the case for it to be permanently in place.

An article on the matter in the UK's 'Daily Mail' in October 2011 stated:

> "Earlier this month a claim for $900,000, (around £500,000) in legal fees was put in front of the judge in charge of her case—just for sorting out the conservatorship.

> "That money will all come from Britney's funds. No wonder she is still working so hard despite her troubles. 'She does love performing,' says one source close to the Britney camp, 'but left to her own devices it's highly unlikely she'd undertake the sort of commitments that her conservatorship has signed her on to.'

> "And there are signs she no longer enjoys the touring as she once did. It is almost a given she mimes throughout most of her performances—something she used to put down to her energetic dance routines. But even they have fallen by the wayside."

Britney later hooked up with another manager, Jason Trawick, who she shortly afterwards described as her 'boyfriend,' and later, fiancé. Trawick joined Britney's father in overseeing her conservatorship. Partners often double as handlers in the world of celebrity mind-control. There were claims that Trawick was effectively chosen for the 'boyfriend' role by Spears' parents. Spears and Trawick ended their 'engagement' in early 2013.

That same year, Lutfi Tweeted what purported to be images of texts sent to him by Britney during their turbulent years together. One reads:

> "My Dad will send me away again. He's soo (sic) mean. I can't believe they hurt me like this . . . my Dad's reading everything right now that I text and everybodys (sic) really scares me. I miss my babies and I'm really still scared I'm never gonna see my babies again."

Another text, which Lutfi alleged was from Britney, elaborated:

'My mom and dad are soo (sic) mean. They don't care about me, they just want my money and my babies. They stole my voice and scarred me for life. I will never forgive them . . . all they care about is $$$$. They makes (sic) up lies about you to all these fucking shady lawyers . . . I'm sad. So very sad. Lost. Very lost.'

How many MCs

It's impossible for outside observers to say with absolute certainty which artists are victims of mind-control. Given the penchant for offering visual clues, however, it's certainly possible to make an educated guess. In this context, a singer who appears as a likely candidate is Mariah Carey.

Carey first emerged in 1990 signed to Columbia Records, a division of the entertainment giant Sony, with her sweeping ballad 'Vision Of Love'. From 1993 to 1998 she was married to Tommy Mottola, himself a former singer and song-pitcher, former manager of the duo Hall & Oates, and by then, CEO of Sony Music Entertainment. Michael Jackson famously branded Mottola a racist and referred to him as 'devilish' in a rant about the Sony corporation, to which he was also signed, at Reverend Al Sharpton's National Action Network event in New York City in 2002.

(Columbia itself is a name to conjure with. Like the country of Colombia, and the District Of Columbia which comprises the city of Washington, it is derived from 'columb,' the Spanish word for dove. The dove is a symbolic rendering of the mother goddess figure of Semiramis in Ancient Babylonian mythology. This is the archetypal figure also represented by the Statue Of Liberty in New York Harbour, which was given to the city by French freemasons in Paris, where a replica of the same figure stands on an island in the River Seine. Masonic and ancient mystery school symbolism throughout.)

Many researchers have questioned whether Mottola was acting as Mariah's handler during their time together. Certainly, their marriage was known to be turbulent and unconventional. Mottola himself addressed this in his book 'Hitmaker: The Man and His Music,' writing: "it was absolutely wrong and inappropriate for me to become involved with Mariah." When interviewed by 'The Hollywood Reporter' on the subject, Mottola remained his notoriously evasive self when asked: "You were accused in the press of 'trapping' Mariah Carey in an unhappy marriage. In 'Hitmaker,' you describe friction at home as she grew 'resentful.' Why divulge such details?"

Mottola replied:

> "I came to the conclusion long ago that I gave the marriage the best that I could, as did she. The good news is that she went on to have a huge career, and so did I. Our personal life didn't work out, but I continue to be her biggest fan and support her."

In 1997, Mariah released an album entitled 'Butterfly'. Although Monarch butterfly imagery was missing from this particular album sleeve, on the cover to her 'Greatest Hits' album, she is indeed pictured clutching one of the distinctively-coloured Monarchs for no apparent reason.

Mariah's apparent obsession with butterflies was taken further in 2011, when she had a butterfly design painted on to her pregnant stomach for her birthday, along with the phrase 'dem babies.' This particular butterfly featured one pink wing and one blue, so wasn't an obvious depiction of a Monarch. But the strange move nevertheless prompts some questions as to why she chose it. She gave birth to twins three years to the day after marrying all-round entertainer Nick Cannon, in another example of an industry-only relationship.

A very interesting turn of phrase comes from a paragraph in Mottola's previously-mentioned book, where he describes the final break-up of his relationship with Mariah. He writes that he went to work and "left a note with lyrics to an Elton John song on the nightstand: 'Butterflies are free to fly. Fly away . . .'"

According to the Vigilant Citizen website's extensive article on Monarch programming, a rainbow is another image that has strong connotations in mind-control circles, linked as it is to the 'Somewhere Over The Rainbow' song from 'The Wizard of Oz.'

> "In each case, the slave is given a particular interpretation of the movie's storyline in order to enhance programming. For example, a slave watching 'The Wizard of Oz' is taught that 'somewhere over the rainbow' is the 'happy place' dissociative trauma slaves must go to in

order to escape the unbearable pain being inflicted upon them. Using the movie, programmers encourage slaves to go 'over the rainbow' and dissociate, effectively separating their minds from their bodies."

In 1999, Carey released an album entitled 'Rainbow', whose sleeve design features her cavorting in front of a rainbow on an all-white background, while the inside gatefold has her reclining on a bed sucking on a heart-shaped lollipop, with an electric-light rainbow overhead.

Two years later came an incident which, on the surface, looks like another of those 'crazy celebs' who have everything in the world going off the edge, but has some darker connotations. In September 2001, immediately prior to the events of 9/11, headlines reported that Mariah had suffered an apparent nervous breakdown and made an attempt at suicide. According to the 'Daily Mail,' (and several other sources who ran an identically-worded article, proving that mainstream outlets work from the same limited and controlled sources!):

"The 31-year-old singer's publicist denied that she had tried to take her own life, but Carey's mother apparently made a distraught call to the emergency services last week after her daughter was discovered in her New York hotel room bleeding from slit wrists and cuts to her body.

"She's cracking up. I think she's going to kill herself,' her mother is quoted as having told police officers before Carey was taken to Westchester North Hospital, where she remains since being checked in as 'emotionally disturbed' last week. Her spokeswoman, Cindy Berger, said Carey had cancelled all public appearances after experiencing an 'emotional and physical breakdown.'

"She dismissed tabloid reports that the singer tried to commit suicide. She said that, just before the breakdown, Carey suffered cuts to her body, but the injuries were unintentional. 'She did break some dishes and glasses, and she may have stepped on them,' said Ms. Berger. 'She is taking it day by day and is resting and improving."

And later in the article:

> *"Last month, Carey made a surreal, impromptu appearance on MTV's 'Total Request Live,' dressed in little more than a lavender T-shirt. She also made a publicity appearance at a Long Island shopping centre, where her publicist eventually took the microphone off her to stop her speaking."*

In what appears to be another example of an arranged relationship of the type the entertainment industry likes to engineer, (see Jay-Z/ Beyonce, Rihanna/ Chris Brown, Nas/ Kelis, Katy Perry/ Russell Brand, etc, etc,) Mariah reportedly had a brief sexual dalliance with Eminem. This seemingly turned bitter quickly, (as they have a tendency to do,) resulting in Mariah taunting Eminem with the song and video 'Obsessed.' This spawned a vicious 'diss' track from Eminem in the form of 'The Warning,' in which he complains of having to 'put up with' her 'psycho ass,' and portrays her as an alcoholic.

The subject of Carey's mental well-being came back to the mainstream in June 2015, when 'The National Enquirer' ran a front-page headline entitled 'Mariah: Suicidal & Insane! Carey's terrified brother tells all.' The article references Mariah's 2001 breakdown, with her brother Morgan detailing how her irrational behaviour, alcoholism and addiction to prescription drugs have prompted fears she could 'end up like Whitney.'

Eager Bieber

Some similarly erratic behaviour patterns came from Justin Bieber's visit to London in 2012. Bieber, another former child star, was pictured around town wearing a gas mask and was late arriving on stage, frequently babbling incoherently. A few days earlier he had sported purple leopard-print harem pants.

A couple of years later, he was arrested for drag racing on Miami Beach, appearing memorably in court in an orange prison suit. The media also reported him verbally abusing and spitting at fans. In 2014, a vintage video emerged of Bieber singing a song about killing black people.

All of this served to demonise Bieber as an obnoxious brat in the eyes of the public, and it begs the question of how much of it was instigated as part of some scheme to humiliate him. For instance, it would take a person of very disciplined morals to be able to watch this video and *not* feel compelled to reach for the nearest baseball bat:

- https://www.YouTube.com/watch?v=CCJ51ibuoIM

The public was further subliminally instructed to hate on Bieber in June 2015, when he was charged with assault and careless driving charges. It also emerged that there was a warrant for Bieber's arrest issued in Argentina, after he had failed to respond to a summons related to an assault accusation dating back to 2013.

Vigilant Citizen posted an article upon the release of Bieber's disturbing 'Where Are U Now' video, positing the idea that the industry that spawned him was now mocking and humiliating him, which you can check out here:

- https://www.facebook.com/events/403201616537938/

It's not the first time the industry has built an artist up to become famous and successful, only to later degrade them by carefully fostering the public's contempt. Chris Brown, another former child star, received this treatment when he was charged with assaulting girlfriend Rihanna. Although hitting women is always indefensible, the amount of scorn and judgement poured on him for months afterwards did seem out of all proportion to the event.

Hollyweird and La La Land

Britney and Bieber's strange behaviour brings to mind stories of actress Lindsay Lohan running wild, crashing cars, getting ejected from celebrity nightspots and going in and out of 'rehab.' Lohan is yet another former child star to have come out of the Disney empire, (is there a pattern emerging here?), and is an example of Hollywood celebs sharing many characteristics with their music industry equivalents.

The Hollyweird scene is reportedly a hotbed of MK-Ultra mind-control activity, as evidenced by a handful of whistleblowers. Best known among these is the actress Roseanne Barr who has been interviewed on a few different occasions on the subject. (The very name Hollywood comes from the 'holy wood' which wizards and druids used to construct magic wands. Highly relevant considering the mind spells that Hollywood films cast over their viewers.)

Barr appears to have first raised the issue of mind-controlled celebrities during an interview on CNN with a cynical Larry King on 16th August, (Madonna's birthday and Elvis's reported death day,) in 2001. During the interview she mentions Nazi scientists being brought to America by the CIA at the end of World War 2. She goes on to suggest that she may have had some kind of chip implanted in her head, and that she feels her moves are being constantly monitored by a group of women including chat show host Oprah Winfrey. She claimed she had suffered intense trauma during her childhood, leading to Multiple Personality Disorder. Barr was raised in Salt Lake City, Utah, home of the Mormon Church, and is of Jewish parentage. Her paternal grandfather changed his surname from Borisofsky to Barr upon entering the US from Russia.

In 2013, by this point having run as a presidential candidate, Roseanne discussed the issue of racism, sexism, the Hollywood class system and the presence of MK-Ultra in an interview with Abby Martin's 'Breaking The Set' on the RT America network. You can watch that video here:

• https://www.YouTube.com/watch?v=8whbmRMw0Bg

The fact that Barr stands as one of only a handful of Hollywood insiders that have come forward should not be taken as representing any lack of credibility for the information. There are obviously great risks involved in speaking out in this way. A best-case scenario is that an actor's career is likely to flop overnight. She has spoken of a 'culture of fear' that permeates the industry and keeps most potential whistleblowers obediently in their place. There's also the strong possibility of mind-controlled slaves undergoing programming that prevents them from speaking out even if they wished to.

The Gospel according to Luke

Just as with the Britney Spears/ Sam Lutfi affair, the issue of A-list pop stars being under the dominance of their mind-control handlers emerged from the murky shadows again in 2014 with an extraordinary story involving the singer Kesha Sebert, known then by the artist name of Ke$ha. Up to that point, she had been just one name in a glut of soul-less industry puppets singing vacuous songs over generic electronic production, and displaying all the usual symbols pertaining to dark occultism and mind-control in her videos. Her stage show at the 2011 Sydney Future Music Festival depicted her drinking blood from a human heart to the song 'Cannibal' in a performance that would have been watched by millions of pre-teen children, such is the target market of 'artists' of her ilk.

Things reached a new moral low–even by the standards of the industry's cesspit of depravity–with her song 'Die Young'. The lyrics offered the basic sentiment that life is all about partying, drinking, having promiscuous sex and living for the moment. There's no point in morality because life is basically pointless, and we're all going to die young anyway.

The video was notable for all the wrong reasons, too, overloaded with esoteric imagery to the point that even regular members of the public with no background in studying occult symbolism were questioning why pyramids containing all-seeing-eyes, upside-down crosses and pentagrams were being flashed on-screen for no apparent reason. Ke$ha is depicted as leading some kind of cult immersed in sex magick as she sings about 'young hunks, taking shots, stripping down to dirty socks.'

Feigned moral judgement came from the mainstream media and government spokespeople, however, when the Sandy Hook school 'shooting,' (which has proven to be yet another staged false flag event involving actors, just as an aside,) occurred a few weeks after 'Die Young' had become a massive hit. The chorus line was felt to be distasteful and inappropriate in the aftermath of what had just happened, (but didn't.) Apparently there was no problem with the song before that, and it was deemed just fine for daytime radio play.

Although Ke$ha is credited with having written the song's lyrics, (its Wikipedia entry makes the statement, in all apparent seriousness, that she "wrote the lyrics after travelling around the world and embarking on a spiritual journey,") in the aftermath of the 'Die Young' controversy, she posted the following message on her personal Twitter account:

> *"Understand, I had my very own issue with 'Die Young.' For this reason I did NOT want to sing those lyrics and was FORCED TO."*

Soon afterwards the Tweet was deleted, but it had already offered the first official indication of the level of control that existed in the Ke$ha camp.

It was the song's producer, who also happened to be Ke$ha's manager, who is of particular interest in this context. This is one Lukasz Sebastian Gottwald, known throughout the music industry by the name Dr. Luke.

Gottwald's Wikipedia entry says that he was born in the US state of Rhode Island in 1973 and is of Jewish parentage, (a fact which will surely surprise no-one by this point in our story!) His father is said to have been an architect who emigrated from Poland. Gottwald's professional music career began as the house band guitarist on the TV show 'Saturday Night Live.' According to comments given by Ke$ha to the entertainment site TMZ, Gottwald earned his 'Dr.' nickname in this period by selling drugs to other artists.

His first music production credit is on Kelly Clarkson's 'Since U Been Gone' in 2004. Since then, pretty much all the A-list artists he has produced and written songs for have been the ones whose lyrics most promote the Illuminati agenda of moral degradation, and whose videos are most laden with Satanic and other dark occult symbolism. These include Katy Perry, Pink, Avril Lavigne, Britney Spears, Nicki Minaj, Rihanna, Miley Cyrus, Jessie J, Juicy J and Shakira. A glance at his credentials shows that Gottwald is a well-connected individual in the corporate music game.

Gottwald had acted as Ke$ha's manager throughout her ten-year career. In 2012, Ke$ha wrote and recorded a song called 'Dance With The Devil' which was said to document aspects of her relationship with Gottwald, and the control that he and the industry in general exerted over her. It included the lyrics:

"I keep on dancing with the Devil,

I keep on dancing with the Devil,

I sold my soul, ain't no turning back,

I keep on dancing with the Devil."

The real shocker came in October 2014 when Kesha, (who by this point had dropped the '$' from her name in an apparent statement of independence,) filed a lawsuit against Dr. Luke, claiming sexual assault and battery, sexual harassment, gender violence, and emotional abuse throughout their working relationship. Ke$ha's mother, Pebe Sebert, had already claimed that emotional pressure from Gottwald had led to Ke$ha developing a nervous eating disorder.

Reading between the lines, the lawsuit gave as strong a public indication as there's ever been, of the relationship between a mind-controlled music industry slave and her handler. Handlers often turn out to be artists' own managers, ('management' in the true sense,) spouses or other family members, their close proximity allowing for constant monitoring of their activities and mental state, and for intervention whenever required. The 24-page lawsuit opens with the following wording:

"At eighteen years old, Ms. Sebert was induced by defendant Lukasz Sebastian Gottwald, (a.k.a. 'Dr. Luke,') a successful music producer, to drop out of high school, leave behind her family, home, and life in Nashville, Tennessee, and come to Los Angeles to pursue a glamorous career in the music industry.

"For the past ten years, Dr. Luke has sexually, physically, verbally, and emotionally abused Ms. Sebert to the point where Ms. Sebert nearly lost her life. Dr. Luke abused Ms. Sebert in order to destroy her self-confidence, self-image, and self-worth so that he could maintain complete control over her life and career."

Further on, it alleges drugging and rape at the hands of Gottwald:

"Ms. Sebert took the pills and woke up the following afternoon, naked in Dr. Luke's bed, sore and sick, with no memory of how she got there. Ms. Sebert immediately called her mother and made a 'fresh complaint,' telling her that she was naked in Dr. Luke's hotel room, she did not know where the clothes were, that Dr. Luke had raped her, and that she needed to go to the emergency room."

To save face—and unsurprisingly—Gottwald responded by filing a countersuit against Kesha and her family, denying the accusations and claiming that the lawsuit had been an attempt to pressure him into releasing Kesha from the confines of her recording contract.

Kesha's attorney Mark Geragos responded to this by stating:

"This is just another pathetic and entirely predictable example of Dr. Luke's continued abuse, and a misguided attempt to keep Kesha under his tyrannical control. This lawsuit has absolutely no basis in fact, the law or reality. Kesha is focused on reclaiming her voice and her freedom. She is determined to move on with her life and her career by putting this dark period behind her."

This was followed by another counter-lawsuit against Dr. Luke's, from Kesha's mother in December 2014. Geragos, meanwhile, seized upon a comment made by Lady Gaga earlier that month that she had been raped by a famous music producer when she was 19, by claiming the rapist in question was Dr. Luke. Although spokespeople for Gaga denied this, Geragos stuck by his allegation.

For many who only obtain their view of what's going on in the world from corporate, mainstream sources, this would have offered their first exposure to the dominance that is exerted over artists by their industry overseers, revealing them to be nothing more than pawns who, in the eyes of the industry, are owned property to be used and abused at will.

Running in the family

Satanic Ritual Abuse, (SRA,) incorporates elements of trauma-based mind-control. A survivor of a lifetime of this at the hands of his own parents and the cult to which they belonged is Jay Parker, who now works as a radio show host, public speaker and counselor for other victims. In his 2015 'Good Vibrations' interview, he elaborated on the importance of keeping the abuse within certain generational bloodlines:

> "My experience was growing up in a family of teachers. Both my parents were schoolteachers. My mother traced her Satanic heritage back to the Amalekite people, from basically 2000BC in what would now be Palestine. My father was ninth-generational Illuminati; I would have been tenth. My family came from Northern Ireland and came to the US back in the potato famine in the 1850s. There were three brothers. They were all Satanic as far as I can tell. One went to Chicago, one went to Philadelphia and one went to New York State. They started Illuminati cells wherever they went. When my grandfather was buried in a small town in New Jersey, 300 people showed up that no-one in the town had ever seen.

> "The religion that they're working with is at least from 2000BC, and it's a religion based on abuse and programming. The human, in a hypnogogic trance for the first five to six years of their lives, is building their subconscious. Your subconscious will run 95 per cent of your adult life. So in the first five to six years of your life, you're having your subconscious built by your society, by your religion, by your parents. None of it's being built by you. None of it's, 'oh, I like that. I'm going to put that in my mind. That's going to be part of my data bank.' Thoughts, images, prejudices. All kinds of things are being thrown in there, by television, through subliminals in mass media."

Jay says that keeping the SRA abuse in the family is to ensure the programme is continued like clockwork through successive generations. He himself would have been expected to continue the trauma had he not risen above the programming and thus broken the long-running chain when he did in 2001.

Pulling triggers

Victims and handlers within Monarch Programming are interchangeable. Many handlers have undergone trauma themselves, and part of their programming prepares them to traumatise new slaves, while remaining in servitude themselves. Arranged marriages never last long as shifts end and new handlers are brought in.

Katy Perry is another whose videos and promotional pictures are littered with all-too-blatant clues. Perry's husband for a short period was Russell Brand, alleged 'comedian,' former BBC presenter, host of the shows 'Big Brother' and 'Brand X,' and The Child Catcher in the massive occult ritual that was the closing ceremony of the 2012 London Olympics. Despite all these red flags, many still accept his positioning as a self-styled hero of the people calling for a 'revolution of consciousness' in the UK. It's amazing the effect some long hair and a beard can have. That and a heavy dose of denial. Brand's controllers are telling us all about his true allegiances through the symbolism they have him place right in front of our faces, and yet still so many make excuses for him, constantly insisting, 'but he says all the right things!' Yes. He's a trained (millionaire) actor, and actors are known to improvise around scripts.

The Youtube user known as Alien Fossil Project posted a video in which Brand and Perry are attending an Oscars Red Carpet ceremony. At one point while he's talking, Brand momentarily flashes a pendant with the word 'Obey' on it, and Perry's demeanour changes as she becomes incoherent. The pendant also features a pentagram design in red, white and black, the same colours the pair are wearing, coincidentally, and echoes a publicity shot featuring 'hip hop model' (it says here) Amber Rose, in which she poses with a massive 'Obey' sign in red on her T-shirt. The former girlfriend of Kanye West, Rose then gravitated towards rapper Wiz Khalifa. Is anyone going to keel over in shock at the news her father served in the US military for 20 years?

You can see the Brand/ Perry video here—https://www.YouTube.com/watch?v=9NaSYrVbH6c.

This has all the hallmarks of a handler/ slave scenario. Shortly after his split from Perry, Brand began dating Jemima Khan, (nee Goldsmith,) an heiress to another banking dynasty heavily connected to the Rothschilds. Brand has been photographed on a handful of occasions throwing up the 'mano cornutto'/ devil horns hand sign that we visited in the earlier chapter. Brand has said that he was sexually abused himself as a child. How many more clues do people really need?

Who's the daddy?

Two works of fiction are frequently cited as providing triggers for those under Monarch Programming, to bring forward certain alters. These are the 1939 movie 'The Wizard Of Oz', and the 'Alice In Wonderland' stories by freemason and occult secret society initiate Lewis Carroll. Both these stories are laden with mind-control imagery in their surface narrative, as well as being allegedly full of trigger phrases, images and colours. A further story subject to the same claim is J. D Salinger's 'The Catcher In The Rye', which Mark Chapman was famously reading when he 'shot' John Lennon.

Fritz Springmeier got further into the question of 'triggers' in his 'Good Vibrations' interview:

> *"Another thing that they're using the music industry for . . . I used to listen to the radio, and whenever they wanted to announce a ritual on the radio, you'd hear the song 'Heartache Tonight'. Or to reinforce the programming there's a song 'Playing With The Queen Of Hearts'. 'Knock Three Times' is another one. Three knocks is a mind-control trigger."*

Springmeier also contends that the US Country & Western music industry was effectively founded on the basis of generational mind-control. Very interesting when you bear in mind that Billy Ray Cyrus, father of the clearly troubled Miley Cyrus, made a name for himself on this scene.

> *"The Country & Western music industry was created by the intelligence services and the Illuminati, and has been a hotbed for this trauma-based mind-control. I've watched these Country & Western performers doing things, and right in front of people, if you understand the mind-control, you see it. So Dolly Parton was out there on stage one time, and her handler came out and she turned around and put her hand on his in submission as a slave does, because I'd been taught by Cisco Wheeler how a slave is to show submission. So she does that and then she turns around and calls him 'Daddy.' Right there in front of millions of people on television! If you understand the*

mind-control you're like, 'whoa, they just did it right in front of us. This isn't even secret!' So once you know how to recognise these things, you see it right in front of you all the time."

Dolly Parton is Miley Cyrus's 'Godmother', as a matter of interest.

When armed with knowledge of the agenda that music artists are being used to propagate, it's easy to fall into the trap of resenting and despising them for it. I've certainly been guilty of that when it comes to the likes of Nicki Minaj and Lil' Wayne and the role they've played in helping turn hip-hop from a once-meaningful art form into the septic tank of toxic garbage it now is. But it remains important to consider what horrors many artists have most likely been through since early childhood, to the point that their minds and personalities really are no longer their own. No amount of mansions, yachts and nice cars can ever be worth such a heavy price paid.

Resources:

Cathy O'Brien/ Trance Formation of America:

- http://www.trance-formation.com/

Conspiro Media: The Rothschild influence on music. Thelonious Monk & Jay Electronica:

- https://conspiromedia.wordpress.com/2012/07/31/
  as-kate-rothschilds-relationship-with-an-american-rapper-
  reportedly-intensifies-conspiro-media-presents-the-first-of-a-
  two-part-feature-on-the-notorious-familys-influence-on-music-
  over-the-la/

Vigilant Citizen: Origins and Techniques of Monarch mind-control:

- http://vigilantcitizen.com/hidden-knowledge/
  origins-and-techniques-of-monarch-mind-control/

Russell Brand busted as Katy Perry's Illuminati handler:

- http://www.YouTube.com/watch?v=9NaSYrVbH6c

Vigilant Citizen series of in-depth analysis of mind-control symbolism in countless pop music videos:

- http://vigilantcitizen.com/category/musicbusiness/

Vigilant Citizen: B.O.B. and Nicki Minaj's "Out of My Mind" or How to Make mind-control Entertaining:

- http://vigilantcitizen.com/musicbusiness/b-o-b-and-nicki-
  minajs-out-of-my-mind-or-how-to-make-mind-control-
  entertaining/

Nicki Minaj: 'Roman Holiday' on Wikipedia:

- http://en.Wikipedia.org/wiki/Roman_Holiday_(song)

Catholic League Blasts Rapper's Grammy Performance, Asking 'Is Nicki Minaj Possessed?':

- http://newyork.cbslocal.com/2012/02/13/rapper-nicki-minajs-
  grammy-performance-raises-eyebrows-with-religious-references/

Freeman Fly on mind-controlled stars/ the occult imagery of Britney Spears:

- http://freemantv.com/
  celebrities-under-mind-control-release-the-stars-weird-stuff/

Roseanne Barr talks about MK-Ultra mind-control in Hollywood:

- https://www.YouTube.com/watch?v=8whbmRMw0Bg

Roseanne Barr: "MK Ultra Rules In Hollywood":

- http://www.collective-evolution.com/2013/08/21/
  roseanne-barr-mk-ultra-rules-in-hollywood/

TV presenter Al Roker snaps into a mind-controlled state?:

- http://www.YouTube.com/watch?v=4jjIDWfWuPE

Kylie Minogue: mind-control?:

- http://mkculture.blogspot.co.uk/2009/02/mkd-km.html

Britney Spears interview with Diane Sawyer:

- http://www.YouTube.com/watch?v=DMpguv7st7s

Freeman TV: Britney Spears and other celebrities under mind-control:

- http://freemantv.com/
  celebrities-under-mind-control-release-the-stars-weird-stuff/

Daily Mail: Mariah has suffered breakdown:

- http://www.dailymail.co.uk/tvshowbiz/article-64099/Mariah-
  suffered-breakdown.html

The Daily Beast: Speed Read: Juiciest Bits From the Tommy Mottola Memoir 'Hitmaker':

- http://www.thedailybeast.com/articles/2013/01/31/speed-read-
  juiciest-bits-from-the-tommy-mottola-memoir-hitmaker.html

Roseanne's America: Interview with Roseanne Barr re Hollywood mind-control:

- https://www.YouTube.com/watch?v=HLTsdC0lasc#t=273

Roseanne World blog: Joe Jackson is an MK-Ultra operative:

- http://www.roseanneworld.com/blog/2009/07/
  joe-jackson-is-an-mk-ultra-ope/

Vigilant Citizen: Michael Jackson's "Secret Drawings" Reveal References to mind-control:

- http://vigilantcitizen.com/musicbusiness/
  never-seen-drawings-made-michael-jackson-hint-mind-control/

Justin Bieber behaving like 'a complete douchebag':

- https://www.YouTube.com/watch?v=CCJ51ibuoIM

Daily Mail: She's miming, lethargic, there are hundreds of unsold tickets–and her parents get all the cash. Britney's humiliating new tour:

- http://www.dailymail.co.uk/tvshowbiz/article-2054471/Britney-
  Spears-humiliating-new-tour-Shes-miming-lethargic--hundreds-
  unsold-tickets--parents-cash.html

Vigilant Citizen: Britney Spears is on Tour and is Still Under mind-control:

- http://vigilantcitizen.com/latestnews/
  britney-spears-is-on-tour-and-is-still-under-mind-control/

Vigilant Citizen: Britney Spears' Former Nanny To Testify in Trial About How the Singer was Manipulated by Handler:

- http://vigilantcitizen.com/latestnews/britney-spears-
  former-nanny-to-testify-in-trial-about-how-the-singer-was-
  manipulated-by-handler/

Daily Mail Onine: Mariah Carey's brother fears she will 'die like Whitney Houston' as he claims the pop star is addicted to alcohol and prescription drugs:

- http://www.dailymail.co.uk/tvshowbiz/article-3109625/Mariah-
  Carey-s-brother-fears-die-like-Whitney-Houston-claims-pop-
  star-addicted-alcohol-prescription-drugs.html

CHAPTER 12

STATE YOUR BUSINESS

Predictive Programming and the manipulation of consent.

'You must give them all fair warning . . . victims.'
  Sir Jimmy Savile (1926-2011) guesting on Sir David Frost's
  'Through The Keyhole'

'To not say no is tacitly say yes in their mentality.'
  Mark Passio

Contracting and consenting

As we approach the next stage in our story, the universal concepts of conscious free-will, tacit approval and consent come into play. These are metaphysical qualities which need to be understood for the tactics of the entertainment industry's dark magicians to make any kind of sense. Without being perceived in their full context, these activities will appear as bizarre, random standalone events, rather than being part of the colossal, interconnected web that they really are.

The concept of consent lies at the very root of the human experience, according to the teachings of many ancient religions, esoteric mystery schools, spiritual mediums and past-life regressionists. Within these lies the notion that, as spirit-souls and expressions of infinite consciousness, each of us 'consents' to be born into physical human form before we get here. We also hear that our higher selves form bonding 'contracts' with other spirit-souls, which have a bearing on what plays out as we go through our lives. In this regard, we can actually choose which other souls will be our parents, partners, children or adversaries. Spirit-souls often 'contract' in this way through several lifetimes, according to the

238

teachings, exchanging roles from one lifetime to another, in order that each can learn the lessons and undergo the experiences that they have pre-chosen for themselves. So your daughter in one life could be your husband in the next.

This truly is a mindblower when you hear it for the first time, and it can take several days of mental assimilation to get your head around it. And I guess there's no way of fundamentally proving this notion one way or the other until we depart this physical realm. Either way, the fact that the idea is so widespread in cultural traditions all over the world, illustrates the importance of free-will consciousness, and giving consent to a situation before you undergo it, so there can be no legitimate claim that it was foisted upon you without you agreement.

As beings imbued with self-awareness, humans are also gifted with free-will–the ability to make decisions which govern our thoughts and behaviours. These have a direct bearing on the conditions that manifest as a result. This is consequentialism, a concept which has been called many names through the ages. Whatever the label, the dynamic is always the same. Humans are unique in being able to shape the reality that we experience as a result of projecting our will. The nature of the energetic intent that we put out comes right back at us in the form of our experiences. By the same process we also reap the appropriate consequences for our actions, (karma.) The dark priest class that has been holding humanity in spiritual enslavement for millennia understand this universal truth only too well. If we are to stand any chance of breaking the spell, therefore, and achieving the freedom that's so long overdue, we also need to understand that these concepts are very real, and start to utilise them for the all-round betterment of humanity.

This concept is documented in the writings known as 'The Kybalion: Hermetic Philosophy,' which was published in 1908 and attributed to unknown writers who called themselves 'the Three Initiates.' It offers an interpretation of the Hermetic philosophies practiced in Ancient Egypt and Greece. On the subject of consequentialism, it states:

> *"This Principle embodies the fact that there is a cause for every effect; an effect from every cause. It explains that: 'Everything happens according to Law;' that nothing ever 'merely happens;' that there is no such thing as chance; that while there are various planes of cause*

and effect, the higher dominating the lower planes, still nothing ever entirely escapes the Law.

"The Hermeticists understand the art and methods of rising above the ordinary plane of cause and effect, to a certain degree, and by mentally rising to a higher plane they become causers instead of effects. The masses of people are carried along, obedient to environment; the wills and desires of others stronger than themselves; heredity; suggestion; and other outward causes moving them about like pawns on the Chessboard of Life.

"But the Masters, rising to the plane above, dominate their moods, characters, qualities, and powers, as well as the environment surrounding them, and become movers instead of pawns. They help to play the game of life, instead of being played and moved about by other wills and environment. They use the Principle instead of being its tools."

Despite so many of their teachings being otherwise full of controlling dogma, the human capacity to make free-will choice is something that's recognised in many of the world religions. I certainly remember having it drummed into me during the four years I attended a Christian church, that people make their own individual choice–independent of 'God'–to either accept Jesus and 'be saved,' or to be led astray by 'The Devil' and go to Hell. These are sensationalist over-simplifications of a universal truth, but the basic principle remains the same. Our capacity for free-will choice that affects our resulting experiences, is our greatest gift as humans. To be able to hijack that ability by manipulating and corrupting free-will choice on a mass scale, therefore, is one of the greatest weapons available to any parasitic enemy.

This is what is happening when we get into the phenomenon known as Predictive Programming.

Predictive Programming

PP is the practice of encoding visual clues and symbols into works of popular culture aimed at large audiences, which depict a real-world event yet to happen, or currently happening. In recognition of the powerful influence of the subconscious mind on an individual's psyche, images are subtly conveyed in encoded form which foreshadow events which are known to be coming. When the individual's conscious mind is then subject to news of the event in question, memories from the subconscious are unknowingly evoked, bringing a type of familiarity with the event. The propaganda of whatever official story the powers-that-be concoct and unleash via a compliant mainstream media, are then more readily absorbed.

It's a variation on the occult symbolism being placed into music videos that we encountered in the earlier chapter, except this method is far more involved, as it relies on the unwitting participation of the audience to achieve its full potential. The power lies in the symbols remaining subliminal. Once they cross the threshold into the conscious mind and their intent is fully understood, their power is lost. This is why it's so important for people in their large numbers to understand how the game—and we ourselves—are being played.

British researcher Alan Watt may have been the first to have coined the Predictive Programming phrase. He explains its workings as follows:

> *"Things or ideas which would otherwise be seen as bizarre, vulgar, undesirable or impossible are inserted into films in the realm of fantasy. When the viewer watches these films, his/ her mind is left open to suggestion and the conditioning process begins."*

PP can be seen at work in music videos, live stage shows, television programmes and Hollywood movies, and has been used for decades. Logic dictates that the only way this can be, is if the forces that control these industries are working alongside those directing the events that are being depicted—or if they are ultimately one and the same. Any sceptics rejecting this dynamic are left with a whole world of 'coincidences' defying all mathematical odds to explain away as 'just one of those things.'

We'll look at some classic examples of this phenomenon in practice, before studying the effects that they have and their reason for being placed where they are.

Doctor's Orders and Legs Eleven

The single event conveyed more than any other in Predictive Programming form has been 9/11. There is a huge array of Youtube videos made by independent users, consisting of clips from Hollywood movies and TV shows made prior to 11th September 2001. Some of these compilations go on for minutes, indicating the sheer number of examples. As a result there are way too many to list, but a few classics to illustrate the idea are as follows:

- In the film 'Independence Day,' released in 1996, there is a split-second frame in which a digital clock is seen counting down hours, minutes and seconds. The clock *just happens* to be at 00:09:11:01.

- In the first 'Matrix' movie, from 1999, the camera closes in on Neo's passport, which *just happens* to show an expiry date of 11th September 2001.

- 'Terminator 2: Judgement Day' (1991) contains a split-second shot showing a low bridge with a clearance sign giving the height '9'11'.

- In a 1997 episode of 'The Simpsons,' Bart holds up a bus leaflet entitled 'New York'. A massive '9,' indicating the $9 price, lines up next to the WTC towers, giving a nice, clear 9/11. (Matt Groening, creator of 'The Simpsons,' is reportedly a 33rd-degree freemason, but I'm sure it's just a coincidence and nothing to worry about.)

Some Youtube videos which chronicle other 9/11 examples are listed in the Resources section at the end of the chapter. The number of aspects of that fateful day evoked–from planes flying into the towers, to bodies apparently jumping from them–will be truly astounding to anyone looking at this subject for the first time.

It's not just the movie industry that has a monopoly on 9/11 imagery, however. There are examples of PP symbolism in American professional wrestling matches. And as further evidence that all aspects of the entertainment business are owned and directed by the same forces, the music game played its part in subliminally preparing the world for what it knew was to come.

One of the key albums in the discography of Jay-Z, the Illuminati's key asset in the corporate hip-hop world, was 'The Blueprint.' Its release date *just happened* to be 11th September 2001. Most albums get released on a Monday, whereas this was a Tuesday. The reason given was that the release date was moved back from the following week to 'combat bootlegging.' Well, that's that all sorted then.

The US author and researcher known as Isaac Weishaupt, (tongue-in-cheek wordplay based around Adam Weishaupt, the founder of the Bavarian Illuminati in 1776!) points out some date significance from Jay-Z's other two 'Blueprint' albums in his great book 'Sacrifice: Magic Behind The Mic'. 'The Blueprint 2: The Gift & The Curse' was released on 12th November 2002, he explains, which *just happened* to be the day that a video tape of Osama Bin Laden was said to have been discovered containing his 'admission' to orchestrating the 9/11 attacks. (If you ever want any tips on preserving your youth, by the way, Osama's your man. In the succession of videos that appeared in the post 9/11 years, he gets progressively younger and his beard progressively blacker with every new appearance. What's his secret, goddamit?!) November 12th was also the date in 2013 when New York's newly-constructed One World Trade Centre building was announced as the tallest building in the US.

It was back to 9/11 for the release of the 'Blueprint 3' album, meanwhile, on 11th September 2009. Weishaupt reminds us that this was around the time that Jay-Z was seen sporting a sweatshirt with the favourite Aleister Crowley phrase 'Do What Thou Wilt' emblazoned across it. Countless researchers have drawn parallels with Crowley's works and the strange, esoteric aspects of September 11th–particularly the fact that the numbers 9 and 11 figure majorly in Crowley's teachings. Many are of the view that the entire 9/11 spectacle was a massive dark occult ritual on a scale the world had never seen before, incorporating numerology and Saturnic death cult symbolism. The author S. K. Bain has an excellent book entitled 'The Most Dangerous Book In The World; 9/11 As Mass Ritual,' which comes highly recommended to anyone wishing to delve head-first into the more sinister aspects of 9/11 symbolism.

A couple of Busta Rhymes' albums in the late 90s, 'When Disaster Strikes' and 'Extinction Level Event,' seemed to show a new-found fascination with large-scale chaotic events. And why did Busta add the line 'there's only five years left' to the lyrics of his track 'Everything Remains Raw,' released in 1996?

It wasn't just in the years and months immediately prior to 9/11 that music industry foreshadowing occurred, however. There are now some very alert researchers whose work has been facilitated exponentially by the internet, and barely a trick gets past some of the more on-the-ball observers. The work of these people has enabled a widespread understanding of the techniques of Predictive Programming. I've no idea what led to someone reversing the sleeve artwork to the British AOR group Supertramp's 'Breakfast In America' album from 1979, but a very interesting phenomenon occurs when you do. The image, designed by one Mike Doud, depicts Lower Manhattan as seen from an aeroplane window, with a waitress in place of the Statue Of Liberty. The word 'Supertramp' appears over the Manhattan skyline complete with WTC twin towers. When the image is mirror-reversed, however, the U and P of 'Supertramp,' partially obscured by the towers, now appear to have become a 9 and an 11.

If this reference is too ambiguous and unconvincing for some, I'd invite them to debunk the sleeve to an album entitled 'Party Music' by a little-known Californian rap duo called The Coup. The original design features the pair paraded in front of the twin towers which are exploding in exactly the same manner as we saw on 9/11. As Pam The Funkstress drums, Boots Riley is seen pressing what looks like a kind of remote-control detonator. The album was scheduled for release in early September 2001. Post 9/11, this sleeve design was pulled by the group's label, Warner Brothers, and never made the stores. The album eventually appeared in November of that year with a new sleeve showing a hand holding a cocktail glass. Group frontman Boots Riley has said that he conceived the twin towers design months earlier, and that it was intended as a statement against capitalism. Either this is one of the wildest examples of coincidence in the history of popular culture, or there's more to the sleeve's background than Riley is letting on.

On the subject of 9/11 foreknowledge, meanwhile, if anyone has any answer as to how the musician Prince seemed to know what was coming back in December 1998, as evidenced by comments made at one of his live shows, I'd love to hear it. He ended one of his overseas concerts of that year with the words: "We got one more, then we gotta get out. I gotta go home, y'all. I gotta go home to America. I gotta go get ready for the bombs. Osama Bin laden gettin' ready to bomb, yeah." This could have been dismissed as a spontaneous and topical comment–particularly as Bin Laden had been indicted for orchestrating the 1995 bombing in Oklahoma City just the previous month–had it not been followed by the phrase "2001–hit me!"

(Of course, the fact that Bin Laden had nothing to do with the attacks is neither here nor there. The plan to pin 9/11 on him is likely to have already been in place in 1998.)

The only options here as far as I can see are that: 1. It was a humorous quip based on Prince's previous references to 'the bomb' in such songs as '1999', and that the '2001' reference was random and *just happened* to end up being highly portentous. Or 2. Prince moved in such social circles as to have obtained inside knowledge of what was to come from those who were in a position to know, and the '2001' reference was highly valid. Who can know for sure?

I also find it interesting that, of all the years in which Arthur C Clarke and Stanley Kubrick could have chosen to base their futuristic sci-fi epic '2001: A Space Odyssey,' it *just happened* to be the year of the 9/11 attacks. The movie was released in 1968, the year that construction of the World Trade Center's North Tower began.

9/11 pre-knowledge theories are exacerbated by accounts of several celebrities who were scheduled to be on one of the doomed flights, but ended up not flying for one reason or another. Among these are said to be actor Mark Wahlberg, singer Patti Austin, Leighanne Littrell, actress and wife of Backstreet Boy Brian Littrell, Seth MacFarlane, creator of 'Family Guy' and 'American Dad,' and Michael Jackson. To be fair, it's unclear how true these claims are, and whether they may in fact be urban myths, but I feel they're worth throwing into the mix of strange 9/11-related questions nonetheless.

Michael Jackson's 9/11 links don't end there, either. On the sleeve to his 1997 remix album 'Blood On The Dancefloor: HIStory In the Mix,' Jackson is pictured dancing on a black and white-chequered floor, with a city in the backdrop which looks a lot like Manhattan engulfed in dust. (In further symbolic curiosities, meanwhile, the design of the tiled floor is that which is found in Masonic temples, representing the duality between light and dark/ good and evil/ night and day, etc. Black and white designs are also said to be mind-control triggers. Jackson is wearing a blood-red suit, which is the principal colour associated with Saturn, the planet of death worshipped by the dark occult priest class. 'Blood on the dancefloor' is taken to be a barely-concealed reference to Masonic ritual sacrifice.

Every cloud...

The insane chemtrailing/ geo-engineering agenda that's now blighting skies the world over also seems to have been foreshadowed using this tried-and-tested method. These days, the reinforcement that skies criss-crossed with clouds of toxic chemicals from dawn, followed by a 'white-out' and a blocking out of direct sunlight a few hours later is totally normal, is hammered home by the drawing in of chemtrailed skies into children's story books and cartoons, and on to packets of breakfast cereals like Weetabix. The Met Office and the TV weather forecasts also pretend they don't exist, when anyone with a pair of eyes and a neck that tilts upwards can see for sure that they do. But in 1984, an episode of the popular sci-fi series 'Dr. Who' made by the BBC, (surely not?!) included a very interesting line of dialogue. In episode 2 of 'The Caves Of Androzani,' (which introduced actor Peter Davidson to the Doctor role,) the character known as Morgus utters the phrase: "as they used to say on Earth, every cloud has a strontium lining." Given that strontium has been identified as one of the main metal particulates of chemtrails, is it beyond the realms of possibility that this was a sly and knowing nod to the widespread agenda that was known to be coming the following decade? You can listen to the clip by scrolling 10 minutes and 44 seconds into the video at the following link, (assuming it hasn't since been taken down amidst the usual bollocks about 'breaching terms of use'!)

- http://www.dailymotion.com/video/
  x2464uf_doctor-who-the-caves-of-androzani-2-4_shortfilms

Terror on demand

The PP agenda in movies has been stepped up majorly in recent years, and for pretty much every 'terror' event in the 'news,' there has been at least one major depiction of what was to come in a blockbuster movie or cartoon.

In the Batman film 'The Dark Knight Rises,' the camera hovers for a second over a map of Gotham City, on which the place name 'Sandy Hook' has been circled. The film was released in July 2012, five months before 'lone nut' Adam Lanza is said to have shot 20 children and six adults at Sandy Hook Elementary School in Newtown, Connecticut. Research from the Infowars.com website revealed that in the earlier movie 'Batman Begins,' a similar map of Gotham City can be seen. In this version, however, the area in question is named 'South Hinkley' and not Sandy Hook.

This particular movie gets two bites of the PP cherry, however. During a midnight screening in Aurora, Colorado on 20th July 2012, a gunman is reported to have burst into the theatre and opened fire on the audience, killing 12 people and injuring a further 70. This is said to have occurred at the precise moment that a trailer was showing for the movie 'Gangster Squad,' in which gunmen are depicted firing machine guns through the movie screen at the audience.

The blame for this was placed on another 'lone nut,' one James Holmes. But the amount of anomalies surrounding the official version of what happened are so numerous that they almost warrant a book in themselves. Conveniently, the gunman was reported to have been wearing a gasmask, obscuring his facial features. There's also the small matter of the individual appearing in court, with hair dyed orange like The Joker in the film, being an entirely different person to the one in the identity photo of 'James Holmes' paraded by the mainstream media. More mind games being played at a bewildered general public's expense.

There's even a third strand to this particular one, which is where the first example of a music video comes in. In the promo for the piece of toxic audio garbage titled 'My Homies Still' by the rapper (it says here) Lil' Wayne, there is a scene entirely unrelated to the song's content, where Wayne is depicted in a movie theatre surrounded by 12 skeletons.

(How many people are said to have been killed in the Aurora shooting again?) 'My Homies Still' was released on 5th June 2012, 45 days before the Aurora incident. In further symbolic links to the Batman movie, meanwhile, the rest of the video is full of bat-related imagery, including a girl in a leather Batman mask, and rappers (it says here) Lil' Wayne and Big Sean hanging upside-down from the ceiling in a bat-like manner. None of these scenes have any connection to the lyrics of the song, of which here's an example:

> *"Man, fuck ya'll with a sick dick, Semi automatic no click click,*
>
> *We don't feel you like an elephant, gettin' fucked with a tick dick,*
>
> *Little nigga with a thick bitch, and before I fuck this bitch,*
>
> *I gotta put that patch over my third eye, Slick Rick."*

Interesting reference to putting a 'patch over my third eye,' don't you think? As for the rest of the song's meaning, answers on a postcard. This is what the kids are getting down to these days, apparently.

As a final aside, Wikipedia's entry on the 'My Homies Still' video tells us:

> *"(It) begins with several shots of white mannequins holding various poses, some with missing limbs . . . After a panda is shown dancing, the elephant then changes colour to pink, and a man and dog are shown to have each-other's heads superimposed onto each-others' bodies . . . Several female heads, (although still seemingly alive,) appear as trophies on the wall."*

No more needs to be said for anyone who has read the previous chapter on dissociative mind-control!

Following the Boston Marathon 'bombings' of 15th April 2013, (almost certainly another staged False-flag event using actors,) it didn't take sharp researchers long to realise that the event seemed to have been predicted in a recent episode of the cartoon 'Family Guy.' In one scene, the character Peter Griffin, 'winner of the Boston Marathon,' is seen dressed in Muslim garb hitting a button on a mobile phone, upon which two huge explosions are heard outside, the second one accompanied by screams. In a separate scene from the same episode, Griffin is seen mowing down other runners in a car at the finishing line of the marathon, echoing what we were told about the fate of one the Tsarnaev brothers in the 'news.' Most clips of this episode that were posted to Youtube have been conveniently removed due to 'copyright' issues, but you can still see one of the analysis videos here: https://www.YouTube.com/watch?v=wYdxWE_JF0Y

Other episodes of 'Family Guy' are said to have predicted elements of the 9/11 and 7/7 attacks.

The event said to have taken place in Woolwich, London, on 22nd May 2013 involving an alleged soldier by the name of Lee Rigby being butchered by two 'Islamic fundamentalists' (what else?), also appears to have been foreshadowed, and in a distinctly British way. The investigative filmmaker Tom Secker has pointed out that several aspects of the official Woolwich narrative were depicted in Series 5 of the British TV drama 'Spooks,' created and screened by the BBC, (surely not?!)

Secker explains that several of the episodes feature a South East London-born British Muslim convert of Nigerian descent—the exact background details of Michael Adebolajo, Rigby's alleged attacker. In the 'Spooks' narrative, the Michael character has a white girlfriend, who gets co-opted by the British 'intelligence' services to infiltrate the terror cell and become an informant. When she is discovered, she gets killed by means of a large kitchen knife. The female character's name *just happens* to be Lee. The same Michael character also crops up in Series 6 of 'Spooks,' having now been recruited himself as an informant. This series features another episode in which a character is murdered by way of a large knife. The BBC is a propaganda arm of the British government, and the idea that it could be working in league with security services such as M15 and M16 on mass mind-control agendas should surprise no-one who has been paying attention to what *really* goes on in the world.

The fact that most, if not all of the 'real life' events above never actually happened the way the official story maintains, and that most have been proven to be faked using actors, doesn't detract from the validity of the Predictive Programming applied. The perpetrators rely on the public's acceptance of what's being portrayed, regardless of whether it was 'real' or not. False-flag events are used to generate a reaction of fear and shock, and the notion from the public that 'something must be done.' This paves the way for the controllers to instil a measure that suits their agenda—waging a foreign war, perhaps, the imposition of further public surveillance, or more restrictions on personal freedoms in the name of 'terror prevention.' They would have a much harder time gaining public compliance for such measures had they not first justified the need by way of a perceived threat.

The nightly BBC 'news' is not to be outdone by works of fiction either, (even though what we're now asked to believe as 'news' crossed the boundary long ago.) There have been a handful of examples of the 'news' announcing stories before the details have occurred in reality. The BBC's coverage of 9/11, where reporter Jane Standley is seen in front of the infamous Salomon Brothers building, better known as 'Building 7,' and announcing it as having collapsed several minutes before it actually did, has now passed into legend in conspiracy circles, and is very much the smoking gun that proves complicity of the BBC and those that control it in the events of that day. That's unless you accept that she *just happened* to get her story wrong, and it *just happened* to collapse unexpectedly at odds of billions-to-one afterwards.

In May 2015 we appeared to get more of the same, when the BBC reportedly announced the 'victory' of David Cameron's Conservative Party in the General Election by beaming an image of the party's 316-seat majority on to the side of BBC Broadcasting House in London, *before* the final count had officially been announced. This bolstered the claims of vast numbers of people that the election was rigged and that it had already been decided that Cameron's Conservatives would get another term in office, regardless of how anyone may or may not have voted.

It's been going on forever, too. In 1898, a novel was written by Morgan Robertson, 'Futility,' telling the story of an 'unsinkable' ocean liner named The Titan which collided with an iceberg in the North Atlantic in the month of April, and sank with huge loss of life, largely through there not being enough lifeboats available. 14 years later, The Titanic sunk in circumstances uncannily similar to what had been depicted in the novel. (Conspiracy researchers will also be quick tell you that the Titanic *just happened* to be carrying Benjamin Guggen-heim, Isador Strauss, the head of Macy's department stores, and John Jacob Astor, all three of whom were providing the main opposition to the creation of the US Federal Reserve. They all died in April 1912. In December of the following year, the US Federal Reserve was instated.)

Another extraordinary 'coincidence' appeared to come from the Pet Shop Boys' 'King's Cross,' a track from their 1987 album 'Actually.' It was released two months before a massive fire devastated the London train station of the same name, killing 31 people and injuring over 100 more. Although the official account of the lyrics was that they referred to 'desperation and unemployment,' they appeared to eerily foreshadow the disaster, with lines like:

"Only last night I found myself lost,

by the station called King's Cross,

Dead and wounded on either side,

You know it's only a matter of time."

What were the chances?

'Uncanny similarities'

During the writing of this chapter, another classic example occurred, straight in at number one on the Top Of The Psy-Ops Hit Parade. In March 2015, a Germanwings Airbus A320 was reported to have crashed into the French Alps on a flight from Barcelona to Dusseldorf, killing all 150-plus on board. The mainstream media quickly ran with the story of how the 28-year-old co-pilot, Andreas Lubitz, had been suffering depression, and decided to take his own life along with those of everyone else on the flight. He used an opportune moment when the pilot left the cockpit to lock himself in, and deliberately steer the plane towards the ground. We're told that the pilot and some passengers tried in vain to break the door down moments before it crashed.

A couple of days later, a UK 'Daily Mail' article appeared, detailing the 'uncanny similarities' between this event and the plotline of an Argentinian film that had been released weeks before, entitled 'Wild Tales.' The first of the movie's six short stories, intended as a black comedy, involves a pilot inviting several people with whom he had grievances–including a lover who jilted him and a troublesome work colleague–on to a flight, then deliberately crashing the plane into the ground, killing himself and everyone on board. He achieves this by locking himself in the cockpit. In panic, a passenger is seen attempting to break the door down. Although the film had yet to be released in Britain, it had already been shown in the US, and in Spain and Germany, the departure and arrival ports of the Germanwings flight. Of course, the 'Daily Mail' article put the similarities down to another of those 'amazing coincidences.'

It wasn't long until there was more of the same. The movie 'Kingsmen: The Secret Service', one of the most blatant pieces of Establishment propaganda ever passed off as 'entertainment,' featured a scene in which Colin Firth's secret agent character, in a mind-controlled state, slaughters the entire congregation of a church. The fact that the mutilation is shown in jerky CGI to give it a comic veneer, and that the general public just passively accepts such things as 'entertainment,' shows the depths to which our collective morals have already sunk. A few weeks later came the news of the mass shooting at a largely black church in Charleston, South Carolina, where yet another 'lone nutter,' Dylann Roof, was said to have slaughtered nine people in what many researchers have concurred was a staged exercise as part of the US government's ongoing attempts to disarm its citizens, and to create further racial hostilities in America.

Different event, same tactics, no imagination.

Knock before entering

It becomes clear that the powers-that-shouldn't be not only plan their moves years (and sometimes even decades and centuries) in advance, but also love to encode their intentions into works of popular culture. Effectively, they tell the truth to the subconscious mind which doesn't have the capacity to properly process the information. They then lie blatantly to the conscious mind. It's their way of trying to cheat the karmic consequences of Natural Law, by, as they see it, giving the public the opportunity to object to what they plan to do, then taking it as tacit approval or implied consent to go right ahead when nobody calls them out on it. Of course, it's a sick, twisted way of looking at it, as no-one could reasonably be expected to have interpreted the clues until after the event happens. What's the likelihood of anyone seeing the Lil' Wayne video, for instance, and going "Hey! Wait a minute! That split-second cinema scene tells me they're planning to stage a shooting in a movie theatre during a screening of the Batman movie, then use it to try and tighten US gun laws and strip Americans of yet more personal freedoms. I'm not having that!" Who are you supposed to write to should you figure this out? And the very idea that you can somehow cheat laws set in place by the creative force behind the universe is egotisic arrogance of the first degree . . . but then we are talking about demented psychopaths here.

In an interview with John Gibbons on his 'Alchemy Radio' podcast in July 2014, Irish researcher Thomas Sheridan went into the reasons why revealing their tactics is all part of the dark controllers' methods:

> *"Telling us is part of the magic. We have to consent. That's why they blow the whistle on what they do through all kinds of books and movies and so on. And they'll often show us a hint of things before they do them. And this is how their sorcery, their black, hexan paganism works. You have to be told.*

> *"This is why Dracula always knocked on the door and asked to be let in . . . The Devil has to be invited in. Then you've forfeited your right to say 'I was taken by surprise.' No, you brought it in. This is why we all have to learn what they're doing to us, we have to learn wordplay, we have to learn neuro-linguistic programming. Because the only thing that's keeping them in power is our acquiescence to their pathological drive. And the best weapon we have against them is our refusal."*

In the movie 'The Exorcist', Linda Blair's Regan character only gets possessed by the demonic entity *after* she's messed about with a ouija board she found in the cellar. Although Regan didn't fully understand what she was doing, this was the entity's 'invitation.' Without it, it could not have entered into her.

In 'The Wicker Man', it is stated that Edward Woodward's policeman character is fair game as a human sacrifice purely because he came to the island of his own free will, (albeit having been coerced into looking for an apparently 'missing' girl.) He wasn't forced. He made the choice. Here are two films subtly conveying the implications of consenting in their narratives.

Some further insight came from Mark Passio on his 'What On Earth Is Happening' radio show on Republic Broadcasting Network in October 2014:

> "The societies that were planning this whole agenda, and had been planning this event (9/11) for decades before this, were using all kinds of occult symbolism and numerology in this event. They stick to this plan and they're very predictable in this regard. They love their symbolism. They love playing with numbers. They love putting this out into other peoples' faces.
>
> "One of the dark principles of their ideological tenets is that, if you tell people what you're doing, even if it's telling them wordlessly through symbols or numbers, then you have somehow gotten their implied consent, because they haven't said no. And to not say no is to tacitly say yes in their mentality. So that, in their mind, relieves the burden of karma that would ordinarily come down upon them for directing these actions, (because they don't actually take these actions, they get their order-following house slave dogs to do it for them.) In their mind, because they told you in a wordless, occult way, then in some way that alleviates the karma, because they did say it in some form. It's a sick, twisted way of looking at it."

The veteran researcher Michael Hoffman expressed these same ideas in more scholarly fashion in a lecture he delivered in 1987, entitled 'The Occult Philosophy:'

"The fallacy of even independent researchers is that, exposure per se of the methods and personnel involved in the cryptocracy's crimes is an ultimate goal. If only we could get some of these facts out into the open, runs the refrain.

"I would reply to that notion that the cryptocracy is not stagnant. It is engaged in a remarkable process set into motion centuries ago, an operation which has accomplished most, if not all of its chief goals with awe-inspiring despatch already. In the beginning and middle stages of this operation, secrecy was a key to accomplishing these goals. Generally speaking, that secrecy is no longer necessary today. Quite the contrary.

"The cryptocracy has actually been determined to reveal many of its greatest secrets to we profane ones for some time now, but very few have noticed."

When you come to understand this underlying need to let us know what they're doing, it makes sense of so many of the control system's tactics. This is why they always announce foreign wars via the mainstream media before going off to invade another country. From their point of view, they've told us their intentions; now they can steam right in. This is why ingredients are listed on distinctly unhealthy food and drink items, and in toxic vaccines. You might think it would suit their purpose more to avoid telling people that brain cell-destroying Aspartame is included in soft drinks aimed at kids, or that a vaccine contains such delights as aborted human foetus, monkey brain tissue and formaldehyde, but they go right ahead and reveal it. (To be fair, these horrors in vaccines are generally hidden under some multi-syllabled scientific name, but their true nature can still be discovered by anyone vigilant enough to do the research.) It's why fat, sugar and starch content and calorie quantities are included on supermarket food labels, alcohol content listed on liquor, and warnings about the possibility of lung cancer on cigarette packets. You can't say you weren't told.

By the same token, this is why 'side effects,' (so, 'effects,' then) of pharmaceutical drugs have to be listed on the leaflets that come with them. If you contract one of them, you were told it could happen, and they're no longer liable for the free-will choice you made to take it. It's the reason you can't get a mobile phone package or a credit card without signing a contract consisting of several pages of small print disclaimers that benefit the corporation rather than the individual, and absolve them of any responsibility in the event of a situation arising. It's the reason we have to be told that CCTV is in operation on buses or in public buildings, or why we have to be warned that speed cameras are in operation on roads, and of what the speed limit is before you can be issued with a speeding ticket. It's why we're told in advance that taxes are going to go up, or new ones are to be introduced. The disclaimers that the manipulators feel allow them to be let off the karmic hook are everywhere you look. Tacit approval and implied consent are the constant name of the game.

It does appear to be the case, however, that in instances where no 'contract' as such has been entered into, they give the opportunity for an opt-out. It would appear to be an extension of the courtesy of revealing their intent in encoded form, by giving those who are alert enough to realise what they're doing the opportunity to say 'no thanks.' This is why, when the new glut of full-radiation body scanners were introduced to US airports in the post-9/11 years, travellers were given the option of avoiding them by announcing they wished to opt out and undergo a thorough groping by TSA officials instead. Taking this option relied upon the individual being sufficiently well-informed to know about the detrimental health effects of the machines, of course, which is why most people still obediently walk through them when coerced into doing so. This concept of 'opting out' is even expressed when police officers read you your 'rights.' (This is a fallacy in itself, since true rights under Natural Law can only be granted by the creative force behind the universe and not by any man or woman.) By informing you that 'anything you say can and will be used in evidence against you,' they're absolving themselves of any burden of responsibility by (as they see it,) putting the onus on to the individual. It's their idea of having given you 'fair warning' of their intent and sufficient opportunity to neglect to consent. There is a very real sense in which the famous phrase 'silence is consent' applies. For as long as we demonstrate no opposition to what's being done to us, (and with no excuse for claiming 'I didn't know' when we're living in the age of the most abundant availability of information humanity has ever known via the internet!) there is a very real sense in which we deserve what we get. Although there will be individual exceptions, the will and the principle of care is not present enough on a collective basis, and so we reap the collective results that we are all experiencing.

Understanding the concepts of consent and free-will approval, and the extent to which the powers-that-shouldn't-be recognise they are bound by it, is where our true power lies. If we, in our colossal numbers, make it abundantly clear that we do not in any way consent to the systems of slavery, oppression and violation that they foist upon us, I feel some very interesting results could manifest. Without our approval, they would stand in full judgement for the crimes they commit against humanity. They know this. Their understanding that they would be taking on the full karmic consequence for actions which they alone chose, would present a very different state of affairs to the one we currently have. This shift can only be achieved through vast numbers of people understanding deeply the methods (such as those outlined in this book) that are being used against us, which is why communicating this information is essential to human freedom.

Great truths are often encoded into works of popular culture such as Hollywood movies, whose surface narratives can appear dismissively trivial. In the film 'The Truman Show' starring Jim Carrey, his controller Christof states: "He (Truman) could leave at any time. If his was more than just a vague ambition, if he was absolutely determined to discover the truth, there's no way we could prevent him." Another reminder that everything we experience is down to free-will choices, either on a microcosmic, or personal level, or the choices that we make collectively as a species on a macrocosmic level.

For a human to have their free-will consciousness hijacked and manipulated is to render them as nothing more than an unthinking flesh robot, and this is precisely the dynamic which is occurring with millions of people on the planet without their knowledge. Freedom is all about breaking the dark magician's spell. Once you understand how an illusionist performs their tricks, you'll never be fooled by them again. So it is with the tactics used in the entertainment industry. Once it's out of the confines of the subliminal mind, and into the conscious, the manipulations no longer work. More people need to be made consciously aware of how they're being duped. When you're no longer making any kind of unwitting energetic connection with the agenda, more discerning choices can be made.

Our very own minds are being used as weapons against us. But we can change it any time we choose. As the late, great Bill Hicks remarked so potently, 'it's just a choice.'

Resources:

9/11 Predictive Programming in Hollywood movies and TV shows:

- https://www.YouTube.com/watch?v=IzLDxP3Qrzs
- https://www.YouTube.com/watch?v=Rd-zOMb3REU
- https://www.YouTube.com/watch?v=roE0sJktfBY
- https://www.YouTube.com/watch?v=rnf7hQE6leU
- https://www.YouTube.com/watch?v=63OdK8ZcrrY
- https://www.YouTube.com/watch?v=OpYWt8yJAoI

The Coup's Boots Riley speaks out about 9/11:

- http://www.daveyd.com/bootsonthewarpolitics.html

Family Guy Predicts Boston, 9/11 & 7/7 London Attacks Weeks in Advance:

- https://www.YouTube.com/watch?v=wYdxWE_JF0Y

Tom Secker talks with Alex G on the BBC's 'Spooks' Predictive Programming of 7/7 and Woolwich:

- http://www.investigatingtheterror.com/audio/The_War_on_Terror_in_the_UK_and_Africa___A_conversation_with_Alex_G.html

Prince: 'Osama Bin Laden gettin' ready to bomb':

- https://www.YouTube.com/watch?v=KzC_GNaf12o

Daily Mail: Outrage over the release of Oscar-nominated movie showing member of aircrew locking himself in cockpit to crash a plane and kill everyone on board:

- http://www.dailymail.co.uk/news/article-3014631/Questions-raised-release-Oscar-nominated-movie-showing-member-aircrew-locking-cockpit-crash-plane-kill-board.html

CHAPTER 13

MINDS AND MACHINES

Music's role in normalising the Transhumanist agenda.

> *'Just beneath the skin, you will hardly know it's in,*
> *Push a button if you want to know our names,*
> *Invented in the labs, to keep the low life under tabs,*
> *Something tells me that there is another aim.'*
>
> *Imani Hekima: 'Just Beneath The Skin' (2011)*

> *'Can't you see, they're trying to plug into our minds,*
> *Trick us with technology and keep us all confined,*
> *Can't you see the signs, we're running out of time.'*
>
> *Nate Featuring Dark Matter: 'Tricknology' (2014)*

> *'In the year 5555,*
> *Your arms hangin' limp at your sides,*
> *Your legs got nothin' to do,*
> *Some machine's doin' that for you.'*
>
> *Zager & Evans: 'In The Year 2525' (1969)*

Instant robot; mix well

In 1998, US singer Cher released a single entitled 'Believe.' It was the chart hit and karaoke favourite it was always destined to be owing to its catchy hook and commercially-orientated production. There was something very distinctive about it, though. Cher's vocals sounded very strange and robotic when she hit the chorus. It was the first time the general public had heard the phenomenon of Auto-Tune.

The technique was developed by California-based Antares Audio Technologies, a company founded by a former geo-physicist by the name of Dr. Harold 'Andy' Hildebrand, who had used sound waves to map oil wells. The company's website points out that it became the largest-selling audio plug-in of all-time shortly after its release in 1997.

Auto-Tune is an audio production method which digitises a human voice, allowing for its automated manipulation. The reason given for its invention is that it allows a singer's voice to hit required notes and tempos with precision. The required notes can be pre-programmed, and the voice is then pitched up or down the scale to hit them spot-on, over-riding any shortcomings on the part of the vocalist. The Wikipedia entry on Auto-Tune describes the process as follows: "Auto-Tune can also be used as an effect to distort the human voice when pitch is raised or lowered significantly. The overall effect to the discerning ear can be described as hearing the voice leap from note to note stepwise, like a synthesizer."

It strikes me that there's an obvious response to this explanation. It's just a thought, but the music industry *could* always employ singers who are skilled enough to be able to hit required notes themselves, without the aid of plug-in technology, and any singers unable to achieve this *could* be sent away to practice until they can. Can't help thinking that this would be a more sensible solution to the problem that Auto-Tune was apparently devised to rectify? I guess I shouldn't be too surprised though, given that the same concept of technology compensating for questionable human skill is now prevalent throughout the DJ-ing profession. Software packages such as Serato and Traktor now come with a function known as a 'sync button.' This allows for two tunes being played off a laptop to have their tempos and beats automatically detected, then to be mixed together seamlessly with no manual input required. An entire generation of young 'DJs' are now being conditioned to accept this as the 'normal' way of making a set flow, rendering them to the status of a machine operative, rather than any kind of artist. It's a testament to how fickle human nature can be, and to the short attention spans in the instant culture in which we now live, that many DJs couldn't wait to ditch the vinyl and embrace this 'cool' new digital technology when it first appeared . . . but that now, a few years down the line, we're witnessing a nostalgic hankering towards real vinyl again and a resurgence in its output, as if laptop DJ-ing is now old-hat and the fashionistas are looking for the next big thing . . . even if in this case that means the last big thing.

Either way, the Cher tune was proudly trumpeted as an example of this great new method of production. There was a small drawback in that it stripped any semblance of humanity out of her voice, making it akin to Stephen Hawking's electronic voicebox. But that didn't seem to matter to anyone at the time, such was the novelty value of this new phenomenon. No-one then could have had any clue as to the proliferation of Auto-Tune, (known popularly as 'the Cher effect' in its early days,) that was due to engulf mainstream music the following decade. Nor how this seemingly innocent and random phenomenon could be connected to a much wider, and extremely sinister plan.

Welcome to the music industry's part in the Transhumanist agenda.

Man and machine: an unholy alliance

Transhumanism is the merging of humanity with technology. For decades, there has been a fascination within the 'elite' class of tinkering with the natural state of what it is to be human—their way of asserting what they psychopathically consider to be their god-like status—and this goes some way to explaining their reverence towards, and fascination for technology. The dark priest class have revealed in their own writings how they fantasise about a society merging its innate human qualities with technological 'improvements.' This is one of the central tenets of the New World Order. It sounds like the stuff of science fiction films, for sure, but hopefully the previous chapter on the workings of Predictive Programming will have gone some way towards explaining why that would be.

The plans that the 'elites' have for themselves and those reserved for the rest of us are rather different, however. They appear to believe that Transhumanism holds the key to immortality on their part. Experiments involving implants and drugs on military subjects have already produced what are known as 'super soldiers'—humans whose natural functions have been so artificially altered that they can go for days without food, water or sleep, are impervious to pain, and display the super-human strength of comic-book heroes. These are the qualities that the dark controllers seemingly wish to retain for themselves in their quest to go way beyond the regular mortality of humans.

For the slave population, however, (that's you and me,) all the evidence points toward a different plan. Here, the aim is to have microchips and brain implants inserted into the population, for remote tracking and mind-control purposes. Attempts have already been made to routinely chip babies as soon as they are born, but these have been met with the suspicious resistance they deserve on the part of parents . . . so far. To get the public mindset used to the idea and to present it as a benign and beneficial thing, pet dogs have been already been getting chipped for years, the RFID signal linked to satellite trackers with the sentiment that 'you need never lose Fido again.' There has been a big push in recent times to extend this method to patients with dementia, with the helpful suggestion that if they should happen to wander off in their pyjamas in the middle of the night, they can be easily traced.

Chipping has become routine in certain facets of the military, whose staff are always the first in line for any new biological experimentation, and some corporations are now following suit, making it mandatory for staff to be chipped as condition of their employment. All on the grounds of 'safety' and 'security', naturally. One such establishment has been the Epicenter hi-tech business block in Sweden, where staff of tenant companies have had to have RFID chips installed under their skin to open office doors and even use the copier. Hannes Sjoblad, who carries the curious title of Chief Disruption Officer at the company which made the chips, was quoted as saying: "we already interact with technology all the time. Today it's a bit messy—we need PIN codes and passwords. Wouldn't it be easy to just touch with your hand? That's really intuitive."

Right on script, Hannes.

Upon first hearing, the idea of 'improving' oneself with technology will be an appealing prospect for many—particularly those with left brain-imbalanced scientific minds. A good example of this is Kevin Warwick, Professor of Cybernetics at Reading University in England. His website biog describes him as 'carrying out research in artificial intelligence, control, robotics and biomedical engineering.' He has been a highly vocal advocate of microchips being inserted into humans and has undergone the process himself, proudly proclaiming that he has had a device implanted into the median nerves of his left arm to link his nervous system directly to a computer, and that he was responsible for the first purely electronic communication between the nervous systems of two humans.

Warwick is either entirely down with the elite agenda, or is what is referred to as a 'useful idiot'—someone oblivious to the big picture, but whose work contributes conveniently towards it. Either way, the plan for a microchipped population remains high on the wish-list of the social engineers. As with all things, however, they realise that were they to try and introduce such a drastic measure overnight, it would likely meet with strong resistance, such is the human mind's in-built aversion to sudden change. What they have long-since perfected, therefore, is a slow and gradual process of incrementalism, a method described by David Icke as 'The Totalitarian Tiptoe.' This advocates making small changes in progressive steps over extended periods of time. Each step gradually moves you closer to your end goal, but covertly enough so as not to raise attention. It has been described allegorically as the 'frog in a pot' syndrome; put a frog into a pot of boiling water and it'll jump straight out. If you put it into a lukewarm pot, however, and slowly turn up the temperature in stages, the changes will be so subtle that the frog won't notice it's being slowly boiled alive.

And so it has been with the desire towards Transhumanism. And the extent to which the Totalitarian Tiptoe has been in place was brought home to me a while back when thinking about the changes in society that have taken place in just the last 20 years. These apply to my home-land of the UK, but will be familiar to readers in pretty much any other country.

Let's take 1996 as a starting point. In that year, very few people had mobile phones, and the internet was still in its infancy. The majority of people who owned PCs would not have been using them to access the internet at that point. Broadband phone lines were yet to be unleashed, the limited amount of internet connections being achieved by tragically slow dial-up modems. E-mail was very much in its infancy, with most business communications still being done by fax or letter.

In 1996, you could still get a landline phone number, with a geographical dialling code, for the local branch of your bank. You could still phone your electricity or gas company and have the phone answered by a human being. (And in the same country as you, too–how about that?!) You could tell the person answering the phone what you were calling for, rather than having to develop Alzheimer's or reincarnate several times waiting for a menu read out by a cheerfully-voiced computer to end. You could still go to a supermarket and have your groceries checked-out by a human cashier, rather than being coerced to scan them on a machine and pack them yourself.

To watch television, you required a television with an aerial connector. The end. As everything ran on analogue signals, digital set-top boxes and the additional wiring involved, was unnecessary. Drivers actually used to be able to find their way from point A to point B utilising map-reading skills in conjunction with a good road atlas, rather than being instructed in which way to go by their car. They could also exercise their judgement in deciding when to put their windscreen wipers on for themselves, and unlocked their car by putting a key in the lock and turning it. Somehow kids managed to get from one end of the day to the other without ringtones, Instagram or Snapchat and didn't lose their minds when they were unable to pick up a wi-fi network to update their Facebook status every half-hour.

All of these major changes to daily life have occurred in less than 20 years, and a glance at the 'then' and 'now' scenarios is a master study in how the Totalitarian Tiptoe works. The technology involved has transformed human society beyond recognition in most countries around the world. A time-traveller from as recent as 1996 teleporting to present day would be left baffled as to what was going on. And yet, because it has happened in small steps over an extended period, and because each societal change has been presented as something that is 'great' for us, it has been readily accepted and absorbed the way the architects always knew it would be. Does anyone really believe it's just coincidence that all major supermarkets adopted self-scan checkouts at the same time as all major corporations adopted automated phone systems? Or that the only factor driving the changes is 'cost-effectiveness?' Is the fact that some restaurants now covertly record their customers' conversations all for their own 'safety,' and is fitting cars with tracking devices at the factory really just about 'efficiency?'

There are many of my generation who can remember clearly the days before 1996 when our daily operations were much simpler and more organic. But 40 years from now, as we die out, the majority of the world's population will only ever have known a life dominated by computerised machines.

Nobody is denying that technology has a positive role to play in some aspects of our lives. Of course, numerous examples could be cited of the genuine benefits to humanity that the world of science has brought. This has nothing to do with the insidious and malevolent agenda being rolled out by the controlling forces, however.

This complete remodelling of the way we humans interact with electronics in pretty much every aspect of our lives, has been slowly preparing us psychologically for what's planned. This is the introduction of technology designed to interact with natural human functions, creating a human-machine hybrid, but with far more emphasis placed on the automated, machine-like aspects than the human ones.

Hopefully anyone whose first instinct is to think it's truly astounding that science has come this far—rather like Kevin Warwick—will do some further research into what this agenda really entails, and why it's being so zealously foisted upon us. Like every other manipulation in human society, from organised religion to the financial system, it's all about control and the perpetuation of human slavery.

The long-term plan, as the work of many researchers has highlighted, is to have a microchipped world population, linked, via remotely-controlled radio signals, to a central computer. David Icke went into the implications of such an arrangement at the hands of, shall we say, those who do not have humanity's best interests at heart, in his book 'The Perception Deception:'

> *"Google is the predominant player in the Transhumanist agenda, and technology like Google Now is designed to track and manage every aspect of peoples' lives with the ability to know if you are walking, driving or riding a bicycle, when you are at home, and able to recognise your voice patterns, which are an expression of your unique vibrational signature. These stepping stones are promoted as an 'ain't it great?' new gadget, when they are systematically taking people down a very dark and dangerous road. The modern Pied Piper has ditched the pipe for a Smartphone.*

"Google executive chairman Eric Schmidt said in 2013 that the company could produce artificial intelligence within five to ten years that would be indistinguishable from the human mind, (the enslaved human mind, that is.) Schmidt is obsessed with the Transhumanist agenda, and has described concepts like sending a robotic clone of himself to social events and swallowing nano-technology to regulate his body. His desire for a society run by robots and Transhumanist technology is shared by so-called futurists such as Ray Kurzweil, who wants to see humans merged with machines and have a global society controlled by computer systems with an artificial intelligence that surpasses that of the entire human race, (the enslaved minds of the human race.) Kurzweil is the director of engineering at . . . Google."

And from Icke's earlier book, 'Human Race Get Off Your Knees:'

"We are now seeing 'eugenics: the final frontier,' with the emerging movement known as Transhumanism. This is developing and promoting various control technologies like microchips, brain chips, brain-computer interfaces, cyborgs and nano-technology. Its advocates talk of 'upgrading' the race by implanting more and more external technologies into the human body.

"The word 'Transhumanist' was first used by Julian Huxley, the eugenics fanatic. The Transhumanists push the benefits of improving health and intellect, but the real idea is to create a master race that is part-human and part-machine."

Anything that can be automated now is. Cars that drive themselves are now a physical reality. Robots are now replacing warehouse workers, and a standard joke in the DJ-ing industry is that human DJs won't be required in the not-too-distant future. In a world where cars modify their speed according to the volume of traffic their sensors detect around them, it surely won't be long before automated DJ systems intuit what tracks to play based on how busy its sensors detect the dancefloor to be. Maybe it won't all be so 'great' when large numbers of people can't get jobs any more on the grounds that a robot can get it done just as efficiently, and doesn't need pay, lunch breaks, sick days or holidays.

We now also have the obsession with 'Smart' everything, from phones to meters. The idea behind a 'smart' network is very sinister, with devices linked to each-other via an endless array of wi-fi networks, flooding the unseen morphogenic field in which we live with disruptive electro-magnetic frequencies, and all the while relaying surveillance data back to a central computer. The UK has now received the news that its first 'Smart' city to be configured in this way is to be Glasgow, and there are now announcements that a stretch of the M6 near Birmingham is to become its first 'smart motorway.' The only smart thing about anything with 'smart' in its name is to give it the widest berth possible. (It's worth noting that 'smart' has multiple meanings, too. As well as meaning 'clever', its dictionary definition is also given as "to be the cause of a sharp, stinging pain; as an irritating application, a blow, etc."

Ray Kurzweil has also predicted that humans, (if they can still realistically be described as such,) will even be able to have internet systems implanted into their heads so they can be organically attached to the worldwide web, and can surf it by way of thoughtwaves, with the results displayed on a small screen implanted into the cornea. The Google Glass invention, where being permanently and personally on-line was normalised, would appear to have been paving the way for this.

While Google frequently eulogises about Transhumanist technology, co-founder of the Apple Corporation, Steve Wozniak, appeared to take a more guarded view in a 2015 interview for the 'Australian Financial Review.' Apparently warning of the dangers of replacing humanity with Artificial Intelligence, he commented: 'Computers are going to take over from humans, no question. If we build these devices to take care of everything for us, eventually they'll think faster than us and they'll get rid of the slow humans to run companies more efficiently." The article goes on to quote Tesla Motors boss Elon Musk as stating that humans could be banned from driving in years to come, with cars instead controlled by robots. This gradual path is already being paved, with some cars now equipped with cameras and programmed to automatically telephone the Police in the event of an accident! The same article also tells of a hotel in China, Pengheng Space Capsules Hotel in Shenzhen, which is staffed and operated entirely by robots. The savings in staff costs apparently allow the hotel to offer rooms from as little as £6.80 a night.

While anyone who has maintained the capacity to think for themselves would surely reject the nightmare of a Transhumanist future, there
are still many who have been duped into a sense of awe at technological
advances, presented as they are with a 'wow!' factor attached. How else
to explain the apparent enthusiasm of Australians to voluntarily take an
RFID chip under their skin to make electronic payments, according to
a 2015 story from 'The Business Insider'?

> *"A mind-boggling 25% of Australians say they are at least 'slightly
> interested' at the prospect of having a chip implanted in their skin
> that could be used for payments, new research has found.*
>
> *"The research by credit card company Visa and the University of
> Technology Sydney, found Australians are open to the prospect of
> paying for items using wearable tech including smart watches, rings,
> glasses and even a connected car."*

Apparently, carrying a wallet or a couple of credit cards around has
become a real problem. Which is convenient for the controllers as it
has long been the plan to eventually ban cash payments in society, (a
move recently introduced in Sweden,) and to coerce the entire general
public into taking such chips. On this basis people will not be able to
pay for essential goods and services unless they are linked to a giant central computer via their unique electronic ID. Those whose first instinct
is to think of this as 'really cool' might like to reflect on what would
happen were they to somehow fall foul of the authorities, and have their
eligibility to pay for essential products and services switched off? They
might also like to picture a scenario where, should the Inland Revenue
or any other government department decide that you owe them money,
they can automatically deduct it from your account and deal with all
the questions later. (That's before you get into the technology where
radio signals can be transmitted via embedded chips to remotely alter
the brainwaves of the wearer, triggering emotional responses and mood
changes. Chemicals can also be remotely released into the bloodstream
by way of appropriately-configured chips.)

This hellish scenario can only transpire if people succumb to it
through their free will, however. The resources do not exist to forcibly

chip an entire world population if mass resistance is encountered. It's humanity's ultimate choice. I wonder what the choice will be?

The ugly face of the cashless society, along with biometrics, clashed spectacularly with the live music industry at the 2015 Download rock festival in Leicestershire, England. The event's organisers had already raised significant concerns over their decision to introduce facial recognition scanning for customers, citing the tried-and-tested justification of 'reducing crime', (they really would be in trouble without that one to fall back on, wouldn't they?)

They then added insult to injury by announcing a cashless payment system for festival-goers, who would have to load credit in advance on to electronic wristbands known as 'dog tags,' (much slave symbolism there?), then have these scanned by a network of electronic readers all over the site. The organisers crowed proudly that "not only will it reduce queues for the bar and food stalls, it removes the faff of cash and makes security on-site even tighter." This is the exact blueprint for the cashless society that the elites want for nations at large, and Download would appear to have been a dry-run experiment, with the attendees as unwitting guinea-pigs, all the while paying for their own experimentation. Given what we've learned about how the dark controllers love their symbolism, I guess we shouldn't be too surprised that the Download logo advertising the wristbands shows a red devil's hand surrounded by fire flashing the Baphomet/ horned hand symbol, with a blue wristband in place. There may be optimism to be gained from the fact that the payment system was a monumental failure, however, with punters branding it 'useless,' 'a farce' and 'a complete joke.' Attendees complained of being forced to queue for hours for entry, to buy food and drink, to check their balances and to top up their credit.

There were similar glitches just a few weeks later with the cashless top-up system at the Digital Dreams Festival in Toronto. Notice how both events' names have electronic/ computer-related overtones.

The 'Daily Mail' reported that European festivals have been using electronic wristbands for years, beginning with the Eurosonic Noorderslag Festival in the Netherlands in 2012. Glastonbury boss Michael Eavis is said to have briefly considered the idea, but feared the technology would attract many external companies making it 'too commercial.'

Auto-Pain

All of which brings us right back around to Auto-Tune, and the *real* reason it's been so enthusiastically adopted by the corporate music industry. It can't be down to just how great it sounds, after all. I've asked countless DJs and musicians their opinions on the sound, and have yet to receive one comment praising it. A rolling of the eyes and a stream of profanities is the usual reaction.

Just like the techniques described in our earlier chapters, it's all targeted at the suggestive subconscious mind—in this case, to bring about a more ready acceptance of human-electronic hybridization by making the merging of the two seem completely normal.

In the past, Auto-Tune has been confused with an earlier vocal synthesis system known as a vocoder, most popularly associated with the musician Roger Troutman of the funk group Zapp. British producer Linslee Campbell once demonstrated to me the vocoder's workings when related to the human voice. He had a type of harmonica in his mouth, connected to an electronic keyboard. He then spoke into the vocoder and used the keys to manipulate the resulting sound. This is the crucial difference between vocoders and Auto-Tune; the former at least still involves a degree of creative human control!

It's unlikely that Hildebrand and his Antares company created Auto-Tune with any malevolent form of usage in mind, and more feasible that his creation was seized upon to be incorporated into the Transhumanist mind game. Hildebrand is quoted as saying "we never thought anyone in their right mind would do that" in response to how Auto-Tune was utilised on the Cher record. He did appear to get with the programme later on though, by announcing a new software programme named Throat Evo. This, according to the Antares website, "processes voices through a meticulously crafted physical model of the human vocal tract," and "allows the creation of vocal tract models well beyond the limits of physical human anatomy, offering the possibility of vocal characteristics that are simply unattainable by any other means."

I'd suggest they should remain unattained then. But that's just me.

Following the Cher hit, little more was heard of Auto-Tune in popular music until several years later. In 2005, an artist emerged on the so-called 'hip-hop' scene by the name of T-Pain, (I suspect the 'T' stands for 'tinnitus.') His debut album, 'Rappa Ternt Sanga', utilised the technology to full effect, notably on the first two singles, 'I'm Sprung' and 'I'm In Love With A Stripper'. It became T-Pain's trademark sound to the point that everything he has ever released incorporates it, and he has become truly synonymous with the effect, even to the point of boldly suggesting he should be paid royalties whenever the technique is used. In 2009 he collaborated on an iPhone app entitled 'I Am T-Pain' with the manufacturer Smule, allowing users to re-create his vocal 'style' for karaoke purposes.

Breaking through around the same time was the singer/ rapper Akon, who claims the dubious distinction of having 'discovered' T-Pain. Akon flooded songs from his second and third albums, 'Konvicted' and 'Freedom,' with the sound, as well as a novelty excursion from his first album, entitled 'Lonely,' which truly has to be heard to be believed. Within months, Auto-Tune was cropping up on the majority of hits in the pop music and 'hip-hop/ R&B' fields, including output from Flo Rida, Ke$ha, Pitbull, Will.I.Am, Black Eyed Peas, David Guetta, Chris Brown, Usher, Ne-yo, Lil' Wayne, Drake, Snoop Dogg, Kanye West, Taio Cruz and Jennifer Lopez to name but a few, (and all those in 2008 alone!) In more recent years, it has become worryingly present in the output of prominent reggae-dancehall artists. It also entered the British consciousness through 'talent' (it says here) show 'The X Factor' in 2010, when producers admitted to having used the effect on the performances of certain entrants to improve their sound. In what was more likely a publicity stunt than anything else, show boss Simon Cowell then imposed a ban on its use in future episodes.

Stories even emerged of hopeful young girls auditioning at 'talent' contests and actually making their voices sound like they'd had Auto-Tune applied, such was their idea of what it takes to have a hit record in these times.

There have been attempts to justify Auto-Tune's use as a form of creative expression. But many of the comments turn out to be quite revealing in light of the *real* purpose for its over-saturation.

The US DJ and producer Jayce Clayton, known alternatively as DJ/ rupture, writes:

"The plug-in creates a different relation of voice-to-machine than ever before ... Auto-Tune operates as a duet between the electronics and the personal."

He added, with possible irony: "As such, it becomes quite humanizing." (!)

And could author, academic and Professor of Black Popular Culture, Mark Anthony Neal, have been dropping a knowing clue when he commented on Lil' Wayne's use of Auto-Tune by saying: "his slurs, blurs, bleeps and blushes of his vocals, index some variety of trauma."? (Readers who may have missed the chapter on the workings of trauma-based mind control are encouraged to go back and check it out!)

Singer Michael Bublé, meanwhile, probably didn't realise the relevance of his vocabulary when he criticised Auto-Tune as making everyone sound the same and "like robots."

Ludovic Hunter-Tilney, writing for the UK's 'Financial Times' during Auto-Tune's explosion in 2008, also nailed it—and was probably equally unaware of the prophetic potency of his words. Reviewing Britney Spears' album 'Circus,' he observed:

"Her heavily-produced voice, as if responding to the turn of a dial, slides from natural-sounding coos to robotically-distorted chirps. In the course of a single song she morphs between flesh-and-blood Britney and automated Britney so seamlessly and frequently, that we grow unsure of the difference. With the all-too-human foibles of her breakdown-prone personal life acting as a backdrop, it makes for a dazzling display of technological enhancement."

He went on to make a reference to "Spears' Android drone."

An album that stands as a showcase of how the Auto-Tune sound can be used to discordant effect is Kanye West's '808s & Heartbreak.' By the time this was released in 2008, Kanye's music had already been degraded and debased beyond hope. The album was released in the wake of the sudden death of his beloved mother, Donda, to whom Kanye was famously close, (he had dedicated the track 'Hey Mama' on his 'Late Registration' album to her,) and his break-up from fiancee Alexis Phifer. '808s' was said to be a kind of cathartic release for

Kanye's grief. It certainly showed in the set's downbeat and unsettling feel, which didn't go un-noticed by critics.

Jody Rosen writing for 'Rolling Stone' magazine, observed:

> "Kanye can't really sing in the classic sense, but he's not trying to. T-Pain taught the world that Auto-Tune doesn't just sharpen flat notes: it's a painterly device for enhancing vocal expressiveness, and upping the pathos . . . Kanye's digitized vocals are the sound of a man so stupefied by grief, he's become less than human."

An interesting choice of phrase within the overall context of this book's story.

Those who know

The Transhumanist plans—and specifically those of the microchipping agenda—have not gone undocumented by some of music's more awakened artists—those *not* owned lock, stock and barrel by corporations who dictate their every move, that is. A brilliant interpretation, with a cracking video to match, came from the British musician Imani Hekima on his song 'Just Beneath the Skin'. Here's the Youtube link—https://www.YouTube.com/watch?v=HE9wbbmQWAM

I can remember back in the mid-90s hearing Rastafarians commenting on microchips and barcodes as being 'the mark of the beast' at the hands of the 'Babylon System.' Back then in my walking sleep-state I had no idea what they meant. In recent years it's become all too clear. The only question remaining is how they had so much knowledge of the plan in the years before the internet. According to many, Jamaicans possess a spiritual connectedness to higher consciousness, which is amplified by their regular smoking of cannabis, and this allows them to channel great truths into their minds.

Similarly, there's a reason why technology is referred to untrustingly as 'tricknology' in hip-hop slang, as exemplified by Jeru Tha Damaja on his tracks 'Can't Stop The Prophet' and 'Revenge Of The Prophet.' In these, various concepts are metaphorically presented as comic book-style super-villains that the hero, The Black Prophet, must combat. Besides Ignorance, Hatred, Jealousy, Envy, Anger, Despair, Animosity and

Deceit stands Tricknology. As conveyed in 'Revenge Of The Prophet:' "Fightin' ignorance everyday, it's gettin' weary. When I think I got him he pulls a slip on me. And there's so many soldiers in his fiendish-ass army. One of the fiercest, is this nigga named Tricknology."

(The track ends with the promising words, "to be continued..." This was in 1996, however, and 20 years on we're still waiting! Either way, the lyrics to these tracks truly convey the potency of *real* rap music to inspire, educate and uplift when in the hands of a responsible and intelligent lyricist, and are about as far from the content of mainstream 'hip-hop' output of the past ten years or more as it's possible to get!)

The British rapper Nate expanded on this on a 2013 track, itself entitled 'Tricknology,' with lyrics like:

"iPads and iPods, forever got your eyes locked on screens that's HD,

Entertainment as a mind fog,

Tapping Blackberries while you're walking,

Arthritis of the hands will have you shaking."

"8 million megahertz of frequencies are passing you,

Better use the eye of consciousness to see you fucking through."

"So don't get caught up in the World Wide Web

Understand why it's called the interNET."

The subjects of hip-hop and Transhumanism found common ground in a 2014 interview by BJ Murphy with two New York MCs by the names of MC Kilch and Maitreya One. The artists appeared to be openly advocating the elites' agenda at first glance, with Kilch stating:

"I would like to see more emcees making music that utilizes Transhumanist thinking, or speaks about concepts such as the Technological Singularity, but I don't think that hip-hop has a duty to promote such."

Maitreya One then appears to offer a more compassionate and human take on the subject by saying:

"Hip-hop's duty is to show the proper use of technology, which is to be used in a humane way, not just to uphold a social order that oppresses and divides us. Hip-hop sees technology's ability to free us from the mundane work-a-day schedule that limits our freedom and holds our bodies captive to a corrupt monetary system that enslaves us. Hip-hop's version of the Technological Singularity is all-inclusive and puts humanity first."

However, the waters then get muddied again when you read that Maitreya cites J Edgar Hoover, the founding director of the FBI, as one of her influences, and praises the covert and illegal COINTEL-PRO programme that he brought in. Then, at the end of the interview, she gives a respectful shout-out to the aforementioned Ray Kurzweil of Google. Whether they're in on an agenda or simply confused, therefore, remains in question, You can read the interview here:

- http://ieet.org/index.php/IEET/more/murphy20140502

Wanted dead or alive

There is a kind of visual variation on Auto-Tune, and it first came to public view in 2012 when a life-size hologram of slain rapper 2Pac was paraded at the Coachella Festival in California, 'performing' alongside a flesh-and-blood Snoop Dogg and Dr. Dre. According to Nick Smith, president of San Diego-based AV Concepts, it took his company four months to create the hologram, at a cost at least $100,000. The idea is said to have come from Dr. Dre himself. Smith boasted about how his company was able to recreate long-dead figures and visually recreate them in the studio: "You can take their likenesses and voice and . . . take people that haven't done concerts before or perform music they haven't sung and digitally recreate it." He also justified the massive cost of producing the hologram by pointing out that it still worked out far cheaper than having to transport a real-life performer around a multitude of venues on tour. Why am I getting flashbacks of the British dark comedy starring Rik Mayall entitled 'Bring Me The Head Of Mavis Davis,' in which a record company owner decides one of his fading stars is worth more to him dead than alive, and plots to kill her in order to pay off his debts? The 2Pac hologram itself was even given its own Twitter page, attracting more than 3,300 followers. Sorry . . . did I mention that the world is insane?

A couple of years later, the 2014 Billboard Music Awards featured a life-size hologram of Michael Jackson in performance, five years after his ritual sacrif . . . sorry, tragic accidental death at the hands of his physician. The technology for this one used an illusory technique dating back to the 16th century, involving mirrors and known as 'Pepper's Ghost,' but like the 2Pac creation, it was said to have taken several months to prepare, and at a similar cost. The MJ hologram 'performed' the song 'Slave To The Rhythm,' (much pertinence to that title?) from his second posthumous album, 'Xscape.' The song was recorded for the 1991 album 'Black & White,' but didn't make the final selection. Do you think there could have been a reason for that?

Call me old-fashioned but I can't help thinking that if the industry didn't kill off its artists, then it could continue to put the real thing on stage rather than needing to create a hologram, but hey, that's just me. To be fair, though, I should mention that the industry doesn't always wait until its artists are dead and buried before making holograms. At the 2006 Grammy Awards, a flesh-and-blood Madonna performed with digitally-projected cartoon members of the Gorillaz. Holograms of Celine Dion and The Black Eyed Peas have also 'performed,' though I'm unsure how you'd ever tell the difference in the case of the latter.

Stooge.he.is

Black Eyed Peas frontman Will.i.am stands as a text-book example of an artist corrupted by the industry machine and co-opted to help push its Transhumanist psy-op. His very name reads like a web address, (as does that of fellow group member apl.de.ap,) and it wouldn't surprise me if his trademark haircut, with a corner chunk cut out, is meant to symbolise a section of his mind that's been lobotomised. This is certainly the effect that his 'music' is designed to have on the masses.

The group, and i.am in particular, became very useful to the agenda once their music had been firmly shifted from the credible hip-hop sound of their 1998 album 'Behind The Front,' into the brainless tripe they were producing by the time of their fourth album 'Monkey Business,' with mind-numbing bile like 'My Humps' and 'Pump It.'

We'll get more into how this process has been repeated time and time again—and with the Black Eyed Peas as an example—in the later chapter on The Systematic Degeneration Of Hip-Hop Culture.

More than most, i.am's image for the past several years has been made deliberately evocative of a robot/ cyborg. This is reflected in his own vocal style on record, (Auto-Tune overload,) and in tracks he has produced for other manipulated puppets such as Flo Rida. Emphasis has been put on explicitly digital/ electronic production styles.

BEP videos have also been laden with robot/ cyborg imagery. A detailed analysis on the Vigilant Citizen website by contributor LVB in 2010 went into this, highlighting in particular the song and video to 'Imma Be.' In terms of the title, this is generally taken to be a street-slang way of saying 'I'm going to be.' Given the blatant symbolism of the video, however, LVB speculates that the real meaning of this could be 'I'm a bee,' as in, an expression of the hive-mind mentality and The Singularity of which Ray Kurzweil speaks so enthusiastically. The same video makes use of the tune 'Rock That Body,' which, the article suggests, could be an alternative expression for improve, or upgrade that body by way of artificial implants.

VC's article picks up the story of how the video's overall theme is set:

> "Will.i.am tells everyone he has something cool to show them, and he busts out one of those high-tech aluminium CIA-type briefcases and opens it up. The other Peas ask what it is, and he tells them that it is a machine with artificial intelligence, (AI,) that will sample your voice and allow you to just type in the lyrics and it will 'do all the singing, talking, rapping.' He says that it is the future and it is what will take the Peas into 3008 . . . which is kind of funny, and very optimistic as far as being able to live that long without some kind of radical technology.

> "This false 'reality' scene continues with another BEP asking Will if this means that he won't actually be rapping in the studio any more, and Will explains that, no, he won't be doing the rapping because the machine will do it all, which Will thinks is very cool.

"Then Fergie gets really mad and puts on a big drama-queen display. She says 'it will take the soul out of it' and 'it's not real,' and finally she says, 'we're not robots!', and leaves the room pissed off."

As the video progresses, subtle visual touches include dancing robots, a graveyard of broken machine parts and signs advertising beer. It could have been any brand in the world, but it *just happens* to be TuBORG. VC breaks down how aspects of human/ machine hybridization being presented as a liberating thing for humanity, are contrasted with those in which it is conveyed with a terrible, doom-laden foreboding, leading to extreme cognitive dissonance on the part of any confused viewer under its spell.

This is just one example of the Will.i.am/ Black Eyed Peas involvement in pushing Transhumanist ideas. In a much-hyped publicity stunt, in 2012, i.am.'s single 'Reach For The Stars' was reportedly released from NASA's Mars Curiosity Rover. As reported by researcher Isaac Weishaupt on the Illuminati Watcher website at the time:

"The quote he provided is quite telling if you look at it from this more sinister viewpoint. If you read it from the view that he is secretly trying to implant the idea that it is acceptable to merge the power of technology into our body and become a Transhumanistic cyborg, then you can see how all of the symbolism found in their videos also helps push the propaganda.

"This is about inspiring young people to lead a life without limits placed on their potential and to pursue collaboration between humanity and technology,' will.i.am said."

Further blurring of the lines between the natural and the artificial, comes from the increasing proliferation of CGI (Computer-Generated Imagery) in the majority of Hollywood movies and in many TV shows. Decades ago, challenging and difficult scenes in movies had to actually be carried out physically by cast and crew, (see William Friedkin's 'Sorcerer' or Werner Herzog's 'Aguirre: Wrath Of God' for two great examples!) Now, some techno-boffin in a darkened lab is given a brief and a salary, and scenes that used to bear some semblance to physical reality appear by magic with a few clicks of a mouse. I'm sure most will also have noticed how airbrushed and photo-shopped magazine covers make their subjects look like plastic dolls rather than real flesh-and-blood humans. All part of the dark mind-control games to allow artificiality to become acceptable and familiar within the general public's psyche.

Making tyranny 'cool'

These scenes tie in with another trend in the popular music videos of recent years. As well as subtle suggestions of Transhumanist elements, an unfeasible number of A-list promos have featured depictions of a militarized Police state in what is always described in prophetic Hollywood movies as a 'dystopian future.' Police and military, often portrayed in the form of cyborgs, are frequently seen interacting with the artists in choreographed scenes. In most cases, of course, the lyrical content of the song bears no relevance to the scenes being acted out on the screen, but the chance to deeply embed certain images into the collective consciousness—accompanied by a catchy hook to make them more palatable—is too good an opportunity for the demented psychopaths to resist. In many countries—the US in particular—the Police have been getting slowly more militarized every year, and there has been a specific drive to recruit psychopathic thugs to the profession, to the point that many officers who joined the force with the genuine aim of 'making a difference' are leaving in their droves. Stories of US Police criminals executing people for crimes such as being homeless or selling cigarettes on the street now come weekly. The outcome is always the same. Despite the apparent 'investigation,' and the frequent availability of video evidence that should convict the perpetrators of murder, every officer walks free with no more than a temporary suspension.

Standard-issue uniform is now all-black, (one of the colours associated with Saturn,) and the assorted accessories that the Police now sport, from shields to helmets to body padding, already gives them the appearance of robots. A 'them and us' society, with 'them' protected by armies of violent, unthinking thugs, is precisely the type of future the social architects have in their plans for 'us.' They would argue that it's not like they didn't announce their intentions in advance. We're just supposed to know that they've done it by way of the latest Beyonce or Rihanna video.

Singularity ladies

One of the biggest pop-R&B hits of the past decade is Beyonce's 'Single Ladies,' a song that has been adopted by women the world over as an anthem of female strength and empowerment. The hookline berates the man in question for not 'putting a ring on it.' He apparently should have shown his commitment to his woman by spending a large chunk of his corporate salary on an engagement ring, and now he's lost her as a result. Right on, sister!

Some time afterwards, however, American musicologist and researcher Lenon Honor stunned many—myself included—when he presented an in-depth analysis of the true purpose of the song's accompanying video. As usual, the on-screen imagery is largely at odds with the lyrical content of the record. The video features Beyonce performing various eye-catching dance routines, flanked by a dancer on either side mimicking her moves. Lenon elaborated in the 'Good Vibrations' interview I did with him in 2013:

> "That song and video went viral, and oftentimes, the social engineering that takes place is global . . . There were people dressing up as Beyonce, and they would have two other dancers that would dress up too, and they would memorise the dance. They would also have their children do it, scantily-dressed, and record them. Little girls doing these very provocative dances. Also males! Males would be doing the same thing. This provides a level of programming, because it's not just mind-control programming, it's also body control. In other words, you can actually programme someone by having them reproduce physical movements, and when these become a repetition, these can also access the subconscious mind."

Lenon points out that throughout the video, Beyonce is wearing a robotic sleeve on her left arm and hand. Although it's right there in plain sight, evoking the merging of the human body with cyborg machinery, it can still go un-noticed given the distraction of the intricate dancing.

At the very end, though, she holds the arm up and strokes it, before making the fingers zing and laughing. Oh it's such *fun*, this Transhumanist stuff!

Viewers are left with a comfortable familiarity with the scenario being depicted. It doesn't matter that they're not consciously aware of it. It's the same concept as when someone hears a piece of major news, but a while later, couldn't tell you what the source was. The only really important thing is that they now know it, and its potency has been firmly supplanted in their mind.

At other times, Beyonce has appeared on stage as a robot, strongly resembling the one featured in Fritz Lang's 1926 movie 'Metropolis,' which was astoundingly spot-on almost 100 years ago in its depiction of the type of technologically-governed 'them and us' society we see unfolding by the day. Kylie Minogue, Nicki Minaj and Michael Jackson have worn similar robotic garb. Miley Cyrus even released a single entitled 'Robot,' in which she is pictured as a mutilated cyborg/ human hybrid on the sleeve.

Beyonce–and the so-called 'R&B' scene of the 2000s–have been useful to the Transhumanist agenda at other times, too. The title of her 2006 song 'Upgrade U,' further pushes the message, and there's little room for confusion with Chris Brown's 'I Can Transform You' from 2008, either, complete with its screeching electronic production and robotic voices. 50 Cent and Justin Timberlake got on the bandwagon, (through coercion, no doubt,) with 2007's 'Ayo Technology.'

Nas was foreshadowing a world he must have had advance knowledge of as far back as 1999 on his track 'New World' (interesting choice of title?) from the 'Nastradamus' album. The closing line: "I might be old-fashioned, stuck in my ways, but nothing makes me more happy than seeing today," suggests a celebration of how wonderful it is that technology has come so far. But other lyrics such as: "while the poor people starve, computers takin' over they jobs," and: "you got CD-Rom, everything operates by computers. Then what happens when circuit breaks?" present a conflicting message.

In the electronic music realm, meanwhile, Daft Punk's song 'Harder, Bigger, Faster, Stronger' leaves little to the imagination in terms of what it is espousing–especially as the duo frequently depict themselves as cyborgs, and their trademark sound consists of robotised vocals over digital beats. The song's video shows four people being 'improved through mechanisation.' The group have also performed stage shows from inside of a pyramid complete with illuminated capstone. This song was later sampled by Kanye West for his track 'Stronger' with its hookline 'that that don't kill me will only make me stronger,' a key part of the process of shifting the sound of 'hip-hop' ever further away from sample-based analogue beats into the electronic realm.

More of that next as the journey continues.

Resources:

Website/ biography of Professor Kevin Warwick of Reading University:

- http://www.kevinwarwick.com/

Music video: Imani Hekima: Just Beneath The Skin:

- https://www.YouTube.com/watch?v=HE9wbbmQWAM

Rolling Stone Magazine review of Kanye West's '808s & Heartbreak.':

- http://www.rollingstone.com/music/
  albumreviews/808s-heartbreak-20081211

The Financial Times: Changing the parameters of pop by Ludovic Hunter-Tilney:

- http://www.ft.com/cms/s/0/bf9b9a96-bcdc-11dd-af5a-
  0000779fd18c.html#axzz3VEZkYdLn

Throat Evo, by Antares Audio Technologies:

- http://www.antarestech.com/products/detail.
  php?product=THROAT_Evo_14

Nate Featuring Dark Matter: 'Tricknology' (with lyrics):

- https://www.YouTube.com/watch?v=RghsWi6uRa0

Hip-hop and Transhumanism: An Interview with M.C. Kilch and Maitreya One:

- http://ieet.org/index.php/IEET/more/murphy20140502

MTV News: Tupac Coachella Hologram Source Explains How Rapper Resurrected:

- http://www.mtv.com/news/1683173/tupac-hologram-coachella/

Michael Jackson 'not a hologram' at Billboard Music Awards:

- http://www.google.co.uk/url?q=http://www.smh.com.au/
  entertainment/music/michael-jackson-not-a-hologram-
  at-billboard-music-awards-2014-20140522-zrl63.
  html&sa=U&ei=JIkVVYinPMnYat-wgsAK&ved=0CCYQFjAG
  &usg=AFQjCNFgc72H7s8CfbTTVSA93Faseez1pg

Beyonce's 'Single Ladies' video:

- https://www.YouTube.com/watch?v=4m1EFMoRFvY

Vigilant Citizen: Transhumanism, PsyWar and B.E.P.'s "Imma Be":

- http://vigilantcitizen.com/musicbusiness/
  Transhumanism-psychological-warfare-and-b-e-p-s-imma-be/

The Transhumanist and Police State Agenda in Pop Music:

- http://vigilantcitizen.com/musicbusiness/
  the-Transhumanist-and-Police-state-agenda-in-pop-music/

Illuminati Watcher: William Continues Secret Agenda for Transhumanism:

- http://illuminatiwatcher.com/
  will-i-am-continues-secret-agenda-for-transhumanism/

Exposing The Matrix: Transhumanism Symbolism:

- http://exposingthematrix.blogspot.co.uk/2012/04/
  transhumanism-symbolism.html

SHTFPlan.com: Trendies Ready for Ultimate Wearable: "Chip Implanted in Their Skin Used for Payments":

- http://www.shtfplan.com/headline-news/trendies-ready-for-
  ultimate-wearable-chip-implanted-in-their-skin-used-for-
  payments_06012015

CHAPTER 14

THE SYSTEMATIC DEGENERATION
OF HIP-HOP CULTURE

From the cream of the crop to the dregs of the cesspit.

"Call it 'black radio'? Don't make me laugh! So is black music all about tits and arse?
    Akala:' Find No Enemy' (2011)

"If you got 22s spinning on your hooptie,
If you got paid and you spent it on a new chain,
If you got Kanye bumping on your two-way,
You've been sipping on some heavy, heavy Koolaid."
    Alais Clay Featuring Payday Monsanto: 'Heavy Koolaid' (2012)

"Uh, . . . we notice you talk about a lot of religious, political, raise up the blacks-type subject matter . . . Nothing wrong with that, don't get me wrong. It's just, if you could kinda tone it down, maybe, a little bit . . . not talk so much about Farrakhan and Al Sharpton and guys like that, and .. If you could do that I see you really making a splash in the mainstream, and on the major radio stations and video networks. Don't you wanna go double-platinum, K? Well, we could make that happen, guy. I mean, get you some nice, friendly production, a few wardrobe adjustments here and there, and bang! You'll be wearing a K-Rino chain in no time! Waddya say? All you gotta do is sign here."
    K-Rino: 'Solitary Confinement' LP opening skit (2009)

In 1993, one of the biggest hip-hop records of the year, to be heard in clubs and on radio stations the world over, was KRS One's 'Sound Of Da Police', a scathing reflection on the modern police force as a contemporary representation of the slavery system in America. Its lyrics included:

"You hotshot, wanna get props and be a saviour?

First show a little respect in your behaviour,

Change your attitude, change your plan,

There could never really be justice on stolen land."

In 2013, one of the biggest hip-hop (it says here) records of the year, to be heard in clubs and on radio stations the world over, was Big Sean's 'Ass' featuring Nicki Minaj. It's a song about a girl with a big ass. Its lyrics included:

"Ass, ass, ass, ass, ass, ass, ass,

Ass, ass, ass, ass, ass, ass, ass,

Stop . . . now make that motherfucker hammer time like,

Go stupid, go stupid, go stupid."

(Is it just coincidence that the 'go stupid, go stupid' hook-line also appears in a separate song from Lil' Wayne, 'My Homies Still,' or is there a message of instruction being sent to the fans here?)
    And later:

"Wobbledy wobble, wo-wo-wobble, wobbin,'

Ass so fat, all these bitches' pussies is throbbin.'

I can think of no better example of the slow-drip debasement of a once-meaningful art-form, into a retarded caricature of its former self over the course of 20 years, than to compare the type of lyrical content that was getting unleashed through the genre then and now. For anyone who might suggest that these are two extreme examples, I would challenge them to find me a mainstream hip-hop record from the past ten years–by which I mean one that was on heavy mainstream radio and TV rotation and released through one of the main corporate labels–which dealt with *anything* other than these general subject areas:

- Having promiscuous sex

- Partying in the club

- Throwing wads of cash in the air

- Girls with fat asses

- A rapper's superior financial status over his or her peers

- The possession of gold rims, chains or other paraphernalia

- The acquisition of high-fashion clothing, alcohol or jewellery brands

- Gun crime

- Selling large quantities of drugs

- Having more sex

The only one that springs to mind for me is Lupe Fiasco's 'Words I Never Said', and you can read more about this particular artist and record in the next chapter!

Has this transition come as the inevitable result of a genre's 'progress' or mutation over an extended period, in response to natural market forces, and reflecting random changes in society and attitudes? Is it just taking the easy option towards vast profits by stripping its lyrical content down to the basest form to appeal to the widest possible demographic? Or has it occurred at the hands of an insidious agenda to subvert a powerful art-form and turn it into immoral, toxic filth as a way of brainwashing a naive new generation of consumers who, with such a long passage of time, will have no recollection of the original values that this genre once stood for?

Before we attempt to answer the question, have another lyrical compare-and-contrast. This is from Nonchalant's 'Five 'O Clock' from 1995:

"Well, Mr. Black Man, tell me where you're heading,

The last few years I watched while you were shedding,

Pounds and pounds of growth from the population,

Soon we won't be able to have a strong black nation,

A shooting here, a stabbing there, when will it stop?

'Cause now you're dying from the dose of the crack rock,

I'm just a Nubian Queen that needs a king to stand strong,

And try to press on."

Now, please enjoy the lyrical wisdom of Lil' Wayne on 2013's 'Million Dollar Pussy':

"If you hating, you just need some pussy,

She fucked up when she gave me some pussy,

Say, 'I fuck you better than that other nigga,'

She say Tune, 'I'm 'bout to cum', I say, 'I'm cumming with ya,'

And she don't like them pretty niggas, diddy niggas,

She ride this dick, her titties jiggle,

That's my pillows."

Shall we move on?

Mark Devlin

The metaphysics of hip-hop

Why should it be that the dark priest-class should have set its sights on hip-hop? As ever, financial considerations will have played a part, but it's far from the whole story. The fact that the corporates have been able to make a killing out of the debasement and commercialisation of hip-hop is a secondary factor to the real likely motivation.

In 2005, the writer, lecturer and MC known as Black Dot released his landmark book 'Hip Hop Decoded—From Its Ancient Origin To Its Modern Day Matrix.' In it, he proposed that there are spiritual and metaphysical components to hip-hop, with strong links to the ancestral history of black cultures. The aspect that most instantly think of is the rap element, which was largely derived from the spoken-word poetry traditions that preceded it, from the likes of Gil Scott-Heron and The Last Poets. (Check out their 'E Pluribus Unum' for the lowdown on the New World Order and the imagery on the US dollar bill from way back in 1973, the same year that DJ Kool Herc is acknowledged as hosting the very first hip-hop block parties.) The remaining elements of the art-form are equally important components, however—B-boying, or 'breaking,' turntablism and graffiti art.

These four fundamental elements, Black Dot proposes, have their origin in four aspects of African culture that were in place centuries before the first slaves were taken to the shores of America. They represent, respectively, the oracle, the dancer, the drummer and hieroglyphics, and combine to form the foundation of the fifth element, which is Knowledge Of Self. These traits lay embedded within the spirit and the psyche of Africans, Dot explains, and were resurrected in The Bronx when hip-hop culture was born from the roots of these earlier traditions. Pioneering artists such as Kool Herc, Afrika Bambaataa, Grandmaster Flash and Grand Wizard Theodore were channelling these ancestral spirits, and applying them to a new generation in a new place and time.

Black Dot expanded on his observations in a podcast interview with me, marking the tenth anniversary of his book's release:

> *"I think the environment was right to bring this about. And these guys were not trying to change reality. They couldn't hold it any more, so they just became the vessels in which the spirit took physical form*

290

and utilised them to bring forth a culture that is the biggest one in the world today. So in my book I make sure I honour them, because they were the first doers, as we say . . . Grand Wizard said this book changed his life, Kool Moe Dee said it's the greatest book he ever read. Afrika Bambaataa said something very similar, because no-one had put them in the proper perspective of their contributions."

As Public Enemy's Professor Griff remarked when expanding upon this principle in one of his lectures:

"We set the hip-hop thing in motion and gave birth to something everyone is affected by. Everyone that comes into music has to contemplate whether or not they're going to deal with the vibration of hip-hop—Higher Infinite Power Healing Our People.

"So in The Bronx, when we gave birth to this vibratory frequency . . . it set something in motion. And during this particular time, those trains that went out, the tracks were like veins in the black community. Then brothers took them spray cans and tagged them trains. Put their hieroglyphs on there and we read it. Something was going on. A baby was born in The Bronx that we needed to bring the gifts to. And it roared out of The Bronx. You can't help it now; the cat is out of the bag. Everyone's been affected by it."

These elements can also be seen to be artistic expressions of the four principal elements inherent in the natural world—earth, air, fire and water, which themselves combine to complement the fifth element of spirit. It is these components that are represented by the five points of the pentagram, an important symbol in occultic circles, with the spirit element pointing upwards. This is why satanists invert the pentagram, to have the spirit element pointing downwards, relegating it to base consciousness status, as far removed from higher spiritual awareness as it's possible to get. (These elements also make an integral appearance in the plotline of Dan Brown's 'Angels And Demons' novel and its Tom Hanks-starring film.

Black Dot's lectures and videos on this subject, available on Youtube, come highly recommended for further understanding of the concepts being conveyed.

The intuitive awakening of these traditions within this beautiful new art-form, and the uplifting effect it was having on black communities, would not have gone un-noticed by the dark controllers. Sure enough, the infiltration intended to debase and degrade its spiritual potency began.

The tactics used were similar to those applied to Rhythm & Blues and Rock & Roll before it, and any number of 'urban' music genres since. Time and time again, the corporates take a beautiful and creative art-form that had evolved naturally, and seek to corrupt it. They can't stand not being in control. The trouble is, in their own machine-minds, they have no creative abilities or imaginations of their own. So they use scientifically-designed blueprints and templates and, once they have completely dominated a genre by throwing huge amounts of money at it to buy everyone out, they unleash all subsequent product according to these formulae. That's why all output from that point forward sounds like completely artificial constructs, devoid of artistic love and passion. Real music fans can tell the difference between a track that was put out because the corporations just wanted to make a whole load of money and keep an agenda going, versus one that was produced because the music-maker genuinely had a message that they wanted to communicate to the world through their art, and they managed to put it out undiluted.

Murder, he wrote

In 2012, a letter started circulating heavily in the hip-hop press, purporting to have been written by a former executive with one of the big music corporations in the US. The writer didn't give his name, but claimed to have been present at a meeting at a private residence in Los Angeles in early 1991, along with representatives from the other big record labels of the time, where the future direction of rap music was on the agenda. This was the spawning of the genre which came to be known as 'gangsta rap.' Also present at the meeting, the writer said, were a small group of individuals that nobody else recognised. Before the meeting commenced, everyone present was required to sign a confidentiality contract, with those that refused being asked to leave.

As the meeting progressed, the guests identified themselves as representatives of the US private prison industry. They outlined a plan in which they invited the major music corporations to work with them on reshaping the lyrical identity of the hip-hop genre, which by then was already proving itself to be a powerful and highly profitable market force. The record labels' job, they were told, would be to systematically change the lyrics going into records, and to shape and mould the image of the artists, the aim being to modify the behaviour of young black males based on the type of lifestyle they heard being propagated by their idols. The resulting crime waves would, in turn, lead to dramatically-increased numbers of inmates filling privately-owned prisons, bringing colossal shares in the resulting profits for all parties concerned. As the letter outlines:

> *"We were told that these prisons were built by privately-owned companies who received funding from the government based on the number of inmates. The more inmates, the more money the government would pay these prisons. It was also made clear to us that since these prisons are privately-owned, as they became publicly traded, we'd be able to buy shares."*

The writer states that he and three others, who by this point were disgusted by what they were hearing and wanted no part in it, were forcibly removed from the house at gunpoint and reminded that they had signed a gagging agreement. The writer says that he battled with his conscience for over 20 years, but finally decided that he could no longer keep the secret and felt the need to share his story with the world.

The letter continues:

> *"As the months passed, rap music had definitely changed direction. I was never a fan of it, but even I could tell the difference. Rap acts that talked about politics or harmless fun were quickly fading away as 'gangsta rap' started dominating the airwaves. Only a few months had passed since the meeting, but I suspect that the ideas presented that day had been successfully implemented. It was as if the order had*

been given to all major label executives. The music was climbing the charts, and most companies were more than happy to capitalize on it. Each one was churning out their very own 'gangsta rap' acts on an assembly line. Everyone bought into it, consumers included. Violence and drug use became a central theme in most rap music. I spoke to a few of my peers in the industry to get their opinions on the new trend, but was told repeatedly that it was all about supply and demand. Sadly, many of them even expressed that the music reinforced their prejudice of minorities.

"... Now that I have a greater understanding of how private prisons operate, things make much more sense than they ever have. I see how the criminalization of rap music played a big part in promoting racial stereotypes, and misguided so many impressionable young minds into adopting these glorified criminal behaviours which often lead to incarceration.

You can read the letter in full here:

- http://www.hiphopisread.com/2012/04/secret-meeting-that-changed-rap-music.html

That's gangsta

Inevitably, the writer's mystery identity has led to claims that the letter is a hoax. Putting oneself in the writer's position, however, if everything he claims is true, it becomes easy to understand why he would choose anonymity. And looking at how the landscape of hip-hop has changed over the past 25 years, can anyone really argue that the claims sound far-fetched and unrealistic?

It's true that lyrical content and the stereotypical images portrayed by rappers changed from the beginning of the 90s onwards. Wikipedia's entry on 'gangsta rap' lists the type of lyrical subjects it expounds as including: "crime, serial killing, murder, violence, profanity, sex addiction, homophobia, racism, promiscuity, misogyny, rape, street gangs, drive-by shootings, vandalism, thievery, drug dealing, alcohol abuse, substance abuse, disregarding law enforcement, materialism, and narcissism."

NWA, (Niggaz With Attitude,) had largely paved the way with tracks such as 'Straight Outta Compton,' 'Fuck Tha Police' and 'Gangsta Gangsta'–although Philadelphia-based Schoolly D's 'PSK: What Does It Mean' is largely credited as the first 'gangsta rap' record, followed by offerings from Ice-T and Just-Ice. By 1992, former NWA member Dr. Dre's 'The Chronic' had appeared, an album considered an all-time classic in hip-hop circles, followed a year later by the debut album from Dre protégé Snoop Doggy Dogg, two sets which continued steering hip-hop in the desired direction with songs such as 'The Day The Niggaz Took Over,' A Nigga Witta Gun,' 'Rat-Tat-Tat-Tat,' 'Bitches Ain't Shit,' 'Murder Was The Case,' 'Serial Killa,' 'For All My Niggaz and Bitches,' 'Gz And Hustlas' and 'Gz Up Hoes Down.'

Back in the early 90s, and all the way through to relatively recent times, you'd have found me defending these trends, and explaining them away as natural artistic expression, and merely a documentary-style reflection of the ghetto street life from which many of these artists emerge. It's clear to me now that it goes way beyond this and involves a long-term, concerted plan set into place with some very clear objectives. The anti-establishment image of 90s hip-hop, along with the perception that it was 'cool' to be into it, was what attracted me to want to be a participant, so I can absolutely understand why the plan to use it as a method of social engineering has been so successful. It's only at this advanced stage in life with the maturity that it brings, that I've been able to break through the brainwashing and see the agenda for what it is–as difficult as it is to admit that I was taken in, and that many artists I previously looked up to were merely manipulated pawns. I can understand, therefore, why so many original-generation fans of The Beatles and the artists that emerged out of Laurel Canyon have such a hard time accepting that there was any kind of Hidden Hand involved in the 1960s scene too.

The release of the 2015 NWA biopic 'Straight Outta Compton,' inspired researcher Lenon Honor to embark on a documentary film of his own, titled 'NWA–A Critical Analysis.' 'Compton' had documented the birth of the 'gangsta rap' era with affectionate nostalgia, portraying Eazy E and Dr. Dre as valiant heroes while conveniently forgetting to mention Dre's woman-beating tendencies, and the fact that Eazy had fathered–and abandoned–many children through his promiscuous sex life, (but with Dre serving as the film's Executive Producer should we be too surprised at this sanitised take on the story?) Lenon undertook an in-depth analysis of NWA's legacy, arming himself with a copy of each of their six albums, and trawling through the lyrics to identify certain themes, trends and vocabulary that were being systematically employed to change the landscape of hip-hop music of the time.

> *"On NWA's first album there were 12 tracks. (Actually there were 11 tracks, but I've counted another song because in the re-release they've added 'A Bitch Is a Bitch'!) You have 177 instances where male NWA members disrespected women, 143 of those by NWA members, 34 of those instances by other members of the group called The Posse. That's in 50 minutes and nine seconds. You also have 87 instances of self-aggrandisement. That means the rapper is trying to make himself out to be greater than he actually is . . . by disrespecting other people. There were 66 negative references to the female body . . . calling black women 'bitches', 65 times. Also, disrespecting of men 61 times. References to alcohol, 59 times, references to drugs, 34 times, the use of the term 'shit' 33 times, the use of the term 'fuck', 28 times, references to money, 21 times, references to cars, 19 times, general violence against black men, 16 times . . . "*

And through the rest of NWA's canon of work, 48 tracks in total.

> *"There were 553 instances of disrespecting black women. The word 'fuck' was used 198 times, 'motherfucker' 197 times, disrespect of black men, 193 times. References to 'dick' or penis, 96 times, references to guns, 93 times. General violence against black men, 88 times, disrespect of other black rappers, 91 times, references to drugs, 87 times."*

Lenon suggests that the appearance of the 2015 movie, far from marking a nostalgic trip down memory lane, was strategically released to glorify the same value system that was pioneered in NWA's early days, to a whole new market.

"Here we are 25 years later, and this programming is being re-presented to the world. So the idea is, if you present a movie to people who weren't even born 25 years ago, if you promote it in the right way, they're going to be inclined to view the movie. So now we have a whole new generation of people who are going to be exposed to the same type of programming that I was exposed to growing up."

By the arrival of Notorious BIG, 50 Cent and Rick Ross, it had become the fashion for rappers to model their entire personas on criminal figures. Christopher Wallace, aka Notorious BIG's alter-ego, was Biggie Smalls, a big-time gangster character portrayed by actor Calvin Lockhart in the 1975 movie 'Let's Do It Again.' When rapper Curtis Jackson became 50 Cent, he was emulating the identity of Kelvin Martin, a street robber from The Bronx. Martin was shot in a project building in 1987, dying four days later, so it seems prophetic that Jackson was himself shot nine times in Queens, New York in 2000. Unlike Martin he survived. The rapper Rick Ross, meanwhile, took his name from a notorious drug trafficker known as Freeway Ricky Ross, who has admitted to running cocaine as part of the Iran-Contra affair on behalf of those nice people at the CIA. The impostor Rick Ross's real name is William Roberts II, and his lawless gangster image took something of a battering when it emerged that, prior to his rap career, he had worked for the government as a correctional facilities Officer, as well as graduating from Albany State University on a football scholarship. Other rappers to have adopted crime-related pseudonyms include the New York duo Capone N Noreaga, named after an Italian mob boss and a Panamanian dictator respectively, Texas MC Scarface, named after Al Pacino's Tony Montana character from the 1983 movie, and Tragedy Khadafi, named after the toppled Libyan leader. For a time, Nas went by the name of Nas Escobar after the Colombian drug lord Pablo Escobar. Murder Inc. label founder Irv Gotti and Dogg Pound rapper Daz Dillinger, modelled themselves on American mobsters John Gotti and John Dillinger.

For many purists, 1996 was the last year in which mainstream hip-hop output held any real credibility, and before the ulterior motives really plunged it into an ever-downward spiral. I'm inclined to agree with that judgement. There seems to be some allegoric potency to the deaths of 2Pac and Notorious BIG in 1996/ 97, as if their murders symbolised the death of the art-form. Hip-hop's obsession with 'bling' culture really took a hold in '97, largely through the names propagated by Sean 'Puff Daddy' Combs and his Bad Boy Records empire. Besides these, artists such as Jay-Z, R Kelly, Lil' Kim, Foxy Brown, Missy Elliott, Cam'ron, 50 Cent and Ja Rule saw to it that the worship of material-ism and big-name brands became normalised, as the original-genera-tion heads who remembered the better days of the genre's youth started to fall away from clubbing and record-buying. The title of 50 Cent's breakthrough album, 'Get Rich Or Die Trying,' summed up the mind-set of the 2000s scene with perfection.

Even the trivial party records of old, going back to the likes of Sugar-hill Gang's 'Rappers Delight' and Kurtis Blow's 'The Breaks', going through to 90s offerings from Nice N Smooth and Naughty By Nature, managed to be creative, lively and fun without resorting to the crude-ness that today's tunes are seemingly required to in order to get put on.

East West

It was a depressing period for hip-hop purists when the so-called East Coast/ West Coast 'beef' occurred during the mid-90s. The benefit of hindsight, the testimonies of insiders, and the resources of the inter-net for independent research, all point to this period as having been manipulated and contrived at the hands of the industry, (with some involvement from the CIA,) rather than being the unfortunate random affair it was presented as. It centred around Los Angeles' Death Row Records, owned by Marion 'Suge' Knight, with Tupac Shakur as its prominent artist, and its counterparts in New York–Bad Boy Records, Sean 'Puff Daddy' Combs and Biggie Smalls, aka The Notorious BIG. The events which led to the murders of 2Pac and Biggie were foreshad-owed by infamous tracks from each of the artists. In 1995, Notorious BIG had put out 'Who Shot Ya,' (with much background goading from Puffy,) apparently taunting his former friend 2Pac over a November '94 incident that had occurred outside Quad Recording Studios in Man-hattan. Shakur had arrived there to meet with Biggie and Puffy. He was attacked by three unknown assailants, robbed of his jewellery and shot five times. In a subsequent interview with 'Vibe' magazine, Shakur stated that he believed Biggie and Puffy, along with a criminal associate of Puffy's known as Jimmy Henchman, to be responsible for the set-up. Henchman is currently serving a life sentence connected to a murder; Biggie is dead; Puffy is alive and well and reckoned to be worth around a quarter of a billion dollars.

This, and the ongoing East/ West tensions, seemingly prompted 2Pac to record 'Hit 'Em Up,' a vicious five-minute tirade in which he threatens to murder the entire Bad Boy Records and Junior Mafia personnel and their children, and boasts of having had sex with Faith Evans, Biggie's wife. He also references the earlier Biggie track by saying, 'Who shot me? But you punks didn't finish.' The suspicion that the shooting was a set-up was also referenced by fellow Outlawz member Hussein Fatal's line 'Frank White needs to get spanked right for setting traps.' (Frank White was one of Biggie Smalls' pseudonyms after the character portrayed by Christopher Walken in the movie 'King Of New York.' Hussein Fatal himself died in a car accident in Georgia in July 2015.)

This period ushered in a new era of hip-hop 'diss' records, where two prominent artists would record tracks specifically to antagonise each-other. While none of them got as close to the mark as 'Who Shot Ya' and 'Hit 'Em Up' had, each glut was used to ignite 'beefs' between the artists concerned. Early examples included Canibus and LL Cool J taking each-other on with 'Second Round K.O.' and 'The Ripper Strikes Back,' Jay-Z and Nas going at it with 'Takeover' and 'Ether,' and 50 Cent re-launching his career by directing a beef record at any other rapper in sight. It all seemed a far cry from the days of MC Shan and Boogie Down Productions arguing relatively peacefully over territorial status on 'The Bridge' and 'The Bridge Is Over' in the 80s. The diss records of the 2000s became a staple part of the corporations' output, with every 'hot' artist having to have some manufactured beef with one of their peers. While it became a marketing gimmick that netted large profits for the labels, it also served to portray hip-hop as a genre steeped in bragging egotism, rivalry and threats of violence, feeding right into the hands of its critics, and tying in nicely with other aspects of the long-term agenda.

The Dark Knight

Inter-coastal rivalries aren't even necessary when there are deadly beefs within the same extended camp. At the time of the 'Straight Outta Compton' movie's release in 2015, a new theory regarding the fate of group member Eazy E was thrown up. Eazy's death in March 1995 had been put down to AIDS after he had been admitted to the Cedars-Sinai Medical Center in Los Angeles, (more on this place later!), apparently suffering from asthma only a month before. From asthma to death from AIDS in a month is quite some going.

Eazy's son, Yung Eazy, told the music press that Death Row Records supremo Suge Knight had deliberately injected his father with the AIDS virus only weeks before he died. As evidence, Yung Eazy pointed to a 2003 TV interview with host Jimmy Kimmel, in which Knight jokes about the stabbing of people with AIDS-infested needles being the new 'Hood' murder method of choice.

You can view the Jimmy Kimmel interview clip here:

- https://www.YouTube.com/watch?v=zxGvS1F0L38

A possible motive became apparent when a 2013 interview featuring former NWA manager Jerry Heller resurfaced two years later. In it, Heller revealed that he had talked Eazy E out of his plans to kill Suge Knight, and that to have done so, was 'a big mistake.' Heller recalled:

> "*One day I came into the office, and (one of my clients) and Eazy were talking, and I said, 'What's going on here?' And Eazy said, 'You know this guy Suge Knight?' And I said, 'Yeah.' He says, 'Well, I'm gonna kill him . . . This guy's gonna be a problem, and I'm gonna kill him.'*"

Heller added:

> "*And you know something? I should've let him kill him. I would've done the world a favour. He would have done it, for sure. By himself.*"

It seems few people who have crossed his path would spend too much time mourning the demise of Suge Knight. His track record speaks for itself—even leaving aside any role he may have had in the murder of Tupac Shakur in 1996. That same year he was jailed for a probation violation. Two years after his 2001 release, he was back in the Big House for another violation after assaulting a parking attendant. In May 2008, out again, he got into a money-related dispute outside a Hollywood nightclub. In August the same year, police were called to a Las Vegas strip club where they found him beating his girlfriend and brandishing a knife.

Another Vegas arrest came in 2012 when he picked up three years' probation for driving on a suspended licence, for traffic violation charges and for being found with marijuana in his car. In August 2014, Knight was shot six times at a music awards party hosted by Chris Brown, echoing a situation nine years earlier where he had also been shot at an awards event hosted by Kanye West. Do you think it's something he said?

Only two months later, he was bailed after a legal case relating to the theft of a female photographer's camera, with a charge of second-degree robbery. He was also implicated in the 2009 robbery of Akon producer Noel 'Detail' Fisher, where five armed men broke into Detail's house claiming they were calling in a debt on behalf of Knight. This incident was reportedly linked to one of the previous month where Knight was extensively beaten at a private party at the W Scottsdale Hotel.

The big crunch, (no pun intended,) came when he was charged with murder and another case of attempted murder in early 2015. Police had received a video tape allegedly showing Knight reversing his jeep over 'friend' Terry Carter, (with friends like him, eh?) and associate Cle 'Bone' Sloan in the car park of a fast-food joint in Compton, LA. The incident is said to have occurred after an argument on the set of the movie 'Straight Outta Compton.' Carter died. Knight was also charged with attempted pre-meditated murder, hit-and-run resulting in death, and hit-and-run resulting in injury, facing possible life imprisonment. What a guy.

As the UK's 'Black Sheep Magazine' observed at the time:

"As the body-count has piled up around him, Knight has displayed a seemingly supernatural ability to avoid death-by-bullet against all the odds, bringing its own brand of bleak comedy and making

him seem more like an invincible cartoon character than a hulking manipulative thug that personifies everything that's wrong with hip-hop culture."

Following his subsequent jailing, Knight complained that he was going blind, and it was reported that he had developed a brain tumour and a blood clot in his lungs. He also complained that the toilet in his jail cell was haunted as it flushed by itself every 20 minutes, keeping him awake. Could karma finally be coming home to roost for Suge Knight?

Yeah, baby

Besides reinforcing criminal stereotypes, there is another aspect to this insidious agenda which has been slowly rolled out over the past two decades. A case could certainly be made for mainstream hip-hop output becoming deliberately infantile and retarded as the 2000s progressed, as the trend for songs coming with their own form of line-dancing emerged. Fans would be required to recite a dance that they'd seen on MTV when the record in question came on in the club, leading to armies of mind-controlled automatons doing as they'd been instructed. The likes of Soulja Boy's 'Crank Dat,' D4L's 'Laffy Taffy,' Lil' Jon's 'Snap Yo Fingers,' Young Dro's 'Shoulder Lean' and Cali Swag District's 'Teach Me How To Dougie' helped push this agenda. Jibbs' 'Chain Hang Low' even appeared to the tune of the nursery-rhyme 'Do Your Ears Hang Low?' as if to publicly announce the tendency to child-like intelligence levels that was being employed. By the time the 'Schmoney Dance' invented by newcomer Bobby Schmurda from his 'Hot Nigga' track had arrived, all hope had been lost.

The same tactics have been applied to what's now laughingly referred to as the 'R&B' scene, a genre which has always sat side-by-side with hip-hop. Where it once referred to Rhythm & Blues, 'R&B' now seems to simply be a reference to Rihanna & Beyonce. (Although 'Rubbish & Bollocks' might be a more fitting description for the 2010s.)

The current glut of urban music A-listers all have infantile nick-names to dumb their followers down yet further, (as if the 'music' itself wasn't enough to do it,) by regressing them back to baby-talk. So Jay-Z, Kanye West and Beyonce are Jay, 'Ye and B, Rihanna is RiRi, Rick Ross is Rozay, and Lil' Wayne, Chris Brown and Drake are Weezy, Breezy and Drizzy! It's all presented as something for those 'in the know,' as if it's cool and 'down' to refer to the artists on these familiar terms.

The dumbing-down agenda was further enforced by a study put together by Andrew Powell-Morse on behalf of Seatsmart. For this, he fed popular song lyrics into a Readability Score software package, which he used to figure out the average reading level against US schooling standards. He concluded that lyrics in contemporary songs, (with offerings by Kanye West, Chris Brown and Beyonce offered as examples,) come in at below third-grade reading level. His report concluded that hip-hop had the lowest lyrical intelligence out of the four main genres analysed, and that the overall reading level in mainstream hits had been declining since 2005.

The Texas rapper Scarface seems to agree with the idea of the deliberate dumbing-down of intelligence levels through hip-hop. In an outburst that's rare to hear from an artist signed to a prominent label, he used his interview time on 'Hardknock TV' in April 2013 to state:

> *"I feel like we're losing it, you know what I'm sayin'? I feel like the people that are in control of what hip-hop does is so fucking white and so fucking Jewish until they don't give a fuck about what the culture and the craft and what it really is about . . . Let me say this shit right . . . 'cos I want this to be as offensive as I can fucking make it for these old-ass, er, punks that's running these record labels, you know, that's in the powerful positions to dictate what the black community hears and listens to . . . like there's no fucking way that you can tell me that it's not a conspiracy against the blacks in hip-hop, because you put out fucking records that make us look stupid."*

As the UK's Conspiro Media site observed at the time:

> *"Scarface has good reason to bemoan the quality of modern-day hip-hop music, a genre that was once teeming with articulate, intelligent voices applying their rhymes to topics worthy of further attention such as inner-city poverty, police brutality, racism, drug-addiction, hidden black history, and the promotion of self-empowerment. This social and spiritual consciousness that once prevailed, has now been*

*minimised and marginalised by spitters of lyrical nonsense who cele-
brate 'bling, big bucks, big-brands and bitches."*

The article goes on to quote Wise Intelligent of the group Poor
Righteous Teachers, one of a number of hip-hop acts from the early 90s
that adhered to the teachings of the Five Per Cent Faction of the Nation
of Islam:

*"It wasn't expected for hip-hop to reach this level, but when they real-
ised that it would, it followed the same format as every other music
genre. Blues, rock—they all had a political edge when they started, but
they eventually were over-marketed and commercialised and became
what they became. And it's necessary because, you have to understand, the powers that exist that are ruling the world, they can't have
too much influence in the hands of musicians. There was a time in
Europe when it was the arts that actually educated the people. The
people were being educated through the arts, through theatre, through
Shakespeare and so-on and so-forth. So they understand that science,
and they don't want to let music expand and let the musicians have
that kind of power."*

The War on Blacks

The insidious control system clearly has contempt for the bulk of
humanity—those it considers to be 'useless eaters.' But it strikes me that
it harbours a particularly hateful brand of contempt towards people
of colour. Lawrence Fishburne's Furious Styles character in the classic
movie 'Boyz N The Hood' nails it when he points out to his son that
a gun store and a liquor store are the two consistent features in any of
LA's black neighbourhoods.

Throughout modern history the system has employed various methods to destroy black communities, create negative stereotypes of black
people in the eyes of others, and to subvert and corrupt its forms of
artistic expression. This stance can be seen from more obvious measures
such as the importing of slaves from Africa and the flooding of black
inner-city ghettos with crack cocaine and laboratory-developed AIDS,
to less blatant strategies. The 'blacking up' of white people such as Al

Jolson and the participants in 'The Black And White Minstrel Show' would be one. The gradual degeneration of hip-hop is another.

As Black Dot's earlier comments emphasise, hip-hop is an art-form which has black cultural traditions built into its very fabric, so any co-ordinated attempt to corrupt it also has the effect of corrupting the cultural identity of its people. Pretty much all evolutionary ties to these past elements have now been cut through the continual phases of corporate artificiality that hip-hop has undergone.

The desecration of moral values relevant to black people has not been immune, either. As if things had not been degraded enough, in his guest verse on the remix of Future's 'Karate Chop,' (itself a master study in the absurd deployment of Auto Tune,) Lil' Wayne included the line 'I beat that pussy up like Emmet Till.' Quite rightly, this incurred the scorn of certain factions of the black community, given that Emmet Till was a 14-year-old African-American who was brutally beaten and murdered by racist thugs in 1955 after supposedly flirting with a white woman. His mutilated body was weighted to a fan blade bound to him by barbed wire and dumped in a river, (which gave rise to Kanye West's lyric on 'Through The Wire' where he states his girl is 'scared to death that her man look like Emmet Till' after his jaw was wired together following a car accident.)

Here, with the Lil' Wayne lyric, was one of the leading figures in contemporary 'black' music, (I know . . . I know,) desecrating the memory of one of the most tragic African-American figures with a throwaway one-liner in a trashy piece of audio garbage. Among the most vocal critics was Airickca Gordon-Taylor, a cousin of Emmet Till and the founding director of the Mamie Till Mobley Memorial Foundation, who said:

> "To compare his murder and how beaten and how bullied . . . and tortured he was, to the anatomy of a woman, was really very disrespectful . . . I just couldn't understand how you could compare the gateway of life to the brutality and punishment of death. And I feel as though they have no pride and no dignity as black men."

Epic Records subsequently issued an apology. To paraphrase the Mandy Rice-Davies character in the film 'Scandal,' 'well, they would, wouldn't they?

Cash Money Records, the label that spawned Lil Wayne, clearly hadn't learned much of a lesson when they released Nicki Minaj's 'Lookin' Ass Niggaz.' In the promo shot, Minaj used a famous photo of the black civil rights leader Malcolm X looking out of a window holding a rifle, while the song's video shows her replicating the pose and shooting at men. Two on-line petitions demanded the picture's removal. The first was worded:

> "You come from a rich legacy. Without the work and life of Malcolm X, you would not be able to do what you do. Unfortunately you have chosen to disrespect and dishonor the legacy that he left us ... We demand that you remove the picture."

The second tackled Minaj's glamorisation of guns, writing:

> "Malcolm X carried a gun as he feared for the safety of his family and himself, and was aware he would someday be killed by political opponents. The image of Malcolm X looking out the window high-lighted that fear. Nicki Minaj's use of guns in her new music video speaks to the gun culture in our society today where gun violence is an acceptable norm."

Minaj issued a part-apology on her Instagram page, worded:

> "What seems to be the issue now? Do you have a problem with me referring to the people Malcolm X was ready to pull his gun out on as 'Lookin Ass Niggaz?' Well, I apologize. That was never the official artwork, nor is this an official single. This is a conversation. Not a single. I am in the video shooting at Lookin Ass Niggaz and there happened to be an iconic photo of Malcolm X ready to do the same thing for what he believed in!!!! It is in no way to undermine his efforts and legacy."

As Black Dot observed in an interview on the subject for this book:

> "I think it arises because Lil' Wayne and Nicki Minaj and them are so removed from African culture, so to speak. Meaning, there's

a generation now, and they are part of that generation, that don't care about Malcolm X, they don't care about Emmet Till. They don't care about anything but themselves. And part of that is this new multicultural thing we have going on in America, where everybody is everybody. As a result, you lose the base of who you are.

"But when you're disconnected through culture, and all this becomes just about money, hoes and things of that nature . . . he probably ran across a picture of Emmet Till and figured, 'oh shit, look how messed up this guy's face is. Let me mention that.' And he mentions it with no kind of connection to it whatsoever. That's why it was easy for him to kick those lyrics. I believe it wasn't until the backlash came that he said, 'oh shit! Wooah! I think I touched a nerve there so let me back up.' And it's funny because, if we as a collective got pissed-off at half the things these guys said, they wouldn't say it. So I think the record label tells them, this is what we're talking about for the most part—money, hoes and clothes, this and that. Stay out of anything political."

David Icke, arguably the world's best-known conspiracy author, turns out to be highly clued-up on the machinations of the corporate music machine, and of hip-hop's role in particular. When I interviewed him for the very first 'Good Vibrations' podcast, he told me that he had once been selected by the manager of Public Enemy to go up on stage at one of their shows, such had been the appetite among hip-hop's free-thinkers to the information he had put out during the 1990s. On another occasion in New York, hip-hop pioneer Afrika Bambaataa had attended one of his lectures, and he spent time explaining to Icke that what purports to be 'hip-hop' in these times is really nothing of the sort. In my podcast, Icke made a striking point about what hip-hop's pres-ent-day obsession with materialism, 'bling' culture and the acquisition of personal wealth really represents:

"One of the things that saddens me among black America . . . is when I see the people who have come through from the families of former slaves, taking on the so-called 'values' of the slave-owners! Not only taking on the values . . . but taking on the religion that was imposed

on them by the slave-owners ... To see people enslaved by a religion that was imposed upon their ancestors after they were appallingly brought from Africa to serve the slave-owners ... And of course, the slave-owners' values are money, wealth, control ... And here's Jay-Z making the point that this is a great thing! Look at the bling, look at my big car, look at my clothes! How much did I make last year? A million dollars here, and a million dollars there!

The long-standing tendency towards rappers boasting about their material possessions is a baffling thing, when you really apply some critical thought to it. An MC taunts their listeners by relaying how much richer they are than them, and how much better they're doing in life, often addressing the listener as 'nigga,' 'muthafucka' or 'bitch' in the process. In many cases, the listener will have paid money to be reminded of their apparent inferior status, (I say 'apparent' because, in a significant number of cases, it's all fiction, and the rapper will no better off than most of the people listening due to the way the recording industry is set up to always work in the favour of the corporation and never the individual ... a bit like the rest of daily life!) Why should it be that people find it entertaining to be lyrically taunted in this way? The outstanding conscious rapper DISL Automatic addressed this on his track 'Here I Stand' in specific reference to Jay-Z when he stated: "ain't it funny how they love it when a grown man brags, 'bout the jewellery and money that none of his fans have?"

The corporations have shaped and moulded the music in line with their larger social engineering plans, reinforcing in the public's mind the notion that life is an inevitable struggle, that money and material possessions are the judge of a person's true worth, and that individuals should know their place in the world. It's an expression of the externalisation of power. Celebrities are placed on pedestals, giving the view that they're more important and worthy than the little people who are merely worker-ants, there to keep their heads down, pay taxes and be grateful to the hand that feeds them. Any tactic that denies people the acknowledgement that their true power lies within themselves is fair game for this control network.

Mobb Deep frontman Prodigy has been extremely vocal on the subject of Illuminati influence on hip-hop. In a letter he penned to 'Urb

Magazine' in the wake of reading the book 'Leviathan 666' by Dr. Malichi Z. York, he stated:

> *"Jay-Z knows the truth, but he chose sides with evil in order to be accepted in the corporate world. Jay-Z conceals the truth from the black community and the world, and promotes the lifestyle of the beast instead . . . Jay-Z is a goddam lie. I have so much fire in my heart that I will relentlessly attack Jay-Z, the Illuminati, and every other evil that exists until my lights are put out."*

The day the Banks failed

The issue of black slavery in America cropped up via another heavily puppeteered artist at the tail-end of 2014, when Azealia Banks felt compelled to call for $100 trillion in reparation payments to the ancestors of former slaves at the hands of white corporate America. Addressing the DeWolf family, who were prominent Rhode Island-based slave-traders, she went on to directly message descendant James DeWolf Perry:

> *"What did you (sic) family do with all the money you made from slavery???? I need to know. Now. Someone should kick your ass, and punch you right in your stupid smiling cracker face."*

Later, in an interview on New York's Hot 97, she offered some further opinions on how black and white artists respectively are treated in the music industry:

> *"I feel like, in this country, whenever it comes to our things, like black issues or black politics or black music or whatever, there's always this undercurrent of kinda like a 'Fuck you.' There's always a 'Fuck y'all niggas. Y'all don't really own shit."*

Banks returned to controversial territory a short while later when addressing rapper Kendrick Lamar about his response to the police shooting of Michael Brown and the Ferguson riots. She messaged:

Mark Devlin

"When we don't respect ourselves how can we expect them to respect us, dumbest shit I've ever heard a black man say."

And:

"HOW DARE YOU open ur (sic) face to a white publication and tell them that we don't respect ourselves . . . Speak for your fucking self."

One of Banks' Tweets during her initial rant about slavery read:

"Please please please do not get distracted with reality tv and rap music and fashion and all that other dumb shit."

As a scathing article in the UK's on-line 'Black Sheep Magazine' observed at the time, the words pot, kettle and black do spring to mind here, given that Banks hardly finds herself in a position of integrity to lecture others on the debasement of moral values, her 'music' acting as a major contributory factor towards the corruption of the scene she represents. She does know a lot about 'dumb shit,' however:

"It seems a good idea to recap a little on Ms. Banks' track record here. She first emerged into the public's consciousness with her track '212' in 2011. The video featured her cavorting in a sweatshirt featuring Mickey Mouse, mascot of the massive, white-owned Disney corporation, also a symbol denoting the trauma-based mind control programming of artists that's endemic throughout the entertainment industry. The video caused controversy for the subliminal message flashed on-screen for a split second throughout. It reads:

"'I guess that cunt getting eaten.'

"Indeed, the line in question does crop up as part of the lyrics of the 'song'. Here's an excerpt:

"And fit that tongue tongue d-deep in,

I guess that cunt gettin' eaten,

310

I guess that cunt gettin' eaten.

"Like most pop market-aimed rappers featured on MTV and main-stream radio stations, Azealia Banks' target audience will be mainly children and teenagers.

"What other gems of wisdom do we learn from '212,' you might reasonably ask? Well, how about:

"I'm a look right nigga,

Bet you do want to fuck,

Fuck 'em like you do want to cum,

You're gay to get discovered in my 2 1 deuce,

Cock-a-lickin' in the water by the blue bayou."

"I can just see the pride on the faces of parents all over the world as their ten-year-old daughters swagger around the house reciting all this good stuff. The 'critics' certainly think it's great, anyway, if Wikipedia's entry on '212' is anything to go by:

"The song received universal acclaim, with critics complimenting Banks' versatile rapping style as well as her songwriting ability. 'The Guardian' gave the song a positive review and placed it at number 2 on their 'The Best Songs of 2011' list."

And doesn't it speak volumes about where we're at that it did?

The twisted morality of the BBC reared its head in 2014, meanwhile, when Radio 1 announced its Teen Awards scheme by asking, 'are you 14 to 17 years old?'–clearly their target audience. They then immediately played Nicki Minaj's 'Anaconda,' (a euphemism for big dicks,) which contains the lyrics:

'This dude named Michael used to ride motorcycles,

Dick bigger than a tower, I ain't talking about Eiffel's,

Real country-ass nigga, let me play with his rifle,

Pussy put his ass to sleep, now he calling me NyQuil.'

Highly appropriate material for 14-year-olds to be listening to, I'm sure any parent of one would agree.

I heard it on my radio

As a radio DJ of 20-plus years, I come with some authority on the type of lyrics that are deemed acceptable for by legal stations in the UK and US. I wasn't greatly surprised to get pulled up by an angry station director for letting the 'street' version of Sporty Thievz' 'No Pigeons' accidentally air, with the lyric 'go home and fuck your babysitter.' It's fair to say the lines of acceptability have been systematically blurred in recent times, however.

In the 90s and early 2000s, words such as 'fuck 'and 'shit' were definite no-gos, and were usually obscured by being spliced into the radio-friendly version of a track backwards, becoming 'cuff' and 'ish' respectively. The intention is to avoid offending listeners who might be upset by hearing explicit language, of course, or to protect children who might happen to be listening. You could certainly debate the effectiveness of such methods, given that hearing the phrase 'cuff all y'all mutha-nickuff ziggin' leaves little to the imagination. But the advent of digital production brought even more questionable 'censorship' methods. A common way of allegedly disguising the word 'fuck,' became to simply render the word so the end of it has a downward inflection, mimicking the sound of a turntable being turned off. This has become something of an industry standard. Even more ludicrous has been the muting-out of just the middle vowel, so 'I don't give a fuck' now becomes 'I don't give a f(silence)ck. Because there's no telling what the original word was from that, right?

The opening lines to Nicki Minaj's track 'Only,' demonstrate the technique, (the *s denoting a split-second of silence.)

"I never f*cked Wayne, I never f*cked Drake, all my life, man, for f*ck's sake. If I did I'd menage with 'em and let 'em eat my a*s like a cup cake.'

Well, now that the 'u' in fuck and the 's' in ass have been muted, it's perfectly acceptable for radio play. Who could possibly get upset now? Feel free to have a listen to the 'clean' version for yourself:

- https://www.YouTube.com/watch?v=FIw4C2yqD5I

Things have become even more farcical, however, with certain non-swear words now being singled out for censorship. The radio version of Snoop Dogg and Pharrell's 'Drop It Like It Hot' mutes the word 'suicide' from the line: 'the interior like suicide, wrist red' as Pharrell describes his Phantom car. On 'Get Right' by Ayo Beats featuring Abel Miller, the word 'cocaine' has its second syllable muted. It makes all the difference, you know.

My favourite absurd radio edit of all, though, has to be the 'clean' version of Jadakiss's 'Why.' The original 'street' version includes the line, (quite reasonably in my view,) 'why did Bush knock down the towers?' Those behind the radio edit deemed it appropriate to mute the word Bush, however, so the line becomes 'why did (blank) knock down the towers?'

Well, that's cleared that one up then. No complicity from the Bush administration in the events of 9/11 after all. Phew.

Selective Morality

These all stand as examples of what I call Selective Morality. According to the corporate entertainment machine, it's just fine for eight-year-old girls to hear their idol Rihanna exclaiming 'whips and chains excite me' and 'bitch better have my money', or Katy Perry advising that 'I kissed a girl and I liked it,' or to watch Disney cartoons with erect penises cleverly disguised into the artwork so as to only be perceived by the subliminal mind. But we can't possibly have these same kids hearing the words 'suicide' or 'cocaine' in a song on the radio. That's just not acceptable at all.

Selective Morality would also have been at work when BBC Radio 1 DJ Mike Read imposed a ban on Frankie Goes To Hollywood's 'Relax' in 1984 in protest at its obscene lyrics . . . right in the era when there would have been massive complicity to cover up the fact that Jimmy Savile and others were sexually abusing children on BBC premises. Did someone say double standards? Read, who for a time revelled in being a lookalike of his friend and tennis partner Cliff Richard, joined a bizarrely-behaving Frank Bruno as a guest at Savile's funeral, gushing their praise for him as 'a great man,' a year or so before Savile's exposure as a sex monster.

I raised the Selective Morality issue with Lenon Honor when we studied the content of Kanye West's extremely dark 'Yeezus' album for a 'Good Vibrations' podcast. We discussed a line in the song 'On Sight', where Kanye states that "we get this bitch shaking like Parkinsons." This had incurred the wrath of the Parkinsons Society, and several other groups, for its trivialisation of the effects of Parkinson's Disease. Elsewhere, offence was caused to some Asian people by a line on 'I'm In It', where Kanye states that he needs some sweet-and-sour sauce before performing cunnilingus on Asian women. I can understand the sentiments in both cases, but what struck me as strange was that lyrics such as these were taken in isolation and scrutinised, while the rest of the album's depraved content completely flew under the moral radar. The album contains multiple references to 'niggas,' 'hoes' and 'bitches,' as well as to dark occultism and demonic possession. It seems all that is just fine in today's scene. The same dynamic was at play when Rick Ross got dropped from a sponsorship deal by Reebok after apparently advocating date-rape on the Rocko track 'U.O.E.N.O.' with the line: "Put Molly all in her champagne, she ain't even know it, I took her home and I enjoyed that, she ain't even know it." (Molly is a slang name for MDMA, or ecstasy.) While this was clearly an irresponsible and insensitive line, it's far from the only morally reprehensible thing Rick Ross has ever had to say!

As Lenon observed:

> *"The nature of the entertainment industry is like social engineering. You bring people along a particular course. If you call black people 'niggers' for long enough, soon enough they'll start calling themselves*

'niggers.' I've been on a basketball court where you have Asian people calling each other 'nigger.' The same with white people. It's social engineering over time. Calling women 'bitches' and 'hoes' is now normalised. And now, we're even seeing dark occultic references in certain lyrics being normalised! It's all been so propagandised that people have been de-sensitised to it. So now when they hear it it's not a big deal. But then when they hear something like 'I got this bitch shaking like Parkinsons,' people are shocked. The only reason people no longer react with shock to hearing references to 'bitches' and 'hoes' or 'niggers,' is because, over time, we have been conditioned to just think of it as 'normal' and acceptable."

With Miley Cyrus simulating fellatio on a blow-up doll at concerts attended by children under ten and sporting a strap-on cock in promo shots, and Nicki Minaj proclaiming on track that 'I'm a bad bitch, I'm a cunt,' ('Roman's Revenge,') it's difficult to imagine how the popular music scene can be debased and degraded any further. But I'm sure they'll find a way.

The weaponisation of sound

Working alongside the degeneration of lyrical content, has been the mutated production methods within 'hip-hop.' A couple of decades ago, sampling was still rife—one of the original hallmarks of the art-form. Popular producers such as DJ Premier, Large Professor, Pete Rock and Q-Tip routinely took select portions of old soul and funk records, and looped them over a newly-created drumbeat to give a track its underpinning rhythm. Those who study the science of sound have remarked that a track employing a sample in this way carries some of the signature energy and ethos of the original record. Either way, the use of samples spelled a creative and imaginative way of making new records; audio train-spotters had a field-day trying to identify the original sounds, and it provided a way for hip-hop to retain a connection to black music sounds and styles that had gone before.

The fashionability of sampling started to wane as the 90s turned into the 2000s. The excuse generally given was that, music law being what it is, it became too expensive for record labels and their producers to keep making the publishing payments that were necessary when old recordings were used. Given the huge profits that A-list rappers generate for their corporations—plus the fact that music giants like Sony and Universal would have had a stake in the original tunes anyway—this seems more like a cover story for the real reason sampling was phased out.

It was part of the plan for the music to be deliberately detached from black music styles of old and to lose its soul. Noughties mainstream 'hip-hop' was designed to have an effect on the subconscious mind. Sample-based beats were replaced by newly-created rhythms, coming in the early 2000s from super-producers like Timbaland, Just Blaze, Swizz Beats, The Neptunes and Kanye West, (before his switch from producer to rapper.) These producers did still employ some sampling, but by-and-large, their trademark sound involved new instrumentation. By the dawn of the 2010s, 'hip-hop' creations relied heavily upon digitised production, bringing artificial electronic sounds. The tempo of tracks started to fluctuate wildly, too. Whereas a standard hip-hop tune from the 80s or 90s would have a steady rhythm of between 90 and 105 beats-per-minute, by the 2010s, tracks were coming in with wildly differing beat patterns, putting a strain on the ear of the listener, not to mention giving DJs a hard time trying to mix them and make a set flow naturally. The 'hip-hop' producer of choice in recent times has been DJ Mustard out of Los Angeles. His signature style, heavy on the synthesised handclaps, is now all over the work of pretty much every A-list artist, from Chris Brown to Lil' Wayne to Tyga to Tinashe to Wiz Khalifa.

As any audiophile will confirm, there are sound frequencies which are harmonious and natural to the human energy field, and which synch with our brainwave patterns, and there are those that do the opposite. When the latter are deliberately used they have an unsettling and discordant effect on the listener. In the same way that sound has been proven to heal and restore the human body to holistic health, it can have the reverse effect, too. Appropriately-structured sounds can generate a range of negative emotional responses, including melancholia, depression and rage.

These can all occur without a listener having any idea that it's as a result of the music they're listening to. We're into the realms of A=440 versus A=432hz here, which is a theme I intend to get into in 'Musical

Truth 2,' (as it's already become clear that there needs to be one!) I've personally been unable to listen to what passes for 'hip-hop' for at least the past eight years. If I'm ever unfortunate enough to have a track by Lil' Wayne, Drake, Big Sean, Future, 2 Chainz, Nicki Minaj or their ilk come on the radio, I have to reach for the off-button in a mad panic, because these tracks actually make me feel unwell. There's something going on at an unseen level. (TV and radio ads have the same effect on me now, too.)

All bases covered

As if to drive home the absolute corporate dominance at all levels of the US market, even those artists commonly thought of as 'conscious' rappers, whose music has stayed outside of the obvious corporate agendas, have offered the odd clue as to the true nature of their industry owners. Common, generally thought of as offering thoughtful and positive rhymes throughout his canon of work, put out the track 'Universal Mind Control' alongside Pharrell Williams in 2008. The title speaks for itself, and it came with a video very much pushing Transhumanist imagery. De La Soul, heralded as the original 'Native Tongues' rap crew, put out a promo pic recently showing frontman Posdnous striking the same tired one-eye pose that all the more obvious puppets of the industry do. De La defendants will claim that the pose is mocking and ironic, but I wonder if this would really be the case? Would a group with a fan base in the tens of millions risk many of them getting it twisted in this way, knowing how it would work against them if their clever joke were to be misunderstood?

Erykah Badu's place, meanwhile, remains as open-for-discussion as her overall image and style always have. She was the girlfriend of the aforementioned Common, in the midst of further inter-industry relationships with Andre 3000 of Outkast, (with whom she had her first son,) and fellow Texas-born rapper The D.O.C, (with whom she had a daughter.) She then had a third child with equally enigmatic rapper Jay Electronica, of whom, more in the next chapter.

Having changed the spelling of her first name from Erica in protest at it having been a slave-name, Badu has always been marketed as something of an Earth goddess figure, very spiritual in nature, showing a reverence for the religions of Ancient Egypt, or Khemet. These credentials were very much cemented by her debut album, 1997's 'Baduizm.'

As the years progressed, however, some suspect symbolism started to creep into her work, some of it hinting at Transhumanism, (a robotic/cyborg headpiece in a promo shot,) and some at the presence of Monarch Programming, (she wears butterfly wings on the sleeve to her 'Erykah Badu Live' album, and guests in the video to the song 'Queen' by Janelle Monae, which is absolutely laden with trauma-based mind control symbology.) Other esoteric and mystery-school imagery has routinely appeared in her promotional material and live shows.

Badu has never been a stranger to controversy. Her most infamous video, to the song 'Window Seat,' sees her stripping naked as she walks the streets of her native Dallas, culminating at the spot of the JFK assassination, at which point a shot is heard and she falls to the ground bleeding blue blood. Go figure.

Move over, Scarface

References to 'The Illuminati' have become commonplace in mainstream hip-hop lyrics, to the point that they have eclipsed the frequent references to legendary gangster characters like Scarface and Don Corleone as a way of courting controversy. There is almost a cachet of 'cool' that has come to be associated with the idea of a mysterious powerful cabal, with rappers dropping hints that they are a part of this elite group. Chat forums and Youtube threads are alight with claims from fans that such-and-such an artist has sold their soul and is 'in the Illuminati.' (And of course, for every such comment, there's another blasting the poster as a 'retard' or a 'fuckwit,' and denying that any such group exists.)

The truth is that, first of all, the 'Illuminati' is a much-misunderstood phrase, in its broadest sense standing as a catch-all term for the networks of secret societies that control human activity from the top down. It's doubtful that a singular organisation by that name is in current existence. Secondly, the elite class to which it refers, reserve membership only for those of certain selected bloodlines, or for deeply trusted associates who have shown themselves to be unquestionably down with the agenda. The idea that they would accept into their ranks former street hustlers and heroin pushers who have sold their soul as a way of escaping their ghetto lifestyle, is laughable. These individuals aren't 'in the Illuminati', they're merely the rank-and-file foot soldiers doing its dirty work, (although it's rumoured that Jay-Z has joined the ranks of The Boule, an elite secret society with membership restricted solely to black people.) It's more likely that the elite controllers harbour nothing but contempt towards those prepared to degrade their morals in exchange for a quick fix of fame and fortune. Either way, the fashionability of 'the Illuminati' has been gradually drip-fed to the current generation of music fans.

One of the earliest references came from Mobb Deep frontman Prodigy, in his guest verse for LL Cool J's 'I Shot Ya' remix in 1995, where he states: "Illuminati want my mind, soul and my body, secret societies trying to keep they eye on me." Later, on the song 'Skull & Bones,' he proclaimed: "I shine, illuminate, yeah, my aura is awesome. Illuminati is us, we are the origin." In the same year, on 'Been There, Done That,' Dr. Dre stated: "Money is the root, I want the whole damn tree. Ain't tryna stick around for Illuminati. Got to buy my own island by the year 2G."

More recently, on 'Holy Ghost,' (featuring P Diddy/ Puff Daddy, appropriately enough,) Rick Ross rhymes: "They say I'm gettin' money, must be Illuminati, talking to the Holy Ghost, in my Bugatti." Fellow Maybach Music artist Meek Mill preferred rhyming 'Ferrari' than 'Bugatti,' meanwhile, on 'Dreamchasers:' "I'm getting money, must be Illuminati. They think I signed up 'cause I just bought a new Ferrari." He then managed to slip in a reference to a Maserati on 'Fender Up': "Illuminati wanted my mind, soul, and body. They asked me would I trade it for all for a Maserati."

On 'Hiipower,' Kendrick Lamar offers: "Who said a black man in the Illuminati? Last time I checked that was the biggest racist party." Fellow new-generation rapper J Cole went all-out on 'Villuminati' from his 2013 album: "These next three bars is dedicated to the retards, keep on asking me about the Illuminati. Is you stupid, nigga? Young black millionaire, old white billionaires. I'm sure that they can do without me. And I ain't really into sacrificing human bodies."

Nas, strongly rumoured to be a high-ranking initiate, blurred clarity somewhat with a line on his verse for the DJ Khaled track 'Hip Hop,' which personifies the hip-hop art-form as a woman. Seemingly stating that suggestions of an Illuminati plot within hip-hop were ill-founded, he states: "Confused fans think that she illuminates, demonic." Either way, Nas certainly seemed to be communicating the agenda when he titled his 2006 album 'Hip Hop Is Dead.' By that point it had been cold in the ground for quite a few years, and Nas would be one to know.

High Priestess of the Industry Madonna then went all the way in 2014, with a song actually entitled 'Illuminati,' presenting the idea that this was some kind of benevolent religious movement dedicated to the uplifting of all humanity.

The lyrics began:

"It's not Jay-Z and Beyoncé; it's not Nicki or Lil' Wayne,

It's not Oprah and Obama, the Pope and Rihanna,

Queen Elizabeth, or Kanye.

And later:

"Rihanna don't know the New World Order,

It's not platinum-encrypted commerce,

It's not Isis or the Phoenix,

The Pyramids of Egypt.

"Don't make it into something sordid."

Phew, that's that all cleared up then.

This was a blatant piece of propaganda at the hands of the industry machine, to give kids the idea that they were now all clued-up on what this mysterious 'Illuminati' is because they heard it in a Madonna song, and that's all they need to know about it.

These are just a few 'Illuminati' namechecks in tracks of recent years. Many, many more are available.

Rue The Day

On 20th March 1969, a meeting took place in Pittsburgh, Pennsylvania, attended by a number of paediatricians who were part of the Planned Parenthood organisation. This, in turn, was connected to the Rockefeller Foundation which was, and still is, heavily involved in eugenics and the long-term mass depopulation programme. A guest speaker, Dr. Richard Day, addressed the delegates. All in attendance were asked to put down their notepads and switch off any recording devices, as the information they would hear was to be top-secret. Thankfully, one delegate, Lawrence Dunegan, did take notes, and almost 20 years later in 1988, recorded some tapes detailing what he remembered of the meeting. In it, Day, (who died in 1989,) had outlined a massive array of changes that were to be introduced into all aspects of human society over the coming years and decades. Being a part of the Rockefellers' inner circle, he was in a position to know. In among measures such as compulsory sterilisation, the destruction of traditional family values, the promotion of homosexual lifestyles, the introduction of genetically-modified crops and fluoridated water, and the suppression of cancer cures as a means of population control, Day's comments regarding the future deployment of music and the entertainment industry speak for themselves. Dunegan recalled:

"Movies would gradually be made more explicit as regards sex and language ... There would be pornographic movies in the theaters and on television ... He said something like: 'you'll see people in the movies doing everything you can think of.' ... Violence would be made more graphic. This was intended to desensitise people to violence ... People's attitudes toward death would change. People would not be so fearful of it but more accepting of it, and they would not be so aghast at the sight of dead people or injured people. We don't need to have a genteel population paralysed by what they might see. People would just learn to say, 'well I don't want that to happen to me.'

"As regards music, he made a rather straightforward statement like: Music will get worse ... Lyrics would become more openly sexual ... Older folks would just refuse to hear the junk that was

offered to young people, and the young people would accept the junk because it identified them as their generation, and helped them feel distinct from the older generation . . . This aspect was sort of summarised with the notion that entertainment would be a tool to influence young people. It won't change the older people, they are already set in their ways, but the changes would all be aimed at the young who are in their formative years, and the older generation would be passing. Not only could you not change them, but they are relatively unimportant anyhow. Once they live out their lives and are gone, the younger generation being formed are the ones that would be important for the future in the 21st century."

You can get a full transcript of Dunegan's tapes here:

- http://100777.com/nwo/barbarians

Resources:

The Secret Meeting that Changed Rap Music and Destroyed a Generation:

- http://www.hiphopisread.com/2012/04/secret-meeting-that-changed-rap-music.html

Vigilant Citizen: Madonna Spreads Disinformation With New "Illuminati" Song:

- http://vigilantcitizen.com/musicbusiness/madonna-spreads-disinformation-new-illuminati-song/

'Conspiro Media' examines the comments of a prominent rapper who's let rip at music-bosses, and spoken of a "conspiracy" against Hip Hop:

- https://conspiromedia.wordpress.com/2013/05/03/conspiro-media-examines-the-comments-of-a-prominent-rapper-whos-let-rip-at-music-bosses-and-spoken-of-a-conspiracy-against-hip-hop/

Hidden Mysteries: Bronfman Manipulating/Controlling Black Youth Artists:

- http://www.hiddenmysteries.org/conspiracy/reststory/bronfmanblack.html

Seatsmart: Lyric Intelligence in Popular Music: A Ten-Year Analysis:

- http://seatsmart.com/blog/lyric-intelligence/

NME: Azealia Banks calls for $100 trillion in slave reparations:

- http://www.nme.com/news/azealia-banks/81961

I'm a casualty of Straight Outta Compton's revisionist history: Female journalist who was viciously beaten by Dr Dre says NWA movie completely whitewashes rapper's violent attacks on three different women:

- http://www.dailymail.co.uk/news/article-3202966/Female-journalist-viciously-beaten-Dr-Dre-says-Straight-Outta-Compton-completely-whitewashes-N-W-rapper-s-violent-attacks-three-different-women.html

Back in 1969, Dr Richard Day made some astonishing predictions about where the world would be today:

- https://henrithibodeau.wordpress.com/2015/06/08/back-in-1969-dr-richard-day-made-some-astonishing-predictions-about-where-the-world-would-be-today/

CHAPTER 15

ME, ME, ME

Satanism 101.

> *"If you want to find the secrets of the universe, think in terms of energy, frequency and vibration."*
>
> *Nikola Tesla (1856-1943)*

> *"What we have called matter is energy, whose vibration has been so lowered as to be perceptible to the senses. There is no matter."*
>
> *Albert Einstein (1879-1955)*

The nature of evil

Before we move on, a little background would appear to be relevant to explain the context in which many of the happenings detailed in the following chapters occur.

Satanism is not what most have been trained to think it is. The religious point of view–particularly within Christianity–holds that it is the worship of a singular supernatural entity known as the Devil, and with such pseudonyms as Lucifer, Beelzebub and of course, Satan. For many, these are expressions of the same entity, and it is a paradigm which the same forces that created the religious systems themselves, find it very convenient to have the majority of the general public believe. It serves to keep large numbers of people uniformly controlled through preying on their primal superstitious fears. Just as importantly, it keeps them from doing any kind of personal research into the *real* concept of Satanism and the black magic ritual practices that go with it. Just blame the evils of the world on 'the Devil,' goes the approach, rather than take any personal responsibility by acknowledging your own part in the dynamic, and how your own behaviour might be continuing to perpetuate the problems that humanity faces.

The word 'Satan' comes from Hebrew, and means adversary or enemy. In the esoteric context, the original Hebrew word can be taken to mean an adversary to the Christ consciousness—nothing to do with the figure of Jesus, but instead concerned with humans accessing higher levels of consciousness and re-connecting to the divine source from which we all emanate. The concept of Jesus and other messianic figures are symbolic of this alchemical process. Satanism stands as the absolute antithesis of humans achieving this, seeking instead to keep them grounded in base consciousness, attached to the ego and all the material trappings of this physical plane. Given that the thoughts of the majority of people in the world today—from the moment they get up in the morning to the moment they go to bed at night—are concerned solely with what they themselves want or need right here and now, without a single consideration towards the wellbeing of others, most people can be said to have been manipulated by society into becoming Satanists. It's a statement that will horrify many and bring instant denial, but it doesn't stop it from being true. Are my immediate and personal needs, whims and desires taken care of right here and now? Am *I* all OK? Yes? Well then, what else in the Universe could possibly matter? *That's* Satanism.

Satanism on an organised basis, is rooted in an understanding of Natural Law, or the law of cause-and-effect, and the recognition that, in this energetic construct in which we find ourselves, every action has a reaction. But Satanism denounces the moral aspect of this dynamic—the idea that there are absolutes of right and wrong behaviour set into place by the creative force behind the Universe. Instead, it teaches that the individual is their own God who gets to make up their own interpretation of right and wrong—or reject any semblance of 'right' at all if they choose. A direct quote from the Church of Satan organisation, (to be found in the FAQ section of its own www.churchofSatan.com website,) sums up this mindset as follows:

"We see the Universe as being indifferent to us, and so all morals and values are subjective human constructions. Our position is to be self-centered, with ourselves being the most important person (the

'God') of our subjective universe, so we are sometimes said to worship ourselves. "

This worldview completely disregards any thought or care as to the effect an individual's self-serving actions may have on any other living thing, and it's summed up in the title of one of the principal ceremonies performed at the annual Bohemian Grove gathering–the Cremation Of Care. Bohemian Grove is a large, privately-owned area of redwood forest in Northern California, where the rich, famous and powerful of the world meet each Summer, dress in robes, and perform various rituals including a mock sacrifice, (it's apparently 'mock', anyway,) in front of a 40-foot stone effigy of an owl, designed to represent the demonic entity known in the ancient world as Moloch. This gathering is a documented fact, and there's a famous photograph of Richard Nixon and Ronald Reagan there in 1957, both of whom would go on to become US presidents. Those who summarily scoff at the idea of 'a conspiracy' without bothering to do an ounce of independent research of their own, might like to ask themselves why the so-called 'leaders' of this world feel the need to enact this stuff every year, and why the mainstream 'news' always forgets to tell us about it. 'Care' is an expression of the sacred feminine principle inherent in the Universe, whereas 'action' is the sacred masculine equivalent. These two values need to be well-balanced and at work in an individual, in order for them to fully observe the two principal tenets of Natural Law. More of this in the final two chapters.

Sequestered understandings

Satanists have a knowledge of the esoteric workings of the Universe, and as in (hijacked) Freemasonry and other fraternal orders, the degrees of knowledge increase the further up the chain of command you go. So an entry-level Satanist will have only the most basic understanding of what their practice is all about. The real knowledge is retained by the high priests. A central tenet of mystery religion magick is to keep this knowledge limited only to those who are deemed worthy of it. There are deliberate efforts to keep great truths about the nature of reality hidden from the vast majority of the population–those considered the profane ones. Dark occultists utilise the power differential that this knowledge gives them over the rest of the population to their tactical advantage. It suits them to have the bulk of the people, on whose life-force energy and tacit approval they rely to be able to carry out their activities, in complete ignorance of how Natural Law and the Universe works. Little surprise then, that this type of knowledge is nowhere to be found in schools, colleges, universities or any other so-called 'seat of learning.'

This is why there are Satanists and other dark occultists at the very top of all professions and walks of life, from politics and commerce, right through to the entertainment business. They've made it their mission to infiltrate these institutions and ensure that Satanic ideology is filtered from the top-down throughout daily human affairs, to a population left absolutely clueless as to how they're being manipulated.

This ideology feeds very much into eugenics. The dark 'elite' practitioners believe that they themselves, through the advanced knowledge that they closely hoard, have the right to decide who in society gets to propagate their genes, and who, conversely, does not. It's a mind-set that's summed up nowhere better than on the notorious Georgia Guidestones in the US, a series of granite monoliths which were erected in a remote location in March 1980, and which were inscribed with certain ideologies in line with what's commonly referred to as the New World Order–the masterplan of the elite controllers for the rest of humanity. The stones contain ten 'guidelines' inscribed in eight modern languages, with a shorter message written in Babylonian, Classical Greek, Sanskrit, and Egyptian hieroglyphs. All of the guidelines feed into what's clearly in place throughout the planet already. But the Satanic ideology of maintaining the human population by deciding who gets to live and who dies, is summed up in the first two–'Maintain humanity under 500,000,000 in perpetual balance with nature.' and: 'Guide reproduction wisely–improving fitness and diversity.'

The fact that this aim is inscribed in stone and put on public display for all to see also ties in with the concepts of free will, consent and tacit approval, as explored in our chapter on Predictive Programming. No-one can say they weren't told.

Heavy vibes

The rituals that form a central part of Satanism (and other forms of dark occult practice,) meanwhile, are based in an understanding of the true nature of this reality–that all apparently 'physical' matter is actually an expression of the same universal energy force, simply in different states of vibration at an endless array of frequencies. The lower the vibratory rate, the more apparently dense the matter in question will be. All living things, and all their surroundings, are expressions of the same energy force. Any individuals or groups with a deep understanding of this knowledge–along with a malevolent intent towards the rest of humanity and a desire to keep this knowledge within their own closely-controlled circle–stand to gain a powerful advantage over the rest of the human population, and this is precisely the dynamic which has been played out in this world for many, many thousands of years.

Satanic rituals, therefore, are all about the manipulation of energy to bring about certain vibratory states, and therefore, to 'physically' manifest certain desired outcomes. The vibratory frequencies involved are extremely slow, which is the realm of fear-based emotions generated by humans. These include guilt, anxiety, hatred, jealousy, regret, despair . . . all negative emotional states which keep humans very much grounded in this 'physical' reality, and very much cut off from their true nature as inter-dimensional spirit-souls. This is why human society is structured to trap the majority of people in these fear-based states, and many researchers have pointed out that these collectively allow for a connection to other realms of existence, in summoning non-human entities. They feed energetically off of fear-based energy which serves as sustenance for them, and they crave a constant supply of it, hence the ongoing need for rituals to be performed in the same tried-and-tested fashion, over and over again. They are performed at key geographical points on the earth's energy grid, too, frequently at vortex points where two or more 'ley' or energy lines cross and the earth energy is naturally amplified. By performing dark rituals at these points, the negative energy is then absorbed into the grid and re-distributed, helping to spread the 'bad vibes' far and wide.

Far-fetched as it may at first sound, this is a concept that has been referenced in ancient texts, legends and religious writings by civilisations from all over the world, spanning vast ages. The entities that are evoked through bringing about an energetic state compatible with theirs, have been known by many names. They are the demons spoken of in The Bible, the Djinn of Islamic lore, the Archons spoken of by the Gnostics, the Chitauri of the South African Zulu tradition, and many, many others. It's the same concept as the over-simplified Christian 'Devil' or 'Antichrist,' only very much in the plural rather than the singular. These entities can only be temporarily brought into this state of existence through being summoned or 'invited,' which is where the concepts of consent and free-will choice come into play again. Satanists make a conscious choice, through their will and intent, to bring these entities into manifestation. In seances, similarly, entities have to be 'invited' in before they can take possession of a human body.

Knock three times

I'm alarmed to realise that I've actually witnessed a Satanic ritual almost first-hand–though I didn't understand it to be such at the time. In 2004 I went to the Czech capital of Prague with my wife to play a DJ gig, and we booked ourselves into lodgings on the recommendation of a DJ mate who'd stayed there shortly before. The venue wasn't a hotel as such. It was a grand restaurant in an old building on the side of a sloping hill overlooking the old city, and accessible by a hillside car on a track. Above the restaurant were two guest rooms, both served by a kind of annexe room with a billiard table in. I noticed that the annexe had a metal spiral staircase in the corner leading to some kind of loft. Our room was tastefully decorated and furnished, with a large four-poster bed.

We spent the evening downstairs in the restaurant where there was an air of celebration, as a musician who looked very much like bearded Benny from ABBA plonked away at the piano, and kept glancing our way with a knowing smile. Hours later, we'd gone to bed, but had both been awoken by something at the same time–around 3am. We heard movement in the annexe outside our room, and suddenly, there were three firm knocks in short succession on our door. This put me on immediate alert as we weren't expecting anyone, and something about the knock seemed unsettling so we didn't respond. Shortly afterwards, we heard creaking floorboards and footsteps from the loft area above us, and a form of low vocal chanting. The atmosphere turned unfeasibly cold. At one point, I sensed what felt like a hand on my shoulder and turned around to see what my wife wanted. She was right over the other side of the bed and couldn't possibly have touched me from there.

By some miracle we did get back to sleep, but remained shaken by the experience. As we headed back downstairs, we noticed the venue was adorned with paintings depicting what looked like grinning demonic entities, lunatic asylums, and variations on Dante's 'Inferno'. We decided to explore further up the hill on which we were situated. Taking the hillside car to the top, we found a large flat area with a massive inverted pentagram etched into the ground. I've trawled the internet for information on this venue for the past few years, but can find no reference to it or the things that go on there. However blatantly it might be advertised by the pentagram, the place appears to remain a best-kept secret strictly for those in the know.

Understanding what I now do about black magick rituals, it's clear that we witnessed one that night. It seems that we were assumed to be there to take part in it, rather than having naively stumbled upon the place by accident as we had, hence the knowing smiles from Benny. The knock on the door was our invitation to take part. The air becoming cold was a reflection of the energetic shift that was being brought about. I don't like to think of what else might have been going on right above our heads.

Max Spiers touched on the power of Satanic ritual in his on-line interview for 'The Bases Project' in 2014:

> "We have in our DNA the ability to conjure and call upon certain entities if a ritual is done in the right way. The reason rituals are so important to them is because whenever you do it, you're then re-activating the morphogenetic field of anybody else who's ever done that ritual before. And if you know what you're doing you can bring them into being."

There's Something About Saturn

Whatever entities it might connect with, Satanism is also very much about the influence of the planet Saturn, whose name would appear to be directly derived from 'Satan'. So many clues are hidden in language and placed right there in plain sight, but get missed through a daily over-familiarity with the words that most never think to question.

There have been many methods of depicting Saturn through the mythology of the ages. In the ancient world, the planet was referred to as 'The Dark Sun,' and has also been known as 'The Dark Lord.' Some scholars have suggested that Saturn was the original Sun of our solar system, before it was displaced by some monumental heavenly cataclysm that gave birth to our current Sun.

Whatever the scenario, Saturn is always depicted as having a negative, controlling effect on humanity. It represents hierarchical structure, order and control. Its ancient symbol resembles an extended lower-case h, with a cross at the top. It has been suggested that this is where the cross seen atop many a supposedly 'Christian' church originates, and that in fact, Christianity, just like Islam, are fronts for much older systems of Saturn worship. Saturn's colours are black and blood-red. This is why judges and priests wear black robes, and why the Trooping Of The Colour ritual of the British monarchy is steeped in black and red. Saturn has also been represented through history as a black cube, from which the Ka'bah at Mecca is derived, (the Muslim followers walking around it in concentric circles mimicking the cloud patterns persistent at Saturn's north pole,) as is the black 'mortar board' hat that university graduates wear. These institutions were all set up in reverence to Saturn, with the vast majority of initiates having no idea that they're a part of it.

Saturn is associated with time, a construct attributable to this 'physical' reality, and which doesn't exist outside of this realm. Saturn is seen as a force which governs the passage of time, and which therefore brings ageing and eventual 'death' to humans and other living things. For this reason, the figure of 'Old Father Time' is actually a depiction of Saturn. It is the Greek figure of Cronus/ Cronos/ Kronos, which was seen to govern time, and from which we get words such as 'chronology,' all concerned with the measurement of time.

It is also a symbol of agriculture and harvesting. Saturn is the figure of the hooded, scythe-wielding Grim Reaper, representing a bringer of death and a harvester of souls. Cronos was also depicted with a scythe, or sickle, and sometimes a harp. The hammer-and-sickle emblem of the Soviet Union is another evocation. Throughout ancient civilisations, Saturn was symbolised as an old man with a white beard, an icon that feeds very much into the festival of Saturnalia, celebrated by the Ancient Romans and based around the 'death' of the sun at the Winter Solstice, from which we got the modern concept of Christmas. No great surprise to find Father Christmas as an emblem of this event, then, another old man with a white beard, and alternatively known as Santa, a none-too-subtle anagram of Satan! The Dark Sun is also the inspiration for the character of Set, (sometimes known as Seth,) in Egyptian mythology. This figure was said to be a god of violence, disorder and upheaval and was the enemy of Horus, representing the Sun (or Son) of Man. In Arabic, the word 'Shatain' means Satan, 'the devil,' or any vicious person or animal. 'Al Shatain Ramad,' meaning 'the Devil of Ramadi,' was the nickname given to Chris Kyle, the inspiration for the Hollywood blockbuster 'American Sniper', who is said to have killed up to 160 alleged 'insurgents' during the second Iraq 'War,' before falling victim to a fatal bullet himself in a classic example of consequentialism in action.

Saturday is, of course, named after Saturn, and is the day in the Western world where people give their energy to celebrating the weekend in a leisurely fashion, unwittingly making a subtle energetic connection to Saturn in the process. It represents the 'holy' day, meanwhile, in certain religious cultures. Saturday is the sixth day of the week, and Saturn the sixth planet in the solar system. From this comes Saturn's strong association with the number 666, 'the number of The Beast,' which goes some way to explaining why this particular number crops up so much in popular culture. The dark priest-class that control the entertainment industries—along with so many other walks of life—worship the energetic influence of Saturn.

As the veteran occult researcher Jordan Maxwell has commented:

"The planet Saturn is very important. The Nazi party were the most Saturnalian Brotherhood of war and destruction. They always knew

Saturn had rings, the Lord of the Rings. Saturn is the God of this world. From that we get the dark side of The Force, Darth Vader. Remember Darth Vader with his Nazi helmet speaking through his masonic triangle? ... The god Saturn was referred to as El. If you continue today to worship the planet Saturn, you become known as an <u>el</u>der, you got <u>el</u>ected, with <u>el</u>ections, now you're one of the <u>el</u>ites, now you've got <u>el</u>evated."

And according to author Fritz Springmeier:

"Saturn is an important key to understanding the long heritage this conspiracy has back to antiquity. The city of Rome was originally known as Saturnia, or City of Saturn. The Roman Catholic Church retains much of the Saturn worship in its ritual. Saturn also relates to Lucifer. In various occult dictionaries Saturn is associated with evil."

An inside story

Author, public speaker and radio show host Mark Passio of www. whatonearthishappening.com, has revealed that he was a low-ranking member of various dark occult groups in his younger years. He has explained that he was born into a typically Catholic Italian-American family in Philadelphia, and was inducted into traditional church cere-monies from childhood, where he gradually came to observe the hypoc-risy of the church and its people, causing him to rebel and seek the absolute antithesis of the institution which he found so repellent. This turned out to be the Church Of Satan, then still under the leadership of its original High Priest Anton LaVey. The young Passio's skills as a writer, communicator and musician had marked him out as being potentially useful to the group. Within a few years, however, Passio says he had become wise to the organisation's true nature, and his con-science could no longer allow him to continue. He stated his intention to leave the Church and start revealing many of the occult teachings that he had learned there to the general public, and was met with no opposition whatsoever. Instead, he says, his former colleagues mocked him and wished him luck in what they considered a futile attempt to wake the masses up from the manipulated trance that they had been collectively placed under, such was their confidence in the worldwide Satanic ideology they had installed. These people referred to the public disparagingly as 'the dead,' such was their view of the almost non-existent state of their spirituality, and their confidence in their own techniques of worldwide mind-control. They were also referred to as 'the unbegun,' as in they hadn't even taken the first steps on any kind of personal journey towards spiritual enlightenment.

In a January 2015 interview with Lee Ann McAdoo on Infowars' 'Nightly News,' Passio related some home-truths about the often misconstrued world of Satanism and Satanists.

"I became aware that this wasn't just an isolated group of individuals that were just working with occulted, or hidden knowledge in order to, essentially, grow their own personal power, but they were inter-networked groups of people who were working together, and they came from an eclectic array of people from every walk of life. In every social institution you can imagine, there were Satanists placed in positions of high influence and power within those institutions, including politics, banking, law, military, law-enforcement, entertainment, technology, medicine, education and every other area of our lives. And they were not isolated individuals who were trying to increase their own power and influence. They were working together as a tight-knit unit towards a common goal, and that common goal was to increase their own power and control at the expense of everyone else's rights and freedoms.

"The occult is knowledge that has been hidden for particular reasons and held by very few people. When you hide and hold very important knowledge tight to yourself, and you try to keep it sequestered from everyone else, what you are doing in that instance is creating a power differential through the knowledge differential you've created. We've all heard the term 'knowledge is power.' I would have a slightly different take and say that knowledge which is applied can be converted into real world power. And that is what these dark occultists do who are using this knowledge, certainly not to uplift humanity. They're using it to create a knowledge differential in the world so that they

can stay in power, and they can take advantage of the ignorant masses who have no idea what that knowledge is or how it works.

"Occultism is effectively hidden knowledge about two over-arching fields of study and endeavour. The first is the human psyche. The mind, and how the mind works. All its inner workings and operations. I would call this 'the inner world,' the inner world of the individual. And in the occult, this is often referred to as 'the lesser arcana,' or the body of knowledge that constitutes the microcosmic world, in other words, the world of the individual.

"Then there's a second body of knowledge that is all about the greater spiritual laws that, ultimately, the entire Universe is bound by and works according to. This would be considered the greater, or major arcana of knowledge, or the macrocosmic knowledge. It also includes the physical sciences, because much of the true knowledge about how the physical sciences work is also occulted or hidden from us, so that our society doesn't progress and advance in ways that the people who currently hold the reins of our society don't want it to."

Separately, on edition 184 of his ongoing podcast series, Passio observed:

"Satanism is about me, me, me, me, all day every day. If I could explain to you what Satanism really is . . . when you say the term, everybody's mind goes to the idea of the Christian devil, the red devil with the horns and the pitchfork and the tail. This has little-to-zero to do with what I am calling ideological Satanism. Satanists chose that name because of the archetypal connection to the Christian 'adversary' or 'opposer,' (which is what Satanism means in Hebrew,) to the Christ consciousness—the higher mind, the connection to the higher self. The real saviour of the world, which is making that connection to higher-self and higher consciousness, and really being aware of what's going on within us and around us. Satanists chose that image, because what they're really trying to do is keep people in low-vibratory consciousness so they can ultimately be ruled and controlled and put into slavery and bondage."

What is it about Satanism and dark occult practices, and the top ranks of the entertainment industry? How and why should they be even remotely connected?

Our story continues . . .

CHAPTER 16

A CERTAIN SACRIFICE?

Blurring the lines between rituals and 'tragic accidents.'

> *"Who do you think you are?*
> *To them you are nothing but a piece of meat, and you're only as valu-*
> *able as your last hit song,*
> *And when you make no more hit songs, nobody cares for you no more."*
> Minister Louis Farrakhan of The Nation Of Islam

On the face of it, the worlds of dark energy/ ritual magic and the entertainment industry should have no interlinking threads whatsoever, and should be about as far removed as it's possible for any two subject areas to get. Yet a never-ending array of hard evidence and revealing symbolism tells a different story, indicating that dark occult elements are a part of the very fabric of this industry, and have been since its inception. Many would go as far as to state that the very reason for the corporate music, film and television industries being set up in the first place, was so they could be specifically used to cast malevolent spells into the minds of the unwitting general public, all the time under the guise of something that's cool, fun, and which people willingly choose to bring into their lives.

The gift that keeps on giving

Ritual sacrifice is a deeply horrific practice which has unfortunately been a part of human society for aeons. It has taken various forms among different civilisations. Although the fine detail of the religious belief systems differ, the common point is that such sacrifices are designed to appease whatever 'gods' or supernatural deities the culture in question believes in, and to attain their blessing or goodwill. Although once a socially accepted part of many cultures, in modern times these practices have been denounced as the barbaric acts that they truly are. At least in the mainstream. Unfortunately, ritual human sacrifice never went away. It just went underground.

There is evidence that the old mystery religion which presides over the entertainment industry–and so many other walks of life–is steeped in a need for the continued offerings of human life-energy to its various deities, and that the untimely deaths of many prominent musicians through the decades can be attributed to this very factor. This claim, understandably, is dismissed by many as outrageous, and a step too far in what might otherwise have been a compelling story. But as has hopefully become clear by this point, the world really is very different to how we were raised to think it is. And, rather inconveniently, many more dark and sinister things go on than most would be comfortable acknowledging. It becomes a question of just how much an individual wants to discover truth, as to what places they're willing to go to pursue it.

The Vigilant Citizen site provided some reflections on the suggestion of industry ritual sacrifices in a 2011 article:

> *"The phenomenon of stars dying at a young age in strange circumstances goes beyond the well-publicised 27 Club. While this Club is 'reserved' to singers dying at the exact age of 27, many other types of artists have died in mysterious circumstances around the age of 30. Recently, the deaths of Heath Ledger and Brittany Murphy followed the same pattern as those described above. Strangely enough, there often appears to be a media build-up around these figures before their death, documenting their odd behaviour or personal problems. Were these deaths pre-meditated and part of some kind of sick ritual carried out by the occult-minded elite at the helms of the industry? Are charismatic stars being risen to fame in order to later sacrifice them, creating a worldwide mega-ritual? Is the wave of shock and grief surrounding these events harnessed in some way by high-powered occultists?*
>
> *"These concepts might sound totally ridiculous to the average person but, to occult initiates, the magical potency of human sacrifices has*

been recognised and documented by the rituals of many ancient civilisations. In 'Secret Societies and Psychological Warfare,' author Michael A. Hoffman II writes:

"The issue of controlling humanity with esoteric words and symbols encoded within a play, a media spectacular or a ritual, is one of the most difficult for people to comprehend. That is why most people are viewed with utter contempt as 'cowans,' 'the profane,' 'the gentiles' and 'the goyim' by secret-society initiates'

"About mega-rituals, Hoffman writes:

"(Some murders) are ritual murders involving a cult protected by the US government and the corporate media, with strong ties to the police.

"Such killings are actually intricately-choreographed ceremonies; performed first on a very intimate and secret scale, among the initiates themselves in order to program them, then on a grand scale, amplified incalculably by the electronic media.

"In the end, what we have is a highly symbolic ritual, broadcast to millions of people, a Satanic inversion; a Black mass, where the 'pews' are filled by the entire nation, and through which humanity is brutalised and debased in this, the 'Nigredo' phase of the alchemical process."

A Professor speaks

One of the most outspoken proponents of the idea that the music industry periodically sacrifices the artists it has nurtured, has been Professor Griff, Minister of Information–a kind of intellectual public face–for the long-standing hip-hop group Public Enemy. PE are one of the few groups to have maintained their integrity and longevity through the drastically-altered hip-hop landscape of the past 30 years, and their overall message of truth, knowledge and empowerment–and the preservation of black culture and heritage–has been largely unchanged in this time. Their 2012 track 'WTF' included the line: "I'm at the age, if I can't teach, I shouldn't even open my mouth to speak," which resonates with me big-time. Griff's personal and passionate messages have been very much in-line with this ethos. Inevitably, though, they have not been without their controversies.

Griff, (born Richard Griffin in New York in 1960,) spent a stint in the US army, before launching a security service to work the hip-hop party circuit in his native Long Island. He was then recruited as an associate member of Public Enemy for its formation and signing to Def Jam Records. Following two successful group albums, Griff hit the headlines in 1989 when he made public comments that were branded 'anti-Semitic' and 'homophobic.' When these labels get applied, it's usually a sign that you've got a little close to the mark and upset some important people. Because of the social stigma systematically created by the Rothschild-controlled Anti Defamation League of saying anything remotely critical of someone who identifies themselves as 'Jewish'–regardless of whether the claim has any foundation or not–the minute the term 'anti-Semitic' comes into play, it spells instant discrediting of anything the individual in question has to say in the eyes of many. The same has become true of criticising homosexuals in recent times, which represents a major 180-degree turn since, as recently as 1967, it was considered a punishable crime in the UK, (1982 in Northern Ireland.) As the old wartime maxim observes, 'if you're copping the flak you're over the target.' And so Public Enemy frontman Chuck D had little choice but to announce that Griff had been axed from the group in the wake of the ensuing controversy. Griff rejoined shortly afterwards, was 'fired' again, and rejoined a second time, since when he has been appearing sporadically at live shows. In his 2009 book 'Analytix', Griff apologised for his earlier comments, admitting they were misjudged.

His position at the frontline of both the music industry, and specifically the happenings within the hip-hop genre, quality Griff as a credible source of information as to what goes on behind the public veil, and his lack of any corporate affiliations has given him the personal freedom to speak candidly. And he has.

Griff's assertion, made many times in interviews and public appearances over the years, is that the hip-hop business–like all aspects of the music industry–is ultimately controlled by a dark priest class steeped in ritual magick, and that aspects of their religious beliefs require them to make sacrifices of carefully-chosen individuals who have signed contracts with them. These contracts go far beyond straightforward business deals, and in effect, represent lifelong binding arrangements where the artist could be said to have 'sold their soul' to the corporation in exchange for a life of promised fame and fortune. This phrase can be taken either symbolically or literally. There would appear to be a clause in some such contracts, however, which allows the controllers to decide how long the life of the performer concerned lasts.

There is a secondary aspect to the sacrificial tenet, too. This involves these artists giving up a nominated family member, close friend or associate, who will become their 'blood sacrifice,' thus enabling them to move up the ladder of success. The first level of this is referred to as the 20 Million Dollar Club, membership of which shows you're on your way. Those who reach the lofty heights of the 100 Million Dollar Club and upwards are considered to have paid the heaviest personal prices, and to have demonstrated just how much they wanted the fame. Many researchers claim that all of the successful A-list stars in music, films, TV and sport will have made some kind of sacrifice of this nature, since they wouldn't have been elevated to such positions of prominence if they hadn't. Certainly, a delve into the fine detail of many celebrities' life stories does reveal the untimely passing of family members and others.

Professor Griff went into this subject area when he guested on an episode of Greg Carlwood's 'Higherside Chats' podcast in 2014:

> "These people have enough influence and power to have your wildest fantasies come true. People that have put themselves into a position where they can do that, oh yeah, they have a lot of power over the average person. You sacrificing a family member is absolutely nothing to these people. It's almost like, if you don't, then you're not loyal to us. And I think that is the conversation that we are not having. What is the price that you will pay to be rich and famous? That is the question we need to ask. What is that price? What does that look like?

> "And we don't know these individuals. Some of us will allow our mom to get sacrificed. Some of us will allow our girlfriends or wives to get sacrificed. Each of us knows what our own threshold is. And

there are certain things that I'm just not going to do. Other people around me will have taken it, and they're probably living a better life. Fortunately or unfortunately, one of mine is that I'm not going to apologise for the truth. Poison me, burn my house down, shoot at me, do whatever you feel you need to do. But I'm not going on record to apologise for the truth. I'm just not.

"The allure of you being rich and famous and successful and having enough money to buy anything that you want, to someone growing up poor and not really having anything—which is the majority of us—the allure of living this kind of life is attractive to any one of us. No-one wants to live poor. So the whole idea of you having two or three cars, and a couple of homes, and living in the finest places, eating the finest food and doing anything you want to do, is very attractive. I think we can agree, Americans are fucking lazy! We want to reap the most benefits for the least amount of work."

Griff wasn't speaking hypothetically in his reference to being shot at, poisoned and having his house burned down, by the way, as all of these have happened to him over the years. Which could well be taken as further confirmation that his comments have touched a few raw nerves which would prefer not to be touched.

The hip-hop genre specifically is said to offer countless examples of blood sacrifices. Even those who scoff at such 'conspiracy theories' are forced to acknowledge that this musical genre, more than any other, has had an above-average quota of casualties who *just happen* to have died prematurely for one reason or another. It's suited the Establishment to have the public put this down to the erratic and edgy lifestyles lived by so many hip-hop artists. But some closer examination of the finer detail, for those who are prepared to go there, throws up a sea of strange anomalies.

All about Puff

One of the most frequently-cited examples is the suggestion that rapper Christopher Wallace, known as Biggie Smalls or The Notorious BIG, was offered up as a sacrifice. Professor Griff has always been direct in his accusations towards Biggie's producer and mentor, Sean 'Puffy' Combs in this regard, as in these comments given on the Amen-Ra Film Productions DVD 'Blood Sacrifice For Fame & Fortune & Freemasonry.'

> *"All the evidence points to the fact that he (Combs) had something to do with it. Puffy wasn't no real rapper like that, but as soon as Biggie was off the scene he came out with his album. Now he's up in the 300, 400, 500 Million Dollar Club. Jay-Z, as I'm told, is the one that was called in by The Hidden Hand, by the Illuminati, and they gave him a $40,000 nice room on a beach somewhere where he spent the weekend with Denzel Washington and some other people sipping $20,000 bottles of Crystal. Him and Beyonce. And when he came back off that trip, the beef between him and Dame Dash began."*

Sean 'Puffy' Combs' father Melvin, was a drug dealer and small-time hustler in Harlem, and was an associate of Frank Lucas, the character portrayed by Denzel Washington in the movie 'American Gangster'. Melvin was shot dead while sat in his car in New York when Puffy was three years old. In a 2013 interview, Puff commented: 'I have his hustler's mentality, his hustler's spirit . . . He was a drug dealer and he was a hustler, so I learned early in life that there's only two ways out of that dead-end jail. It made me work even harder."

The young Combs first found success in the music industry as an intern at MCA Records, under the mentorship of executive Andre Harrell. Combs was charged with launching his own imprint, Uptown Records, through which he launched such artists as Mary J Blige and Jodeci. Harrell had hired Combs on the advice of Dwight 'Heavy D' Myers, whose act Heavy D & The Boyz were among the artists on Uptown. Tragedy loomed in December 1991 when Puffy, together with Heavy D, staged what was billed as their Celebrity Charity Basketball Game, with many high-ranking black music artists scheduled to perform at The Nat Holman Gymnasium at City College, New York. The promoters had oversold tickets, and the commotion that occurred through large numbers of people trying to force their way in, resulted in a stampede in which nine people were trampled to death. Andre Harrell hired the celebrated lawyer William Kunstler to defend Combs, and his team fought the families of several victims over wrongful death charges for years. Harrell subsequently fired Puff, describing him as 'too arrogant' for his own good. It is an incident largely missing from official biographies of Sean Combs, and an early encounter with death marking the very start of his long career. (Heavy D died aged 44 in Los Angeles in November 2011 shortly after returning from a tribute concert to Michael Jackson in Cardiff. The cause of his death was cited as complications from deep-vein thrombosis in the leg, with heart disease also a factor.)

Ultimately, the tragedy did little to harm Combs' career. From Uptown, he went on to found his own Bad Boy Records label through Clive Davis' Arista, the vehicle through which he launched the career of The Notorious BIG, arguably the number one hip-hop star of the mid-90s. In 2009, former Bad Boy recording artist Mark Curry released his book 'Dancing With The Devil: How Puff Burned The Bad Boys of Hip-Hop,' in which he gave an insider's account of how every artist that ever recorded on Bad Boy has ended up either dead, broke, in prison, a drug addict, or has turned to religion, (Ma$e became a Christian minister, Loon converted to Islam, Shyne to Judaism.)

Curry documented some of Puff's favourite operating tactics in his book:

"Puff has an annoying habit of inserting himself into the songs and videos of all the artists on his label, and it was common knowledge that many Bad Boy acts resented him for this. Asked about the practice in the July 1995 edition of a magazine aimed at black teenagers, Puff said: 'I like performing with my artists, I like talking on the records, and I like being in videos.'

"But he also revealed an ulterior motive: 'It protects my interests in terms of what I'm going to do in the future. Say if a company tries to remove me. It's going to be hard to remove me and still have all my acts and the same level of intensity and the same flavour and feeling.'

"Even worse, Puff charged the artists for his appearances on their records and videos, usually without them realising it until they received their paltry publishing royalty statements. That's when they discovered that a large sum of their money had gone to fees which

were doubled, tripled and even quadrupled because of Puff's 'special guest appearance.' He charged artists, for example, for having his Bentley in their videos—which he insisted upon—then took a tax credit for business use of the car.

"A few had complained publicly that Puff was upstaging them as much as he was promoting them. They felt that his presence was more of a distraction than an attraction, since critics considered Puff a mediocre rapper and marginal dancer at best."

Aside from the moderate success of singer Faith Evans, who was briefly married to Notorious BIG and pregnant at the time of his murder, the only success story to emerge from Bad Boy Records has been Puffy himself, who consistently crops up in the top three of the annual Forbes Rich List in hip-hop, his personal wealth estimated to be in the hundreds of millions. He must be doing something right.

The strong implication that Puff had earned some friends in influential places came from a well-publicised incident in December 1999. Puff was in attendance at Club New York in Manhattan alongside Jennifer Lopez, said to be his girlfriend of the time, bodyguard Anthony 'Wolf' Jones, and Shyne, one of the artists signed to Bad Boy Records. A shooting ensued in which three people were injured. Witnesses said the incident erupted when Puffy walked into someone in the club and a drink was spilled. An argument followed in which the other man taunted Puff about his wealth and threw cash at him as an insult. This caused a commotion among the crowd. Shyne is claimed to have drawn a gun and attempted to fire at the man, but ended up wounding three bystanders instead.

Puffy is said to have been seen firing a gun into the ceiling of the venue. As Puff and his entourage hurriedly left the club, their car got pursued by cops and ran through 11 red lights, at which time a gun was seen being thrown from the window. Shyne, then 21, was charged with, and later convicted of, attempted murder, assault, and reckless endangerment. He was sentenced to ten years in prison in June 2001, getting released in October 2009. Shortly afterwards, he announced that he had converted to Judaism, was studying the Torah 12 hours a day, and had moved to Jerusalem under the new name of Moses Michael Levi.

For his part, Puffy was facing a possible 15 years imprisonment for illegal gun possession and bribery charges. He stood accused of offering his driver, Wardel Fenderson, $50,000 in cash to say the gun was his.

In the event, Puff walked away scot-free. There has been much suspicion that he was cut a behind-the-scenes deal allowing for his career to continue undeterred, and that his VIP status had marked him out for special treatment. (He has been strongly rumoured to be a Freemason.) This 'favour' would have left him beholden to his superiors, however, as there's no such thing as a free lunch in this game.

Puff's name re-emerged in intriguing fashion in 2013, when music industry executive-turned cocaine druglord Jimmy Rosemond was interviewed by federal agents. According to an article on the Smoking Gun website, Rosemond reported being quizzed about the sexual activities of many music industry key players, which included being asked directly whether Sean 'Puffy' Combs was "having sexual relationships with under-age boys." Where did that question come from?!

Tupac & Biggie

Biggie was gunned down in the early hours of 9th March 1997, shortly after leaving an after-party for the Soul Train Music Awards in Los Angeles, hosted by Quincy Jones's 'Vibe' magazine and Qwest Records. As the SUV he was travelling in pulled up at a red light, a Chevrolet Impala was seen to draw up alongside. Shots were fired and Biggie was hit four times. He was pronounced dead shortly after being rushed to Cedars-Sinai Medical Center, (more on this place later!) He was 24. Puff, Biggie's mentor, manager and apparent best friend, happened fortuitously to be riding separately in the car ahead. It seems he didn't handle the situation well. In his book, Mark Curry reports that Puff ran over to Biggie's car distraught, crying "Oh God, please let him pull through." Puff claimed to have been the one to call Voletta Wallace, Biggie's mother, to break the bad news, but this turned out to be a lie. Curry adds:

> *"Puff was freaking out,' (Junior MAFIA group member) Lil' Cease said in a recent documentary. Cease said that while he and members of Junior MAFIA were trying to figure out how to get Biggie back*

home, Puff went back to his hotel, grabbed his stuff, and was on a plane to New York in less than three hours."

There have been multiple claims as to the responsible party in the years since '97. The theory that it was rogue elements within the LAPD crops up repeatedly, as does the suggestion that Biggie was the victim of warfare between rival street gangs in LA. Either way, despite the shooter being identified as a black male by witnesses, and sketches being drawn up, no-one has ever been charged with The Notorious BIG's murder.

Biggie's death occurred almost exactly six months after that of his one-time-friend-turned-opponent, Tupac Shakur, in startlingly similar circumstances. Tupac had been attending a boxing match alongside Death Row Records supremo Suge Knight at the MGM Grand in Las Vegas on the evening of 7th September 1996. He, Knight and their entourage were reportedly involved in assaulting a member of the Crips street gang, Orlando 'Baby Lane' Anderson, upon exiting the MGM Grand lobby. After stopping at a venue known as Club 262, Tupac and entourage left in their Sedan. As they were at a red light, a Cadillac was seen to pull up at the vehicle's side and a series of gunshots were rapidly fired. Tupac was hit several times and Knight was reportedly hit in the head by fragmentation. As in the Biggie case, the shooters' car sped off never to be heard of again. Unlike Biggie, Tupac did not die instantly. He remained in a critical state in hospital for a further six days, largely in an induced coma, eventually being pronounced dead on the afternoon of Friday 13th September at the age of 25.

(It's interesting to note that prominent music industry deaths often occur in groupings. Brian Jones and Jim Morrison died exactly two years apart, for instance, in 1969 and 1971. In between were the deaths of Jimi Hendrix and Janis Joplin within days of each other in 1970. T-Rex frontman Marc Bolan's death occurred in 1977, when the mini being driven by his girlfriend Gloria Jones crashed into a fence post and a tree in Barnes, South West London. I hadn't uncovered any bizarre elements to this one, suggesting that it may have been that rarest of things—a genuine 'tragic accident'—until I learned that the registration mark on the car was FOX 661L, with FOX corresponding to 666 in Pythagorean numerology! A few years before, Bolan had released the song 'Cosmic Dancer' which included the possibly prophetic lyric 'I danced myself into the tomb.'

There was then a gap of three years until John Lennon's assassination in December 1980 was followed by the death of Bob Marley five months later. Reggae legend Peter Tosh and hip-hop pioneer Scott La Rock were both shot dead in 1987. Tupac and Biggie then occurred within six months of each other in 1996/ 97, with Michael Hutchence shortly after in late '97. Aaliyah and Lisa 'Left Eye' Lopez' 'accidents' occurred within 8 months of each other in 2001/02, followed by Jam Master Jay later that year, then Michael Jackson, Amy Winehouse and Whitney Houston, in 2009, 2011 and 2012 respectively.)

Just as with the Biggie case, no-one has ever been charged with Tupac's murder. Two police forces from two separate cities just don't seem to be able to solve two murders committed in busy public streets in front of dozens of witnesses. I wonder if the cases would have remained 'unsolved' had it been, let's say, Rod Stewart and Mick Jagger as the victims? Again, with the Tupac murder, there have been allegations of police corruption and/ or organised crime affiliations. A popular alternative theory, however, is that Tupac's murder was arranged by Suge Knight and served as his own ritual sacrifice to the industry. He was certainly taking a chance by riding in the same car as Tupac if he did indeed have prior knowledge of how the events of that night were going to go down.

In what would appear to be a couple of examples belonging right in the earlier chapter on Predictive Programming, both Tupac's and Biggie's deaths appeared to be eerily foreshadowed on a pair of now-infamous record sleeves in the months leading up to their murders. Earlier in 1996, Tupac had released an album by the intriguing title of 'The Don Killuminati: The 7-Day Theory,' credited to his new alter-ego of Makaveli. The image depicted his naked body being crucified. The artist name was in homage to the Italian writer and philosopher Niccolo Machiavelli whose works Tupac had studied while in jail. Machiavelli lived from 1469 and wrote the book 'The Art Of War.' It is claimed, (but equally disputed,) that he faked his own death at the age of 25 to fool his enemies, returning in public 18 years later at the age of 43. This led to speculation that Tupac may have somehow faked his death and would do the same. He would have been 43 in 2014. The last entry on the sleeve notes on the reverse of the album reads 'Exit–2Pac, Enter–Makaveli.' Meek Mill, an affiliate of rapper Rick Ross and an artist on his Maybach Music Group label, released a track entitled 'Tupac Back' in 2011.

A highly-detailed examination of the theory that 2Pac may have somehow faked his own death resides here:

- http://real-eyes-realise-real-lies.blogspot.co.uk/2013/12/2pac-amerikaz-most-wanted-dead-or-alive.html

In Biggie's case, all three of his albums appeared to indicate a morbid fascination with his own death. This has even led to claims that he may have somehow been complicit in his own sacrifice. These rumours have been fuelled by the bleak track 'Suicidal Thoughts' which depicts him killing himself, and includes lyrics like: "When I die, fuck it, I wanna go to hell. Cause I'm a piece of shit, it ain't hard to fucking tell. It don't make sense, going to heaven with the goodie-goodies. Dressed in white, I like black Timbs and black hoodies." And: "I swear to God I want to just slit my wrists and end this bullshit. Throw the Magnum to my head, threaten to pull shit." The voice of Puff Daddy is heard at the end of the track saying, "ayo, Big . . . ayo, Big."

Either way, his breakthrough LP was titled 'Ready To Die,' the double-album that was completed, but only released after his murder, was titled 'Life After Death,' and the collection of previously-unreleased tracks that seems inevitable in the case of a deceased artist, (do you think there could have been a reason why these tracks in particular were unreleased?) was titled 'Born Again.' What many distraught fans found so strange about 'Life After Death', was that the gloomy sleeve image showed Biggie in a funeral suit standing next to a hearse with the licence plate 'B.I.G.' This album included the songs 'You're Nobody 'Til Somebody Kills You,' and 'Somebody's Gotta Die.'

A very interesting article appeared in 2012 on the egotripland.com site, based on an interview with Ebon Heath, who was the art director for the photoshoot that spawned the cover image for 'Life After Death.' Heath revealed that, of the many pictures and themes that were considered for the album, it was Puff's ultimate decision for the funeral theme to be used. He recounts:

"In the beginning we spoke about the album. Puff was really his own art director–it was more us supporting his vision and coming up with it from the conceptual stages. And he was like, 'Life After Death' is gonna be bright. It's gonna be about blue skies and green grass. And this isn't some dark shit, this is really about the 'life' part, not the 'death' part.

". . . Then the graveyard location came up where we shot–my partner Michele thinks it was Cypress Hills Cemetery on Jamaica Avenue in Brooklyn . . . I don't know, it was weird. Like it somehow switched. We were out there in the middle of the graveyard at the end of the day, and it sort of switched just as a concept just in the process of us shooting in this graveyard. And it was bugged, too, because it was a cold day. Big had messed up his leg in a car accident, and he was on a cane. So he was already sort of grumpy. So already that was a weird vibe."

The King is dead, long live the King

Often when prominent artists are removed suddenly, they are quickly replaced by another who has been groomed for stardom, and is swiftly moved into position. It seems to be an additional twisted component of the process. The long-held suspicion in this regard is that Biggie Smalls' murder paved the way for Jay-Z to be ushered into place as the number one hip-hop star, a role he's pretty much held ever since. (When it comes to Tupac Shakur, meanwhile, Professor Griff's idea is that DMX and Ja Rule were ushered into place shortly after his murder, to fill the vacancy for an edgy 'thug-style' rapper that had been left.)

Biggie and Jay-Z recorded the track 'Brooklyn's Finest' together, which appeared on Jay-Z's LP debut 'Reasonable Doubt.' It included the line: 'the number one question is can the Feds get us?' Jay-Z then cropped up on the track 'I Love The Dough' from Biggie's second album 'Life After Death,' which by that point was a posthumous one. 'The City Is Mine,' a track from Jay-Z's follow-up album 'In My Life-time Vol. 1,' released in February 1998, is said to be dedicated to Biggie's memory and includes the line 'you held it down long enough, let me take those reins.'

There's some crossover in theories here, as some have speculated that Biggie may also have served as a sacrifice on the part of Jay-Z, given that his own monumental success only occurred after Biggie's removal. Other theories point to Jay-Z's nephew, Colleek D. Luckie, serving as his sacrifice. Luckie, (a morbidly ironic name in the circumstances,) died in an accident in the Chrysler 300 that Jay-Z had bought him as a graduation present. Jay-Z addressed this in his song 'Lost One' with the lyrics:

> *"My nephew died in the car I bought,*
>
> *So under the belief it's partly my fault,*
>
> *Close my eyes and squeeze, try to block that thought,*
>
> *Place any burden on me, but please, not that, lord."*

Whatever the circumstances, Jay-Z was evidently chosen by the elite controllers as 'their man,' and he went on to faithfully serve the agenda for the next 20-years-plus.

The young Jay-Z—real name Shaun Carter—spent years as a struggling rapper before making it big, and has made no secret of his early years selling crack out of his home in the Marcy housing projects of Bedford-Stuyvesant, Brooklyn. It's a story which continues to provide the basis for his rhymes to this day. He is acknowledged to have been put on in the rap game by an older mentor from the Marcy, a rapper by the name of Big Jaz, later renamed Jaz-O, thus inspiring the similarly-formatted Jay-Z moniker, (also said to be a variation on his nickname as 'Jazzy.') It's not hard to see why a glittering contract offered with the promise 'you'll never be poor again' would have been so attractive. It's often stated that 'there's no way out of the ghetto.' Maybe there is but, as it turns out, you'd have been better off staying there.

1996 was the year chosen for Jay-Z to blow up. He emerged with a fully-formed record label co-owned by himself, Damon 'Dame' Dash and Kareem 'Biggs' Burke. The name chosen was the eyebrow-raising Roc-A-Fella Records, named after the German-Jewish Rockefeller family, (Rockenfelder in the original German,) cited as one of the principal Illuminati bloodlines. The three partners split in 2004 when they sold their 50 per-cent interest in Roc-A-Fella Records to Def Jam Recordings. Jay-Z was appointed President and CEO of Def Jam by this point. Dash and Biggs went their separate ways. Little more has been heard of Biggs. Dash, however, very much fulfilled the role of entrepreneur, involved as he was in the label's Rocawear street clothing spin-off, two film companies, Armadale Vodka, and the Pro Keds sneaker brand. At his peak, he is said to have been worth an estimated $50 million. In his early years he swept floors in a barber shop and sold newspapers to earn enough to buy sneakers.

It has been observed that Dash's own success would not have been facilitated without his own heavy price to pay, and Professor Griff and others have remarked that his own blood sacrifice to his masters may have been the singer Aaliyah, to whom he was engaged.

Aaliyah and Left Eye

Aaliyah was a child star, appearing on a TV talent show aged 10. She signed to Jive Records aged 12, where she was moulded as a singer in the R&B genre. Almost immediately, she was embroiled in controversy over the nature of her relationship with R Kelly who was described early on as her 'mentor,' and producer of her first album titled, perhaps tellingly, 'Age Ain't Nothin' But A Number.' Rumours began to circulate that Kelly was involved in a sexual relationship with the underage Aaliyah. Paedophilia in the entertainment industry yet again. The Quincy Jones-owned 'Vibe' magazine uncovered a marriage certificate showing that the pair had wed in 1994 while Aaliyah was only 15, and that she had lied about being 18 in order to obtain it. This marked the first of many allegations against R Kelly involving sexual relationships with underage girls. In one, a video emerged purporting to show Kelly having sex with a minor, and urinating on her. Despite several allegations, however, he always managed to avoid jail. Could he have friends in high places?

On 25th August 2001, Aaliyah was in the Bahamas to film the video to her song 'Rock The Boat.' She and eight others were killed when their twin-engine Cessna light aircraft crashed close to the runway upon leaving Marsh Harbour Airport. The official account of what happened had the pilot, Luis Morales III, down as unlicenced, and with traces of cocaine and alcohol in his system, implying that the crash was a tragic accident due to pilot error. (Why am I getting flashbacks of what was said about Princess Diana's driver Henri Paul at this point?) Alternative theories have emerged, however, including the suggestion that the plane was somehow intercepted by remote-control using technology known to be in the hands of the CIA, and deliberately flown into the ground. Either way, accusations have persisted that the murder was somehow connected to Damon Dash.

The video had been directed by high-ranking industry favourite Hype Williams, who did not board the plane. Aaliyah's family also had a lucky escape, as her brother Rashad, now a writer, film director and screenwriter, revealed that one or more members of her immediate family were almost always present at her video shoots, but that all had been fortuitously absent from this one.

Back with the strange stuff, Germany's 'Die Zeit' newspaper published posthumous excerpts of an interview with Aaliyah, in which she appeared to be relating premonitions of her death:

> "It is dark in my favourite dream. Someone is following me. I don't know why. I'm scared. Then suddenly I lift off. Far away. How do I feel? As if I am swimming in the air. Free. Weightless. Nobody can reach me. Nobody can touch me. It's a wonderful feeling."

Could these be the memories of a Monarch-programmed alter?

It has been noted that shortly before her death, Aaliyah had been filming the macabre movie 'Queen Of The Damned,' in which she portrayed a vampire queen by the name of Akasha whose blood ends up being drained by her successors as her powers diminish. It was commercially released six months after her death.

Aaliyah was a close friend of Kidada Jones, the daughter of Michael Jackson producer (and 'Vibe' magazine founder) Quincy Jones. (Jackson and Aaliyah both died on the 25th of the month, as did Lisa 'Left Eye' Lopes.) Kidada Jones had also been engaged to Tupac Shakur, who also died an untimely death. There are interconnecting links between key players everywhere you look in these stories.

Left Eye's own story is another riddled with dark and strange elements. She died in another 'accident,' again just outside the continental United States, this time in Honduras on 25th April 2002, when she swerved and flipped the SUV she was driving on a busy road. All eight of the passengers she was carrying survived, while she herself died from a massive blow to the head and a fracture at the base of her cranium.

Lopes provided the 'L' part of the group TLC's name, generally providing the rap verses while bandmates T-Boz and Chilli sang the verses. The 'Left Eye' nickname is one that will spark the curiosity of anyone who has read the chapter on symbolism, with all its connotations to the infamous all-seeing eye, and she would often appear in videos and in photos with her eye highlighted or painted around. Many interpretations of Egyptian mythology maintain that the Eye of Horus is a sign representing sacrifice and rebirth. Her private life was not without turmoil, and she's remembered for having burned down the house of Atlanta Falcons football player Andrew Rison in 1994. Inevitably, the mainstream media portrayed her as an alcoholic with mental health issues in the wake of this.

Left Eye had gone to Honduras in 2002, at the tail end of a turbulent career with TLC that involved much in-fighting and legal wrangling, seemingly in a bid to 'detox' and clean up her life. She was reportedly engaging in yoga, hiking and natural dieting. A film crew was following her movements for 27 (!) days for a 'VH1 Rock Docs' film, which came to be titled 'The Last Days Of Left-Eye.' The crew were reportedly filming at the time of her death.

The author known as Isaac Weishaupt goes into much detail on Left Eye's passing in his fascinating book 'Sacrifice: Magic Behind The Mic:'

"Some theorists speculate that she could have been triggered to actually wreck the SUV through an elaborate mind-control program, similar to the film 'The Manchurian Candidate,' where the victim has a small section of the mind take over and perform an automated action without the conscious ability to stop it. The support for this theory is that she appears to have a calm, trance-like demeanour, (although I disagree with all of that because the documentary seems to show otherwise.) If she actually wrecked the car on purpose, the only thing that would support the theory would be the fact that she believed she

was possessed by a spirit named Nikki. During the documentary she says: "Anytime I got drunk this girl Nikki would show up. When I got drunk I was just a different person. When these two started battling it out, I had to create a third person to straighten them out.'

"She later details an evil twin named Nina as well, and that she was creating all these different personalities, and that's when her problems started. This sounds like the problems that occur when people start dabbling in magic and evoking other people's spirits. This also happens in ghost hunting or ouija board sessions where people try to contact the spirit realm and become possessed. It's possible that Left Eye was plagued by these spirits before she went to Honduras and was truly trying to cleanse them away."

The website PanacheReport quoted Left Eye's mother, Wanda Coleman, as having said: "Her death was pre-destined. The Lord had already prepared me for Lisa's death two years in advance."

Her own fatal accident wasn't Left Eye's only tragic encounter during her time in Honduras. Almost three weeks earlier, a vehicle in which she was riding, driven by her personal assistant, knocked down and killed a ten-year-old boy, Bayron Isaul Fuentes Lopez, as he stepped off the sidewalk into the road. In the VH1 documentary, she states that she felt the presence of a spirit following her, and that it may have been a mistake that the boy died and not her—particularly in light of the similarity of their surnames. Left Eye was widely reported to have keenly dabbled in the occult, and right before her moment of death, the VH1 film shows her holding a tin that seems to have housed a set of Tarot cards. A passenger in the back is heard asking for 'the cards,' right before the SUV veers out of control.

Additionally, Isaac Weishaupt observes that:

"The final few scenes before the day of filming Left Eye's fatal accident included a chilling shot of Left Eye in her room, saying that whatever you fear gets manifested when you're in Honduras. She said it's like going down a hill in a car and not hitting the brakes. Meanwhile, on the wall of the room, you can see that she spray-painted a giant All-Seeing-Eye of Horus.

"She was also seen holding the dead boy's shoes, and says that she felt the spirit that is haunting her had killed the child by mistake. She also said she doesn't believe in death, but rather transformation ... The fact that she was in possession of the dead boy's shoes is of concern because this is a practice known as Sympathetic Magic. Practitioners believe that this use of a material-world object would physically link a person to it. This is also used with voodoo dolls when they inflict pain upon the doll and the person feels it in a similar manner. In fact, this concept holds even more value when you consider that Honduras has a population known as the Garifuna, who practice a religion that some compare to Haitian Voodoo. Left Eye's aunt had suspicions of voodoo because, not only did Left Eye die in an odd sequence of events, but her uncle, Anthony Lopes, also died. He accompanied her to Honduras and stayed after the fatal accident, only to succumb to congestive heart failure just months later."

One implication is that Left Eye's death may have been some form of industry ritual sacrifice, but equally, it may have been the result of her dabbling in the dark occult magick that seems to permeate so much of the music game, and where certain artists seem to be possessed by, or at least in contact with, entities from outside of this physical plane. Who can really say what the case here? Either way, portents and a general air of unease are present throughout.

The Proof is in the Programming

Another untimely and suspicious death in the hip-hop world is that of Proof, a member of the Detroit group D12, and a close childhood friend of Eminem. Proof was shot dead during an altercation outside a nightclub in Detroit's infamous 8 Mile district. The usual confusion and conflicting stories arise when it comes to the fine detail of what went down. Proof's death could well be dismissed as the consequence of fights occurring in a dangerous part of town, were it not for another piece of bizarre and unsettling Predictive Programming, which appeared to portray the incident in advance. The video to Eminem's 2004 single 'Toy Soldiers,' depicts Proof getting shot and killed outside of a night-club in very similar fashion to what came to pass on 11th April 2006.

Did Eminem and those who control him have prior knowledge of Proof's demise? The cover to Proof's 2005 album, 'Searching For Jerry Garcia,' (named after the Grateful Dead frontman and CIA asset who had died exactly ten years earlier,) shows him clutching a skeleton, as if symbolically embracing death.

Hold the Ambulance

Intriguingly, Cedars-Sinai Medical Center in Los Angeles figures heavily in the strange deaths of many celebrities, causing some to question whether it houses some kind of mind-control facility. The Notorious BIG was 'rushed' there after being shot, despite a closer hospital being reportedly available, Whitney Houston's daughter Bobbi Kristina was 'rushed' there after being 'discovered unconscious' the first time around, Britney Spears was 'rushed' there for a 'medical examination,' actor Charlie Sheen, who achieved notoriety for publicly questioning the official story of 9/11, was 'rushed' there with a hernia pain. (He's since been rumoured to be HIV Positive.) Others who have died there include Heavy D, Barry White, Minnie Riperton, George Gerschwin, Brittany Murphy and the film-maker Aaron Russo, another researcher whose work questioned the official story of 9/11 and implicated Nick Rockefeller as being complicit. Russo *just happened* to contract bladder cancer shortly afterwards. It's not necessarily the place to be 'rushed' to, in my humble opinion.

Blood Sacrifice 101

An indication of how far the idea of celebrities giving up loved ones in exchange for engineered fame and fortune has reached, came with a news story that is shocking, yet carries an air of morbid hilarity. In 2013, it emerged that a struggling would-be rapper from Virginia with the catchy moniker of Wafeeq Sabir El-Amin, had attempted to kill his best friend, since he believed this would qualify as an acceptable sacrifice to 'the Illuminati,' who would in turn facilitate a successful career. After a night of smoking weed together, the friend reported waking to find El-Amin pointing a gun at him. There was a struggle in which the friend was shot in the hand. He then grappled to grab the gun, with

El-Amin getting shot in the stomach in the process. The news story, on the Red Ice Creations website, stated:

> *"Deputy Commonwealth's Attorney Thomas L. Johnson noted that El-Amin had become obsessed with the Illuminati and truly believed that there was a link between hip-hop and the secret-society. In El-Amin's mind, he believed that a 'sacrifice' was expected of people that wished to join the ranks of the Illuminati. Johnson went on to say that El-Amin believed the Illuminati controlled the careers of popular hip-hop musicians, and that they were the key to success. Johnson also stated that before El-Amin shot his friend, he supposedly exclaimed, "You are my sacrifice."*

Body count

The idea of blood sacrifices is obviously extremely difficult territory to tread, given that there's no direct proof for anyone outside of the circle that any individual cases may have taken place or not. There are also a wide variety of death methods involved, many of which would require complicity from other parties in order to be kept secret if foul play is indeed at work. This is not beyond the bounds of possibility, of course, particularly when you come to an understanding of how inter-connected everything is in the world of secret-societies. It's never the intention to cause undue hurt or offence to the families of those involved, however. Any researcher into the subject, therefore, is only able to speculate on possibilities, rather than being able to lay claim to the definitive truth. With this in mind, the following are further examples of *possible* blood sacrifices in the music industry that have been cited from various sources. They remain suggestions only, of course, rather than provable fact, and readers must make up their own minds about each one, and do further research of their own if they wish. Any, or all of these deaths may indeed be down to the factors given in the official story, but it would have been remiss to have left them out of a chapter discussing matters of this nature.

A perennial suggestion concerns the sudden death of Kanye West's mother, Donda. He was famously close to her, even dedicating a song on his second album to her, 'Hey Mama,' while she was still alive, in which he spoke of his appreciation for her having instilled moral values in him. Donda died as a result of complications following surgery for liposuction and breast-reduction in November 2007. Kanye was visibly affected by her death, occurring as it did a few months before his split from fiancée Alexis Phifer. These events largely dictated the dark mood of his subsequent '808s & Heartbreak' LP, and as previously discussed, his music changed dramatically from this point on.

Kanye used a very interesting turn of phrase when interviewed for 'Q' magazine in June 2015. When asked what was the biggest sacrifice he had made for his massive level of success, he replied: "my mom." He went on to add: "If I had never moved to LA she'd be alive . . . I don't want to go far into it because it will bring me to tears."

Kanye isn't the only artist to have lost their mother quickly and unexpectedly in recent times. Outkast frontman Andre Benjamin, better known as Andre 3000, had his mother Sharon die one day after his 38th birthday in May 2013, aged 58. She was said to have died in her sleep of 'natural causes,' with no further information having been made public. Just a few days later came the news that Bruno Mars was putting on a brave face and managing a smile as he arrived in Washington for a show, some days after his 55-year-old mother Bernadette had died of a reported brain aneurysm in Hawaii.

NWA rapper-turned-super-producer Dr. Dre is another titan of the hip-hop scene who has had rumours follow him around for years. Most of these surround the untimely death of his son, Andre Romelle Young Jr., in August 2008, who was discovered dead in his bed by his mother. The coroner's report blamed it on an overdose of heroin and morphine. An earlier death in Dre's family had been the passing of Tyree Du Sean Crayon, Dre's half-brother from his mother Verna's second marriage. The sombre track 'The Message' on Dre's '2001' album is dedicated to Tyree's memory, (although it is claimed that the track was ghost-written for Dre by rapper Royce Da' 5 '9 who receives no writing credit in the sleeve notes.) There appear to be no pictures of Tyree on the internet, or information about when or how he died.

Some have also suggested there is a connection between Dr Dre's phenomenal levels of success and the death of the singer Nate Dogg, who had collaborated with Dre on his single 'The Next Episode' along with other projects . . . although the same claim is often made with reference to fellow Long Beach rapper Snoop Dogg, with whom Nate was equally collaborative. Nate, real name Nathaniel Hale, died on 15th March 2011 from what were said to be health problems brought on by multiple previous strokes.

Others have suggested the early deaths of rappers Big Pun and Pimp C may have been connected to associates Fat Joe and Rap-a-Lot Records proprietor J Prince respectively.

Rapper T.I. and Tameka 'Tiny' Cottle, formerly of the R&B girl group Xscape, lost their second child together when their daughter arrived stillborn six months into the pregnancy in 2007. The previous year, T.I.'s personal assistant and lifelong friend Philant Johnson died when he was gunned down outside a Cincinatti nightclub.

Among other music-makers to have lost children young are Prince, whose son Boy Gregory was born with Pfeiffer's Syndrome and died a week later, Led Zeppelin vocalist Robert Plant whose five-year-old son Karac died of a severe stomach infection in 1977, and Marie Osmond, whose son Michael is said to have committed suicide by jumping out of an eighth-floor window in 2010. A story that devastated the public in 1991, meanwhile, was the tragic death of Eric Clapton's four-year-old son Conor, who plunged from the open window of Clapton's 53rd-floor apartment in Manhattan. Clapton fathered Conor with Italian model Lori del Santo while he was still married to Patti Boyd, who had previously been the first wife of George Harrison. Conor's death came during an unlucky period for Clapton; seven months earlier fellow musician Stevie Ray Vaughan, plus Clapton's manager, agent, bodyguard, assistant tour manager and a pilot, had all keen killed in a helicopter crash after leaving a gig in Wisconsin. Clapton dedicated the song 'Tears In Heaven' to the memory of Conor. Inevitably, however, rumours have persisted that there may have been foul play involved in the boy's fall.

The subject of infant deaths also ties into other areas of human society since, as I hope has become apparent by now, all are ultimately linked at their very upper levels. Something that seems to have flown under the radar of most of the British public, is the fact that the country's last three Prime Ministers have all lost children in tragic circumstances. First off, Cherie Blair, wife of PM (and so many other things,) Tony Blair, suffered a miscarriage in 2002. In her recently-published memoirs, Cherie actually revealed that her husband and his PR guru Alastair Campbell, had strategically timed the announcement of the miscarriage to 'avert false speculation about an early invasion of Iraq,' embroiled as the UK was at that time in the second engineered Gulf War (massacre.)

Next up for the PM role following Blair's departure in 2007 was the highly forgettable Gordon Brown. He and his wife Sarah announced the death of their firstborn, a daughter named Jennifer Jane, on 7th January 2002. She was said to have suffered a brain haemorrhage ten days after being born.

Brown's successor in 2010 was (distant cousin of the Queen—but don't worry, it's just another coincidence,) David Cameron. The previous year, he and his wife Samantha had announced the death of their firstborn son, Ivan, who was said to have been born with a rare combination of cerebral palsy and a form of severe epilepsy. Like the Blair and Brown children concerned, Ivan had been born in 2002.

Unlucky lot, these politicians.

Hip-hop oddities

Among other deaths in the world of hip-hop that have raised suspicions are the murder of Run DMC co-founder Jason Mizell, aka Jam Master Jay, at a recording studio in Queens, New York on 30th October 2002 during the season of Halloween, (which in Pagan traditions, is always an important season for sacrifice.) Numerology is thought to be an important factor in other cases, with the date of the death holding special significance, as are planetary conjunctions and other astrological influences. Many suspected a connection to fellow rapper 50 Cent. As Wikipedia puts it:

> "In 2003, Kenneth 'Supreme' McGriff, a convicted drug dealer and longtime friend of Murder Inc. heads Irv and Chris Gotti, was investigated for targeting Mizell (Jam Master Jay,) because the DJ defied an industry blacklist of rapper 50 Cent that was imposed because of 'Ghetto Qu'ran,' a song 50 Cent wrote about McGriff's drug history.

Randy Allen, a former business partner of Jay's, one of the witnesses to the shooting, was also named as a suspect. Later, a man named Ronald 'Tenad' Washington was named as a suspected accomplice in the murder, as well as that of Randy 'Stretch' Walker, a close associate of Tupac. Washington was never convicted, however, and no-one has been further investigated or charged with Mizell's murder."

A rapper whose early demise was highlighted by author Isaac Weishaupt as possibly having an element of foreshadowing was Ol' Dirty Bastard, known as ODB, one of the original members of the Wu Tang Clan collective. Weishaupt points out the tellingly paranoid nature of some of his lyrics leading up to his death in November 2004, such as: "I need help because the black man is God, the government is after me, and the worst is, black man is the devil" on the song 'Diesel.' And later: "They already did 2Pac, my children, all six billion humans, Biggie Smalls on the planet Earth, somebody help me!" And on his pop hit with Kelis, 'Got Your Money:' "I'm the ODB as you can see, FBI don't you be watchin' me." As Weishaupt continues:

"ODB said Bush had a personal beef with him and that the government was out to assassinate him. Similar to other artists and their downfalls, his last few years were spent in jail stints, legal issues and eccentric behaviour. Some claimed that the government microchipped him because he made his way on to a list of the influential people that were outspoken enough to cause too much commotion. Officially he died from an accidental drug overdose of cocaine and Tramadol, but others claim foul play. They say he fell on his knee at a show and asked for a painkiller, which a mysterious stranger gave to him, but he never woke up again.

"A few years after his death, it was revealed through a Freedom of Information Act request that the FBI did in fact have a file on him, which included statements that the Wu Tang Clan was 'heavily involved in the sale of drugs, illegal guns, weapons possession, murder, carjacking and other types of violent crime'."

There was also the murder of the phenomenally-gifted Big L, a member of the Diggin' In The Crates crew, who was gunned down in February 1999 just a few blocks from where he had grown up in Harlem. His slaying was seemingly connected to the criminal activities of his brother; L was either mistaken for him, or was shot in order to make a point. The prime suspect was a man named Gerard Woodley, one of L's childhood friends, who was arrested by police but later released without charge. Big L's murder, therefore, remains yet another from the black/hip-hop community that has been chalked up as 'unsolved.'

The enigma of Guru and Solar

While endless scrutiny has gone towards the murders of Biggie and Tupac, (and to a lesser extent to the deaths of Jam Master Jay and others,) there is another legendary hip-hop MC whose death is full of strange and dark factors and a glut of unanswered questions, but who rarely gets discussed at all any more. Guru, the former frontman of the group Gang Starr, is very much the forgotten candidate when it comes to premature deaths that smack of foul play. Guru was one of my personal all-time favourites due to his smooth-voiced monotone delivery, and incredibly incisive lyrics, which have meant all the more to me since I 'woke up.' As far back as 1992 he made devastatingly candid observations on the true nature of the corporate music industry on the Gang Starr track 'Conspiracy,' with lyrics like:

> *"Even in this rap game all that glitters ain't gold,*
>
> *Now that rap is big business the snakes got bold,*
>
> *They give you wack contracts and try to make you go pop,*
>
> *Cause they have no regard for real hip-hop."*

And later, on the title track of Gang Starr's 'Moment Of Truth' album, Guru came with lyrics so on-the-money that they deserve to be taught in schools:

> *"Actions have reactions, don't be quick to judge,*

You may not know the hardships people don't speak of,

It's best to step back, and observe with couth,

For we all must meet our moment of truth."

Guru, known in his early days as Guru Keithy E, was born Keith Elam in Boston, into a middle-class family that was far removed from the ghetto lifestyle of many of his peers. His father was a judge and his mother a co-director of libraries in the public school system. Having honed his rapping skills, he found fame alongside the Texas-born, New York-based producer DJ Premier and rapper Big Shug as the group Gang Starr, which released its first album in 1989, and went on to be one of the most consistent and well-respected hip-hop acts of the 90s. In 1993, he released the first of his three solo 'Jazzmatazz' albums, fusing jazz influences with hip-hop rhyming, as a side project.

By the early 2000s, Guru had reportedly fallen out with DJ Premier and ceased their working relationship, instead beginning collaborations with a self-proclaimed 'super-producer' by the name of Solar, (real name John Mosher, and not to be confused with the French rapper MC Solaar.) Solar had appeared with very little to show by way of a track record in hip-hop production, and he took up the mantle of producing Guru's ongoing 'Jazzmatazz' series, as well as his 'Version 7.0: The Street Scriptures.' Many Guru fans commented on the decline in the standards of his music. By this point, it had become common knowledge that Guru was an alcoholic and was suffering from other health issues, including depression and severe asthma.

According to Guru's family members and friends, Solar seemed to gain a manipulative and controlling hold over him at this point. They have claimed that Solar took any opportunity to reinforce the rift between Guru and Premier by telling Guru that Premier hated him, and that he worked to cut Guru off from his family. Guru's sister Patricia said: "My brother and I were extremely close. Remained that way until he started working with Solar. So I know that Solar's presence was the thing that caused our relationship to be different." Solar publicly referred to himself as Guru's 'teacher' and 'healer,' also referring to himself as a 'God,' and on one occasion, comparing his own life mission with that of Jesus.

According to Guru's close circle, Solar's relationship to the rapper was an abusive one. 'Jazzmatazz' collaborator Nick "Brownman" commented: "I've seen Solar hit Guru full-on in the face. And the next day, Guru looked me in the eye and said that he dropped some weights and hurt himself in the gym." Former employee of Solar, Tasha Denham, states: "I had to get in-between them fighting, because Solar wouldn't quit . . . Guru had severe asthma, and I had to break it up. If I didn't, I think Solar would've kept beating him."

Other strange things were happening, too. Guru no longer gave interviews or made any public appearances without Solar by his side. In many cases, Solar answered Guru's questions for him, and cut interviews and shows short on a whim. Fans commented that Guru appeared increasingly withdrawn, vacant, thin, and ultimately ill.

On 28th February 2010, Guru suffered a cardiac arrest and went into a coma from which he never regained consciousness. He died alone in hospital on 19th April amidst reports that a clumped afro now appeared on his usually slick-shaven head. Guru's family complained that Solar was preventing them from visiting him in hospital. After Guru's passing, Solar became CEO of 7 Grand Records, the label that Guru had started.

Much of Solar's activity from this point was documented on a website, www.fucksolar.com, set up by a collective of Guru fans. Hacked e-mails from Solar were posted on the site. This may have been the factor that enabled him to get fucksolar.com taken down after a few weeks.

Among the site's claims were that Solar had attempted to embezzle hundreds of thousands of dollars out of Guru's various business interests, that he had used Guru's social media accounts to chat up and arrange sex with women, (despite being married,) and that he had made exaggerated, self-aggrandising claims about his own status as Guru's 'saviour.' Solar had also claimed that Guru had awakened temporarily from his coma, the site reported, and had composed a letter appointing Solar as his sole representative. The authenticity of this letter was challenged by Guru's family, who accused Solar of faking it. The family also accused Solar of having announced Guru's death to the media before telling them, and of travelling with his body to the funeral home, passing himself off as Guru's brother.

Much scorn, along with direct accusations, were directed at Solar on-line in the weeks following Guru's death. At first, Solar replied to everything that had been written about him. Fans claimed that he was using false names to pass himself off as some third party, but giving himself away by his consistently appalling grasp of spelling, punctuation and basic grammar. Throughout, they said, he displayed a level of self-denial and a complete lack of conscience for anything he had done.

It all raises the question of just where Solar came from, and whether he drifted into Guru's life in some random, haphazard fashion, or whether he was sent into Guru's inner circle by some outside party. It wouldn't be the first time that those who control the music game have turned against artists who espouse positive, conscious music. The air of gloom that pervaded Guru's last days have led many to ask whether he had been put under some kind of dark, voodoo-like spell.

Reflecting on the question, however, does tend to suggest that Solar was following a personal agenda, since the Satanic secret-society network does tend to reward those who play ball by elevating them up the ladder to fame and fortune, whereas Solar's career hasn't exactly flourished since 2010. In fact it's probably safe to assume that there isn't an artist in the industry that's keen to work with him given his track record.

Ultimately, there has been no justice for Guru, and the tragic end to his life remains a largely-forgotten and under-discussed chapter in music history. His words live on eternally, however, allowing for reflection on their potency. Particularly the line from 'Moment Of Truth' that runs:

"Just as you get what's coming to you, everybody else is going to get theirs too."

Legends revisited

There are many who accept the idea of the music industry deliberately offing many of its key artists, but who reject the suggestion of any ritual element to the killings. They claim instead that the motivation is purely financial, stemming from the old adage that an artist is worth more to a label dead than alive. There's certainly evidence to demonstrate how an artist's popularity can shoot way beyond what it might have been if they'd remained alive, with Tupac often cited as an example, and the cynical ploy to increase the retail price of Whitney Houston's back catalogue after her death in the run-up to that year's Valentine's Day offers further credibility. I'm not denying that corporate greed is a factor—particularly in the context of the lousy publishing deals that artists often complain of, where contracts see to it that the corporations retain the lion's share of the profit from their intellectual property while they themselves are left with crumbs. (It can be like that with book publishing deals, too!) But I see no reason why both elements could not be at play in tandem with each other; a decision is taken to take out a particular artist in line with the ritual magick of the dark religion, and the fact that the corporations stand to make a killing, (no pun intended,) serves (for them) as a very happy consequence. This would also serve as a mutually beneficial way of destroying troublemakers who had become a thorn in the side of the Establishment.

Viewing things from this informed perspective does tend to cast new light on a number of legendary rock music deaths. Here are just a handful of the most high-profile ones, with a brief summary of some of the anomalies and unanswered questions surrounding the official accounts. (For more on the deaths of Elvis Presley and Brian Jones see the earlier chapters.) These are quick overviews only and don't claim to be comprehensive, as to delve into the fine detail of each case would justify several entire books in their own right. But hopefully, these at least get across the fact that nothing about the official versions adds up, (as ever,) and the truth is highly obfuscated with all manner of foul play at work. To be entirely clear, I'm not saying that every one of these deaths definitely constituted some form of ritual sacrifice—just that in each case it does at least remain a possibility.

Jimi Hendrix

Like Jim Morrison, Jimi Hendrix had taken on mythical status as an icon of pro-peace, anti-war activism and youthful rebellion by the time of his death in London on 18th September 1970. Like Morrison, he was 27. His birthdate, 27th November, was the same as that of Bruce Lee, another iconic figure who died young in mysterious circumstances. As author Alex Constantine commented in his book 'The Covert War Against Rock:' "As the music of youth and resistance fell under the cross-hairs of the CIA's CHAOS war, it was probable that Jimi Hendrix–the tripping, peacenik 'Black Elvis' of the 60s–found himself a target." An FBI file obtained by a group of tenacious students from the University Of Santa Barbara in 1979 confirmed that Hendrix had been the subject of FBI surveillance, and furthermore, that he had been placed on the federal 'Security Index,' a list of 'subversives' to be rounded up and placed in detainment camps in the event of a national emergency.

Hendrix's is another death blamed on the sex, drugs and Rock & Roll lifestyle. It has gone down in the official record that he asphyxiated on his own vomit, as a consequence of ingesting barbiturates.

It's widely acknowledged among alternative researchers that Hendrix's death occurred at the hands of his manager, Michael Jeffery, who hired a gang to break into Hendrix's Notting Hill hotel room and murder him. Jeffery was born in London in 1932, and after a brief bout of military service, embarked on a career as an 'intelligence' agent. According to Hendrix biographers Harry Shapiro and Caesar Glebbeek, Jeffery often boasted of "undercover work against the Russians, of murder, mayhem and torture in foreign cities." Jeffery was also acknowledged to have ties with organised crime networks. Quite how these credentials qualified him as a rock musician's manager over all other contenders, therefore, remains unclear. It seems Jeffery was deliberately sent into Hendrix's inner circle by parties unknown. Jeffery reportedly exercised a manipulative hold over Hendrix, and, having come to realise his true nature, the musician became desperate to escape his binding contract with him. In May 1969, Jeffery reportedly planted heroin on Hendrix, leading to his subsequent arrest in Toronto, as an intimidating reminder of the control he could exert. Through his Mob connections, Jeffery is said to have embezzled and laundered large amounts of Hendrix's income. Plus, as Alex Constantine adds:

"Some of Hendrix's friends have concluded that Jeffery stood to make a greater sum of money from a dead Jimi Hendrix than a living one. There was also mention of a one-million-dollar insurance

*policy covering Hendrix's life made out with Jeffery as the benefi-
ciary... Crushing musical voices of dissent was proving to be an
immensely profitable enterprise, because a dead rocker leaves behind
a fortune in publishing rights and royalties."*

Many researchers into the Hendrix enigma have speculated that Jeffery was commissioned to keep tabs on him, once his profound ability
to pen revolutionary lyrics had been noted, and at the point where it
became clear he stood to have a profound effect on the spirituality and
consciousness of his fans. Hendrix was another highly vocal opponent
of the Vietnam War and had voiced his support for the Black Pan-
ther movement, a group that the government and FBI of the day had
marked out as dangerous subversives that they were determined to put
down. The lyrics to 'Black Gold', one of a series of unreleased demo
tracks recorded early in 1970, give an insight into the type of lyrical
dexterity that a draconian control system might prefer didn't get out
into the mainstream. You can check out the lyrics here–http://www.
metrolyrics.com/black-gold-lyrics-jimi-hendrix.html

According to many, the official account that Hendrix 'asphyxiated' is
code for the truth that he effectively drowned in red wine. The method
could even be described as 'waterboarding' in modern parlance. This
was confirmed by Dr. John Bannister, the on-call registrar at St. Mary
Abbot's Hospital in Kensington. 'The Times' reports Bannister as
saying:

> *"We had a sucker that you put down into his trachea, the entrance to
> his lungs and to the whole of the back of his throat. We kept sucking
> him out and it kept surging and surging. He had already vomited up
> masses of red wine and I would have thought there was half a bottle
> of wine in his hair. He had really drowned in a massive amount of
> red wine."*

Alex Constantine adds:

> *"... Hendrix was, the evidence suggests, forced to drink a quantity of
> wine. The barbiturates, as (Hendrix biographer) Tony Brown notes,
> "seriously inhibited Jimi's normal cough reflex." Unable to cough the*

wine back up, "it went straight down into his lungs ... It is quite possible that he thrashed about for some time, fighting unsuccessfully to gain his breath." It is doubtful that Hendrix would have continued to swallow the wine in 'massive' volumes had it begun to fill his lungs."

Michael Jeffery was said to have been behaving oddly in the days following Hendrix's death. He refused to go inside the church in Seattle for Hendrix's eulogy, instead sitting in a limousine outside. He appeared to be consumed by guilt, and at one point, according to recording engineer Alan Douglas, even confessed. A further claim came from James 'Tappy' Wright, a roadie for the group The Animals, who Jeffery had also managed. Wright stated that he had been with Jeffery a year after the Hendrix death, and that he had confessed to murdering Hendrix by plying him with pills and red wine in order to claim on his life insurance.

It seems karma came calling for Michael Jeffery on 5th March 1973, when the Iberia flight that he was aboard was involved in a mid-air collision over France with another plane. Unfortunately, the remaining 60 passengers and seven crew on Jeffery's flight were also killed. All on the second plane survived. Jeffery had been on his way from his home in Majorca to London for a court case related to Hendrix's affairs.

As with the Jim Morrison story, Hendrix's girlfriend was present in his room on the night he died. However, the testimony that Monika Dannemann gave contradicted the findings of medical personnel on the scene in many respects. Dannemann herself, like Jim Morrison's wife before her, came to an untimely end when her body was discovered in April 1996 in a fume-filled car near her home in Sussex, England, in what the police dismissed as 'suicide.'

Sixteen days after Hendrix's passing, singer Janis Joplin was discovered dead in her Hollywood motel room, the official cause of death given as 'an overdose of heroin, possibly compounded by alcohol.' She was also 27. Her being a musical associate of Hendrix has led to inevitable suspicion that her death may in some way be connected to knowledge she may have had of what had really happened to him.

It suited those involved to see to it that Hendrix's legacy was tarnished with images of another tragic, self-destructive drug addict. As author John Holmstrom concludes in his book 'Who Killed Jimi?':

"He didn't die from a drug overdose. He was not an out-of-control dope fiend. Jimi Hendrix was not a junkie. And anyone who would use his death as a warning to stay away from drugs should warn people against the other things that killed Jimi—the stresses of dealing with the music industry, the craziness of being on the road, and especially, the dangers of involving oneself in radical, or even unpopular, political movements ... Whenever Jimi Hendrix's death is blamed on drugs, it accomplishes the goals of the FBI's program. It not only slanders Jimi's personal and professional reputation, but the entire rock revolution in the 60s."

Jim Morrison

As detailed in the earlier chapter on the psychedelic era, Jim Morrison's family background is a factor which has been conspicuously missing from official biographies over the years, his father having been a high-ranking US naval commander. In this regard, there are many parallels to the upbringing of Rolling Stones founder Brian Jones on the other side of the Atlantic, whose own father was a government military intelligence officer. Both Morrison and Jones went on to die in suspicious circumstances at the age of 27, both on 3rd July, two years apart. As a matter of curiosity, this date turns out to be the Feast of St. Thomas the Apostle, occurring a day before the Earth is said to be at its furthest annual point from the sun.

Morrison, (often known as 'The Lizard King' in a piece of imagery that will raise the eyebrows of anyone familiar with the work of David Icke!) was found dead on 3rd July 1971, in a bathtub in the Paris apartment he shared with his common-law wife Pamela Courson. There are no police reports, emergency call logs, medical examiner logs, reports or records related to his death, and no autopsy was ever performed. The official cause given was 'heart failure.' According to Wikipedia:

"The absence of an official autopsy left many questions regarding Morrison's cause of death. In 'Wonderland Avenue', Danny Suger-man discussed his encounter with Courson after she returned to the United States. According to Sugerman's account, Courson stated that Morrison had died of an accidental heroin overdose, having snorted what he believed to be cocaine. Sugerman added that Courson had given numerous contradictory versions of Morrison's death, saying at times that she had killed Morrison, or that his death was her fault. Courson's story of Morrison's unintentional ingestion of heroin, resulting in an accidental overdose, is supported by the confession of Alain Ronay, who has written that Morrison died of a haemorrhage after snorting Courson's heroin, and that Courson nodded off instead of phoning for medical help, leaving Morrison alone and bleeding to death."

Some contradictions arise from the fact that, according to paramedics from the local fire brigade, they found Morrison's body with a smile etched on to his face, something which is entirely inconsistent with the stated manner of death. There are also reports of The Doors' manager, Bill Siddons, arriving at the Paris apartment to find the body already in a coffin which had been sealed shut. Courson apparently notified the US Embassy of Jim's death only three days later, and listed him as having no living relatives. (He had plenty.)

Morrison was very much the iconic rock star of his era, viewed as a figurehead of rebellion against the establishment status quo, and the-oretically viewed as a dangerous role-model for a control system that wished to keep the youthful generation within its remit. He was out-spoken in his music, his poetry and his interviews, and many have argued that it's not difficult to understand how Morrison's popularity would have been seen as a problem, and that this could have been a motive for his engineered death. Indeed, Morrison is reported to have been the target of much harassment and intimidation at the hands of the FBI during his final years. Some confusion arises with this theory, however, taking into account the recent revelations about Morrison's connections to military intelligence via his father.

In 1975, rumours that Morrison had somehow faked his death and had launched a new life as the proprietor of a communications agency, surfaced with the book 'The Bank Of America Of Louisiana,' supposedly written by, and credited to, Jim Morrison. The book has since been discredited as a hoax by almost all commentators. As Alex Constantine notes:

"The rumour was a deliberate obfuscation concocted by unknown covert operators. The proper question is 'who killed Jim Morrison?,' not 'is he still alive and working for the Bank Of America?'"

Given that Pamela Courson was the only other person supposed to have been present when Morrison passed, any chance of establishing further truth disappeared when she herself died of what was reported to be a 'drugs overdose' on 24th April 1974. As 'The Covert War Against Rock' observes, this was: "a few days before a judge would have ruled in her favour concerning a dispute over the distribution of the Morrison inheritance, a decision that would have brought her, as Morrison's common-law wife and sole heir, a quarter of The Doors' income and an immediate payout of half a million dollars." He adds: "Dr. Max Vasille, the medical examiner, consistently turns down all interviews related to Morrison's death."

There are some very esoteric aspects to Morrison's character which have to be considered, meanwhile, in order to get a full picture of what he was all about. According to the book 'The Lost Writings Of Jim Morrison,' he had married Pamela Courson in a Wiccan ceremony, where they stood inside a pentagram and drank each-other's blood. Morrison is quoted as saying: "I met the Spirit of Music, an appearance of the Devil in a Venice canal. Running, I saw a Satan, or Satyr (Pan,) moving beside me, a fleshly shadow of my secret mind . . ."

In rock groupie Pamela Des Barres' book 'Rock Bottom,' she quotes Doors bandmate Ray Manzarek as saying of Morrison: "He was not a performer. He was not an entertainer. He was not a showman. He was a shaman. He was possessed." And later: "While he, (Morrison,) was staying at the Chateau Marmont, he spent a few wild nights with a buxom neighbour . . . , once waking up in a tangle of bloody sheets after they shared champagne glasses of each other's blood."

John Lennon

The official version of events has it that John Lennon was shot dead by Mark David Chapman, who has been presented by the media as a deranged fan, very much fitting the profile of the classic 'lone nutter.' (See Lee Harvey Oswald, Sirhan Sirhan, Adam Lanza, James Holmes, etc, etc.) Lennon was returning to his home at the Dakota Building in Manhattan, (the setting for Roman Polanski's dark gothic horror 'Rosemary's Baby,') with Yoko Ono on the evening of 8th December 1980. Earlier in the day, Chapman had approached Lennon and got him to sign a copy of his new album 'Double Fantasy'. At 10.50pm, Chapman is said to have assumed a trained marksman's position and fired at Lennon's back five times, hitting him with four bullets. He is then said to have calmly waited until police arrived, who found him reading a copy of JD Salinger's 'Catcher In The Rye.' Chapman has been in jail for the crime ever since, and despite consistent appeals for parole over the years, these are always overturned, making it very unlikely that he will ever be released.

There has been much speculation to the effect that Chapman was a classic Manchurian Candidate-style mind-controlled assassin, his behaviour showing all the signs that would be expected. Chapman has consistently stated that he can't remember anything about that fateful night, which certainly fits the model. The consensus of a great many researchers is that it was not Chapman that killed Lennon, however, but that he had served as a diversion, and therefore a 'patsy' to take the rap for the murder, while the real perpetrator disappeared into the shadows.

That real shooter has been named on several occasions as Jose Sanjenis Perdomo, a long-standing CIA operative and trained assassin, who was posing that night as a doorman at the Dakota Building. Even the highly-controlled Wikipedia confirms this, describing him as a 'witness' to Lennon's murder. Perhaps checking up on the effectiveness of his programming, Perdomo famously asked Chapman if he knew what he had done, to which Chapman replied that he had just shot John Lennon. Perdomo has been named as a key member of an elite and very secret squad of assassins codenamed Operation 40, whose personnel have been linked to an extraordinary array of high-profile assassinations, among them John and Robert Kennedy, Martin Luther King,

Bob Marley and Swedish Prime Minister Olof Palme. The official story of Operation 40 tries to convince that it was a secret operation limited to the early 1960s for the purpose of overthrowing the Fidel Castro's Cuban regime, but the evidence suggests that it has extended way beyond that timeframe. George HW Bush is a name that crops up time and time again with relation to Operation 40 and the many assassinations it is said to have been responsible for. Bush has been proven to have been present in Dallas on the day of the JFK assassination. When asked in an interview decades later where he was on that fateful day, he stated he 'couldn't remember.'

The most common motive given for Lennon's murder was that it was sanctioned by the Nixon Administration, which had tried without success to have Lennon deported from the US on several occasions. Lennon had been a highly vocal critic of the government's stance on the Vietnam War. The timing is said to have paved the way for Ronald Reagan, who had been voted in as the 40th US President just a month before. Lennon was equally unpopular with J Edgar Hoover's FBI, and had fallen victim to its COINTELPRO programme of surveillance. Some conspiracy researchers have even suggested that Lennon was about to blow the whistle on the deception surrounding the replacement of Paul McCartney back in 1966, (see this book's 15,000-word chapter on that subject!,) confessing to George Harrison that he could no longer live with the lie, and so had to be quickly removed to keep the secret safe. It's also fair to assume that Lennon hadn't exactly ingratiated himself to the British Establishment when, in 1969, he returned the MBE awarded to him by the Queen four years earlier, in an apparent statement against Empire and the Vietnam War.

The waters get muddied still further, however, when you hear claims from some quarters that, not only was the original Paul McCartney replaced in 1966, but all four Beatles were at some point replaced! According to this theory, it wasn't the real John Lennon who died in 1980, but an impostor. We then have the claims of the American researcher Miles Mathis that in fact, Lennon somehow faked his death, Elvis Presley-style, and has been living all these years under the assumed identity of Mark Staycer, and still performing as a musician. Mathis' comprehensive essay on the subject can be found here–http://mileswmathis.com/lennon.pdf

If Mathis is correct, it presents the infuriatingly perplexing case that Paul McCartney died but is pretending to be alive, whereas John Lennon lived but is pretending to be dead!

Whether there's any truth to the Lennon replacement theory or not, it's always struck me as an enigma how a man known for his mischievous sense of humour and prone to the regular Rock & Roll vices during the Beatles years, could have transformed into the profound spiritual poet he had become by the following decade. Lennon's output between 1970 and 1980 stands among the most captivating, esoteric and truthful of any mainstream musician's material, with songs such as 'Instant Karma,' 'Gimme Some Truth,' 'I Don't Want To Be A Soldier,' 'Woman Is The Nigger Of The World,' 'God,' 'Love,' 'Working Class Hero,' 'Mind Games,' 'Watching The Wheels' and 'Borrowed Time' resonating with so many as the conscious awakening of humanity starts to affect more and more people. Lennon was writing songs 40-plus years ago whose lyrics are even more relevant today. It's possible that this period served as a kind of personal redemption for him, perhaps motivated by a sense of guilt over the excesses and deceptions of the Beatle years, and wanting to make amends. It's equally possible that these songs simply marked a coming-of-age, a maturing as he progressed into his thirties. Some have suggested that the influence of Yoko Ono brought about a kind of spiritual awakening. Others, of course, will tell you that the reason these songs are so potent are because it's someone other than the real John Winston Lennon churning them out!

Either way, he certainly appeared to have got a handle on the reality of the world when he made what's become one of his most famous quotes:

> *"Our society is run by insane people for insane objectives. I think we're being run by maniacs for maniacal ends, and I think I'm liable to be put away as insane for expressing that. That's what's insane about it."*

Theories abound about the true nature of Yoko Ono, too, and how it was that she came to be so influential in Lennon's life. The suggestion that she was responsible for breaking up the Beatles through luring John away from his bandmates is a well-known one. Less familiar are aspects of her background. Her great-grandfather, Zenjiro Yasuda, was the founder of the Yasuda banking conglomerate, with her father having been a descendant of the Emperor of Japan. Yoko was reportedly enrolled at Tokyo's Gakushuin, one of the most exclusive schools in the country which, before World War II, was open only to the Japanese imperial family and aristocrats of the House of Peers. She spent a brief spell in a mental institution in Japan, just prior to her marriage to the American jazz musician and film producer Anthony Cox.

Claims have also persisted that she was a practitioner in the dark occult, probably helped by the title of her 1974 song 'Yes I'm A Witch.' There have also been theories that Lennon, like so many other prominent musicians, was under a degree of MK-Ultra mind control, and that Yoko was sent into his life as his approved handler, to ensure he remained 'on-script' and to report any issues back to her superiors. This may have some connection to John's 'lost weekend' episode in 1973/4 where, with Yoko's apparent blessing, he embarked on a sexual relationship with their personal assistant May Pang, living with her in New York and LA before eventually returning to his marital home. The singer Harry Nilsson is on-record as having been present during much of Lennon's Lost Weekend period. Associations with Nilsson would appear to be bad luck for other musicians, given that both Mama Cass of the Mamas & The Papas and Keith Moon of The Who were discovered dead in the same room of his flat in London's Mayfair in 1974 and 1978 respectively, during his absence. A reportedly devastated Nilsson subsequently sold the flat to Pete Townshend of The Who. Nilsson himself died of heart failure in January 1994, aged 52.

Backmasking crops up again in this particular story, with claims that the Yoko-voiced 'Kiss Kiss Kiss' from their collaborative album 'Double Fantasy,' has lyrics which emerge as "Satan is coming . . . six six six," and later, "We shot John Lennon" when played in reverse.

Numerology, too, seems to have played a big part in the life and death of John Lennon. He was said to have been obsessed with the number 9, inspiring his songs 'Number 9 Dream,' 'Revolution 9' and 'One After 909.' (9 incidentally, was always an important number in the occult work of Aleister Crowley, as well as figuring majorly in the dark magick ritual that was 9/11.) Lennon was born on 9th October 1940, and died forty years and two months later on 9th December

1980, (still 8th December in New York, but already into the early hours of the 9th in his British homeland.) Lennon and Yoko's son Sean was born on 9th October 1975, Lennon's 35th birthday. John's first home was at 9 Newcastle Road in Liverpool.

Bob Marley

Some tenacious delving into Bob Marley's back-story throws up the usual oddities present when it comes to music legends. His father, Norval Sinclair Marley, was part-Jewish, served in the British Royal Marines, and was employed as the overseer of a plantation in Jamaica. Yet more establishment/ military links. Bob's musical stance, like Jim Morrison's, could well have represented rebellion against what his father stood for. But equally, maybe his father's status made Bob rife for manipulation, the way Morrison seemingly was? The Jewish link was alluded to when Ziggy Marley, (real name David,) Bob's third child, married an Israeli woman and gave Hebrew names to each of his three children. He courted controversy when he refused to support a boycott against Israel in the wake of its incursions into Palestine, and proceeded to play a series of dates in Israel, despite being petitioned not to. This could be considered an odd stance for the son of an artist whose entire persona was steeped in rebellion against worldwide oppression, of the type enforced by the Zionist regime. Justifying himself, Ziggy commented: "Rastafarianism has a lot to do with the Old Testament and Solomon and David and Moses, so we have a strong connection from many years back."

Bob Marley is another artist whose activism and ethics saw him fall foul of the CIA. It seems artists with an international fan base of millions whose music preaches love, unity and opposition to tyranny, don't chime too well with the spooks in Langley, Virginia. If the agency had had its way, Marley would have died sooner than he did. This was the planned result of the violent gun attack upon his home on 3rd December 1976 in which he, his wife and his manager were all wounded. It occurred two days before Marley's scheduled appearance at Smile Jamaica, a free concert designed to ease tension between the two opposing political groups, and organised by Jamaican Prime Minister Michael Manley. The CIA were present in Jamaica at the time, and had reportedly been working to destabilise the country's political system ready for a takeover. Messages of unity weren't really on their agenda.

Despite the attack, the concert went ahead, as did Marley's scheduled appearance, elevating him to heroic status. When asked why he had still performed, Marley responded: "The people who are trying to make this world worse aren't taking a day off. How can I?"

Marley and his entourage kept an understandably low profile after this event, installed at their compound with heavy security, and would have been cautious of all around them. Marley was presumably flattered, however, when he was approached to be the subject of a documentary. One of the film-makers reportedly visited the compound, walking past machete-wielding rastas with a present for Marley—a pair of boots. Some accounts of the story say that they were football boots, others that they were cowboy boots. Either way, according to witnesses, when Marley pulled one on he yelped in pain, and upon examination, one of the boots was found to have a sharp protruding copper wire which had pierced Marley's big toe. The wire would appear to have been laced with some kind of cancer-causing agent. A few months later, in Summer 1977, Marley just happened to break his toe while playing soccer. When the bone wouldn't mend, doctors found that the toe had cancer, which went on to spread throughout his body.

The identity of the gift-bearer is very interesting. According to reports he turns out to have been Carl Colby, who just happened to be the son of the former CIA director William Colby. In 2011, Carl Colby produced, directed and narrated a Hollywood movie, 'The Man Nobody Knew,' documenting his father's life and career in the 'intelligence' services. William Colby died in very mysterious circumstances in April 1996. He was found drowned in the Potomac River after taking his canoe out near his home in Rock Point, Maryland, in what the state coroner inferred was a 'tragic accident' owing to a heart attack or stroke. Inevitably, there has been speculation of foul play, particularly since during Colby's time leading the CIA, he had revealed the existence of documents describing illegal activities by the agency, (surely not?!), and had shown a willingness to be more transparent than previous directors. Steven Greer of www.disclosureproject.org also revealed to Art Bell on Coast to Coast AM Radio in a 2004 interview, that Colby was about to reveal the existence of extraterrestrial energy devices that were being suppressed.

Colby had reportedly left his house unlocked, his coffee-maker brewing and his computer switched-on when he suddenly felt the need to go out on a spontaneous boating trip. Greer also pointed out that the circumstances surrounding Colby's death mirror those of a Senator who was about to become a whistleblower in the movie 'The Manchurian Candidate.' The character is murdered while out kayaking in Chesapeake Bay and it's made to look like an accident. Life imitating art once again? Colby was replaced as CIA Director in 1976 by one George HW Bush. Heard of him before anywhere? Carl Colby, meanwhile, cropped up many years later in the trial of OJ Simpson, (the two had been neighbours,) testifying against him. A poster on the Godlike Productions website on the subject commented wryly that Colby 'seems to be bad luck for black people.'

Marley lived for another four years, eventually succumbing on 11th May 1981. The ability of cannabis to cure cancer has been well-documented in recent times, (but was less well-known in the 1970s,) causing some to speculate that Marley's daily smoking habit may have prolonged his life way beyond what would otherwise have been the case.

The plan was presumably that he would die much sooner. This certainly seemed to be in the intentions of a German doctor, Joseph Issels, recommended to Marley by the Jamaican doctor Carl 'Pee Wee' Fraser. Issels practiced what he referred to as 'holistic immunotherapy' in Bavaria, Germany, and Marley travelled to his clinic for treatment. Unfortunately, according to accounts, Issels was a veteran Nazi and had worked alongside the notorious Josef Mengele at the Auschwitz concentration camp during World War 2. As author Alex Constantine observes: "Bob Marley, the 'dangerous' racial enemy of fascists everywhere, had placed his life in the hands of a Nazi doctor.' Issels' 'treatment' included the administering of vaccines delivered by long needles plunged into Marley's stomach until they went through to his spine. Issels also starved him. On the day of his death, Marley's emaciated body is said to have weighed only 82 pounds.

Marley's death was followed in 1987–on September 11th, intriguingly–by that of Peter Tosh, fellow bandmate in the group The Wailers, and political activist in Jamaica. Tosh and Marley had converted to

Rastafarianism together in the late 1960s, and both had become thorns in the side of the political establishment with their outspoken comments and attempts towards civil unity. Tosh was murdered when a trio of thugs led by Dennis 'Leppo' Lobban, walked in on a party he was throwing for a small group of friends at his Westmoreland home. The gang detained Tosh and his guests for several hours and demanded money from him. Tosh repeatedly told them he had none. Lobban eventually shot him in the head. A gunfight ensued in which DJs Doc Brown and Jeff 'Free I' Dixon were also killed. Lobban was jailed for life, but many of Tosh's associates suspected he was yet another convenient 'patsy,' with Wayne Johnson, producer of 'The Red X Tapes' documentary film, citing an un-named government official who had told him that one of the gunmen was a police officer. Whether or not there was foul play beyond a simple robbery gone wrong, reggae music had lost another of its most prominent and celebrated musicians, and the control system was rid of one more influential freedom activist. It didn't end there, either. Several other Jamaican musicians known also as political activists have been murdered in one fashion or another in the intervening years, among them Major Worries, Tenor Saw, Nitty Gritty, Pan Head, Dirtsman and Garnett Silk.

Michael Jackson

On any level, there can be few life stories as captivating, and ultimately tragic, as that of Michael Jackson. The old cliché 'you couldn't make it up' has never been more apt. It seems clear that Jackson and his siblings were forced into a life of show-business at an early age by their bullying and abusive father, Joe. In one of her interviews on the subject of MK-Ultra in the entertainment business, Roseanne Barr brought up the subject, claiming Joe Jackson to be an asset of the CIA. In her 'Roseanne World' blog she wrote:

> *"Joe Jackson is a child abuser, and catherine (sic) looked the other way while he beat their kids and tortured Michael mentally. Keep them both away from Michael's kids."*

There has been widespread speculation about Michael having been a mind-control victim since his early childhood, and this appeared to be borne out when a series of his drawings were seen for the first time in public when they were put up for sale by a private collector in 2014. Many of them offer disturbing hints at Monarch Programming. Included are the image of a smiling face with wires coming from the head connected to what appear to be electrical switches, a self-portrait under the word 'seven,' in which the bottom half of the face appears deformed as if in the midst of an electric shock, and a composite self-portrait depicting a male, female and child all merged into one.

Although Michael towed the line expected of him for many years, performing dance routines on cue and releasing albums with regularity, by the late 1980s the cracks were starting to show. His various eccentric behaviours are well-documented and need no repeating here. It would appear that he started to go off-script when the lyrical content of his music changed from the relative innocence of his early tunes, to containing conscious messages, from the conspiratorial 'They Don't Really Care About Us,' to the paranoid 'Leave Me Alone,' to the environmentally-conscious 'Earth Song.' His public statements appeared to deviate, too, when he criticised the Sony music empire and the draconian hold it had over its artists in terms of their publishing deals, when he branded Sony CEO Tommy Mottola 'the Devil,' and when he stated that the history books had been re-written to present the version of events that suited the worldwide Establishment, (the origin of his 'HIStory' project.) There have been suggestions that these comments stand as an indication of Jackson's mind-control programming starting to wear off. Either way, it's easy to understand how such behaviours would have made enemies in certain quarters. Many saw the two allegations of child-abuse levelled at Jackson as warnings to him to get back on-track, and as a reminder of what those that control him can do to those who don't play ball. Once again, the spectre of child-abuse hangs ominously above this particular story, as it has over so many others throughout the years. Evan Chandler, the screenwriter and dentist who brought the first of the molestation charges against Jackson, 'committed suicide' five months after Jackson's own death.

Jackson's death, on 25th June 2009, is no less strange and full of unanswered questions than his life ever was. With the blame placed solely on Dr. Conrad Murray for reportedly administering a cocktail of prescription drugs and painkillers that proved fateful, the spotlight has fallen away from any other parties. Murray has become this story's version of the 'lone nutter' blamed for so many false-flag terror hoaxes. The dictionary.com definition of 'a conspiracy' is given as 'an evil, unlawful, treacherous, or surreptitious plan formulated in secret by two or more persons,',(with the word itself coming from the Latin, meaning 'to breathe together.') By restricting the blame for Jackson's death to Murray alone, the official version of the story eliminates any suggestion of a 'conspiracy' and, as with the case of Princess Diana, can be chalked up as yet another 'tragic accident.' (Michael was a close personal friend of Diana, incidentally—but with his social circle also including spoon-bender and admitted Mossad and CIA agent Uri Geller, he could be considered to have had poor judgement in this area. He also recorded twice with 'Paul McCartney,' of course, before going on to purchase the Beatles back catalogue, and married Elvis Presley's daughter Lisa Marie.)

In 2012, a heavily-circulated video appeared of a bald white man sitting at a desk, who claimed his name was Robert Conners, and that he had been a high-ranking officer in the US Department of Defense. During his time with the department, 'Connors' claimed to have worked on a project known as Operation Sedgwick, which he says was a continuation of the CIA's MK-Ultra that was specifically aimed at subverting the African-American population through the strategic use of music. He stated that after much internal struggling, his conscience would not allow him to continue in his work, and that he had decided to become a whistleblower. In the video, he gives an ultimatum to his former employers to publicly admit the existence of this project, or he would release incriminating material to back up his claims. "To show I'm not bluffing," he said, the first item was a recording of a tapped telephone conversation between 'Michael Jackson' and a friend named Dieter Weisner. The video included what purported to be the audio of this conversation, featuring a voice that sounded similar to Jackson's, appearing fearful and paranoid and voicing concerns that his life was in danger.

Despite his claim that he would produce new material each subsequent week, nothing further was heard from this 'whistleblower.' While the view could be taken that something may indeed have happened to him, it seems far more likely that this video was a hoax and that the 'Michael Jackson' phone call was faked, either as someone's warped idea of a joke, or as a deliberate attempt to confuse and confound genuine truth researchers, and ridicule the idea of MJ 'conspiracy theories' in the minds of the masses.

In 2013 it was reported that Paris Jackson, Michael's 'daughter,' was not in fact his biological offspring. On 5th June of that year, she was admitted to hospital after attempting suicide by cutting her wrists and taking an overdose of pills.

Still think the star-spangled world of celebrity is all glitz and glamour?!

There have been rumours among those who would always advise you to 'follow the money,' that at the time of Jackson's death he was about to end his long-standing publishing deal with Sony, which would have seen him taking back the sole rights to not only his own back catalogue, but also that of the Beatles, in an arrangement worth potentially billions. This claim remains unsubstantiated, however.

The very best death conspiracies continue beyond the grave, and so it is with MJ. Just as with Elvis, (his one-time father-in-law,) Jim Morrison and Tupac, some have claimed that, with massive complicity from others, Jackson faked his own death to evade the glare of celebrity life, and possibly to escape his massive financial debts. One such clue is said to be Jackson's comment at the press conference where he announced his gruelling series of live dates at London's Wembley Arena under the 'This Is It' brand, where he states: 'This is the final curtain call.' This was his last public appearance before the announcement of his death.

On the day of Michael's funeral, a character known as 'Dave Dave' guested on 'Larry King Live' on CNN. The back-story given was that his real name was David Rothenberg, and that his father had doused him with kerosene and set him alight when he was six years old in 1983, resulting in 90-degree burns. 'Dave' stated that Michael Jackson befriended him while he was undergoing surgery, and had remained a loyal friend ever since. 'Dave' certainly gave the appearance of being a serious burns victim . . . or the subject of some very elaborate plastic surgery. He told King that he had changed his name 'to liberate myself from my father's criminality.' Was this story genuine? Or, (despite pictures being shown of Jackson with what is said to be a childhood Rothenberg,) could 'Dave Dave' have possibly been a heavily-altered and 'reborn' Michael Jackson, with CNN complicit in one of the entertainment industry's favourite tactics—telling you what's really going on right there in plain sight?

Whitney Houston

In the days following Whitney Houston's death, R&B DJs everywhere rushed to put together their own personal 'tribute mixes' to mark the occasion. In absorbing a few of these, something struck me. With only a handful of exceptions, the songs throughout Whitney's career were all about love; love of the romantic kind in most cases, but also love of the 'agape' kind in the spiritual tradition, of love for all humanity as exemplified on 'Love Will Save The Day' and 'The Greatest Love Of All'. It certainly seems symbolic that an artist whose music was, on the whole, inspirational and uplifting, was possibly chosen as one to be taken out by a dark priest-class that stands for the very antithesis of these qualities. The timing of her death certainly served her record label well, coming as it did three days before Valentine's Day. The resultant outpour of grief led to massively increased sales of her back catalogue, for which retail prices had been specially marked-up.

Those looking for dark symbolic clues can have a field-day with this one, as everything about it comes with a deeply unsettling tone. Whitney's death occurred at the time of the 2012 Grammy Awards, just a few days after the US Super Bowl half-time show, an event which was itself loaded with occultic imagery for those with the eyes to see it. As a 'Vigilant Citizen' article commented at the time:

> "When we look at the facts and the occurrences surrounding Whitney Houston's death, coupled with the symbolic elements of the 2012 Grammy awards, the entire 'event' has the looks of an occult ritual, complete with a blood sacrifice, a celebration and even a 're-birth.'

> "As in the cases of Michael Jackson, Amy Winehouse, Heath Ledger, Brittany Murphy and many others, bizarre events preceded and followed the death of Whitney Houston. After reviewing all of those

accounts, one cannot help but wonder: Was Whitney's death truly an
accident, or was it a deliberate sacrifice planned by 'unseen forces"?"

Whitney's lifeless body was discovered in a bathtub in Suite 434 of LA's Beverly Hilton Hotel in the afternoon of 11th February 2012. She was pronounced dead at 3.55pm. The official coroner's report stated that she had 'accidentally' drowned in the bathtub, with heart disease and cocaine listed as contributing factors. Yet another strange music industry death chalked up as a self-inflicted, drug-induced 'accident.' In this case, the implication was that Whitney's downward spiral from wholesome church girl to self-destructive substance-abuser, was the result of her turbulent relationship with her 'bad boy' husband Bobby Brown. There are reports that Whitney's body was cold when it was pulled from the warm water of the bathtub, indicating that she had already been dead for several hours, despite the time of her death being officially given as earlier that afternoon.

An industry pre-Grammys party had been scheduled to take place just four floors below, hosted by music industry veteran Clive Davis. Like so many executives, Davis comes from a Jewish family. He was the founder of Arista Records and is credited with having launched Houston's career. Despite the news of Whitney's death being publicly announced, and her body still lying a few floors above, the party went on regardless and is said to have had a celebratory air about it, whereas you might think that the appropriate response to such terrible news would have been to cancel the party, or at least move it to another location. In a speech to the crowd, Davis claimed that Whitney's family had said that they wished for the party to continue. Despite having been discovered in the late afternoon, the coroner had reportedly received orders from above that her body was not to be removed until shortly before the party ended at around midnight. Whitney and Bobby Brown's daughter, Bobbi Kristina, was among a group of people said to have been present in the suite throughout, and was reported to have been in a hysterical state.

An item seldom reported in the mainstream media, is that Bobbi Kristina herself was discovered unconscious in a bathtub only a day before her mother's death, in the same group of rooms at the Beverly Hilton, in an event that eerily foreshadowed what was to come. At around 2.50am that night, a man staying directly below the Houston entourage's suite, called reception to complain about water cascading through his ceiling from above. When he went upstairs with security to investigate, they reportedly found a bathtub overflowing, and noticed that a large-screen TV had been smashed. This incident presents the strong suggestion that Whitney may have died sometime during that night, rather than the following afternoon, which would make sense of why her body was reportedly cold when it was pulled out of the bathtub.

The whole affair appeared to get symbolically re-enacted on 31st January 2015, when Bobbi Kristina was again discovered face-down and unconscious in a bathtub, on this occasion by her 'husband' Nick Gordon at her Georgia home. This time, there was no official claim of drug or alcohol abuse, and no tangible reason given for her condition. She was placed in a medically-induced coma after she was described as having undergone irreversible brain damage. The date of this announcement piqued the interest of Isaac Weishaupt, proprietor of the Illuminatiwatcher.com website, as he observed that the start of February was a time of ritual sacrifice known to Pagan societies as Imbolg. Weishaupt points out that actor Philip Seymour Hoffman was also found dead in strange circumstances at the beginning of February the year before, (in a bathroom, though not reportedly in a bathtub.) Gordon's status as Bobbi Kristina's apparent husband was later called into question when the subject of inheritance arose. It later emerged that Bobbi Kristina had been found with bruising, and that Gordon had been investigated as a suspect.

A few days after her 'discovery,' it was announced that Bobbi Kristina's family had decided to turn off her life-support machine on 11th February, the date on which her mother had died three years before, 'so they could be together.' The suggestion had apparently been made by veteran Gospel singer Cissy Houston, Whitney's mother. This did not happen, however, and Bobbi Kristina eventually passed away on 26th July after six months in a coma. By this time, the official cause of death seemed to have been revised, as reported by the mainstream media, to a 'drowning.' Death-by-bathtub seems to be a common component in the music industry. Whitney, Bobbi Kristina and Jim Morrison were all discovered in them. The fact that Bobbi Kristina was in a bathtub at all was considered strange by her friend Debra Reis Brooks, who told the site RadarOnline.com that she had been terrified of baths ever since her mother's discovery in one, and never ever took one. The Illuminati-watcher.com site goes further regarding the possible mystical relevance of celebrities in bathtubs, meanwhile, suggesting this may represent a symbolic ushering-in of the astrological Age of Aquarius, and highlighting the dumbfounding amount of music stars and actors that have been pictured in them in recent times, not always bathing in water. Lady Gaga seems to be particularly fond of them. You can read a totally fascinating article on the subject here:

- http://illuminatiwatcher.com/
  decoding-illuminati-symbolism-water-and-the-occult-bathtub/

Bobby Brown could be considered to be one of the unluckiest men in show business. Notwithstanding the tragic deaths of his wife and daughter, his nephew Shayne, alongside two of his entourage, were stabbed when a fight broke out at a party celebrating his father's birthday in 2005. The man indicted for the attacks, Marque Dixson, was shot dead in a parking lot the following year in a case that remained 'unsolved.'

Fellow singer Chaka Khan was particularly outspoken about the tasteless aspects surrounding her friend Whitney's death, (a young Whitney had been one of the backing singers on Chaka's 'I'm Every Woman' in 1978 before going on to cover the song herself in 1992.) Speaking on a CNN interview with a clueless and by-the-book Piers Morgan about the continuation of the Clive Davis party, she commented:

> *"I thought that was complete insanity. And knowing Whitney I don't believe that she would have said 'the show must go on.' She's the kind of woman that would've said 'stop everything! Un-unh. I'm not going to be there.'... I don't know what could motivate a person to have a party in a building where the person whose life he had influenced so enormously and whose life had been affected by hers. They were like... I don't understand how that party went on."*

She added:

> *"A more honest tribute, in my opinion, would have been, maybe, call everybody together, say a prayer, let's eat dinner and go home."*

Chaka may or may not have been speaking literally when she commented in the same interview:

> *"I think we all, as artists, because we're highly sensitive people and this machine around us, this so-called 'music industry,' is such a demonic thing. It sacrifices people's lives and their essences at the drop of a dime . . . I had a manager once say to me, 'you know you're worth more money dead than alive'."*

Meanwhile, there's more Clive Davis-related strangeness from the fact that, two days before her death, Whitney visited fellow Arista singers Brandy and Monica, who were with Davis at their rehearsals for the pre-Grammys party. Whitney was seen to slip a note to Brandy, the contents of which Brandy has refused to reveal, and appeared to be saying her goodbyes to the three, leading to speculation that she may have been aware of her imminent demise. She beckoned Bobbi Kristina to 'come and say hi to your Godfather' in reference to Davis. Whitney's last public appearance was on-stage alongside Kelly Price, singing 'Jesus Loves Me,' which was a far cry from the tone of the rest of that year's Grammy event, including as it did Nicki Minaj's stage show depicting demonic possession and the 'exorcism' of her character Roman Zolanski!

The day after her death, it was announced that former 'American Idol' finalist Jennifer Hudson would be performing the official Grammys tribute to Whitney. Two days earlier, Clive Davis had told Piers Morgan that Jennifer Hudson was "the next Whitney." Hudson herself had undergone her own personal tragedy in 2008 when her mother, brother and seven-year-old nephew were shot to death in Chicago. The estranged husband of Hudson's sister Julia was charged with the murders, and sentenced to several life imprisonment terms. Inevitably, there have been claims that these deaths constituted some form of ritual sacrifice in exchange for the fame and fortune that Hudson would go on to receive–though it has to be said her career has not been as prolific in recent years as many in 2009 expected it would be.

Clive Davis now has a theatre named after him in Los Angeles. It seems his lifetime of service to the industry has not gone unrewarded.

Also entering the Whitney Houston story, is an enigmatic character who appears to go by the name of Raffles Van Exel, though he has been known to use several other pseudonyms including Raffles Dawson and Raffles Benson. According to an article written by 'Forbes' contributor Roger Friedman:

> "He was on the fourth floor of the Beverly Hilton Hotel in one of Houston's suites when she died. He appeared downstairs in the lobby shortly thereafter, wearing aviator sunglasses, sobbing.

> "... Despite the shock of Whitney's death, Raffles still made it downstairs to Clive Davis's party. He was dressed in formal wear, had Whitney's tickets in his hand, and intended to sit at her table. Just inside the ballroom, he was comforted by celebrities to whom he related his story–"I found Whitney." Gayle King hugged him. Quincy Jones listened patiently to his story. A security guard told me later, 'Well, he was up there.' He was also hanging around with Houston all week prior to her death. On Tuesday, when she emerged from a nightclub looking dishevelled, Raffles appears in a photograph on TMZ like a deer in headlights. He is standing right behind her in a powder blue suit.

> "But who is Raffles Van Exel? He's one of Hollywood's mysteries. I first met him in 2005 hanging around the Jackson family during Michael Jackson's child molestation trial. After Michael went abroad, Raffles was often seen with Michael's father, Joseph Jackson. He trades on being an 'insider' when there's a scandal. No-one really knows him, but he's always where there's action and celebrities ... On Twitter he claims to be managing "'my girl,' Chaka Khan.

> "... Look for Raffles at Whitney's funeral tomorrow. In the old days he used to wear a yellow jacket full of black question marks, like The Riddler. On Saturday night, as he pulled in various guests to

Clive Davis's party past the velvet ropes, he was wearing a Michael Jackson-like tuxedo. He lives in West Hollywood now, but his official domicile–and where he's been sued–is Chicago. He has not responded to countless e-mails and phone messages."

Finally, anyone armed with an understanding of how Kabbalistic numerology figures so heavily in the plans of the entertainment industry's dark occultists, will find it intriguing that the number 11 crops up many times in the circumstances surrounding this story. 11 is known as a master number, and represents the completion of one cycle and the birth of a new one. It is an extremely significant figure in the works of Aleister Crowley, and another crucial component in the details of 9/11.

Whitney died on the 11th of the month, two years to the day after British fashion designer Alexander McQueen was found hanged at his London home, in a death which Metropolitan police described as 'not suspicious.' McQueen was said himself to have been a practitioner of the dark arts, (For the dark occult elements in his designs see: http://justifytheory.blogspot.co.uk/2011/05/occult-fashion-alexander-mcqueen.html) and was reportedly related to three of the Salem witches, as well as *just happening* to have been awarded a CBE by the Queen.

The suite in which Whitney died was number 434, with 4 + 4 + 3 equalling 11.

Michael Hutchence

The story of the premature demise of the Australian frontman of the group INXS is yet another tangled web of strangeness and unanswered questions. Hutchence was discovered dead on the same date as the JFK murder, 22nd November, (22/11–22 + 11 = 33,) in 1997. He was found in his hotel room at the Ritz Carlton in Sydney, (Room 524 which also corresponds to 11 in numerology–5 + 2 + 4,) and was said to have 'committed suicide,' with the ever-present elements of drugs and alcohol added to the picture. Hutchence was said to have been depressed, largely as a result of an ongoing dispute with Bob Geldof, the former husband of British TV presenter Paula Yates, with whom Hutchence was now involved. There was no inquest, and the coroner's report implied that Hutchence had taken his own life by hanging himself with a belt from a doorframe. Rumours quickly emerged that Hutchence had died as the result of a sex act gone wrong, and that he was into auto-asphyxiation–a sexual thrill achieved by bringing oneself almost to the point of death by strangling, but letting go at the last moment. These claims were rejected by the coroner.

Suspicion that all might not be as it seemed, came from further details in the report which most mainstream media outlets chose to leave out of their coverage; Hutchence's body bore the signs of a beating, and he had a bleeding lip and a broken hand, which would have made hanging himself quite an achievement. Suddenly suicide begins to look less likely. On the evening prior to his death, Hutchence had been dining out with his father and stepmother, who said that he had seemed in good spirits. Furthermore, Paula Yates later commented that Hutchence thought suicide was the most cowardly act in the world and that he would never do it. As with the Amy Winehouse story, Hutchence was heard to be arguing loudly with somebody in his room during the early hours, according to the occupant of the adjoining room.

Much of the speculation of foul play came from comments given by Hutchence's father, Kelland, who told Australian TV that Geldof had been intimidating Hutchence and Yates in his attempts to gain custody of Tiger Lily, the daughter they had together. Geldof began his actions after opium was found in Hutchence's property while he was out of the country, in what many believe was a set-up. Kelland stated: "He made their lives miserable. It's like he was on a vendetta . . . I think it contributed very much to what happened." Kelland remarked that his son had had an argument over the phone with Geldof just hours before he died.

Yates herself went further, in an apparent outburst at an airport lounge in Bangkok. The UK's 'Daily Express' quoted her as saying: "Bob Geldof murdered Michael Hutchence. That bastard killed Michael. He is called 'Saint' Bob. That makes me sick. He killed my baby. We have had three years of this." She also claimed that Geldof had frequently threatened Hutchence and herself by saying "don't forget, I am above the law," a comment similar in nature to what Jimmy Savile used to say when challenged. Yates later stated that she refused to accept the coroner's verdict on Hutchence's 'suicide,' telling Australia's Channel 9 TV: "I will be making it abundantly clear that, because of information that I and only I could know about Michael . . . I cannot accept the verdict.

And I won't have my child grow up thinking that her father left her, not knowing the way he loved her . . . I just don't think he killed himself, I really don't."

Like earlier rock stars who met untimely ends, Hutchence was known for his political activism, and his Will named Amnesty International and Greenpeace as major benefactors of his assets.

Paula Yates was another product of generational show business connections. It emerged late in her life that her biological father was the veteran television presenter Hughie Green, rather than the previously-assumed Jess Yates, the presenter of religious TV programmes. She has long been suspected by researchers into mind-control of being a subject of Monarch and/ or Beta programming, her permanently-dyed peroxide hair fitting the stereotype perfectly.

Paula Yates was herself found dead on 17th September 2000, aged 41, the official line being that it was the result of a heroin overdose. The very next day, Bob Geldof filed for custody of Tiger Lily, even though he is not related to her in any way. Hutchence's family objected to this, but say they were not given Geldof's permission to join the custody proceedings. They also objected to Geldof's attempts to legally change her surname to his. A compromise was reached whereby she is now known as Tiger Hutchence-Geldof. Hutchence's mother, Patricia Glassop, complained in 2007 that Geldof had been preventing her from seeing her granddaughter, and branding him "Satan" and "very cruel." She claimed he was only interested in raising Tiger for the inheritance she would receive from her father's estate when she came of age.

In what appeared to be another case of history repeating itself, Peaches Geldof was found dead on 7th April 2014, aged 25. As with her mother, her death was blamed on a heroin overdose. Peaches had been married twice, first to American musician Max Drummey, then to Thomas Cohen, the singer with the English pseudo-punk band S.C.U.M. Despite stating that his family was "beyond grief" at the news, 'Saint Bob' somehow managed to pull himself together within a few weeks and announce his marriage to his long-term girlfriend Jeanne Marine. On the Beltane ritual festival date of 1st May.

Peaches was a member of the dark occult secret-society known as the OTO, Ordo Templi Orientis, (translating as Order of the Temple of the East,) another of the many organisations linked to Aleister Crowley, and one which has proven a strange attraction for a great number of celebrities. Peaches had the initials OTO tattooed on her left forearm. She had also professed to being a Scientologist, and had become interested in her second husband's religion of Judaism. There are promotional pictures of both Peaches and one of the two sons she had with Cohen wearing the Mickey Mouse ears that were covered in the earlier chapter, a symbol hinting at the presence of trauma-based mind control.

There has been much speculation that Peaches was privy to information on a far-reaching paedophile ring connected to the entertainment industry, and that she was preparing to go public with information she had on it. A little over four months before her death, she had faced criminal investigation after she re-Tweeted the names of the two mothers who had allowed their babies to be sexually assaulted by Ian Watkins, the singer with the Welsh band Lostprophets, who was convicted in 2013 of 13 charges of sexual assault on children, receiving a 29-year jail sentence. Child-rape and the entertainment industry merge *yet again*. The two mothers concerned were allegedly fans of Watkins, and had allowed him access to their infants in full knowledge that they would be sexually abused, but were not allowed to be named in court to protect the children. The two, who were referred to in the case only as Woman A and Woman B, received sentences of 14 and 17 years' respectively. I wonder what kind of welcome they can expect from their grown-up offspring when they get released?

Amy Winehouse

Amy Winehouse's demise on 23rd July 2011 makes her the most recent high-profile member of the infamous 27 Club. This is the macabre acknowledgement of the many prominent musicians who, through the decades, *just happen* to have passed away at the age of 27. Among its members are the aforementioned Jimi Hendrix, Jim Morrison, Janis Joplin and Brian Jones, alongside Kurt Cobain, Robert Johnson, and founding member of The Grateful Dead, Ron 'Pigpen' McKernan. If there is a sinister aspect attached, what could be the significance of the age 27? The general consensus seems to be that, in the science of numerology, double figures are added together to get a single value between 1 and 10, in this case 9, (2 +7), with all the occult significance that number seems to bring. Also interesting to note is that 27 is the first number in a very notable cosmic sequence. Doubling it each time gives you 54, 108, 216, 432, 864, etc, and these combinations crop up time and time again in the dimensions and movements of the Sun, Moon and Earth, as well as 432 hertz representing the harmonic frequency for music. There's far more to say about all of this in a future volume!

Many of the same elements as with her fellow members are present in Amy Winehouse's own life story; artistic genius coupled with a turbulent personal life; a difficult childhood; chaotic relationships; the continued presence of drug and alcohol abuse, and contradictory reports and vague police evidence regarding the circumstances of her death. Winehouse had a Jewish family background, which may be neither here nor there, but there's no evidence of any connections to military 'intelligence' or any other type of government institution.

The official line regarding her death is that it was the result of alcohol poisoning, accentuated by the eating disorder Bulimia. This was an explanation that was accepted without question by the general public, who had observed her tragic downfall into alcohol-dependency in recent months, and before it, her dabbling with many varieties of narcotics. It was yet another death put down to the trappings of the live-fast-die-young Rock & Roll lifestyle.

Possibly the strangest aspect surrounding Amy's death, however, were the reports from one of her neighbours of noises, including what sounded like a loud drum beat, coming from her apartment the night before her body was discovered. The official story has Amy's live-in bodyguard Andrew Morris observing her "laughing, listening to music and watching TV" at 2am on the day of her death, after which she was apparently alone. She is said to have texted a friend at 3.30am. Morris next reports seeing her apparently asleep at around 10am, but when she had not moved by a little after 3pm, the alarm was raised. Three bottles of vodka were reportedly found in her room. The news site 'London 24' reported on the day of her death that:

> "One of her neighbours said he is convinced she died in the early hours of Friday because he heard screaming. 'I think something happened that night. It sounded like some weird sexual game. There was screaming and howling.' The man, who would not be named, said he

was woken by the sound at around 2am that night. 'It just sounded really weird and my son said he heard some kind of drum beating.'

"This afternoon he heard one of Winehouse's friends crying in the house, and realised she was dead. He believes a friend left her at home after a night out, and returned this afternoon to find her body. 'She's been quite low-profile and that's why, when I heard these sounds–screaming–I thought it was unlike her. I said to my son 'maybe she's taken a bad drug'.'"

Winehouse appeared to stay outside of the regular industry machine, making non-agenda music that fell well outside of formulaic templates. On the whole, she displayed none of the Illuminati symbolism which many of her contemporaries did–although one picture in particular has to raise the curiosity of any truthseeking researcher who has followed the story so far. In 2008, an art sculpture of Amy was unveiled in which she is playing dead, lying in a pool of fake blood having been apparently shot. By her side is a set of Mickey Mouse ears.

Dionne Bromfield, Winehouse's god-daughter and singing protégée, appeared employing the infamous 'one-eye' symbolism at the end of the video for her song 'Foolin,' released two months before Amy's death.

Reportedly, Amy was well-aware of the fabled 27 Club, and had expressed her fears in advance at becoming a part of it. Her personal assistant, Alex Haines, gave an interview to the now-defunct UK tabloid 'News of the World' in December 2008, stating: "It was my job to look after her. But it was impossible. She had to have a heroin and crack-pipe near her or she freaked out. She'd keep taking drugs until she passed out. Cutting herself was her favourite pastime. She reckoned she would join the '27 Club' of rock stars who died at that age. She told me, 'I have a feeling I'm gonna die young'."

As a footnote to the strange business of The 27 Club, Matt Sergiou published a piece on his 'Conspiro Media' blog concerning its possible links to a phenomenon known as 'Saturn's Return:'

"It's believed this affects a person's life during their late-twenties. Veteran astrologer, Rob Tillett states: 'Giant Saturn, the outermost planet in our solar system visible to the naked eye, spends some

two-and-a-half years in each sign, taking about twenty-nine years to complete his journey around the Zodiac. Long experience shows that there are two (or sometimes three) especially significant periods of transition in a human lifespan; these are when Saturn returns by transit to the place in the Zodiac he occupied when you were born. Astrologers call this dimensional shift the 'Saturn Return.' Each twenty-nine years naturally presents us with the challenge to rise to new levels of awareness, or face the consequences of having failed to gain the wisdom required to do so. This critical phase only happens once every 29 years, so at around age 28-30, 57-59, and, (if you live long enough,) 86-88, you have a Saturn Return. It signifies a definite time of transformation, an emotional transition from one life-phase to the next."

Tillett's knowledge of the Saturn Return is featured in the 2008 book, 'The 27s: The Greatest Myth of Rock & Roll.' It's written by Eric Segalstad.

David Bowie

When the death of David Bowie was announced to an unsuspecting world on Monday 11th January 2016, the wave of emotion that swept through the collective consciousness was largely unparalleled in history. Certainly, the deaths of John Lennon and Elvis Presley were felt just as deeply, but they were in a pre-internet era. With Bowie, there could hardly have been anyone in the world with a phone or a PC who wouldn't have been aware of the news within minutes of its release. The fact that his death dominated worldwide corporate news schedules, too, has inevitably led some to question whether Bowie's apparent demise wasn't some kind of mass human-energy-trawling ritual along the lines of the Super Bowl or Grammys.

If ever an artist were to be selected for such an occulted harvesting of consciousness, few of the modern age would have more relevance than Bowie, an enigmatic performer whose entire persona was steeped in mysticism. In an age where all A-list artists now conform to corporate templates, and where maverick individuality has been completely snuffed out, Bowie was a remnant of an era where personal creativity was still allowed to flourish, and although much of his may have been co-opted into the dark agendas of the industry, he at least managed to demonstrate how a life's work can be fascinating, enthralling and utterly original when an artist is left to express themselves unimpeded.

This factor was evident from the very start. Can anyone name a chart hit of this millennium which comes anywhere close to the genius creativity of 'Space Oddity,' Bowie's breakthrough single from 1969? In his article immediately in the wake of Bowie's announced death, Vigilant Citizen pointed out that the Major Tom character from 'Space Oddity' could well be symbolic of the ascension of man to higher realms of consciousness, given that he begins on Earth and ends up transcending boundaries as he floats through outer space - just as the David Bowman character did in the film '2001: A Space Odyssey.' VC points out how interesting it is that Bowie's next creation, Ziggy Stardust, represents a reversal of this. As an entity from deep space who descended to live among humans, there are parallels to messianic figures such as Jesus coming down from the heavens. It has since been announced that a constellation in the vicinity of Mars has been named after the Ziggy Stardust character, after Belgian astronomers noticed that the stars could be linked to form the lightning-bolt shape that was a Ziggy motif.

So straight away in Bowie's career, there are mystical/ spiritual/ occultic elements. These only get taken further when you factor in Bowie's own stated interest in occult traditions. In 1976, he addressed the fascination he held for the Jewish mystery-school teachings of the Kabbalah on the track 'Station To Station:'

"Here are we,

One magical movement,

From Kether to Malkuth 1."

Kether and Malkuth are *sephirot*, or points, on the Kabbalah's Tree Of Life. The Tree itself is symbolic of the process of attaining higher levels of consciousness through re-connecting with the divine. Kether and Malkuth are the highest and most grounded points on the Tree, so here Bowie is talking of descending from Godliness down to lowest consciousness.

Bowie also expressed a lifelong fascination with the works of Aleister Crowley, (why would that surprise anyone by now?!) Crowley and one of the occult organisations that he helmed, got a namecheck on 1971's 'Quicksand:'

> *"I'm closer to the Golden Dawn,*
>
> *Immersed in Crowley's uniform,*
>
> *I'm not a prophet or a Stone Age man,*
>
> *Just a mortal with potential of a superman"*

Occult symbolism pervaded Bowie's work to the very end. Much scrutiny was applied to 'Blackstar,' his final album, portentously released just two days before his reported death. Even fans who usually reject anything vaguely supernatural, were struck by how the album seemed to show Bowie acknowledging his own imminent passing. There are overtones of a resurrection or a rebirth, too, such as in the lyrics to the title track:

> *"Something happened on the day he died,*
>
> *Spirit rose a metre and stepped aside,*
>
> *Somebody else took his place, and bravely cried,*
>
> *(I'm a blackstar, I'm a blackstar.)"*

The album's first single was 'Lazarus,' in reference to the biblical character who died, but was resurrected to life by Jesus four days later.

Amid the emotional surge of grief and shock, there was confusion among many when Sky News brought on a character by the name of Jack Steven to join in the Bowie tributes. Viewers were immediately struck by the unsettling similarity that Steven seemed to have to Bowie, causing many to question whether the death could possibly have been a hoax, with Steven being the man himself following some plastic surgery, and with a new eye and hairpiece. Steven was introduced as a director of Fortress Music, a company which certainly does exist in London, and he was said to have come with a long history of A&R work. Although the internet throws up no record of Steven's work from decades past, there are at least references to him from earlier in the 2000s, suggesting that he is, after all, who he was presented as. Given that the dark controllers of these industries love to mock the gullible masses and place elements of the truth in plain sight, however, given the strange business of 'Dave Dave' in the wake of Michael Jackson's death and the whole Paul McCartney replacement theory, and given Bowie's own attachment to dark occult practices, it's not hard to understand why some were ready to consider that possibility.

The puzzling elements don't stop there, however. The world was told that Bowie had died following an 18-month battle with cancer, and the media made a point of continually emphasising his age, 69. Within days, the announcement came of the death of actor Alan Rickman, also as the result of cancer, and also at the age of 69. Before long, astute researchers had unearthed an episode of 'The Simpsons' going back to 2013, in which a depiction of Rickman's character from the 'Harry Potter' movies is shown, while the song 'All The Young Dudes' by Mott The Hoople plays, for no apparent reason, in the background. The song was written for the group by David Bowie. Within days of the Bowie and Rickman deaths, came the announcement that Dale 'Buffin' Griffin, the drummer from Mott The Hoople, had died aged 67.

Either the connection between all three of these being shown by 'The Simpsons' was a complete coincidence with odds of several-billion to one, (the option preferred by mainstream media such as the UK's 'Daly Mail,' implying, in all seriousness, that this really was an 'inadvertent' tribute,) or there was foreknowledge of what was to come on the part of the programme-makers, ('The Simpsons' does have previous in such matters,) ... or the Universe is speaking to us in a very profound way through the workings of Synchro-mysticism. Which of these three factors could be at play?

A pertinent question raised by many in the wake of the news that Bowie had secretly been battling cancer, is why someone of his creative, Bohemian, maverick persona would not have sought out alternative treatments for the disease, since cannabis oil and other natural compounds have been proven to cure cancer and many other diseases. It's hard to imagine someone of Bowie's ilk opting for the conventional treatments of the pharmaceutical corporations, such as chemotherapy. The fact that the public only learned that Bowie had cancer at all when it had already apparently claimed his life - plus the fact that pictures subsequently emerged of him in his final weeks laughing, dancing, and seeming to glow with good health - has inevitably called the official story into question. A week after the death announcement, the UK's Odeon cinema chain announced that special screenings of Bowie's movie 'Labyrinth' were to be shown, with the proceeds going to the Cancer Research UK charity.

As befits Bowie's very persona, the scenario surrounding his announced death remains an enigma. Was it an elaborate hoax, allowing him to live out his final years in seclusion? Was there a sacrificial element to it, either against Bowie's will or with his complicity? Or did things happen exactly the way the mainstream media told us, (which would be something of a first.) It's beyond the capacity of any researcher who was not directly involved in Bowie's world to say with absolute certainty. Until direct proof comes along one way or the other, as ever, we're left with a handful of clues, our best guess based on the available evidence, and a strong dose of intuition.

And there's more

A post on the pinballking.blogspot.com site really put into perspective the massive number of deaths that the general public has always seemed satisfied to chalk up as 'the way it goes' in this particular industry. This list, exhaustive as it is, doesn't even include the many early demises in the hip-hop game, but is still shocking in its fullness:

"Have you ever noticed how all the major groups and artists are surrounded by premature deaths? the Beatles (Stuart Sutcliffe, Brian Epstein), the Rolling Stones, Robert Johnson, Bill Haley & the Comets, Buddy Holly, the Yardbirds, the Doors, Jimi Hendrix, Janis Joplin, the Grateful Dead, the Byrds, the Temptations, Deep Purple, T. Rex, Elvis Presley, Lynyrd Skynyrd, Chicago, Pink Floyd, the Who, the Sex Pistols, AC/DC, Joy Division, Led Zeppelin, Bob Marley, Ozzy

Osbourne, the Pretenders, the Beach Boys, Marvin Gaye, Thin Lizzy, the Band, Metallica, Rainbow, Styx, Red Hot Chilli Peppers, the Velvet Underground, Mother Love Bone, Steely Dan, Stevie Ray Vaughan, Creedence Clearwater Revival, Def Leppard, Small Faces, Guns N' Roses, Kiss, Queen, Steppenwolf, Black Sabbath, Nirvana, Hole, Blind Melon, Smashing Pumpkins, INXS, the Cars, the Ramones, Run-DMC, the Clash, the Bee Gees, Tom Petty & the Heartbreakers, Pantera, Crowded House, Boston, Bruce Springsteen & the E-Street Band, Marilyn Manson band, Manic Street Preachers, Michael Jackson, the Misfits, Amy Winehouse, Warrant, Weezer, Gwar, Beastie Boys, Whitney Houston, etc. This list does not even include family members or crew members.

One last strange death is worthy of a mention in the circumstances, I feel. It may well have been the freak accident against all the odds that the mainstream news presented it as. Or it may not. On 27th February 2015, the death of Charmayne 'Maxee' Maxwell, one of the singers with the 90s R&B group Brownstone, was announced. Initial reports stated that she had collapsed after attending one of her son's soccer games in Los Angeles, but this quickly morphed into her having fallen backwards out of the back door of her LA home while holding a wine glass, with the broken shards having 'caused fatal puncture wounds to the back of her neck.' Maxee's husband was the Danish record producer Carsten Soulshock who is said to have arrived home to find her bleeding to death.

Resources:

2Pac: Amerikaz Most Wanted, Dead or Alive?:

- http://real-eyes-realise-real-lies.blogspot.co.uk/2013/12/2pac-amerikaz-most-wanted-dead-or-alive.html

AmenRa Film Productions: Blood Sacrifice For Fame & Fortune & Freemasonry:

- https://www.youtube.com/watch?v=-JAONLsyyec

Celebrity Blood Sacrifices For Fame and Money:

- http://beforeitsnews.com/alternative/2013/03/blood-sacrifices-for-fame-and-money-2597260.html

Government Whistleblower releases what he claims is Michael Jackson's final phone call:

- https://www.youtube.com/watch?v=ssz-qS20B3M

Is Dave Dave Michael Jackson? My Body Language Analysis. CJB:

- https://www.youtube.com/watch?v=v-meOpZeTDk

  Dave Dave is really Michael Jackson:

- https://www.youtube.com/watch?v=zxM_gRSADO0

Q Magazine: Kanye West Blames Himself for Mom Donda West's Death:

- http://www.usmagazine.com/celebrity-news/news/kanye-west-blames-himself-for-mom-donda-wests-death-2015266

Michael Jackson's Mother Proves His Death was a Hoax:

- https://www.youtube.com/watch?v=9r59poA4dYU

Whitney Houston last kiss goodbye to Clive Davis, Monica and Brandy at interview:

- https://www.youtube.com/watch?v=1kGZ5q8YYrE

Vigilant Citizen: Whitney Houston and the 2012 Grammy Awards Mega-Ritual:

- http://vigilantcitizen.com/musicbusiness/
  whitney-houston-and-the-2012-grammy-awards-mega-ritual/

TMZ: Whitney Houston's Daughter Frighteningly Similar Incident Day Before Whitney Died:

- http://www.tmz.com/2012/02/13/
  whitney-houston-dead-bobbi-kristina-bathtub/

Illuminati Watcher: Decoding Illuminati Symbolism: Water and the Occult Bathtub:

- http://illuminatiwatcher.com/
  decoding-illuminati-symbolism-water-and-the-occult-bathtub/

Illuminati Watcher: Conspiracy Theories Regarding Bobbi Kristina's Passing:

- http://illuminatiwatcher.com/
  conspiracy-theories-bobbi-kristinas-passing/

Alexander McQueen: Occult Fashion:

- http://justifytheory.blogspot.co.uk/2011/05/occult-fashion-
  alexander-mcqueen.html

'Satan' Geldof: Bob is only interested in Tiger Lily's inheritance, says granny:

- http://www.thisislondon.co.uk/showbiz/article-23412995-
  Satan-geldof-bob-is-only-interested-in-tiger-lilys-inheritance-
  says-granny.do

The Coleman Experience: The mysterious death of Peaches Geldof and the VIP child-abuse connection:

- https://thecolemanexperience.wordpress.com/2014/04/07/the-
  mysterious-death-of-peaches-geldof-and-the-vip-child-abuse-
  connection/

Vigilant Citizen: Amy Winehouse and The 27 Club:

- http://vigilantcitizen.com/musicbusiness/
  amy-winehouse-and-27-club/

London 24: Amy Winehouse death: Neighbour in Camden heard 'screaming and howling:

amy_winehouse_death_neighbour_in_camden_heard_screaming_
and_howling_1_972931

Daily Mail: Amy Winehouse Said She Always Knew she'd Join The 27 Club:

- http://www.dailymail.co.uk/home/event/article-2360326/Amy-
  Winehouse-said-knew-shed-join-27-club.html

Amy Winehouse Joins the Notorious 27 Club:

- http://mediaexposed.tumblr.com/post/7984782005/
  amy-winehouse-joins-the-notorious-27-club

Miles Mathis: Proof that John Lennon Faked his Death:

- http://mileswmathis.com/lennon.pdf

Did the CIA murder John Lennon?:

- http://www.consciousape.com/2012/10/08/
  did-the-cia-murder-john-lennon/

Beatles Bible: John Lennon and the number nine:

- http://www.beatlesbible.com/features/
  john-lennon-number-nine/

Wikispooks: Jose Perdomo:

- https://wikispooks.com/wiki/Jose_Sanjenis_Perdomo

NME: Jimi Hendrix's doctor says guitarist 'may have been murdered':

- http://www.nme.com/news/jimi-hendrix/46213

Chanting Down Babylon: The CIA & The Death of Bob Marley:

- http://hightimes.com/read/
  chanting-down-babylon-cia-death-bob-marley

Professor Griff: Blood sacrifice for fame and fortune: P Diddy & Notorious BIG:

- https://www.youtube.com/watch?v=-JAONLsyyec

Professor Griff Says Puff Had Biggie Smalls Killed + Speaks On Jay-Z:

- https://www.youtube.com/watch?v=GDsESHmf4-o

Druglord Claims Feds Quizzed Him About Sex Life Of Sean "Diddy" Combs:

- http://www.thesmokinggun.com/buster/sean-combs/rosemond-proffer-sex-claim-657409

Daily Mail: Was Jimi Hendrix Murdered By His Manager?:

- http://www.dailymail.co.uk/tvshowbiz/article-1193752/Was-Jimi-Hendrix-murdered-manager.html

Daily Mail: Puff Daddy 'fired shots in club':

- http://www.dailymail.co.uk/tvshowbiz/article-18903/Puff-Daddy-fired-shots-club.html

Justify Theory: Sean Diddy Combs: "Bad Boys" Of The Occult:

- http://justifytheory.blogspot.co.uk/2010/01/bad-boys-of-occult.html

egotripland.com: The Notorious B.I.G.–"Life After Death" with art director Ebon Heath:

- http://www.egotripland.com/notorious-b-i-g-life-after-death-album-cover-ebon-heath/

Jay-Z devastated by nephew's death:

- http://uk.askmen.com/celebs/entertainment-news/jayz/jayz-devastated-by-nephew-death.html

Die Zeit: Aaliyah Funeral Set; Pilot Probed:

- http://uk.eonline.com/news/42093/aaliyah-funeral-set-pilot-probed

Rapper Attempts To Sacrifice Friend To Join The Illuminati:

- http://www.redicecreations.com/article.php?id=24288

Bob Geldof's Cult of Mysterious Death:

- http://www.anomalies.net/bob-geldofs-cult-of-mysterious-death/

Village Voice: The 10 Most Shocking Revelations About The Tragic Last Days Of Gang Starr MC Guru:

- http://www.villagevoice.com/music/the-10-most-shocking-revelations-about-the-tragic-last-days-of-gang-starr-mc-guru-6648003

Suge Knight Jokes About Eazy E's Death On Jimmy Kimmel, 2003:

- https://www.youtube.com/watch?v=zxGvS1F0L38

N.W.A.'s manager Jerry Heller says not letting Eazy-E kill Suge Knight was "a big mistake":

- http://consequenceofsound.net/2015/08/n-w-a-s-manager-jerry-heller-says-not-letting-eazy-e-kill-suge-knight-was-a-big-mistake/

Eazy-E's son thinks Suge Knight murdered his father by injecting him with AIDS:

- http://consequenceofsound.net/2015/08/eazy-e-suge-knight-murdered-his-father-aids/

Suge Knight May Have a Brain Tumor, Claims Prison Toilet Is Possessed:

- http://theboombox.com/suge-knight-brain-tumor/

The Occult Universe of David Bowie and the Meaning of "Blackstar":

- http://vigilantcitizen.com/musicbusiness/occult-universe-david-bowie-meaning-blackstar/

David Bowie and the Occult:

- http://www.parareligion.ch/bowie.htm

CHAPTER 17

THE ENEMY WITHIN

Can demonic possession explain many of music's alter-egos?

> *"I don't know if I'm a medium for some outside source. Whatever it is, frankly, I hope it's not what I think it is . . . "*
>
> *Ozzy Osbourne*

> *"I made a bargain with . . . the chief commander . . . of this earth and then the world we can't see."*
>
> *Bob Dylan*

> *"When two of the biggest rock songs of all time, Led Zeppelin's 'Stairway To Heaven' and The Eagles' 'Hotel California' both contain the same elements, it deserves a closer look. I mean, both songs contain a lost or confused traveller, a path or a road, a lady shining a light to show the way, Heaven or Hell, wind, spirit, and a piper whose voice is calling."*
>
> *Wayne Bush on 'The Higherside Chats' podcast, June 2015*

We saw in the earlier chapter on trauma-based mind control how many artists—particularly those in the hip-hop genre—show a penchant for having alter-egos. While much of this is undoubtedly due to the presence of Monarch programming and other methods, there is another explanation for the high prevalence of alternate personalities.

If the world in which we live were truly three-dimensional and solid, there would be no possibility for the phenomenon of demonic possession—the presence of outside forces that interact with the human energy field, allowing them to merge with and temporarily 'take over' an individual's very being. But, as even mainstream science is now acknowledging, this is not the type of reality in which we find ourselves. The apparently 'physical' world is in fact illusory, and only appears to be solid because of the way we perceive it through our consciousness. In its base state, everything in existence is energy vibrating at an endless array of frequencies. The lower the frequency of vibration, the more dense and solid an item will appear to be, including ourselves. As implausible as this will seem to anyone encountering this subject area for the first time, as with so much else, this is knowledge that has been understood by mystics, secret-societies and religious orders the world over for millennia, and which has been systematically occulted (hidden) from the general public. Understanding how synchronising energetic frequencies can be achieved through carefully contrived rituals, is key to understanding how possession of a human body–and some would say, soul–is a genuine reality. There is much evidence to suggest that the dark priest-class at the helm of the corporate music industry are in possession of this knowledge, and use it to puppeteer and manipulate many of their key artists, who they see as their possessions, in line with their religious doctrines.

When hip-hop went to the darkside

We've already explored the systematic degradation of hip-hop, but the sinister direction that the art-form seemed to take a short while after the engineered East Coast/ West Coast 'beef' of the mid-90s is worth a mention here. Within ten years, mainstream hip-hop had gone from lyrics mainly concerned with partying and celebrating life, plus MCs bragging about their lyrical skill and dexterity, to tracks dealing with evil, sin, death and the presence of dark parasitic forces. Having been an active radio and club DJ through this period, I can say that this strange transition went largely un-noticed by the majority of hip-hop fans, (as it did to myself,) who chalked it all up merely as interesting artistic expression. Viewing the situation with the benefit of hindsight, however, suggests that this was a trend that happened anything but by chance.

In 1998, DMX released his album 'It's Dark And Hell Is Hot.' The title alone is enough to raise curiosity, and more of it comes from the track 'Damien.' This depicts DMX becoming affected by a character who enters his life at a low point and promises to turn his fortunes around, so long as he will 'be his friend.' DMX has conversations with Damien, to whom no-one else seems to be privy. The track ends with his new mentor coercing him into murdering one of his old friends. DMX laments the situation with the final line, "I see know, ain't nothin' but trouble ahead."

Damien appears very much to be a reflection of DMX's own 'dark side,' brought about by the presence of an outside force. This wasn't the last we heard of him, either. The pair engage in a more hostile conversation on the track 'The Omen' from the album 'Flesh Of My Flesh, Blood Of My Blood', part of which goes as follows:

"Yo, I ain't ask you for shit,

Oh yes you did, when you really needed something then you allowed me to give,

You sold me your soul when you didn't say no,

Just let a nigga go, and gimme what you owe,

Fuck was you thinking? Ain't shit for free,

Ain't a motherfucker you know, can defeat me,

Forgive me Father, for I have sinned,

And with your help, I know the Devil won't win."

In true movie style, the trilogy is completed with 'Damien III,' in which DMX prays to Jesus for salvation from the evil that has possessed him.

Within weeks of the DMX album, Cam'ron had appeared with his debut LP 'Confessions Of Fire.' The track 'Death' sees Cam'ron in conversation with a Grim Reaper character, imploring him not to take his soul:

"Come on, chill man, don't take me,

Don't take you? Why not? Cause you rhyme now?

Listen here muthafucka, lie down,

Yo yo, chill, it ain't my time now,

Come on, last year you had me duckin' the blaze,

What about that bitch that you fucked wit' AIDS?

Aww shit, come on, Death, I ain't know that,

You know I wouldn't have went up in that bitch Kojak."

Elsewhere, on the track 'Confessions,' Cam'ron is heard consumed with guilt over his sins as he confesses to a minister:

"See, my two-year-old nephew, I swear I was holding him well,

'Til he cried, and he cried, and he cried, I had to scold him and yell,

You know, one thing led to another, I said, 'oh what the hell',

Then I threw him against the wall. His parents I told them he fell,

That's why I'm going to hell."

And later:

"I don't wanna talk about that Sunday evening, that cold November weekend,

When I had to grab that deacon, and put him into my dungeons of heathens,

And then in tongues I was speakin."

One of the earliest tracks which Kanye West produced for Jay-Z was 'Lucifer' from 2003's 'The Black Album,' which sampled the Max Romeo reggae tune 'Chase The Devil,' (also used on The Prodigy's 'Out Of Space.') Lucifer has been identified as a deity worshipped by the dark priest-class which controls the entertainment industry—along with so much else—and this tune appears to employ their favourite trick of placing the truth right there in plain sight, all dressed up as 'entertainment.' Some have speculated that this track was announcing Kanye's induction into the dark fraternities, as his own career as an artist took off shortly afterwards. In the lyrics, Jay-Z addresses the by-now-common subject of spiritual possession by outside forces:

"Lord forgive him, he got them dark forces in him,

But he also got a righteous cause for sinning,

Them a murder me, so I gotta murder them first."

And:

"Man, I gotta get my soul right, I gotta get these Devils out my life,

These cowards gonna make a nigga ride,

They won't be happy 'til somebody dies."

By the time Eminem appeared on the scene with his debut 'The Slim Shady LP' in early 1999, hip-hop's fan base had been nicely primed to accept lyrics about murder, mayhem, mutilation, rape, death, sin, guilt and parasitic evil forces as 'normal.' The Totalitarian Tiptoe in full effect. Looking back from an informed perspective, it's incredible how all this stuff was so neatly ushered in with, on the whole, very little objection. Listeners had been conditioned towards extreme lyrical scenarios being passed off as 'just a bit of fun,' and Eminem had been very much groomed as the key player in this role. What was shocking when first heard, had become completely normalised into popular culture by just a few years later, the bar being raised ever higher in terms of what was fair game by way of lyrics. Given the subject matter that has already made it into rap tracks, it's difficult to imagine how things can possibly be degraded any further. But I'm sure they'll find a way.

Explaining the Slim Shady pseudonym, Eminem, (already a pseud-onym for his government name Marshall Mathers,) said in the early days: "Slim Shady is just the evil thoughts that come into my head. Things I shouldn't be thinking about." This absorption was referenced on 'The Bad, The Sad & The Hated,' the Lil' Wayne track on which he guested, with the lines:

"No one knows what it's like,

To be the bad man, (when Eminem created Slim Shady,)

To be the sad man, (and began to explore his dark-side alter-ego in his lyrics,)

Behind the lies, (DJ Cinima,)

No one knows what it's like to be hated, (he really started to connect with people across the world,)

To be faded, (but the violence, rape, and murder in his lyrics,)

To telling lonely lies, (have outraged just as many people as they won over.)

The debut album's second single was 'Guilty Conscience.' It portrays three scenarios in which Dr. Dre appears as the voice of each individ-ual's morality, while Eminem portrays their dark side, coercing them into robbery, murder and date-rape. By the end of the track, Dre's voice of reason has turned dark too, as he also advocates murder. The chorus hook runs: "These voices, these voices, I hear them. And when they talk, I follow, I follow, I follow."

Elsewhere on the album, Eminem takes his three-year-old daughter along with him to a lakeside on '97 Bonnie & Clyde,' where he dumps the body of her mother whose throat he has slit, as well as that of her new lover and his baby son, getting his daughter to help him tie rocks to her mother's foot to help weigh her down. Equally telling as to the agenda that was being slowly unfolded was 'Bad Meets Evil,' where Eminem talks of being a ghost that inhabits rapper Royce Da 5'9's head:

"Trapped him in his room, possessed him and hoist his bed,

Till the evilness flows through his blood like poisonous lead,

Told him each one of his boys is dead,

I asked him to come to the dark side. He made a choice and said . . . "

A similar scenario was depicted on the track 'Murder Was The Case' on Snoop Doggy Dogg's 1993 album 'Doggystyle,' the common denominator between Snoop and Eminem being that both artists are credited with having been 'discovered' by Dr. Dre, who executive-produced both albums. The track depicts Snoop being critically shot in a drive-by shooting, with echoes of a real-life incident that occurred during the recording of 'Doggystyle,' (in a rare case of apparent Predictive Programming occurring *after* the event rather than before!) Snoop, real name Calvin Broadus, was arrested in connection with the murder of Phillip Woldermariam, a rival gang member. Snoop was charged with murder along with his bodyguard McKinley Lee, as Snoop was driving the vehicle from which the shots were fired. Both Snoop and Lee were later acquitted.

On 'Murder Was The Case,' Snoop is in a coma and on the brink of death, when he is visited by a demonic entity who offers to restore him to life and grant him all his wishes, but all on the condition that he remembers 'that ass is mine.' The following year, a short film directed by Dr. Dre and Fab Five Freddy was released, also entitled 'Murder Was The Case.' In the narrative, Snoop dies, but is resurrected after making a deal with the Devil.

Dr. Dre appeared with Cypress Hill frontman Be Real on a 1997 track tellingly titled 'Puppet Master,' laden with imagery straight out of a horror movie. Dre appears as a demonic skeleton in a pope's mitre hat, with Be Real as a horned, clawed and bearded depiction of Baphomet/ Pan/ the Devil, (and in his regular guise looking much like Church Of Satan founder Anton LaVey.) Cypress Hill had released their album

'Black Sunday' a few years before. Although most of the songs were about smoking weed, the sleeve image offered more horror film imagery, showing a rotting skull at the foot of a gothic cemetery.

As if to assert his demonic credentials still further, Dre had also appeared with former NWA groupmate Ice Cube on 'Natural Born Killaz,' a track narrated from the perspective of a crazed, psychopathic murderer who hints at being possessed, all set to a dark, twisted beat.

Other references from rappers to having sold their soul in exchange for fame and fortune are legion. In 2Pac's 'Good Life' he states: "Picture a nigga on the verge of livin' insane, I sold my soul for a chance to kick it and bang." DMX addresses soul-selling again on 'Let Me Fly' with: "I sold my soul to the Devil and the price was cheap." On 'Eyes Closed,' Kanye West told listeners: "I sold my soul to the Devil, that's a crappy deal, Least it came with a few toys like a Happy Meal." Later, on 'Black Skinhead' from his extremely dark 'Yeezus' album, he remarks: "They say I'm possessed, it's an omen."

Lil' Wayne, an artist whose back-catalogue is a one-stop-shop in *everything* that has gone wrong with "hip-hop," slipped a reference to 'Satan' into his unsettling track 'Love Me' in 2012, with barely anyone batting an eyelid. In between Future boasting that "I got some down bitches I can call," and Drake advising us that "long as I got my bitches I couldn't give a fuck about no haters," Wayne's line states: "And these hoes love me like Satan, maaan." A question has always occurred to me—why is it taken as a given that the hoes in question would love Satan in the first place? The video contains split-second frames where Wayne is depicted as a horned entity in another blink-and-you-miss it exercise in subliminals, designed to implant an image in the viewer's subconscious mind. As Black Sheep Magazine observed on the subject:

"If "rapper," (we're told,) Lil' Wayne had emerged with his current style of "music" 15 to 20 years ago, he would have undergone mass ridicule, been laughed off the scene and would never have been taken seriously in the business again.

"It's bad enough that Wayne's records are mind-numbingly vacuous and instantly disposable—and that he and his fellow Young Money/ Cash Money freaks, by manipulation, dominate what is laughingly

passed off as a 'hip-hop' scene now. All this is before you get into the deeply sick nature of the lyrics and imagery employed in his output, with most of his followers so brainwashed hat they've probably failed to even register it, and would laugh off explanations such as this as paranoid and delusional, as they go back to having their sense of normality and world-view dictated to them by this demented trash."

I guess they're not fans then. You can watch the video to 'Love Me' here:

• https://www.YouTube.com/watch?v=KY44zvhWhp4

Just the two of us

The concept of prominent artists having alter-egos has been slowly normalised into the culture in the past few years. Some years ago, Beyonce announced her alternate identity known as Sasha Fierce. The album, titled in no uncertain terms 'I Am . . . Sasha Fierce,' appeared in November 2008. It was a double-disc set, with the first said to represent Beyonce's own character and consisting mainly of slow and mid-tempo ballads, while the second disc was said to be the domain of her Sasha Fierce side, consisting of more uptempo and energetic songs. In comments that smack of covertly revealing the presence of a possessive entity, Beyonce explained the juxtaposition of her character at the time as:

> *"I turn into Sasha. I wouldn't like Sasha if I met her off-stage. She's too aggressive, too strong, too sassy, too sexy. I'm not like her in real life at all. I'm not flirtatious and super-confident and fearless like her.*
>
> *"What I feel onstage I don't feel anywhere else. It's an out-of-body experience. I created my stage persona . . . so that when I go home, I don't have to think about what it is I do. Sasha isn't me. The people around me know who I really am."*

(During the writing of this book, an interview with a New York singer named Gianna, who was being tipped for big things in the mainstream, came across my radar. In it, she talked of having an alter-ego named

417

Lola Grey, of whom she said: "it's just a different side of me that some-times comes out when I write my music. She's more forward and a bit braver than me." Gianna's early publicity pictures featured her wearing polka-dot trousers, with one shot featuring multiple representations of her face with one eye obscured. Why am I getting a strong sense of *deja-vu?*)

Beyonce's performance at the 2013 Super Bowl half-time show came under scrutiny by many researchers who pointed out how, at a key point, her appearance started to change. This, they suggested, was a key point at which she actually came under the possession of an outside entity. The photos of the moment in question are certainly unflattering and a far cry from Beyonce's usually carefully-managed image. In fact, their sharing on social media brought a forceful request from Beyonce's management that they be taken down and no longer used.

There were alternative headlines of a similar nature when Beyonce arrived with Jay-Z to perform a show in New Zealand in October 2013. Part of their welcome involved a group of local Maoris performing a traditional *Haka* in their honour—an ancestral war dance used to intim-idate enemies before a battle. The ritual involves synchronised danc-ing along with purposeful grimacing and sticking-out of the tongue. Beyonce immediately got into the spirit of the dance, her contorted facial expressions looking very similar to the ones that appeared during the Sasha Fierce show, prompting some to question whether an element of spiritual possession was going on here too, (and whether this, in fact, is what is happening to the Maori warriors when they engage in their ritual.)

Jay-Z has gone by various personas over the years, the most common being 'Jiggaman' and 'Hove,' the latter being an abbreviated form of Jay Hova, a name which has been considered arrogantly blasphemous by some of a religious persuasion. The concept of rappers portraying themselves as 'gods' was continued by Kanye West when he adopted his 'Yeezus' persona in 2013.

The Atlanta rapper T.I. put out an album in 2007 titled 'T.I. Vs T.I.P.' The sleeve designs showed a suited, business-orientated side of him, juxtaposed with his street/ ghetto representation, with the content depicting the conflict between his two 'sides.'

Nicki Minaj's Roman Zolanski alter-ego, which she publicly 'exorcised' at the 2012 Grammys, and Lady Gaga's Jo Calderone character, were documented in the earlier chapter on mind control.

Enter the Rain Man

There is one fictional character from the world of movies which has appeared in more hip-hop tracks of recent years than any other, inspiring several song titles. Given rappers' enthusiasm for identifying with gangsters and street hustlers, you might expect this to be 'Scarface's Tony Montana, 'The Godfather's Don Corleone, or someone of that ilk. So why does the honour go to a dysfunctional, autistic *savant* played by Dustin Hoffman instead?

Welcome to the strange and unsettling world of Rain Man.

On the surface, Rain Man would appear to be a reference to Hoffman's character in the 1988 Hollywood movie of the same name, also starring Tom Cruise. At least, this is the publicly-acceptable guise of the character that goes by that name. As many have demonstrated, however, there seems to be a far more sinister agenda at work. Rain Man is actually an other-worldly entity that seems to be revered by the sick occult practitioners manipulating the music industry, and which many artists appear to be channeling through themselves via carefully-crafted rituals. The movie merely offers plausible deniability.

US researcher Lenon Honor commented on the subject in my 'Good Vibrations' interview with him in 2013:

> *"I did a film entitled 'The Workings Of Evil Revisited,' and I have a whole bunch of references even going back 20, 30, 40 years where they were referring to this 'Rain Man' entity . . . And when you really get into it, you realise that part of what goes on with the mind control of the masses, is to indoctrinate them into deifying particular beings that most people would consider 'demonic.' So you have children singing these songs, and they're getting these embedded images, subliminal messages, etc, where they're using particular symbols. They're using skulls, they're using this Rain Man entity, these lyrical references. People are steadily being indoctrinated into a level of occultism that is quite dark and sinister. And I have to say, when I went into*

doing my analysis of all this at the beginning, I had no idea how sinister it all gets."

Lenon was first alerted to the infiltration of Rain Man by the video to Rihanna's international smash 'Umbrella.' In a split-second frame that can only be properly analysed by pausing the video, Rihanna appears inside a pyramid, apparently striking an unusual pose. Close examination, however, shows this has been digitally manipulated, and that Rihanna's body has been made to look like the Baphomet entity, her arms representing outstretched horns, her head and shoulders digitally altered to form a snout and eye sockets, and her legs representing the jaw structure. Lenon has speculated that this may be a representation of the Rain Man entity, however, particularly given some of the lyrical clues in the song. It starts with Jay-Z proclaiming "Jay, Rain Man is back," also reminding us that Rihanna is the "good girl gone bad." There are then multiple references to the character narrating the song, offering shelter "under my umbrella." An excellent article on the Rain Man entity in music appeared on the Spiritsspeakstruths blogspot site, which analyses the significance of the umbrella imagery further:

"Umbrella in Latin also translates to 'shadow' ... Umbra can also mean Phantom or Ghost. The name Umbra appears in the Necronomicon, which is a 'fictional' occult book of demonology by H.P. Lovecraft. In the book, Umbra is one of the thirteen globes of Yog Sothoth, a celestial body ... Basically, Umbra is a Devil.

"In 'Umbrella', Jay sings "Rain Man is back, with little Miss Sunshine, Rihanna where you at?" Notice 'Rain Man' and Jay are two separate people in that lyric ... The entity introduced itself as Rain Man, and Rihanna responded saying, "you had my heart, and we will never be a world apart. You're part of my entity, here for infinity."

"This song is not about love for a man, but a spirit, (a fallen spirit named Rain Man.) Rihanna herself stated on the set of the 'Umbrella' video, that this song "has a deeper meaning to it. You have to really listen to it." Is it possible that Rain Man is a Devil?"

Jay-Z announced his Rain Man pseudonym around the time of his appearance on the Rihanna track. Attempting to explain his ability to intuit lyrics when in that mode, with no need to write anything down, he commented:

> *"I look at it like a puzzle. Like, I try to figure out what Imma say on there, figure out the emotion on the track, what it's saying . . . then I go through my Rain Man. I can't explain it to y'all. It just comes out of the air for me. You start mumbling."*

In a separate interview with MTV News, he said:

> *"I started doing hidden messages into music to remove the technical, then it evolved from there . . . I guess I'm an idiot savant as well."*

Jay is far from the only corporate rapper to have, for some reason, demonstrated an affinity with Rain Man. Around the same time, Eminem recorded a track, itself entitled 'Rain Man.' Introducing it on-stage alongside soon-to-be-slain fellow rapper Proof, he told the crowd:

> *"My name isn't going to be Slim Shady no more. No more Eminem either. I don't even go by my government name Marshall Mathers . . . If I do come back, you know what my new name gon' be? Rain Man."*

The track itself, performed for good measure alongside Dr. Dre, (who else?!), includes the lyrics:

> *"My name was not to become what I became with this level of fame,*
>
> *My soul is possessed by this Devil, my new name is . . . "*

Eminem is no stranger to the subject of soul possession, a concept he has explored several times on record. 'My Darling,' an extra track from the 'Relapse' album, is among his darkest and most disturbing of all—and that's saying something given the vast array of competition! It sees Eminem and his alternate personality of Slim Shady arguing and taunting each other. It all puts me in mind of the movie 'Identity' starring John Cusack and Ray Liotta, in which a disparate group of characters are brought together at a motel during a storm and die one-by-one . . . until the film reveals they were all creations in the mind of a dangerous mental patient.

Elsewhere, the pushing of the Rain Man character into the collective subconscious of hip-hop's audience was far from over. By the time Gucci Mane and Lil' Wayne had both produced tracks entitled 'Rain Man,' (what are the odds of this being just 'by chance?') an alternative attempt at an explanation had been offered. Lil' Wayne's breakthrough track was 'Let It Rain' by Fat Joe, (released, appropriately enough, on Hallowe'en in 2006!) In hip-hop street slang, 'let it rain' has come to refer to the throwing of wads of cash into the air at strip-clubs, causing the notes to flutter down individually as rather generous tips for the girls. Hence, recent references to it raining and an individual being a 'rain man' have been passed off in this regard. The dark agenda has continued at an unseen level, however, with the seemingly plausible cover story merely offering an excuse for puppeteered artists to continue pushing the same ideas.

In his book 'Sacrifice: Magic Behind The Mic,' Isaac Weishaupt offers some insight into why the music industry's controllers might be so set on having their key artists invoke other-worldly entities through their performances:

"The reason why magic practitioners perform spirit evocations, (and internal invocations,) is to pull energy or information from another realm. The artist can pull knowledge, lyrics or energy through the ritual. Any energetic being can be evoked, and that is why even fictional characters like H.P Lovecraft's Cthulhu are used in evocation. So long as you have a defined set of characteristics, you can perform magic to have an energetic connection with them in order to gain their insight . . .

"It takes an incredible amount of energy and focus in order for these people to get in touch with this other realm of existence, so it drains them emotionally and physically, perhaps explaining the overwhelming amount of drug abuse found in the industry."

The world is a stage

A key method of putting rituals right in the public's face–and gaining their energetic input to the possible evoking of supernatural entities–has come from the large-scale stage shows of recent years. Events such as the Grammys, the MTV and VMA Awards and the US Super Bowl half-time show, have been getting more occultic and esoteric with every passing year. These televised shows benefit from audiences numbering several million, allowing for a scale of participation from the unwitting audience never before seen in human history. Among the most infamous have been the 2014 Grammy Awards, which featured industry puppet-of-choice Katy Perry apparently performing an actual witchcraft routine to her song 'Dark Horse.' Her 'act' is prefaced by a sinister voiceover saying; "She cast spells from crystal balls. Invoking spirits. She put me in a trance." It's all there–horned and cloaked demonic figures, fire, esoteric sigils, a supernatural black horse with glowing red eyes reminiscent of the one in the deeply sinister Denver International Airport. The imagery at these shows is now so blatant–and so unconnected to the lyrical content of the songs–that it's even starting to grab the attention of those not known for their acknowledgement of 'conspiracy'-type subjects. The Katy Perry Grammys show prompted a Tweet from former University of Alabama quarterback A.J. McCarron, saying:

> "Is it just me or are some of the Grammy performances so far (sic) seem to be really demonic? Looks like there is a lot of evil in the world."

No, it's not just you, mate. Even 'E! Online' mainstream entertainment news Tweeted:

> "Um, did we just witness actual witchcraft during Katy Perry's Grammys performance?"

Another classic was the 2012 Grammys, held in the wake of Whitney Houston's highly suspicious death. This one hosted Nicki Minaj's apparent black mass and public 'exorcism' of her Roman Zolanski entity. She entered wearing a blood-red robe, (representing one of the principal colours associated with Saturn,) and accompanied by an actor portraying the Pope. The performance went on to mock traditional Christian church services.

As Isaac Weishaupt observes:

> *"That night she performed her song 'Roman Holiday,' in which she channels a spirit named Roman, one of the many spirits that she claims takes over her body. During the controversial performance, she conducted a Satanic ritual and was depicted receiving an exorcism."*

Only days before, Madonna had set tongues wagging with the over-the-top occultic nature of her act at the Super Bowl half-time show. She had presented something of a teaser for this when she had commented in a recent interview with CNN/ CIA's Anderson Cooper that:

> *"The Super Bowl is kind of like the Holy of Holies in America. I'll come out halfway of the 'church experience,' and I'm gonna have to deliver a sermon. It'll have to be very impactful."*

Madonna has earned the unofficial nickname of 'Grand Priestess' of the music industry, in reflection of her faithfully serving her corporate masters for over three decades, and this status certainly seemed to be exploited in the show, appearing as she did in full Babylonian goddess regalia, with rappers Nicki Minaj and M.I.A. in subservient supportive roles to their Queen.

While most of the ritual stage magick occurs at US shows, a British institution which has grabbed the attention of occult researchers is the long-established Glastonbury Festival, held in the wake of the Summer Solstice each June. Of the great many UK music festivals that happen annually, this is the only one that is given hours and hours of live coverage by the BBC. Why would that be, I wonder? Its ritualistic relevance was explored in a fascinating and highly recommended blog entitled 'The Illuminati, Satanism, Drugs & The Music Industry.' Not really one for the kids, then. The article observes:

> *"Glastonbury is famous for its Pyramid Stage. At night you can see the apex fully illuminated, and nowadays, they have a laser beam*

coming straight through the centre of the apex and up into the night sky ... The structure was built close to the Glastonbury Abbey/ Stonehenge ley-lines, and over the site of a blind spring. The pyramid shape is a very powerful structure, the apex of which draws energy up and transmits it still further, while the energy from the stars and sun are attracted to it and drawn down.

... This pyramid grew to symbolise the magic of Glastonbury Festival before it famously burned down in 1994, shortly before the Festival. In 2000, the phoenix rose from the ashes, and a glittering 100ft steel structure was erected with a massive footprint of 40m x 40m—four times larger than its previous incarnation. This current structure was designed and built by local Pilton villager Bill Burroughs, and is based on the Great Pyramid of Giza in Egypt. It's the most instantly-recognised festival stage in the world, and for 40 years, those who have been going to Glastonbury and dancing and singing in front of the Pyramid, are participating in an occult pagan ritual whether they know it or not."

Kali Cyrus

In 2013, it was Miley Cyrus's performance at the MTV VMA Music Awards that came under scrutiny. Quite apart from the alternative media's interpretation of what was going on, this one caught the attention of the mainstream news, tabloids and gossip magazines, setting tongues wagging (pun intended) around water coolers across the US and beyond. This show demonstrated the most blatant transition from Cyrus' previous persona as the squeaky-clean, girl-next-door Hannah Montana, (another creation of the Disney Corporation,) into the debased, sluttish, pornographic persona she has employed since.

According to the outstanding US researcher and film-maker Freeman, Cyrus' continual extending of her tongue was no random thing. In fact, he claimed on his Youtube video on the subject, she was invoking the spirit of the Hindu goddess Kali.

"Once you start to discover the esoteric roots of these rituals—and this is going back all the way to Ancient Greece, or the Egyptian

425

stories . . . The actors would always be the representations of the God forms, or even invoke these God forms into themselves to then give the performance. And this really was the purpose of an actor. So when I started to elaborate on these high-profile rituals, one of the first was, of course, Britney Spears kissing with Madonna. Madonna in a top hat coming down 13 steps to the song 'Hollywood,' which is based on a magician's wand, the holly wood, and then presenting Britney to the world and giving her the kiss of death, if you will. Madonna is a classic example of how this is all inter-worked into the system, because she is a High Priestess within Kabbalah, even going out and perform-ing ceremonies with the Rabbi in Israel. She takes it to the ultimate. She's even removed the vowels from her name, being MNDA now. This is to give her name a more Kabbalistic bed because Hebrew doesn't have these vowels.

"So each one of these celebrities has been brought to us as a God form or a Goddess form. So I have a depiction of Britney as Athena on my website, with a bunch of the other celebrities and the different variations they've used with these God forms. So when I saw Miley Cyrus coming out of that giant teddy bear at the VMAs, it was clear to me, with the amount of tongue gesturing she was doing, that she was to evoke Kali."

Kali was frequently depicted as sticking her tongue out, in the same way that New Zealand Maori warriors do during their previously-men-tioned *Hakas*. A protruding tongue is also a feature of the deity on the sun calendar of the Aztecs. Kali's fearsomeness was enforced by the fact that she wore the heads of vanquished enemies on a belt around her waist. She was always symbolised with long, flowing hair, and as Free-man observed in his written article on the event, Miley appeared to be stroking an invisible mane of hair during her performance.

"Kali, consort of Shiva, symbolises the 'Time of Death;' 'The Black One.' Once Kali had destroyed all the demons in battle, she began a terrific dance out of the sheer joy of victory. The unleashed form of Kali often becomes wild and uncontrollable. Kali was so much involved in the killing spree that she got carried away and began

destroying everything in sight. Kali is the fearful and ferocious form of the mother Goddess."

Freeman's view is that the Miley Cyrus act was a subtle, psychological way of implanting an idea into the minds of the viewing world public–that America has become a completely debased and immoral society, a modern Babylon, inviting the scorn and contempt of the rest of the world, whilst at the same time, representing the sick, twisted values of the control system running it.

Miley's tongue act continued long after the VMA event, as she would continue sticking it out spontaneously on TV and at live appearances. It certainly lends weight to the idea that she had been programmed into doing it ahead of the VMA show, and that the habit took some time to wear off. By late 2015, a publicity photoshoot saw her appearing bare-breasted and wearing a strap-on cock. Many observers commented on the empty and soulless look in her eyes by this point.

Whenever celebrities go off the rails like this, the first question that occurs to members of the public is, 'where are the parents? What are they thinking of, letting this happen to their daughter?!' As we've discussed in a previous chapter, the entertainment world is *nothing like* the rest of human society when it comes to family relationships. Many mind-controlled artists come from generational bloodlines of such activity, with parents doubling as their exploitative handlers. In Miley's case, her father is the country music artist Billy Ray Cyrus, best known for his hit 'Achy Breaky Heart.' Considering what Fritz Springmeier told me about the country scene being a hotbed of trauma-based mind control, perhaps we shouldn't be too surprised at the path his daughter has taken. (The Mormon Church operating out of Salt Lake City which spawned The Osmonds, and the Church of Scientology with its celebrity endorsers like Tom Cruise and John Travolta, are also said to be strongly involved in the mind control agenda. Hip-hop pioneer Doug E Fresh is said to be a member of the Church of Scientology, as are Will Smith and Jada Pinkett, and Priscilla and Lisa-Marie Presley. Charles Manson was a former member.)

Bones, Boards and Spells

In 2004, a multi-volume video series titled 'They Sold Their Souls for Rock 'n' Roll' appeared in the US. Although the heavy Christian bias delivered in the form of church sermons will prove offputting for many non-Christians, the series did make a number of salient points about the demonic influences that had been sweeping the music industry for decades. The ministers involved were content to put this all down to 'the Devil's work,' of course, missing the point that there's far more to these dark, malevolent agendas than a singular entity. Among the acts scrutinised by the series was the rap crew Bone Thugs N Harmony, who were signed by NWA's Eazy E to his new Ruthless Records label in 1993.

From the start, the group displayed a fascination with witchcraft and the dark occult. One of their earliest tracks, 'Hell Sent', has the then-teenage group rapping about coming out of Hell to Earth 'to destroy all worshippers of peace.' Krayzie Bone states: "Sold my soul to the Devil, but I changed my mind, now I want it back. But he won't co-operate, so now it's time to jack."

The intro to their debut album, 'Creepin' On A Come Up,' features a demonic voice at the end stating: "Now, let's run through the doors backwards, my friends, and play with the ouija board." This leads into a song entitled 'Mr Ouija,' where the group ask the board to predict their future, with constant talk of 'a bloody murder' given in response.

Working with the group appears to be bad luck for their collaborators. It has been pointed out that 2Pac, The Notorious BIG, Eazy E, and Lil' Boo of The Graveyard Shift, (Krayzie Bone's cousin,) all died in the same years as their collaborations.

'Tha Crossroads' was the Bone Thugs tribute to their mentor Eazy E after he died, reportedly of AIDS, in 1995. The title alludes heavily to the legend of bluesman Robert Johnson selling his soul to the Devil at a crossroads in exchange for great musical talent. Eazy E himself has been rumoured to have been a practitioner in the dark occult.

The 'They Sold Their Souls' documentary chronicles a witchcraft spell included on the sleeve to the Bone Thugs album "E. 1999 Eternal.' It is written backwards and can only be deciphered when held up to a mirror, working in much the same way as the back-masking audio messages from our earlier chapter. The film states that this is the same tactic used by the witches involved in the Salem trials of the 17th century, who would send people a letter written backwards containing a curse, or hex. The dark energy behind the spell would supposedly be absorbed into the person's soul once they had been tricked into reading it in a mirror.

Three sixes

A crew that has to raise eyebrows in a similar way to Bone Thugs, is the Grammy Award-winning collective known as Three 6 Mafia out of Memphis, Tennessee. The group have explained away their choice of name by saying it represented the fact that there were originally three members, before three more were added to make six. Placed into the overall context of the corporate entertainment industry, however, (they're signed to the Columbia Records imprint of Sony, after all!) it seems far more likely that the group name is to be taken to mean '666 Mafia'–especially as 'Triple Six Mafia' was one of their many early names. In separate interviews, group member Juicy J, whose father is a Christian preacher and mother a librarian, has said that they chose the group name to be deliberately controversial and get noticed.

There's also the matter of their lyrical content, such as on the track 'Fuckin' Wit Dis Click:'

> *"I'm on a cross, Lucifer, please cut me free, (cut me free,)*
>
> *I'll draw your portrait if you pull these nails out my feet, (nails out my feet,)*
>
> *My cross turns upside down"*
>
> *"No Lord could stop us now,*
>
> *Cause the demons reborn again"*
>
> *"Follow me into the trees,*
>
> *Watch me rob Adam,*

And watch me rape Eve"

And in the song 'Sleep:'

"Satanic in scent were wrote on the scent,

It's so sacred, created by Lucifer slaves."

Of very much the same ilk, (as highlighted in an article on hip-hop's Satanic agenda by the Canadian writer Henry Makow,) is the Kansas rapper Tech N9ne, who took his name from the Tec-9 semi-automatic handgun. The Wikipedia entry on him includes the intriguing sentence: "He never met his father, and his mother suffered from epilepsy and lupus when he was a child, which emotionally affected him and inspired him to 'search for God.' He would explore abandoned buildings with his best friend, hoping to catch a ghost on film."

In his article, Makow points out Tech N9ne's trademark ability to rap backwards, with the phrases only making sense when the recording is played in reverse. This puts us right back into realms of back-masking, of course, and Aleister Crowley's teaching of "let him . . . listen to phonograph records reversed . . . " It's claimed that a phrase in his track 'Demons,' which features the chorus "There's a demon inside of me, can I kill it? Hell no! Can I kill it? Hell no! Can I kill it? Hell no!," when reversed comes out as:

"Ahh . . . Slowly die . . . I don't wanna,

Ahh . . . Slowly die . . . I don't wanna,

Hell is coming! Onward . . . Hell is coming! Onward . . .

Hell is gonna keep us enemies my friend . . . Onward!"

The word of Todd

A shocking series of claims of what goes on behind closed doors at major record labels surfaced on the internet a few years ago. It was a recording of a lecture reportedly given some time in the 1970s by a man known as John Todd, who claimed to have been an employee at several of the big corporations of the time, and as the manager of Zodiac Productions. This was described as 'the largest music conglomerate in the world, owning RCA Records, Columbia Records, Motown Records, and almost all the concert-booking agencies in the United States.' In turn, Zodiac is said to have had ties to Chase Manhattan, Standard Oil and Lloyds of London.

In Todd's now-famous monologue, he tells of dark magic spells being cast on master recordings of popular music, and relates this to an encounter with David Crosby of Crosby, Stills, Nash and Young, sometime after Todd says he exited the industry.

> "I saw David the day before Christmas last year and talked with him. I got him away from this witch he was with. He told her to go shopping. We were in West Hollywood. We got talking. I said, 'David, I'd like to ask you a couple of questions.' I said, 'I already know the answers.' I said, 'I've been gone five years. I need to know if certain things are still the way they were when I left.

> "I said, 'do they still bring the master to the Temple Room?' Dave said, 'yeah'. I said, 'do they still have the coven conjure demons into the master?' He said, 'of course.' I said, 'now I gotta know something. What's the main reason for rock music?' . . . He said, 'the same as when you were in. So that we can place spells on people that we couldn't cast spells upon.' I said, 'OK, one last thing. I've been hearing that you must be an initiated witch now to get a record contract.' He said, 'that's right. Many of us that weren't total witches have to be witches now in order to produce music.'

Todd goes on to explain that a master recording of a song or album, which provides the content for every vinyl, CD or cassette copy that gets released to the public, gets taken into the Temple Room that all the major record companies have in their HQ, on a full moon. The master is placed on an altar in the North of the room, he states, with a pentagram engraved in the floor. A coven of thirteen hand-chosen witches and wizards then come in, and conjure up a demonic power, then order it to tell the demons under it to follow every individual copy coming off the original master.

> *"Rock music is not just a song. It is supernatural music that witches carefully design by their spirit guides, in the form of spells. Much of the songs are written in what we call Witch Language. To give you an idea, many of you talk on a CB. Unless you know what a 'smokey' is, and a '10/4' and a 'front door/ back door rocking chair' and these type of things, you don't know what you're talking about. Same with witches. When you're in the first or second level, you have to learn over 2,000 words that, said by anybody else, means something totally different than when you say it."*

Todd cites The Eagles' 'Hotel California' as an example of a song which most people have heard on the radio, but whose lyrics most would be at a loss to explain on the surface:

> *"Stop and think how many songs are out there that you really like, but you don't have any idea what the person was taking about? 'Goodbye Yellow Brick Road? How about 'The Destroyer' by Kiss? . . . The Beatles song 'Helter Skelter,' in witch language, nobody knew what it meant. Manson did because he belonged to the Process. 'Helter Skelter' is a several-thousand-year-old word. Most of the music is either about Helter Skelter or a place called The Night Winds, which is what 'Hotel California' is about, and different doctors of witchcraft. Kiss openly bragged how they were gaining control of people through their music because the people played their music. They told how they didn't form their own group. Their church—because they were ordained ministers of a Satanist church—placed them together. And that's how most of the music is done."*

The speech in question is available here–https://www.YouTube.com/v/Otti-82jEAc

Inevitably, there have been claims that John Todd's testimony was some kind of hoax, as well as doubt as to how reliable his revelations can be taken to be given his questionable past. He has been known by other identities, including John Todd Collins, and 'Lance.'

Todd appears to have come from a long-running bloodline of witches using the family name Collins, who are said to have come to the US from England and brought witchcraft to the Salem Mass. He was reportedly initiated as a witch at the age of 13, becoming a High Priest at 18, then joining the military, (here we go again.) Later, he reportedly became a born-again Christian, and his conversion is said to have prompted his defection. Following his becoming a whistleblower, he claimed that a $200,000 bounty had been put on his head by his former elite paymasters, and that he had been forced to go underground. It's not clear whether or not he is still alive.

The transcript of a taped interview apparently made by John Todd Collins is available here–http://www.beyondweird.com/occult/jtc1.html

Whatever the case with Todd in particular, however, his is far from the only voice that has come forward with such claims about the darker side of the corporate music business, and the gist of what he said has been backed up by other industry insiders and whistleblowers. In particular, many have confirmed the presence of temples within record company HQs. Some corporate head offices are built on the site of former Masonic temples, such as the MTV Canada building in Toronto before it was sold in 2013, as are some recording studios, including Vanguard Records in Brooklyn and Village Studios in West LA.

Resources:

Rain Man in music:

- http://spiritspeakstruths.blogspot.co.uk/2009/11/rain-man-in-music.html

Vigilant Citizen: Whitney Houston and the 2012 Grammy Awards Mega-Ritual:

- http://vigilantcitizen.com/musicbusiness/whitney-houston-and-the-2012-grammy-awards-mega-ritual/

Vigilant Citizen: Madonna's Superbowl Halftime Show: A Celebration of the Grand Priestess of the Music Industry:

- http://vigilantcitizen.com/musicbusiness/madonnas-superbowl-halftime-show-a-celebration-of-the-grand-priestess-of-the-music-industry/

Beyonce was Demon-Possessed at Super Bowl Halftime Show:

- https://www.YouTube.com/watch?v=-dYE5_mJtTA

The Illuminati, Satanism, Drugs & the Music Industry:

- http://12160.info/profiles/blogs/the-illuminati-satanism-drugs-the-music-industry

Bone Thugs N Harmony: 'Creepin' On Da Come Up':

- https://www.YouTube.com/watch?v=n5vwBhJquZo

John Todd: Demons behind the music industry:

- https://www.YouTube.com/v/Otti-82jEAc

The Testimony of John Todd Collins, Part 1:

- http://www.beyondweird.com/occult/jtc1.html

Rock and The Occult:

- http://www.inplainsite.org/html/rock_and_the_occult.html

Vigilant Citizen: MTV VMAs 2013: It Was About Miley Cyrus Taking the Fall 1418:

- http://vigilantcitizen.com/musicbusiness/mtv-vmas-2013/

Freeman Fly: Miley Cyrus Invokes Kali VMA 2013:

- https://www.YouTube.com/watch?v=GLndTfzdtG4

Henry Makow: Rap Music's Blatant Satanism:

- http://www.henrymakow.com/
  satanism_is_explicit_in_rap_mu.html

CHAPTER 18

THE PRICE OF FAME

When the Industry makes you an offer you truly can't refuse.

"I sold my soul to the devil, that's a crappy deal. 'Least it came with a few toys, like a Happy Meal"
Kanye West

I swear I wanted to be, like, the Amy Grant of music, but it didn't work out, And so I sold my soul to the Devil."
Katy Perry

"You sold your soul for material things,
I give a fuck if people think that you're a lyrical king!
Ain't it funny how they love it when a grown man brags,
About the jewellery and money that none of his fans have?"
DISL Automatic: 'Here I Stand' (2013)

The Faustian principle

The German legend of Faust is one which has been seen for decades as having more than a little allegorical relevance to the entertainment industry. Dating back almost 500 years, it tells the story of a scholar who, bored by his life and craving great knowledge and all manner of worldly pleasures, makes a pact with the Devil. The price he pays for these gifts is nothing less than his eternal soul. The term 'Faustian' now describes a situation where an individual has traded their moral integrity in exchange for fame and success at the hands of another party.

The music industry has long had its own re-telling of the legend, in the story surrounding the blues musician Robert Johnson. 'The

436

Crossroads' was the title of his fabled song in which he documents having made a deal with the Devil at a crossroads in exchange for great musical talent. It is widely assumed that the song, far from being fictional, was a real-life account of Johnson's soul-selling experiences. According to Wikipedia: "In folk magic and mythology, crossroads may represent a location 'between the worlds' and, as such, a site where supernatural spirits can be contacted and paranormal events can take place." Johnson died in extremely strange circumstances in 1938, an early member of The 27 Club.

It becomes clear with only a little digging beneath the glossy surface, that this is the type of scenario that governs the corporate entertainment industry, and determines who gets to become its celebrities. The results lie in just how desperate its initiates are for fame and fortune, and how far they are prepared to degrade their morals accordingly. An encounter with 'the Devil' may be assumed to be allegorical, but the concept is still the same. Multiple accounts from first-hand insiders demonstrate that real 'success' comes at a price higher than most would imagine. An observer might be left with the notion that, as an aspiring musician, actor or any other kind of celebrity, the best thing that can ever happen to you is *not* making it big in the ranks of the Illuminati-owned industry machine!

Louis Farrakhan, long-standing Minister for the Nation Of Islam organisation, nailed it in a speech which was later sampled by rapper Cormega on his 2015 track 'Industry,' when he said: "Who do you think you are? To them you are nothing but a piece of meat. And you're only as valuable as your last hit song. And when you make no more hit songs, nobody cares for you no more!"

As Lenon Honor commented in one of his 'Good Vibrations' interviews:

> *"You have to sacrifice something if you want the entertainment industry to work on your behalf . . . So there's a trade-off. It's not that any particular artist is special, because there's plenty of other singers and rappers and music producers, both currently and in the past if you want to look at it historically, who were far more gifted musically than those that 'make it.' That's not the point. The point is; what are*

you willing to sacrifice, and how far are you willing to let the industry push you in a certain direction?

" . . . It's not that Kanye, or Jay-Z or Rihanna or anyone else is special. It's just that they were willing to sign not only a physical contract, but also an ethical contract that says; 'OK, I agree to being manipulated, I agree to being moved along a particular course."

Nothing happens by accident, and the scenario governing the entertainment industry applies just as much to the worlds of politics and big business. Politicians and world leaders aren't there just because they worked really hard, stayed focus and had a bit of good luck. The notion that 'anyone can be President,' 'any rapper can be the next Jay-Z,' or that your little sister's business selling home-made lemonade during the Summer could be the new Schweppes, are there to make you believe that the world is a fair and just place where each individual is judged on their own merits, and where hard work brings success. Individuals and corporations enjoy fame and mega-fortune because they're chosen for it. In some way, each of them is serving the overall agenda. If they weren't, they wouldn't be where they are. Plain and simple. The old maxim 'Presidents aren't elected, they're *selected*' can be applied to the pop music world too.

British researcher and activist Tony Kilvert, otherwise known as Tony Z, dropped a reminder that the same rules that apply to the entertainment game also govern the world of politics, on his 'Good Vibrations' interview in 2014:

"If you understand how the system works, you'll understand that the first thing they do is to get control of you. They get you by the balls, basically. So they use Masons . . . and all sorts of other means to induct you into these dark, Satanic areas, whereby they've got the goods on you. They've got blackmail on you. And it's only when you get to that level and you agree and you go along with it that you'll get in any position of power. It's the same with aristocracy and royalty and all the rest of it. Everybody is a slave to somebody else higher up the chain. And within this system of slavery, they use trickery, bribery, corruption, etc. But it's coming apart at the seams, because it's

becoming so obvious to those that are looking at it. It's right there in front of your face."

Agreement came from Canadian writer and researcher Henry Makow in my 2015 interview with him:

"Now, the people who become successful are the people who essentially agree to promote the Illuminati line in exchange for fame and fortune, in the same way that politicians agree to promote the line in exchange for political success. So in a sense they've made a contract. They've sold their soul. It can be compared to when you join the Masons and you sign an oath that you're never going to divulge the secrets."

It appears that the industry machine has always selected its favourites—those it wishes to elevate to the top of the game to the exclusion of all competitors. As British author John Hamer points out in his book 'The Falsification Of History':

"In the early eighteenth century, there is recorded to have been around 8,500 composers of music in Europe alone, and yet around 8,400 of them, despite the fact that their music may have been brilliant or innovative, have never had their music extensively published or played, other than in small, localised concert halls. And much of it is today now long-forgotten, lost or deliberately buried.

"Why should this be?

"Mainly because, as today, the music industry then had its favourites, and certain personalities including the likes of Mozart, who, whilst feted as a celebrity of his time, probably did not compose much of the music attributed to him then and since.

"The involvement of occultists in the creation of the 'superstars' of their day, such as Mozart, Beethoven and Haydn, cannot be ignored. Indeed, the occult influence in music has always been a factor, and today is absolutely rife throughout the whole of the music industry."

'Eyes Wide Shut' and then some

The specifics of exactly what it is that celebrities are required to go through for the gift of engineered fame are not for the faint-hearted. The Illuminati retains positions of power for its own kind, but is not beyond awarding such perceived fame and fortune to 'outsiders'–those not of a generational bloodline key to their ongoing plans, but who have shown themselves so hungry for fame, and devoid of personal morals, that they will literally do anything in exchange for their idea of 'success.' Initiation of this nature is always at the discretion of the demonic controllers, however–they choose you, you can't choose them. Chosen individuals are required to take an oath to The Brotherhood, (the myth about signing a contract in their own blood may not actually be as far-fetched as it may seem,) to prove their loyalty. It's reasonable to assume that the controllers harbour nothing but contempt for those who would debase themselves in this way, such are the levels of humili-ation that they must endure.

This is the realm of initiation rituals which mimic the sex magick practices of Aleister Crowley and his followers, where every deviant per-version imaginable is fair game, and no bodily excretion is excluded. It makes the orgy scenes in Stanley Kubrick's 'Eyes Wide Shut' look like a girl guides' picnic. The rituals are Satanic in nature, and the sum-moning-up of entities through dark occult practices–including sodomy, paedophilia, group sex and bestiality–are said to be a part of things, as is the occasional human sacrifice. Base sexual activity rooted in the fre-quency realm of the lower chakras, are compatible with the low-density energy zones in which non-human entities are said to reside, and allow for a connection.

According to the insights, the higher a star's earnings and the more high-profile their persona, the more depraved and degraded the acts they will have taken part in. Many insiders state that those members of the $20 million club and above will have had their morals cor-rupted beyond belief. The series of Youtube videos from Black Child Productions listed in the Resources section at the end of this chapter, come highly recommended for more on this whole area. Only for the headstrong.

Public Enemy's Professor Griff has had much to say on such initiations. One he has described is based on the ritual said to be employed within the Skull & Bones fraternity at Yale University which was attended by, among others, George HW and George W Bush, and Senator John Kerry. Reportedly, this involves the initiate lying naked in a coffin and masturbating while recounting their sexual history, while his peers look on. There is one particularly high-profile producer and artist within the hip-hop genre who Griff claims has undergone this process in exchange for his colossal engineered 'success.'

One of the most vocal celebrities to have exposed these practices in recent times, has been the American comedian, screenwriter, producer and actor Dave Chappelle. There are many videos to be found on Youtube of his various interviews on the subject. Chappelle had been highly successful on the US TV circuit, hosting three seasons of his own 'Chappelle's Show' on the Comedy Central network.

Like all A-listers, he reached a point where it was spelt out to him that the next level of success came with certain requirements. To his great credit, unlike so many of his peers, he was so shocked and disgusted by what he had found out that he wanted no part in it, and was prepared to abandon his career in order to escape. Chappelle famously took off to Africa for an extended period, during which the mainstream media attempted to demonise him as having gone 'a bit crazy'—a standard tactic with those that don't play ball. Chappelle has since given many interviews explaining his experience, and documenting the sick activities that go on beneath the glitzy surface of Hollywood and its music industry equivalent.

In an interview with Oprah Winfrey upon his return from Africa, Chappelle raised the issue of the sheer number of black male celebrities who had been forced to cross-dress in order to further their careers—another aspect of the agenda to specifically humiliate and degrade black people as discussed in our earlier chapter. You can view that interview here:

- https://www.Youtube.com/watch?v=gHhxnIEsSlw

A fellow comedian to have undergone a similar wake-up call, and to have had the courage to speak out about it, is Katt Williams. In recent years, Williams has undergone financial problems, a string of altercations with law enforcement, and has been portrayed as mentally unstable by the mainstream media—all strong indicators that you might have said something that somebody higher-up would have preferred you hadn't. In an interview on the subject, Williams commented:

> *"Some of us are against the Illuminati, and we're against it at our own detriment. When people are against the Illuminati then they get punched in the face all the time, the press hates them, and nobody likes them.*
>
> *"Dave Chappelle has never been a part of the Illuminati. They don't want him or me or people like us. But now, it's not necessary for us to stir up that hornet's nest unless we intend to get stung a million times. I didn't understand that. They had to sting me a million times. I'm still not going to join. But I respect it a little more."*

A series of Youtube videos documenting the nature of 'elite' rituals and initiation ceremonies has come from the US researcher Yash Qaraah. Several of his videos feature the voice of an anonymous industry insider, who claims to be blowing the whistle on what goes on. The following are extracts from his various insights:

> *"Just because it's looking good and they look like they're glamorous, it's not like that. This shit is all about rituals, demons, Babylonian Gods, and screwing a man in his ass. Particularly in the music indus-try. They start taking you on these crazy party trips . . . 'Gravy' is a Hollywood slogan for someone who just got popped in their behind! 'Oh, so how's it all going? How's your career going?' 'Oh, I can tell you right now, baby, everything's gravy.'*
>
> *" . . . and what they do, they video-tape that shit. Why would they want to video-tape it? To sell it later? Nah. To keep your mouth closed . . . Now a lot of times, what they'll do while they're doing this thing to you, the men won't be recognisable. They have either a mask on, or they just have their face blacked out. Why do you think they do it? They put that shit in a special index box. Because if you get out of line, they're going to say that you were a homosexual, you were*

a paedophile, you did things but never got caught, and they're going to put this crazy-ass video out of you getting boned by men up your ass . . . And they do the women worse than the men.

"You know why they're so bold with the truth? Because they know the majority of people in society are so dumbfounded and so beat down on these jobs, that they'll take anything. And they do not have your best intentions . . . they have to keep negativity, negative energy to make money. If everybody's happy, they're going to start thinking. And when people start thinking, then people start asking questions. And when they start asking questions, the questions can't be answered. Now you got a society of people waking up. And they can't have that."

Nobody need think the hip-hop game is any different to the situation with Hollywood movies, television, or any other part of the music industry either, this apparent whistle-blower adds, also shedding some light on hip-hop's penchant for 'industry friends' and large entourages.

"98 per cent of hip-hop is gay. There's no other way to say it. 98 per cent of them are gay. Two per cent of them got out. That's not many, because the majority of them love that lifestyle. All actors and actresses sleep with the same sex for roles, contracts, commercials, sitcoms, and that's the truth. The industry does nothing for free, y'all.

"Once you're in, they prefer you not to hang around anyone you know. Why? Because people that's not in the industry can see BS. They can see demonic things happening. They don't want you around folks like that because they can influence you to get out, or not participate. So usually, they pick your girlfriend, they pick your boyfriend. So when you get ready to date somebody, they prefer you to date somebody in the industry because they're wicked, and they got to keep you wicked."

Anyone still want to be rich and famous? Is it any wonder that artists such as Tupac, Michael Jackson, Elvis and Jim Morrison are rumoured to have faked their own deaths to escape the clutches of the industry? It becomes clear that once you sign on the dotted line, you're in for the rest of your days. You're doing what they say now and there's no way out.

Birds of a feather

It turns out that a sordid personal history full of grubby little secrets is the basis on which many politicians are promoted, because it offers the real controllers pulling their strings the capacity for blackmail or humiliating public exposure should their lackeys fail to perform their duties on-script. It's been working this way for a very long time, and is a strategy employed in most countries around the world. There is evidence to suggest that it's no different with certain key artists in the music scene, too, whose personal backgrounds may be rather different from the public image they've carefully cultivated.

Another reason for dark energy *just happening* to permeate the upper levels of the music industry, is again down to the true nature of the energetic field in which we all live. Like attracts like, and artists existing in a very negative state of low consciousness, will attract more low-density energy into their existence. Heavy drug use, sexual depravity, and dabblings in the dark occult have never been conducive towards positive life experiences in the long run.

Additionally—as is the case in so many other areas—a significant number of musicians appear to have been groomed for fame on the basis of their ancestry. The fact that royalty and aristocracy breed within their own circle, usually marrying cousins, is acknowledged even in the mainstream. But this is also the case with 'celebrities,' whose bloodlines can be traced back many, many generations. How many realise, for example, that Madonna, Alanis Morisette, Celine Dion and Angelina Jolie are genetically linked to Hillary Clinton? Or that Britney Spears is related to Laura Bush and Senator John McCain? This has even been admitted to in the mainstream media. As a UK 'Daily Mail' article naively put it:

> *"Researchers at the New England Historic Genealogical Society found some remarkable family connections for the three presidential candidates."*

I'll bet they bloody have. For some reason these particular lineages are deemed important, with very precise records kept of where in the world the descendants are located, so that new generations can be recruited and put to work in prominent public positions by the elites. It's no accident that Brad Pitt and Angelina Jolie ended up together, for instance, as they're reported to be related as 21st cousins. It was always part of the plan for them to become a couple, presumably, with Billy Bob Thornton and Jennifer Aniston having been temporary distractions. Pitt, according to research, is related to Barack Obama, as is George W Bush, and Pitt is also the ninth cousin twice-removed of the outlaw Jesse James, and the twelfth cousin of both Prince William and the movie director Spike Lee. This would explain why Pitt gets so many Hollywood roles, and why Jolie has been given her extra-curricular job as a United Nations ambassador/ Eugenicist. Cherie Blair, wife of the war criminal Tony Blair, is said to be a descendent of John Wilkes-Booth, the man accused of assassinating US president Abraham Lincoln. Woody Harrelson's father, Charles, was accused by a lawyer of being a contract killer who murdered his brother. The researcher Freeman added to this by claiming Harrelson was one of the three 'tramps' detained after the JFK assassination, and had been directly involved in the shooting! (In a neat piece of art imitating life, Woody himself portrayed a serial murderer in the movie 'Natural Born Killers.')

The bloodline plot makes sense of the otherwise overwhelming 'coincidence' that British Prime Minister David Cameron *just happens* to be a cousin of the Queen of England, who herself, *just happens* to be a distant descendant of Vlad Dracul, aka Vlad The Impaler of Transylvania, and inspiration for the 'Dracula' stories. Cameron also *just happens* to be a cousin of London Mayor Boris Johnson, (and is said to be distantly related to Kim Kardashian; now you know why she's famous-for-being-famous and never off TV or out of the gossip magazines!) Cameron, Johnson and UK chancellor George Osborne were all part of the Bullingdon Boys' Club at Oxford University in the same year, a fraternity that employs its own sick and perverted rituals according to recent headlines. The Uni also counted Osama Bin Laden and Bill Clinton in its ranks in previous years.

In a neat piece of segueing that brings us full circle, meanwhile, it's also widely suggested that war criminal George W Bush's mother,

Barbara, wife of George Bush Senior, is in fact the illegitimate daughter of Aleister Crowley. There's certainly a family resemblance when you compare photos. (Bush Junior's farcical appointment as President of the United States demonstrates the bloodline agenda perfectly. Does anyone on the planet truly believe that he earned the role through being the best man for the job, and that the appointment had absolutely nothing to do with who his Daddy was? Really?)

In this regard, an interesting movie to absorb is 'Six Degrees Of Separation', released in 1993 and starring Will Smith. The film's narrative examines the theory that anyone in the world is no more than six steps away from any other individual in terms of familial or social connections. Smith's character claims to be the son of Hollywood actor Sidney Poitier, but is revealed later to be a confidence trickster. This plotline, (heavy on homosexuality,) is particularly intriguing given that Smith is often cited as being descended from a long-running bloodline of particular interest to the Illuminati, which is how his relationship with Jada Pinkett came about, and why his son Jaden and daughter Willow have also been pushed into the celebrity limelight.

As Max Spiers, a whistle-blower from a long-running bloodline of interest to the Illuminati commented in an interview on Miles Johnston's 'Bases Project:'

> *"With a lot of these high-level Kabbalistic celebrities . . . There are lists at the highest levels, and they know where all the bloodlines have migrated to from the beginning. They know where they're all at. If you're connected to a bloodline, you're being tracked. Project Oaktree was all about that, tracking bloodlines from the 1950s onward."*

(It's also said that this is what the National Health Service in Britain was partly set up to do.)

None of these people achieve their positions by accident, or even by merit of whatever talent they have. They're there because they've been placed there.

Extra-curricular activities

The industry controllers clearly see their artists as owned possessions, to be deployed in any way that suits. Celebrities are treated by their industry overlords in the same way that members of the military are treated by their superiors. The same assumed ownership would also appear to apply to their offspring, which is why so many musicians turn out to have fathers who were employed in military intelligence, as we've already discovered.

The idea that no-one ever really leaves the military is well-known, and how many times have you watched a film where a grizzled old former Marine or secret-service operative is supposed to have been retired but gets commissioned for 'one more job,' complaining, 'just when I thought I was out, they pull me back in.' Military personnel are regarded as owned pets. They're often used as unwitting test subjects in biological experiments, it's a condition of their employment that they take certain vaccines, and plans are in place for microchipping to be mandatory before long. There are parallels in the entertainment world, too, which is why A-list celebrities rarely get to retire. Hollywood actors and musicians continue to work into their 70s and 80s when they would have earned enough money to have retired decades earlier. They're fulfilling their lifetime commitment to the hand that has fed them. Bob Dylan alluded to this in the now-infamous '60 Minutes' interview with Ed Bradley when he was asked what the key to his longevity had been. Dylan replied: "I made a bargain with . . . " (at this point Dylan pauses before resuming) " . . . a long time ago and I'm holding up my end." Bradley asks, "what was your bargain?" Dylan replies, "to get where I am now." He adds that he made the bargain with "the chief commander . . . of this earth and then the world we can't see."

Besides puppeteering them as required within their respective fields–whether that's as an actor, television presenter, musician, model or sports star–'celebs' are often called on for sideline assignments that serve the wider agenda in some way, too.

In 2015, by that point a pathetic caricature of his former 'gangster' self, making records with the likes of Katy Perry and TV commercials for Moneysupermarket.com, Snoop Dogg appeared on a TV interview endorsing Hillary Clinton in her bid for the 2016 US presidency! He stated: "I would love to see a woman in office, because I feel like we're at that stage in life to where we need perspective other than the males' train of thought." Some of Snoop's previous tracks have included 'Bitches Ain't Shit,' 'For All My Niggaz & Bitches,' and 'Gz Up Hoes Down,' so maybe he's right? He used an interesting turn of phrase for a separate 2015 interview with Sky News, stating: "I am more sensitive and more vulnerable writing-wise, and accepting a woman for being a beautiful person, as opposed to me saying she is a bitch or a whore, because that was how I was *trained* when I first started . . . " At the start of his career, such an idea would have been laughable, but the slow-drip effect over time that is so skilfully employed, gets a celebrity so familiar within the public's mind-set, that they can later be used to steer people in whatever direction has been laid out for them.

In the wake of his smash hit 'Happy,' Pharrell Williams got in on the act with the United Nations, announcing a 'Happy Party,' designed to get 'the whole world dancing for a happy planet'–a loosely-coded reference to the plans for a One World Government, gaining familiarity for the idea by making it 'fun' and 'cool.'

In late 2015, actor Ewan McGregor was wheeled out–not for the first time–to front a TV appeal imploring the public to give money to help Syrian children affected by airstrikes being conducted there by Western governments. This was after the same general public's tax money had already been used to help fund the massacres in the first place, of course. I wonder how much the Queen gives personally to such appeals?

British TV chef Jamie Oliver, who had previously claimed to be all about organic food, gave a hint as to his true colours in early 2015 when he publicly voiced his support for the Bill & Melinda Gates Foundation, saying he was 'super-excited' to be working with them, and talking about the need for 'a new food system.' Could be have been alluding to Genetically Modified Crops of the type peddled by Monsanto, which the Gates' are pushing as part of the UN's Agenda 21 plans? Does anybody believe that these multi-millionaires genuinely give a shit about regular people when they announce 'campaigns' such as this? How much of their fortunes do any of them personally give to the causes they claim to be passionate about?

Gates himself has been a key figure in the Eugenics movement and the drive towards massive world depopulation. In a 2003 interview with

PBS' Bill Moyers, he admitted that his father, William H. Gates Sr., had been head of the Planned Parenthood organisation which had evolved out of the American Eugenics Society. Its founder, Mary Sanger, had publicly declared immigrants and poor people as "human weeds," "reckless breeders," and "spawning . . . human beings who never should have been born."

What if, coming from such a strategic bloodline, this was always the route that Gates was pre-determined to go down, and the Microsoft empire was gifted to him by much higher powers simply to get him famous, rather than being his own personal invention? (And on that note, does anyone *really* believe dorky college kid Mark Zuckerberg invented Facebook in his Harvard dorm?! That one pales even further into farce in the light of recent claims that Zuckerberg is actually the grandson of David Rockefeller.)

In 2013, an unbelievable TV commercial emerged for the Toilet Strike fresh water project, which was headlined by Hollywood actor Matt Damon, (though it was almost certainly not his own concept but one which he had been instructed to become the public face for.) As part of this, a ragtag bunch of control-system assets consisting of Sir (say no more) Richard Branson, actress Olivia Wilde, and New World Order bagman Bono appeared on-screen, laughing, joking and generally taking the piss by making constant references to 'the Illuminati.' "I remember when Matt first brought up the idea. It was at a meeting of the Illuminati", says Bono. "Oi, Damon! Who let you into our secret Illuminati meeting?" mocks Olivia Wilde. "Illuminati, assemble!" adds Branson. So hilarious. Bono adds: "because this is one conspiracy we can all agree on." (I can never hear Bono's name without thinking of a comment an Irish rapper friend of mine once said. I warned him that an article I was publishing did not paint Bono in a favourable light. "Ah, don't worry," he said. "Everyone in Ireland knows Bono's a cunt.")

The aim was obviously to address the rumours of celebrity involvement by laughing it off, conveying to the general public how ridiculous the claims are, and making those who continue to push them look a little foolish. For those with eyes to see, a mind to think, and the capacity to do independent research, however, the motives were obvious, and it was these three owned stooges who looked more than a little sad and pathetic. The Toilet Strike project is also connected to Agenda 21 which,

in turn, ties into the elites' long-held plans for massive human population reduction, (see the Georgia Guidestones.) Bono and his mates were
merely providing a friendly public face for a very sinister agenda. Along
the same lines as the aforementioned ad., is the website illuminatioffi-
cial.org, (apparently illuminati.com was already taken,) which purports
to be the official site for that particular organisation, and includes such
helpful tools as a guide to deciphering its commonly-used symbols, a
link through to their Facebook and Twitter, and a section titled 'Join
the Illuminati,' where you can leave your e-mail address and sign up
for regular newsletters and updates. I wonder if they do Snapchat too?

There are further connections between Agenda 21 and the myth of
'global warming,' which has now had to be re-named 'climate change'
in the face of so much scientific evidence to the contrary. In a desperate
attempt to still sell the notion that we everyday humans are to blame
for the earth warming up, 'Blackadder' co-writer and 'Four Weddings
And A Funeral' director Richard Curtis, was called on to produce a
TV commercial for a project known as 10:10 in 2011. Imagine, one
minute you're a producer of 'feel-good' comedy films in which posh
people hilariously say 'fuck' a lot. The next, you're called on to direct
a piece of One World Government propaganda. Never a dull moment,
eh? This one seriously backfired when it produced the large-scale outrage it always should have done. The ad. shows children in classrooms
being asked what they are doing to help combat 'global warming.'
When any children decline to commit, the teacher is seen pressing a
button causing them to explode in a mass of blood and gore. The basic
message, therefore, is: 'buy into the official lie about global warming, or
you deserve to be murdered.' It remains utterly unfathomable how this
could ever have been deemed an acceptable stance, and how the mentally-ill individuals behind it ever thought they'd be able to pull it off.

In Summer 2014, it was all about the Ice Bucket Challenge, where
millions worldwide poured buckets of icy water over their heads and
posted the video on Youtube before nominating two others to do it, just
because a bunch of pointless celebrities had been deployed to do the
same. The stunt was supposedly in aid of raising awareness for ALS, aka
Lou Gehrig's Disease, but many members of the public showed themselves to be clueless as to this factor, the idea of emulating a beloved
superstar being far more of a motivating factor. The jury's still out on

what the real reason was for deploying these celebrity pets in such a way, but there were theories concerning the ritual symbology of immersion in water as some kind of 'cleansing.' It's interesting to reflect that the controllers hatch plans such as this every now and again, just to test the degree of mind-control and celebrity worship that the general population is under, and to gauge how ready they would be to adopt a particular stance just because it comes with a celebrity endorsement. The 'Kony 2012' video which went viral on the internet in that year, (and was shown later to be an orchestrated hoax,) showed just how readily something could be communicated around the world if it comes with an air of fashionability and a Twitter hashtag attached. The same happened when millions changed their Facebook profile picture to a French flag following the Paris 'terror attacks' of November 2015.

In the same year, the Smart Meter agenda got a new public face to endorse it in the form of Sir (could he have been anything else?) Bob Geldof. Much scrutiny among truthseeking researchers has gone towards the true nature of the Band Aid and Live Aid projects that Geldof helmed. Curiosity has been raised about many well-known charities, and the fact that the bulk of public donations, made in well-meaning spirit, actually go towards paying executive salaries and 'administration costs,' with only a small fraction being put to use at ground level. Addressing the Geldof-helmed Live 8 concerts of 2005, LC Vincent, writing for henrymakow.com, observed:

> "Most casual observers might assume that the money generated by corporate sponsors, DVD sales, performance royalties, and direct contributions, would be funnelled into various charitable organisations aiding the poorest people of developing nations around the world. They would be wrong.

> "... The money was instead used to pay off the corporate creditors of indebted countries. In effect, the entire focus of the money generated by Live 8 was to provide direct assistance to corporations owed money by these impoverished nations.

A 2010 report from the BBC, no less, alleged that money given by the public to the Band Aid/ Live Aid projects, was used to buy weapons for rebel groups rather than for famine relief. That story resides here–http://www.bbc.co.uk/blogs/theeditors/2010/03/ethiopia.html

In November 2008 it was reported that Geldof was paid $100,000 in Australia for a brief speech addressing Third World Poverty. You couldn't make it up.

Geldof is generally thought of as a full-blooded Irishman. In fact, his paternal grandmother, Amelia Falk, was an English Jew from London, while his paternal grandfather was an immigrant from Belgium. 'Gelt' is the Yiddish word for money. Geldof achieved his 'honorary knighthood' from the Queen in 1986. In 2011, he accepted an honorary doctorate from Israel's Ben Gurion University. In contrast to his claims that he came from 'a poor, Irish, not particularly well-educated background,' those who knew him in his youth have stated that he enjoyed a privileged upbringing in an affluent district of Dun Laoghaire, and that he attended a middle-class private school. One of his early jobs was as a slaughterman in an abattoir. He cares, you know.

Geldof's New World Order activities raise all kinds of interesting questions about whether his emerging as the lead singer of The Boomtown Rats was merely a way of thrusting him into the public eye, (particularly given that he was such an appalling singer!) so that later, once his familiarity had been established, he could start doing the *real* work for which he had been groomed.

The same suspicion could be levelled at his aforementioned mate Bono, who has followed a similar path in recent years, hobnobbing with world leaders and endorsing various NWO projects, (and proudly earning a knighthood for services rendered in the process.) Bono is certainly more of a convincing singer than Geldof. Something else becomes interesting here, though. Many of U2's early songs had meaningful lyrical content, the likes of 'Sunday Bloody Sunday' and 'Pride (In The Name Of Love)' standing as conscious protest songs of their day. Only later down the line did Bono start taking a different path. This is a pattern we've seen with many different artists. They start out in what seems to be a spirit of well-intentioned independence, making songs that carry some sort of message to the people. After winning over fans on this basis, at a strategic point, their music begins to conform more to corporate templates, and this often coincides with changes in their personal lives where they start to get with the Establishment programme. Muse are another group that seem to have followed this path in recent years. Their song 'Uprising' appeared to be a genuine anti-Establishment rant coming from the heart, but pretty soon afterwards, they showed signs of having been neutered back into corporate conformity. Singer Matt Bellamy, who had previously penned a track titled 'MK Ultra', named one of his albums 'HAARP', and had spoken critically of the incoming microchip agenda, had claimed in a 2006 interview that 9/11 was 'an inside job,' but by 2012, said he had changed his stance and now accepted the official story. He added: "I still read about political history, the influence of corporations and the military, but I make sure I'm reading from credible sources. I think my political views are a bit more nuanced now."

Along similar lines, Blur and Gorillaz frontman Damon Albarn, who had previously been outspoken and critical of the (second) Iraq War, went on to accept an OBE in the Queen's 2016 New Year's 'Honours.' The irony of an opponent of wars-of-conquest receiving an award from the figurehead of the very regime that has endlessly perpetuated such events, was not lost on many observers.

Red flags, anyone?

The fall from grace of Kanye West

When it comes to the engineered debasement of an artist and their values, there can be no better example in the contemporary era than that of Kanye West. Studying the nature of his output from his entry point into the industry, to what he stands for today, offers a masterclass in the corporate music industry's tried-and-tested tactics.

Coming out of Chicago, Kanye first emerged as a producer, rising to prominence through his work within Jay-Z and Damon Dash's Roc A Fella Records empire. His early productions, (on and off the label,) saw him making beats for artists such as Memphis Bleek, Beanie Sigel, Ludacris, Rhymefest, The Game, Cam'ron, Twista, Brandy and Keyshia Cole, as well as several for Jay-Z himself.

Kanye harboured ambitions to be a rapper himself, and in 2004, his debut artist album appeared, entitled 'The College Dropout.' With the degradation of the hip-hop genre that we addressed earlier already in place, this album was viewed as a breath of fresh air by pundits, owing to the sample-based, soulful production on many of the tracks, and lyrical themes pursued, which steered away from the stereotypical subject matter of the time. Tracks included 'Jesus Walks,' in which Kanye spoke candidly of his struggle to stay true to Christian values in the wake of the temptations that lay all around, 'Through The Wire,' in which he documents the serious car accident that he felt blessed to have survived, and 'All Falls Down,' a devastating reflection on materialism in society. It included the lyrics:

> *"The prettiest people do the ugliest things, on the road to riches and diamond rings."*

And:

> *"We shine because they hate us, floss 'cause they degrade us,*
>
> *We trying to buy back our 40 acres, and for that paper,*
>
> *Look how low we stoop,*
>
> *Even if you in a Benz, you still a nigga in a coop"*

The follow-up project, 'Late Registration,' appeared in 2005. This set was commended for its more elaborate production and sampling methods, including many string arrangements in conjunction with instrumentalist Jon Brion, giving the album a texture not normally associated with hip-hop product. Themes explored included the blood diamond trade, the superficiality of society, the effects of crack cocaine on black communities, and the expression of love and appreciation to his mother Donda on 'Hey Mama.' It seemed as if the scene had a talented, thoughtful and creative new voice, doubling as a skilful producer, to represent the more meaningful side of the artform.

It was all about to go very, very wrong.

Kanye had become known for his philanthropic work outside of his music, and in September 2005, appeared live on a US telethon in the wake of the Hurricane Katrina disaster that had devastated the city of New Orleans, and drawn criticism of the Bush Administration over its poor efforts in organising relief. Kanye was on-screen with 'Austin Powers' actor Mike Myers, and both were reading from prepared scripts. At one point, however, Kanye improvised and dropped the spontaneous phrase, 'George Bush doesn't care about black people' live on television. As Myers stood shocked, the producers cut quickly away from the scene.

It's always struck me that this incident stood as a turning point in Kanye's career, since from that moment forward

the moral standards in his lyrics began to deteriorate, regressing further with every passing year. At the same time, his music and production styles became gradually darker, reaching an all-time low with the '808s & Heartbreak' album discussed in the earlier chapter on Transhumanism. Clearly, his off-script comment criticising Bush wouldn't have gone down well with the music industry's ultimate controllers, and you have to wonder whether this was chosen as the point to start debasing his output, as a form of 'punishment' for exercising his maverick spirit. It's either this, or that the timing was coincidental, and the blueprint was already in place for the subsequent years.

An artist that had started out lamenting the obsession with fashion brands on 'All Falls Down,' had joined every other A-list rapper in worshipping those very brands and lifestyle habits. Things had hit rock-bottom by the time of Kanye's collaboration with label-mate and mentor Jay-Z on their duet 'Niggas In Paris':

"What's Gucci, my nigga?

What's Louis, my killa?

What's drugs, my deala?

What's that jacket, Margiela?"

On 'Clique:'

"Break records at Louis,

Ate breakfast at Gucci."

On 'Power:'

Mark Devlin

"My furs is Mongolian, my ice brought the goalies in,

I embody every characteristic of the egotistic."

In his guest verse on Keri Hilson's 'Knock You Down:'

"Keep rockin', and keep knockin'

Whether you Louis Vuitton-ed up or Reebok-in"

And on the remix of Rihanna's 'Diamonds:'

"The Delorean parked in front of Armani Emporium,

And parties at Richie is getting risky,

Victoria's Secret show, they miss me."

As if to puzzle and confuse, Kanye has come with the occasional meaningful and reflective lyrics in the midst of all the retarded garbage, such as on 'New Slaves' from 2013's 'Yeezus.' On this, he was back to addressing societal slavery and subjugation of blacks, and sharply criticising the very material obsessions he had embraced on his other recordings:

"My momma was raised in the era when,

Clean water was only served to the fairer skin,

Doin' clothes, you would have thought I had help,

But they wasn't satisfied unless I picked the cotton myself,

You see it's broke nigga racism,

That's that "Don't touch anything in the store,"

And it's rich nigga racism,

That's that "Come in, please buy more,"

456

"What you want, a Bentley? Fur coat? A diamond chain?

All you blacks want all the same things."

It gave the impression that there was still an element of humanity and conscience within his being, and that, for whatever reason, he'd been allowed to express it in this one solitary instance. All around it on 'Yeezus,' however, was the usual depraved toxicity that had become his trademark. Kanye's tendency towards ego and arrogance in interviews, plus his constant appearance in pointless celebrity gossip magazines—particularly since his engagement to famous-for-being-famous Kim Kardashian—earned him as many detractors and critics as it did fans. Either way, it's tragic for those that have followed his career from the beginning, to have seen him become just another manipulated asset of the corporate machine, dancing to whatever tune his higher-ups have dictated, with almost all of his conscientious creative talents having been dumbed down beyond hope.

It's also worth reflecting on Kanye's behaviours of recent times in this regard. He has famously been branded as 'difficult' in interviews, and this has generally been put down to the eccentric nature of an individualistic artist. But behaviours such as lying down on the floor and refusing to answer any interview questions, as he did following a performance on the 'Jonathan Ross Show' on the UK's ITV, hint at other possibilities, as anyone who read the earlier chapter on mind-control will doubtless recognise.

The Fiasco of Lupe

There are echoes of Kanye's fall from grace in the story of another contemporary US rapper. Lupe Fiasco is a name who has generally steered clear of hip-hop's A-list set. It's a safe bet that many young kids raised on a diet of more heavily-marketed names such as Jay-Z, Lil' Wayne and Rick Ross won't even have heard of him.

For a while, Lupe stood as that rarest of entities—a rapper with a mainstream deal, (Atlantic Records,) who went against the grain, and unlike his mainstream peers, actually maintained some integrity and resisted chatting about the same tired, vacuous subject matter. By the time of

2010's long-awaited 'Lasers' album, he had raised the bar by several notches. The obvious example was its first single, 'Words I Never Said.' The homogenised electronic production and grating Skylar Grey hook was unfortunate, but it was the lyrics that packed a sobering punch. Who else in mainstream music was making statements like, "Gaza Strip was getting bombed, Obama didn't say shit?," "9/11, Building 7, did they really pull it?," and, "I really think the silence is worse than all the violence, fear is such a weak emotion, that's why I despise it?" This stuff was the closest that the contemporary mainstream had got to the likes of Marvin Gaye on 'What's Going On' or Prince on 'Sign O' The Times,' and there was more anti-establishment rhetoric with the likes of 'State Run Radio,' 'I Don't Wanna Care Right Now' and 'Out Of My Head.'

You have to wonder whether 'Words I Never Said' was one that accidentally slipped through the net, or whether it was deliberately allowed to be put out as part of an agenda that was already in store for Lupe. It's hard to imagine his superiors at Atlantic, who would have had to have approved the album in listening sessions before releasing it, *just happening* to miss a line like the one on Obama and Gaza. Is it possible he could have been 'allowed' to make a statement like this, only to be seen to atone for it shortly afterwards as a way of the industry effectively saying, 'see what happens when artists try to express themselves?'

Things were kind of patchy in the years following 'Lasers.' Tracks like 'Lamborghini Angels' raised some intriguing, if slightly off-kilter subject matter, but lacked energetic punch. Other outings were confusing at best, bland and weak at worst. But in early 2014 came the crunch, with Lupe dropping the toxic Satanic bile 'Thorns And Horns'. And so the alarm bells rang. You can check out the track on the link below:

- https://www.Youtube.com/watch?v=f0Vxw0ou_dQ

What is clear is that Lupe's music of then and now cannot be perceived as any kind of artistic 'development.' The output smacks of two completely different artists, and not one on a path of musical progression. A pattern is emerging.

Regression: the new progression

The tactic employed with Kanye West—to start an artist off with a particular image to gain a fanbase, then at a selected point to send them suddenly off in a different direction—is one that has been rolled out frequently in the past decade or more. In the face of her overtly sexual and aggressive image and lyrics espousing the usual—sex, materialism, partying, etc—it's easy to forget that Rihanna's entry on to the scene back in 2006 was marked by her single 'If It's Loving That You Want,' a bright and breezy piece of Caribbean-flavoured pop from an album that offered more of the same, 'Island In The Sun.' Similarly, Beyonce was first presented to the world as part of the teen group Destiny's Child, largely addressing standard relationship issues before being sent down a similar path to Rihanna.

These two and their contemporaries represent the strategy now routinely employed with A-list pop stars. They start out as respectable, with family-friendly images and singing innocent pop songs, building a international fanbase of children in the process, and putting potentially vigilant parents off their guard. A year or two down the line, however, the switch occurs, and the star in question ditches the wholesome image in favour of an adult-orientated, sexually explicit one more suited to soft porn or strip-club shows, than to a fan-base of children. Because an affection for the artist has already been established, the fans that have grown to adore them naturally follow any direction they is seen to take, and mimic the behaviours they see. We saw it with Britney Spears, Christina Aguilera, Katy Perry, Taylor Swift, and, most controversially of all, with Miley Cyrus.

There's a time and a place for most things in life, and pornography is no exception. I would just suggest that pop videos and stage shows lapped up by the under-tens are not among those times and places, and I suspect 99 per cent of parents of children of that age would be with me on that one.

The Misrepresentation of Lauryn Hill

It would seem the overwhelming majority of celebrities either end up embracing depraved lifestyle habits, or put up with them for fear of losing their careers, or worse. Occasionally, however, certain high-profile individuals do break the ranks and come forward to expose what they've been a part of. What happens to these people? Often there seems to be a reliance on such stories sounding so outlandish to the general public that they're simply written off as being 'impossible.' In other cases, however, the controllers have ways of picking-off individuals and completely trashing their careers, whilst attempting to discredit them in the eyes of the public. Dave Chappelle and Katt Williams have certainly fallen foul of the industry controllers. Attempts have been made to smear Chappelle as something of a loose cannon and a crackhead, while Williams has been arrested and harassed by the police on assorted claims several times since becoming outspoken. The rapper DMX, who showed signs of trying to break away from his corporate stranglehold a few years ago and dropped a devastating track called 'Industry,' has similarly been in and out of jail on various charges. Coincidence?

There's another artist whose life story over the past 15-plus years provides some of the answers, too.

Lauryn Hill was formerly known as L-Boogie, the extremely talented singer/ rapper member of the chart-topping Fugees in the mid-90s. After the group's short-lived heyday, she broke out with her highly-lauded solo album 'The Miseducation of Lauryn Hill' in 1998. It included several remarkable lyrical outings, such as on 'Everything Is Everything:'

"I wrote these words for everyone,

Who struggles in their youth,

Who won't accept deception,

Instead of what is truth,

It seems we lose the game,

Before we even start to play,

Who made these rules? We're so confused,

Easily led astray."

And on 'The Lost Ones' came an encapsulation of the eternal truth of Universal Law:

> *"Now don't you understand, man, Universal Law?*
>
> *What you throw out comes back to you, star,*
>
> *Never underestimate those who you scar,*
>
> *Cause karma, karma, karma comes back to you hard!"*

All seemed to be going well, and the hip-hop scene had a high-profile, conscious artist expressing great truths through message music. Soon afterwards, however, Lauryn faded from the limelight in a period of what appeared to be self-imposed exile. She hinted at this with comments in later interviews, such as:

> *"For two or three years I was away from all social interaction. It was a very introspective time because I had to confront my fears and master every demonic thought about inferiority, about insecurity or the fear of being black, young and gifted in this Western culture."*

No further music was being released, and the gossip rags started running stories about her going off the rails, acting erratically and being addicted to assorted substances. On the industry grapevine, meanwhile, came stories of Lauryn desperately trying to escape the grip of the Sony Corporation, through which both the Fugees' and her own solo material had been released. The rumours implied that she'd become disillusioned with the sinister, mind-controlling aspects of The Industry, and that she was keen to break free as it was affecting her sanity. Allegations of racist comments emerged, which in retrospect, would appear to be a standard tactic in character-smearing by an industry that doesn't like renegades trying to go their own way. Lauryn articulated the whole experience with the excellent acoustic track 'I Get Out,' with lyrics such as:

> *"No more compromises,*

I see past your disguises,

Blindin' me through mind-control,

Stealin' my eternal soul,

Appealin' through material,

To keep me as your slave. "

You can hear her live performance of the song here:

- https://www.Youtube.com/watch?v=28rNFm2ZtLE

Sadly, it seems there's a price to pay for an artist that a corporation like Sony considers its owned property, putting out a song such as this. Sure enough, in 2012, the story emerged that Lauryn was being pursued by the IRS for a total of $968,000 in unpaid taxes, in an affair which smacks of being an orchestrated set-up. In her apparent defence, she mentioned that she had received death threats to herself and her family, (although it's difficult to see why this would have any connection with her failing to pay her taxes.) The tabloids reported that Lauryn could be facing a long prison term if she was unable to pay off her debts by the given deadline. In the event, she served three months in 2013. A solution then emerged; to pay her debts, she was set to sign a brand new million-dollar recording deal with Sony, the very corporation she'd spent the previous 15 years trying to escape!

Robin Thicke: new recruit

A more recent example of an artist who started out with musical integrity, but has been degraded into yet another corporate marionette, comes with the recent history of Robin Thicke. The same blueprint and tried-and-tested formula can be seen as with so many of his contemporaries.

Robin's father, Alan Thicke, was himself an entertainer. He is best known as a US quiz and talk show host, and as an actor. His mother, Gloria Loring, was also a singer and actress, and his maternal grandparents were a singer and trumpet-player respectively. Robin was therefore well-groomed for a showbiz career himself. Appropriately, his brother

Brennan also became an actor, and Robin went on to marry the actress Paula Patton.

Robin's own success seemed to be a long time coming. I interviewed him for 'Blues & Soul' magazine in 2007 at the time of his album 'The Evolution Of Robin Thicke.' He explained then how he had already been in the business for 14 years trying to make it. He had been mentored early on by the R&B singer Brian McKnight, who had introduced him to Interscope Records supremo Jimmy Iovine. Thicke's 2002 album, known alternately as 'Cherry Blue Skies' and 'Beautiful World,' had been a critical success among his peers, attracting the attention of Pharrell Williams, who subsequently produced him on the track 'Wanna Love You Girl' and signed him to his Star Trak label, but it had flopped commercially. At times, Thicke's lack of success had brought severe bouts of depression. "So I was borderline suicidal," he commented. "I was drinking for breakfast, and the only thing that kept me going was that piano in my house. I'd go over to it and write every day."

Thicke's real breakthrough came with the 'Evolution' album, which showcased his distinctive and classy soulful style, heavy on the falsetto, and drawing on retro black music influences. "Producing the 'Evolution' album was a highly therapeutic experience," he said. "Even up to writing the last few songs, it was all a part of still helping me to believe in myself. Everyone had pretty much written me off and given up on me for the tenth time."

His comments certainly imply a frustrated artist ready to do whatever it takes to emulate the success of his father. Wikipedia's entry on Robin observes: "Thicke has noted that while his parents did not attempt to dissuade him from his desire to be in the music industry, their own experience with the nature of the entertainment business made them leery in the beginning."

Things continued along the same musical path with the albums 'Something Else,' 'Sex Therapy' and 'Love After War.' As previously noted, with artists whose entire personas switch, it's possible to pinpoint the moment where this upgrade is being announced to the watching public. We can only speculate on what has occurred behind the scenes, but an informed guess would be that the artist in question, allowed to go their own path for a while, has shown themselves to be someone that could be of use in the controllers' ongoing agenda, and they've been either invited or coerced into accessing new levels of success. Inevitably, the fast-tracking comes with its own price to pay. You're doing what they tell you now.

With Robin Thicke, a symbolic announcement to the world that he had been recruited as one of the Industry's chosen ones, came with his guest appearance alongside Miley Cyrus at the 2013 MTV VMA Awards. This event was announcing Miley Cyrus' new slutty makeover, as the audience saw the former Hannah Montana star in porn=star mode, 'twerking' and flicking her tongue, as Thicke emerged in a black-and-white striped suit and began to grind against her to his song 'Blurred Lines.' Cyrus said in a later interview that Thicke was very much involved in the planning of the performance, and 'wanted me as naked as possible,' even helping choose her rubber outfit.

The performance attracted the scrutiny of 'Vigilant Citizen' who, in a thorough dissection, stated that the design of Thicke's suit, besides evoking the black-and-white/ dark-and-light/ good-and-evil imagery alluded to in Freemasonry, was also a mind-control programming trigger. This, VC observed, gave the impression of Thicke and Cyrus's relationship as that of a mind-control subject and her handler:

> *"Things got even stranger when Robin Thicke came out to perform 'Blurred Lines.' As its name somewhat stipulates, that song blurs the line between being flirty and all-out creepy. Its video has a strange handler-slave vibe, where Robin, Pharrell and T.I. are all sharply dressed, while the women dancing around them are completely naked . . . and being sung lines such as "you're an animal."*

> *" . . . Forcing slaves to be naked while the masters are dressed is a classic psychological ploy to make slaves feel powerless, vulnerable and inferior."*

'Blurred Lines' marked the end of Thicke's previous mellow, soulful style, casting him in new light as a sleazy kind of pimp. The lewdness of the imagery was further enhanced by the flashing of the slogan 'Robin Thicke's got a big dick,' (thanks for the information,) on a balloon, and the lyric "you wanna hug me . . . what rhymes with hug me?" in a video frequently aired on shows watched by children. The sexualisation of ever-earlier age groups continues on.

Shortly after the VMA performance, Thicke's marriage to actress Paula Patton came to an end amidst claims of his infidelity. He was reported as being in a new relationship with 20-year-old April Love Geary, 16 years his junior.

VC was back on the case with Thicke's follow-up song and video, 'Get Her Back,' observing:

> *"Get Her Back' appears to be about Robin Thicke trying to win his wife back by being nice and apologetic. However, when one adds the imagery of the video into the mix, it becomes a creepy, disturbing tale of a stalker with violent and suicidal tendencies pathetically harassing an ex-lover ... all laced with one-eyed Illuminati symbolism, of course."*

Having cited soulful greats such as Stevie Wonder, Marvin Gaye and Smokey Robinson as his influences, by 2015, Thicke had begun collaborating with garbage pop artists like Flo Rida and Nicki Minaj, (who had previously guested on another Thicke song, 'Shake It For Daddy.' No comment.) The signs that something had happened to Robin Thicke, going way beyond what could be written off as an artist's 'natural progression,' could not be more blatant.

The strange enigma of Jay Electronica

When resolving to discover the true nature of an artist and what motivates their actions, there are few examples full of more apparent contradictions and paradoxes than the case of Jay Electronica. His very persona has an air of unexplained mystery about it, and those who have met him have talked of a magnetic aura that seems to draw in those around him.

Born Timothy Thedford in New Orleans in 1976, official lore has it that he grew up in the city's Magnolia Projects, and that his early life was the ghetto struggle that is the case with the majority of rappers. He is said to have left the city at the age of 19 and taken up something of a Nomadic lifestyle, moving from place to place to pursue his craft before settling in Detroit, where he was introduced to producers J Dilla and Mr. Porter. He signed with Jay-Z's Roc Nation imprint in late 2010.

It wasn't his music that first propelled him into the domain of the mainstream media, however, but rather his high-profile relationship with London-based Kate Rothschild, heiress to the Rothschild banking dynasty. This wasn't the first time a black musician had embarked upon an affair with a Rothschild; as mentioned in an earlier chapter, jazz musician Thelonious Monk had been involved with a Rothschild baroness in the late 1950s. 'Nica,' Monk's partner, was said to have been an obsessive jazz fan. Kate, meanwhile, was a music producer among her various activities, running her Round Table record label.

Electronica is a stated Five Per Center–a radical pro-black faction of the Nation Of Islam–and this would appear to be at odds with him dating a member of the family that is so often cited as the ultimate representation of the white Illuminati power structure. It seems wonderfully ironic that the Nation Of Islam's teachings are frequently described as 'anti-Semitic,' and the Rothschilds refer to themselves as Jewish. It's the type of story which, if presented as a work of fiction, would be dismissed as 'a bit far-fetched.'

The Jay Electronica/ Kate Rothschild relationship began while she was still married to Ben Goldsmith, son of the late billionaire financier Sir (there's another one) James Goldsmith. For a time, Ben and Jay went back and forth on Twitter, taunting each other. In June 2012, Ben was arrested on suspicion of actual bodily harm against Kate, thought to be as a result of her affair. He was later released without charge and subsequently filed for divorce on grounds of adultery. They had three children together. Electronica already had a child with fellow enigmatic music-maker Erykah Badu.

This unlikely union has drawn all manner of speculation from truth-seekers and hip-hop fans alike. Some have attested that, in striking up the relationship, Electronica had 'infiltrated the enemy,' and was working to expose the elite bloodlines from the inside. The opposing view, however, is that at the moment he first found fame and fortune, he went the same way as every other artist does in terms of being owned, and that the relationship is likely to be an arranged one, in the way that all other high-profile celebrity couplings are. Could there be any significance to the lyric 'brunch with the Rothschilds, dinner with the Carters' on Jay's track 'Call Of Duty' in this regard?

The Electronica/ Rothschild relationship was hitting headlines around the same time as the one between Russell Brand and Jemima Goldsmith, daughter of Sir James Goldsmith, and brother to Ben. She married cricketer Imran Khan, taking his name, divorcing before she embarked on her affair with Brand. This seemed an equally unlikely pairing that smacked of being set up, leading to exactly the same kind of scrutiny among vigilant onlookers. By 2014, the relationship between Electronica and Rothschild seemed to have fizzled out. The 'Daily Mail' reported in August of that year that Jay had moved back to America, while Kate was living in a cottage next door to the Georgian mansion of her former mother-in-law, Lady Annabel Goldsmith.

Electronica's music has at times been particularly potent and touching, most notably on the stunning 'Better In Tune With The Infinite,' where he includes lines such as, "the name on that birth certificate, that ain't the real me," and including an opening quote from long-time leader of the Nation of Islam, Elijah Mohammed. At other times, however, his lyrics have been more in-keeping with the general glut of mainstream rappers. There's also the apparent paradox of his appearing in promo shots with one eye covered, and his working relationship with the Grand Master of Illuminati Puppets, Jay-Z.

Conspiro Media writer Matt Sergiou delved right into the Electronica enigma when he guested on my 'Good Vibrations' podcast in 2013, which threw forward some further interesting revelations. Among them was that Jay Electronica's background was not necessarily as had been generally assumed.

A UK 'Mail On Sunday' article centred around the claims of a man named Virgil C. Tiller, who claims he grew up with the young Timothy Thedford. Tiller claimed that, although Electronica did indeed start out in the Magnolia Projects, when he was six, he and his mother moved to a two-bedroom flat in a Victorian house in an affluent district of New Orleans. Tiller also claimed that Thedford received an education at St. Augustines, a private Catholic boys' school which would have cost, at the time, the equivalent of £3,500 per year in school fees.

Matt went on to address another anomaly surrounding Electronica—the issue of his album, 'Act II: Patents Of Nobility' which, like Dr. Dre's mythological 'Detox,' had been promised for years but was still showing no signs of release. A letter had appeared on-line from an individual giving his name as Carter Whitelow. As the initial release date for the album approached, Whitelow commented that it would never come out. The reason, he claimed, is because the lyrics and stories contained were actually based on a book of poetry that he, Whitelow, had written years before when he was in high-school, and entitled 'Act II: The Life And Times of Carter Whitelow.' He had credited the works to his alter-ego, Trademark Legacy, aka the Black Adam.

Electronica had plagiarised the content, he claimed, through a mutual, wealthy college acquaintance who had connections within the Def Jam/ Roc Nation empire. The unnamed friend, if Whitelow's story is true, had given the poetry manuscript to someone within Def Jam, who had held on to it, then seen an opportunity to use it as the basis of Electronica's debut album. Whitelow claims to have recognised his own lyrics when he heard Electronica's material on the radio, and threatened to sue. Little else has been heard in the music media to support Whitelow's claim, but then again, something has to account for the fact that Electronica's album has still not appeared, despite reportedly being completed in 2012, and shows no sign of doing so any time soon.

If Whitelow's story turns out to be true, it casts doubt on the authenticity of any of Electronica's lyrical content, just as the claims about his schooling and housing have to cast doubts upon the consistent claims of a ghetto upbringing. The net result is way more questions than answers when it comes to this most perplexing of artists.

Is nothing sacred?

People often say, "Surely such-and-such an artist isn't corrupted and compromised? I know all the others are, but surely not *them?*" Sadly, from the evidence we can now see, it would appear that any artist who has achieved fame, fortune and great success has attained it at a price. In some cases, an artist can flourish for years without any obvious signs of their ownership, but these indicators are eventually put on public display.

Kate Bush is an act who, from day one, was an original one-off. From the moment she first appeared with the supernatural overtones of the ghostly 'Wuthering Heights,' after reportedly being discovered by Pink Floyd's Dave Gilmour, she has been feted for making wildly creative music that defies conventional categorisation. She has also explored esoteric themes, from addressing Wilhelm Reich's suppressed orgone technology in 'Cloudbusting,' to the weaponisation of sound in 'Experiment IV,' to revering the language of the cosmos in 'Pi.' It was therefore a great disappointment for many when she willingly accepted a CBE from the Queen late in her career in 2013, remarking jovially, "now I've got something really special to put on the Christmas tree."

The following year, Kate played her first solo gig in 35 years at London's Hammersmith Apollo. Alert researchers were quick to spot much of the symbolism that was being displayed, including the depiction of lizard-like reptilian entities, a guitarist sporting a creepy bird face-mask, and a model aeroplane buzzing from one side of the stage to the other dispersing vapours very reminiscent of Chemtrails. All unwelcome hints at Kate being yet another manipulated commodity of the Establishment, and being used to normalise certain agendas in the same way as so many of her lesser-established peers. What is it that happens to all these artists?

Just don't mention the R-word!

Besides the Thelonious Monk/ Jay Electronica affairs, the Rothschilds have largely managed to stay out of the music industry spotlight—just as they manage to avoid the glare of the wider media. They are alluded to on the sleeve to a Rick Ross mixtape from 2012, however, titled 'The Black Bar Mitzvah,' the cover of which has the rapper luxuriating in a fur coat inside the symbol that the Rothschilds adopted as their family logo. It's known as the Seal Of Solomon and is the symbol on the flag of modern Israel, (which the Rothschilds founded,) representing a fusion of the blade and chalice symbols—a unity of the male and female principles inherent in nature. Why Ross chose this title and imagery remains unexplained. Maybe he plans to re-name himself Rick Rothschild?

Around the same time, Boy George appeared showing off a new (temporary) tattoo on the crown of his bald head. This was of a lotus flower and assorted other designs, with the same Seal of Solomon/ House of Rothschild symbol emerging out of it. The significance of this is anyone's guess.

Resources:

Fitzpatrick Informer: The Hollywood Kabbalah Cult Unmasked:

- https://fitzinfo.wordpress.com/2014/05/12/
  the-hollywood-kabbalah-cult-unmasked-part-iii/

Sherry Shriner on Sherry Talk Radio:

- http://www.sherrytalkradio.com/transcribe/2012/01-16-12.htm

Professor Griff & Katt Williams Presents . . . Illuminati Rituals & the Consequences:

- https://www.Youtube.com/watch?v=JLcL0spncTs

Justify Theory: The Crazies Pt. III: The Katt Williams Persecution:

- http://justifytheory.blogspot.co.uk/2012/09/the-crazies-pt-iii-katt-williams.html

Bob Dylan Admits He Sold His Soul to the Devil:

- https://www.Youtube.com/watch?v=IqvvOD4bdRs

Vigilant Citizen: When Insiders Expose the Ugly Side of the Entertainment Industry:

- http://vigilantcitizen.com/vigilantreport/when-insiders-expose-the-ugly-side-of-the-entertainment-industry/

Black Child Production: Hollywood Casting Couch; Satan's Playground:

- http://www.dailymotion.com/video/
  x2az5g0_hollywood-casting-couch-satan-s-playground_news

Black Child Production: Satanic Hollywood: The Ritual Sacrifice:

- https://www.Youtube.com/watch?v=K_5qEvos69M

Black Child Productions: The Gay Ritual

- https://www.Youtube.com/watch?v=Id642i9c3HI

Yash Qaraah's Youtube channel:

- https://www.Youtube.com/user/wobsymphony1619/videos

Professor Griff Calls P.Diddy Gay & Illuminati Scum:

- https://www.Youtube.com/watch?v=OSIq5JPNEX8

Druglord Claims Feds Quizzed Him About Sex Life Of Sean "Diddy" Combs:

- http://www.thesmokinggun.com/buster/sean-combs/
  rosemond-proffer-sex-claim-657409

Lauryn Hill: I Get Out:

- https://www.Youtube.com/watch?v=28rNFm2ZtLE

Daily Express: Kanye West throws himself on the floor and refuses to speak on The Jonathan Ross Show:

- http://www.express.co.uk/celebrity-news/560794/
  Kanye-West-strop-The-Jonathan-Ross-Show

DMX: The Industry:

- https://www.Youtube.com/watch?v=LHmQokVlmpo

Fitzpatrick Informer: The Hollywood Kabbalah Cult Unmasked:

- https://fitzinfo.wordpress.com/2014/05/12/
  the-hollywood-kabbalah-cult-unmasked-part-iii/

Vigilant Citizen: Robin Thicke's Video "Get Her Back" or How Pop Culture Keeps Promoting a Culture of Death:

- http://vigilantcitizen.com/musicbusiness/
  robin-thickes-video-get-back/

Illuminati Video, Olivia Wilde, Bono and Richard Branson Join Matt Damon's Toilet Strike:

- https://www.Youtube.com/watch?v=56PpsudMnC8

Vigilant Citizen: Bono, Richard Branson, and Olivia Wilde Make Fun of "Illuminati Conspiracies" in Ad for Clean Water:

- http://vigilantcitizen.com/latestnews/bono-richard-branson-
  and-olivia-wilde-making-fun-of-illuminati-conspiracies-in-
  charity-ad/

Richard Curtis' withdrawn 10:10 video:

- https://www.Youtube.com/watch?v=5-Mw5_EBk0g

Margaret Sanger, Founder of Planned Parenthood, In Her Own Words:

- http://www.dianedew.com/sanger.htm

Daily Mail: Obama is related to Brad Pitt, while Hillary Clinton is cousins with Angelina Jolie:

- http://www.dailymail.co.uk/home/article-1001741/Match-heaven-Obama-related-Brad-Pitt-Clinton-cousins-Angelina-Jolie.html

Brad Pitt's genealogical links:

- http://www.geni.com/blog/look-whos-related-brad-pitt-and-angelina-jolie-375036.html

US researcher Freeman on the bloodline links of celebrities:

- http://freemantv.com/occult-symbolism-of-madonna-at-superbowl-halftime/#sthash.wRWHauph.dpuf

The wild Rothschild heiress, her rap star lover and the photo that's alarmed her friends:

- http://www.dailymail.co.uk/femail/article-2568763/Kate-Rothschild-heiress-rap-star-lover-photo-thats-alarmed-friends.html

Jay Electronica denies stealing rhymes:

- http://hiphop-n-more.com/2010/10/jay-electronica-denies-stealing-rhymes/

Mail On-Line: The Rothschild Rap: After THAT MoS revelation about Kate Rothschild leaving Ben Goldsmith for a rapper called Jay Electronica, we now reveal the clue to the break-up played by DJs all over Britain:

- http://www.dailymail.co.uk/news/article-2157046/After-Kate-Rothschild-Jay-Electronica-clue-break-played-DJs-Britain.html

Conspiro Media blog: Thelonious Monk/ Jay Electronica/ Rothschild links:

- https://conspiromedia.wordpress.com/2012/07/31/as-kate-rothschilds-relationship-with-an-american-rapper-reportedly-intensifies-conspiro-media-presents-the-first-of-a-two-part-feature-on-the-notorious-familys-influence-on-music-over-the-la/

Vigilant Citizen: Robin Thicke's Video "Get Her Back" or How Pop Culture Keeps Promoting a Culture of Death:

- http://vigilantcitizen.com/musicbusiness/robin-thickes-video-get-back/

CHAPTER 19

AND NOW FOR SOMETHING
COMPLETELY DIFFERENT

Humanity, we have a problem.

> *"To be honest with you I don't really know how,*
> *We're gonna change this,*
> *But we have to."*
>
> *Alais Clay: 'Wake 'Em Up' (2010)*

> *"Freedom is directly linked to morality. As a society becomes more*
> *moral, freedom increases. As a society becomes less moral, freedom*
> *declines."*
>
> *Mark Passio*

Truth bombs

Despite the validity of everything else you'll have read here, you've just reached the most important two chapters in the entire book. Although the information that follows is best read at the tail-end of everything else for the full context, these can be taken in isolation and absorbed in their own right. I certainly urge anyone to *not* stop reading here, or the true nature of everything else they've read will be lost, and if there's only one section they choose to share with others, I would urge them to make this the one.

Having spent the rest of this book looking at so many of the strange things that go on in the music industry and beyond, it's now time to start addressing the *why*. Any such story that ends without going there is like getting to the summing-up of an Agatha Christie murder-mystery and finding the last few pages have been ripped out.

I'm going to spend the remaining pages sharing with you what I've come to understand. I'll be dispensing with phrases like 'I believe that . . . ' or 'it's my opinion that . . . ' It'll be pretty clear that this is the case, and to state that every time would detract from the readability of the information. How anyone chooses to react is of course up to them. A significant part of the human suffering that's endured for so long has been as a result of certain individuals telling everyone else what they must believe. The information will speak for itself, anyway, and will resonate with those it's destined to resonate with.

As I mentioned at the very start of this book, it is impossible to truly understand the manipulations of the music industry without putting them into the full context of what's really going on in this world—and what this reality is in the first place. The understandable reaction of so many when they come to grudgingly accept the conspiracy is to ask, 'but what can we do about any of this?' It's only an understanding of what follows that offers the empowerment to do anything to counter it.

The same could be said for any number of subjects within the truth/ conspiracy realm. There are many full-time experts on 9/11, for instance, who have taken apart the official version bit-by-bit and could talk for hours about the many anomalies. The case will be the same with the truth about vaccines, GM food, Chemtrails, institutionalised paedophilia, Satanic Ritual Abuse, trauma-based mind control . . . the list goes on. Each of these may seem like an isolated subject area in its own right, but when you come to understand the bigger picture, it becomes clear how they're all connected, and how each of them serves its own purpose within the system, in tandem with all the others. As music is my thing, I've attempted to show with this book how the manipulations of the music industry are just one of these cogs in the wheel.

Many feel overwhelmed by the dark nature of these subjects, reasoning that the control system has been so deeply embedded into our reality for so long, that deconstructing it step-by-step seems impossible. Those of a New Age persuasion, meanwhile, will argue that paying any kind of attention to a dark or negative subject only helps to keep it manifested in reality, due to the energetic connection that individuals make when applying their conscious attention. This is ultimately a cop-out and an abdication of personal responsibility, since the first step towards resolving any problem *has* to be understanding the full nature of it as far as it's possible. Only then can any solution come. And attempting to dismantle the hugely complex and multi-tiered control system brick-by-brick, clearly *is* impractical. The real solution lies elsewhere.

There can surely be no-one of an appropriate thinking capacity in the world, who hasn't given at least the smallest amount of reflection to the big questions in life: Who are we? Where do we come from? Why are we here? What, actually is 'here?' What happens when we leave it? Although discussion of such subjects is rarely heard around the water cooler at work or over the average family meal, they are enigmas which have puzzled and confounded humanity for millennia, and must surely occupy the thoughts of all people on Earth at least occasionally during their solitary quiet time.

For as long as I can remember, they've certainly plagued my mind, from the first mentions of 'Jesus' and an undefined entity called 'God' in my primary school days, to my four years attending an Evangelical Christian church under the delusion that this might bring answers to the strange feelings I started getting at the age of 19 that the world wasn't quite what we'd been led to think it was, to my ultimate depar-ture, disillusioned at not having found the answers but instead a whole set of new questions. This set me on the path to many years of bitter Atheism, genuinely believing that there is no divine plan, that human life is a cosmic accident, and that beyond death lies oblivion and noth-ingness. As I mentioned at the start, it was around 2008 that this belief system started to crumble, in the face of new evidence that was coming my way as to the true nature of this world and the forces that currently have it in their grip.

The activities of the dark occult priest-class are well-documented in the rest of this book. The power that they've been able to exert over humanity has only been possible through *their* deeply-studied under-standing of the profound nature of reality. What it all comes down to is the fact that everything in creation—from the planets and stars, to black holes in deep space, to animals, plants, mountains and humans—is made up of the same universal energy, vibrating at different frequencies. In its base form, everything is this energy. It's each expression's unique vibratory pattern that gives it its form in the apparently physical realm. (I say 'apparently' physical, because what we understand to be the solid world only appears that way because of how we, as consciously-aware beings, interpret and decode the energetic patterns that we experience.)

I'm under no illusion as to how bizarre or unfeasible that information sounds when it's encountered for the first time, and I was in lasting denial of it myself when I first came across it. But there are many, many researchers, authors and scholars, from many different ages and walks of life, and from civilisations in all corners of the world—and all corroborating each-other's information—who can explain the whole phenomenon way better than my soundbite version can. This understanding is also the basis of many of the religions and belief systems of cultures from all over the ancient world, before many of these great truths got corrupted and deliberately occulted by the institutionalised religions that we see at work in the world today. It's not for nothing that the word 'religion' is derived from the Latin word 'ligare,' meaning 'to bind or tie back'.

You can also see this great truth about the nature of our reality encoded into popular movies in the form of allegory. The original 'Matrix' is one of the most frequently-quoted examples. Beneath its surface gloss and CGI action sequences, lies the revelation that what we think of as physical reality is actually electrical and digital information waves, which get decoded into 'reality' by our minds acting as receivers/ transmitters. In other words, the world only exists this way because we perceive it to be so. Without observers in place to decode the information, everything would remain in its base form, as energetic information codes. It occurred to me a while back that this must be the origin of the often-heard phrase, 'if a tree falls in the woods and there's no-one there to hear it, does it make a sound?' These seemingly nonsensical phrases don't come about by accident.

When I came to my ultimate acceptance of this great truth, it had the opposite effect of the previous belief systems that I'd embraced; it *answered* more questions than it raised. Only the understanding that this apparent reality—and all others—are expressions of energy resonating to different frequency patterns, can explain the concepts of timeless eternity, the survival of spirit-souls after death, reincarnation, out-of-body and near-death experiences, remote viewing and astral projection, and even the relatively trivial phenomenon of premonitions and *deja vu*. The atheistic/ Darwinian view that the world is basically a cold, heartless rock floating in space, and that we're mere biological entities that *just happen* to have mutated out of nothingness against all the odds, is another cop-out. It's a belief system for habitual sceptics, and is there as an alternative to all the man-made, mind-controlling religions of the world to keep humanity away from the *real* truth of our existence. If they can't get you with rigid, superstitious dogma, they get you with the opposite–absolute denial of anything vaguely spiritual or esoteric.

Imagine then, that a small section of the human population, back in the mists of pre-history, had come to understand that the Universe works in this way, and, devoid of the normal characteristics that prevent most of us from acting in such a way, (conscience,) had decided that they could gain a tactical advantage over the rest of the population by putting their knowledge to work, while deliberately keeping the rest of humanity in complete ignorance through an assortment of malevolent efforts. If we assume these individuals to not have humanity's best interests at heart, and to be ruled by a psychopathic mind-set, we can start to see how this is going to spell a pretty raw deal for everyone else. This, in fact, is the dynamic that has been at play in our world for thousands of years, and the conditions we find ourselves living in during these times are as a direct, long-term consequence of this process.

It's only a psychopathic approach to the world that could keep a control system formed on this basis in place for as long as it has been. Most people when thinking of psychopaths, have visions of the Norman Bates character in the Hitchcock movie, or a knife-wielding frenzied serial killer from some teen slasher flick. But this is a caricature of the extreme end of psychopathy. For the most part, it's determined simply by a complete lack of empathy and compassion towards other beings, and an inability to understand–or care–about the impact that your actions might have for the rest of creation. A psychopath can quite happily give the order for a village-full of women and children in some far-off land to be slaughtered in a drone bomb attack, and sleep like a baby that very night without a single troubling thought. The world's governments are full of them, and not by accident. A very small proportion of the human population–between one and five per-cent depending on which researcher you listen to–are reckoned to be primary psychopaths. They're born this way, with the section of the brain that gives rise to compassion and empathy broken and dysfunctional. It's a mental illness, and at its primary level, it cannot be cured.

Secondary psychopathy, meanwhile, is a condition that can be pro-grammed or cultivated into an individual, usually from early childhood. Growing up in a family or social environment which is characterised by psychopathy–in conjunction with suffering personal abuse and trauma oneself–can bring about a psychopathic approach to the world. These are the methods that the controlling 'elites' use on their own children to produce the type of mindset that will be needed for a lifetime spent serving the system and oppressing the rest of humanity. Psychologists say that this level of psychopathy can actually be reversed and cured, however, if an individual is taken out of this type of conditioning early enough, and if there is some level of personal will on their part to break free of it. There are examples of many who have done this.

Exiting the asylum

Over the years phrases such as 'conspiracy theorist' and 'tinfoil-hat-wear-ing nutjob' have been created to dismiss anyone questioning the official line as a wide-eyed, unhinged lunatic. Exercising the ability to think for yourself and asserting your individuality have been made a social crime, and because the majority of people are constantly seeking the approval of others, and trying to 'fit in' to a world that has been deliberately made insane, they play ball and act in line with 'normal' behaviour, not wishing to step out of the security and comfort-zone of the box.

It becomes clear then, that understanding great truths, then taking on the responsibility to communicate what you've learned to others, can never be possible for anyone still stuck in that systematic mind-set. Anyone wishing to embark on a path towards true knowledge and understanding–and therefore freedom–has to first let go of any concern of what others might think of them for what they do, say or think. Most people are shackled by worries of what the blokes down the pub might think if they stopped talking about football and started speaking about the mysteries of life and reality, or what their Mum or Dad or partner might think, or what their boss at work will say. Fear of becoming a social outcast is what keeps so many silent and inactive about informa-tion that needs to be put out there as widely as possible if humanity is ever to break free of the slavery and servitude that's been imposed on us.

Overcoming this is certainly a difficult process for most that come to truth. I know this from personal experience. Burning those first bridges is always the most difficult step. As you start to speak out, you realise that the paths back to your previous way of life are disappearing and that the only way now is forwards. It didn't take long until I reached the stage where I no longer gave a shit what anyone might think of me for what I was starting to say, however, and for that which I instinctively knew to be true. I couldn't be writing this book otherwise.

A way of thinking which certainly helped me overcome any worry about how people might perceive me, was to consider what anyone actually gets in exchange for worrying what their mate, or sister, or dad, or colleague, or some random stranger might think of them. In each case, the value that you draw from censoring what you say, or modifying the way you act for fear of how it might go down with somebody else, is exactly the same. Absolutely nothing. No value or benefit at all. Why then, do we do it?

Another way I like to look at it all is: I've never appreciated being taken for a mug. And who really does? Who can honestly say they enjoy the idea of being duped, of being treated by others as a chump, of someone else considering them so dumb and ignorant and stupid, that they can feed them a constant crock of lies, disinformation and deception, knowing they'll lap it all up like an unthinking moron? Not me, thanks.

Yet this is what's going on in the world. Every day the bulk of humanity is spoon-fed lies by the corporate-controlled mainstream media, by the professional paid liars in government, and by those in other aspects of the Establishment. All these lies can be proven to be such by the application of critical thought and evidence-based research. Yet most choose to commit absolutely none of their time–through free-will choice–to looking into such matters, and remain too afraid to talk about it to friends, family, neighbours and colleagues. "Well, I'd *like* to let people know about human slavery and about how our thoughts and perceptions are not our own, and about how things are never going to get any better for any of us until there's a massive shift in awareness of these things and a huge change in human behaviour and thought as a result . . . but whatever would the lads at the job think?"

Who, honestly, can look at the world we live in and think it to be 'normal' or sane? A world where human labour is exploited in the form of taxes, stolen by an institution called 'government' on the premise that it's needed to help maintain the infrastructure of the land? (although the truth is that much of it is covertly siphoned off to fund some overseas war or other.) A world where such taxation methods are only necessary in the first place because, instead of printing and circulating money themselves, the governments of the world commission cartels of private bankers operating under such names as the Federal Reserve and Bank Of England, to loan the government money with debt automatically attached, obliging the government to use the energy and the labour of the people as collateral against the loan?

Then, when more money is needed to pay off the debts that come with each new transaction, the banking cartels issue new money with yet *more* debt attached, meaning there's *never* enough money in circulation to pay off the accrued debts, and in turn, that there will *always* be those in society that will go bankrupt and lose money, property and land. It's built into the very fabric of the system that this is the case, and yet people accept this with no fuss as 'normal.' Just the way it is. And anyone suggesting that it might be in humanity's best interests if we found a new way to do things is written off as a 'nutter' or a 'conspiracy theorist.' If this is 'sane,' I'm very happy to remain in 'nutter' territory, thanks all the same.

How can anyone truly justify one family sitting on sickening, colossal levels of wealth purely as a result of their genetics, and expecting the rest of the population to be servile to them? How many question what 'Royal' even means in the first place? What excuse can there be for hundreds of thousands in the very land they claim to 'reign' over, living in shocking levels of poverty and hardship that could be eradicated overnight if the wealth were distributed fairly, in line with humanity, compassion, and straight common-sense, rather than being tied up in gold-plated carriages, pointless regalia, and other mindless expressions of pomp and grandeur that benefit no-one except the soulless parasites that are permitted to use them? The Queen of England, (not that there's anything English about the whole Saxe-Coburg-Gotha and Battenberg bloodlines that pass themselves off under the stolen name of 'Windsor,' of course,) is so obscenely rich that she's reckoned to 'own' what equates to around a sixth of the planet, including the sea-beds that lie underneath oceans! How can any one human-being, (a status which

is debated by some!) own a sea-bed, for fuck's sake!? Or any other natural resource on the planet for that matter, which in reality is freely and
abundantly available to all who occupy the Earth for the few decades
that they're in their bodies, before it falls under the custody of the next
generation?

Another expression of pure insanity when you really get down to the
grass-roots of it. And another which is not only tolerated, but is actively
propped-up and allowed to continue by so many of *the very people* it
exists to enslave and exploit so contemptuously! Witness the hordes of
brainwashed morons waving their plastic flags and queuing for hours to
catch a glimpse of the figurehead of a system that is enslaving them and
their families. That's sane? I'll stay crazy, please.

Who, outside of the realms of the propaganda and hyperbole that's
peddled in its favour, can really offer *any* kind of moral justification for
war? Who, apart from career military men, soulless bankers or psychopathic politicians with a salary to earn and an agenda to serve, have you
ever met who wanted a war? Who thought that killing and mutilating
other people and causing unending ripples of human suffering, was a
reasonable, sensible and justifiable way of resolving a conflict? And yet
we're conditioned from the earliest age to meekly accept that war is an
inevitable by-product of human nature, that we're tribal beings that just
can't get along, and that we're inherently warlike and aggressive in our
nature.

We live in a society of double-standards where, if an everyday civil-
ian picked up a machine-gun and slaughtered a group of women and
children in cold blood, they would, (quite rightly,) be branded a dangerous criminal and incarcerated/ executed, depending on the state or
country in question. Yet, when a military soldier, (or increasingly now,
a cop,) does the same, this act of straight murder can be written off as
'collateral damage' involving 'casualties of war,' and the perpetrator will
not only escape justice, but is highly likely to be decorated for 'bravery'
or 'service in the line of duty!'

We hear constantly of the 'War on Cancer,' as promoted by the many,
many charities in this field. "One day we'll beat cancer," they say. But it
always comes with the proviso that to do so, they need money from the
general public on a never-ending basis. Lots of it. When cancer charities
have been working on 'finding a cure' for well over 50 years, you have to

ask yourself where exactly all that money is going when the cure never seems to appear. The truth is that the majority of the funds go towards making the senior executives of these charities very, very rich. As difficult as it is for people to come to terms with, sadly, it turns out that many cancer charities are money-making scams, cynically manipulating the good nature of well-meaning people by dangling the ever-present carrot of 'hope.' The last thing this organised racket wants is to find a cure for cancer. This would put hundreds of thousands of employees out of business, and deprive the pharmaceutical industry of millions of customers every year, along with the huge profits they generate through conventional treatment.

The truth is that natural cures for cancer have always existed. Nature provides the remedies for all human ailments, usually in the form of the appropriate plant correctly administered. This is knowledge that has been understood for millennia by the shaman and priest-doctors of indigenous populations around the world. You know, the very same shaman and priest-doctors that have been mercilessly slaughtered by the colonialism that has ravaged so many civilisations, destroying their culture and knowledge in their wake.

Isn't it interesting, given that cannabis is cited as the principal alternative cure, that it's demonised in Western society as a dangerous 'narcotic' that's illegal to cultivate, whereas pharmaceutical drugs and vaccines loaded with toxic ingredients like mercury and formaldehyde, are absolutely fine? How could this be in a situation where governments 'care' about people and 'represent their interests?'

Can any world where this sort of thing happens be judged as 'sane'? Clearly not, I'd suggest. And yet it goes on being tolerated by most, without a second thought towards the sheer injustice and madness of it all.

The brainwashed state of low-level consciousness that we are manipulated into from birth—and which few ever take it upon themselves to break out of—was communicated with poetic brilliance in a 2015 Facebook post by Mats Rickard Lagnevall. It's hard to know how to express this great truth any more effectively than this:

"In a materialistic Westernised country of choice, a young boy cries out loud to express his great anguish because, for reasons beyond his

comprehensive ability, he cannot have that big red toy located in a large Toys 'R' Us. His mother says he can have this yellow toy instead. But it's so small compared to that toy, and thusly, he displays his emotions in the most natural manner available to him. The tears of disapproval fall seemingly unending in quantity.

"To no avail does the mother tell the boy to be silent. She says that it is not a matter requiring tears. But why should he be silent? He is sad, and he must therefore express it so that he can move beyond it. In her unconsciously-accepted shame, she angrily commands him to be silent! Although this proves to be an equally futile act. His tears continue to fall.

"The boy simply cannot understand. After all, there are so many toys here, why can't he have that red toy? Why are all these toys here if not to be played with? Why must he be silent when he is sad? Why is his mother now angry at him? His tears are starting to give way for shock and confusion.

"Strangers passing by the mother and her boy stop in their paths to whisper to each other, whilst pointing their fingers—something that the mother almost instinctively responds to by grasping the boys arm firmly and inflicting slight pain, as she threatens him with not receiving any toy at all unless he stops his crying and sobbing. And of course, at this outlook, the boy mentally musters up all the force he can in an effort to stop the tears. The only sound remaining to break the silence is intermittent snivelling as he assumes mental posture and looks around at the people now quickly losing interest, as there's no longer anyone upsetting the status-quo.

"The boy records everything, yet in his conscious mind, he can understand none of it.

"As the years go on and he grows older, he learns that displaying emotions is largely frowned-upon in this society, and during his years in school, he also learns that questioning authority is duly forbidden, as the authority will punish you for such transgressions.

"In his teens, the boy is introduced to different ways of intoxicating himself. He habituates smoking, as it relieves his worries by granting slight sensory stimuli, blatantly disregarding all the long-term potential hazards outweighed by the instant gratification.

"He grows up to become a mediocre man, taught to keep most of his opinions to himself and do what he's told. He eventually marries a woman who doesn't demand too much from him, and he drudges through the work weeks of the year only really looking forward to the next weekend and its subsequent pleasures of intoxicating himself to a sufficient degree as to forget his worries, and to numb the ever-growing pain in the furthest reaches of his being.

"The boy is now a man, his life as inconspicuous and insignificant as any of his fellow colleagues or friends. One week is merely replaced by another. The joy that used to arrive every weekend is now scarcely available but more than once a year during the first few days of vacation. It is at this point that he completely loses all outlook on life. He succumbs to a deep and dark place wherein years of suppressed emotions haunt him in every waking moment. The strength of his mind is shattered under the sheer force of the emotional re-emergence, and his life falls asunder.

"He seeks help from society in how to handle these emotions. But the modern inquisition under the guise of Psychology does not exist to alleviate the issues created by the societal norms in the first place. It's only meant to assure that the people are able to work another week, and thusly he receives no actual assistance. He is given one drug after another, all of which numb his mind, and essentially remove the sensations elicited from his suppressed emotions. But he continues taking them, because he's learnt not to disobey authority and to do what he's been told.

"At this point, the man is largely dead. He's still able to perform within his monotonous work, but all of life has lost its colours, the taste across his palate is bland, and he no longer has a mind with which to worry. His spinal column is left to live out the remaining

years of his so-called ordinary life. And one day, he is found dead in his favourite chair.

"Is this really what we want?"

And so, it becomes clear that a major change in the human mind-set—brought about by a radical shift in consciousness—is vital if this planet is to ever come close to being a just and moral place to live. Losing the fear of what others might think is the first change that has to happen on a major scale. But an understanding of the moral laws of the Universe—on a scale that rivals the knowledge that's been hoarded by the dark occultists who have held humankind in slavery for so long—is also essential.

Resources:

Rick Simpson's site regarding natural cures for cancer:

- www.cureyourowncancer.org/rick-simpson.html

John Assaraf: Why You Should Be aware Of Quantum Physics:

- http://johnassaraf.com/law-of-attraction/
  why-you-should-be-aware-of-quantum-physics-2

CHAPTER 20

IF NOT YOU, THEN WHO?

IF NOT NOW, THEN WHEN?

How the story ends is down to us. It always has been.

> *"Some men see things as they are and say why?*
> *I dream things that never were and say why not?"*
> *George Bernard Shaw (1856-1950)*

> *"Our future may lie beyond our vision, but it is not completely beyond*
> *our control. It is the shaping impulse of America that it is neither fate*
> *nor nature, nor the irresistible tides of history, but the work of our*
> *own hands—matched to reason and principle—that will determine our*
> *destiny. There is pride in that, even arrogance, but there is also expe-*
> *rience and truth. In any event, it is the only way we can live."*
> *Edward Kennedy, eulogy to his brother Robert F Kennedy, 1968*

The Truth will set you free–but first it will piss you off

The outstanding activist, researcher and humanitarian, Santos Bonacci, had some wonderful words to say about seeking the path to truth when he guested on the Vinny Eastwood Show in November 2014:

> *"I'm a researcher, and have been all my life. I've always studied and*
> *uncovered truths, facts, evidence, proof, because that's what I love*
> *doing. I love the truth, I want the truth, I need to know the truth,*
> *and I speak the truth. It's the best way to go. When you start lying, you*

have to create more lies to cover the original lie. And we know that lies create a lot of hurt among humanity. We see how politicians lie, lawyers lie—in fact, that's what being a lawyer is all about, lying—and we see businessmen lie and never coming up with the goods. So it's a very hurtful thing to do. And the only thing you should never do in the Universe is never injure or harm another living thing. So to uncover the truth is a very beautiful thing, and I've always been a very zealous truthseeker, and I've uncovered many, many lies that are happening.

"So because of this, and because of the presentations that I've put out on Youtube, I've come to the attention of both good people, and people who would love to continue perpetuating the lies, because it does help their agenda and their money-making schemes. So when you start uncovering things that you know you should—because otherwise you would occasion those wrongs—this does hurt the ones that are perpetrating the great lies."

"He who knows of a wrong but does not uncover it, occasions it."

Just as truth is absolute, unwavering and eternal—regardless of whether any one individual believes it or not—so there are laws set into place in the Universe by whatever force it was that created it. The outstanding US researcher Mark Passio refers to this as Natural Law, as do many others. The same dynamic gets expressed under other names, however. The concept is known variously as Universal Law, Karmic Law, the Law of Cause and Effect, and through the notions of 'what goes around comes around,' and 'every action has a reaction.' Parents of young children will recognise the concept played out in the Choices and Consequences method of parenting, where kids are taught that the free-will choices they make carry a resulting consequence, whether good or bad. I prefer to use the Natural Law reference. Mark Passio has a wealth of information on the phenomenon—and so many subject areas related to it—in the many podcasts, videos and articles that are accessible via his hugely resourceful website at www.whatonearthishappening.com

My own understanding of how Natural Law works was summed up in just three words by the Australian researcher Max Igan, (whose equally outstanding work all resides at www.thecrowhouse.com,) offered by way of a simplistic explanation–'Do No Harm.' I'd always had it drummed into me that you should 'treat others the way you'd like to be treated yourself.' But on one of Max's podcasts I heard him point out the logical fallacy behind that often-heard statement. Supposing for argument's sake, Max suggested, you happen to be a homosexual who enjoys bondage, and you happen to live next door to a man who you find sexually attractive, but who doesn't share your preferences. Using the above statement's advice, presumably you would then be justified in forcing yourself and your preferences on that individual, on the grounds that you'd quite like it if one day he came over to your place and did the same to you.

I feel the point was well-made.

In fact, it's an apparent reversal of that statement which holds true to Natural Law, and which can be expressed as: "Do not treat others in a way you would not wish to be treated yourself." The ultimate inherent human right is to be left alone to live your life however you choose, so long as your chosen behaviours do not cause harm to another living being. This way of approaching life has universal applications, and if observed by everyone on the planet, would involve a better way of life for all concerned, with no exceptions. At the most extreme, (except in unavoidable cases of self-defence,) no-one would kill or physically harm another being, on the grounds that no-one, (barring the odd mentally-ill psychopath,) would want that done to them by another.

With characteristic vitriol, Mark Passio illustrated the point wonderfully on a radio interview with David Whitehead on the Truth Frequency Radio network in 2014:

"The bottom line is, if you wouldn't want a person doing a certain behaviour to you, don't do it to another person. The end. And people can't get that simple message. That's the golden rule in the apophatic sense. Do not do to others what you do not want done to you. State the golden rule like that, folks. It's infinitely more powerful than 'do unto others as you would have them do unto you.' When you say it in the negative, in the apophatic sense, it's way more powerful. Because everybody knows how they don't want to be treated.

"Let me pass the buck, let me say it's somebody else's fault. It's because of this reason, it's because I didn't know this, it's because this circumstance was in place, it's because I had to pay this bill, it's because I was worried about what this person would think of me, it's because my wife might leave me, it's because I have a kid to feed . . .

"<u>None</u> of that matters! Zero! I would look every single human being in the face, no matter what their circumstance was, and say it does not matter! And that's not me being on some sort of moral high-horse. It's not me putting myself up on a pedestal. I can make mistakes. What I'm saying is, there is no justification. Everybody, ultimately at some level knows when you're harming someone else, and you have no right to do that to another person. I don't care how much you thought you were allowed to do it, because someone told you, or you believed in this law or that law or the other thing."

And expanding on the principle on Episode 180 of his What On Earth Is Happening podcast:

"The solution is so simple. It always has been. Don't treat others the way you yourself wouldn't want to be treated. State it that way and it becomes real unambiguous, and so simple that a child could figure it out. You don't want to be harmed, defrauded, stolen from, raped, have your rights taken away? Don't do that to other people. Period. <u>The end</u>. It's so simple it's almost stupid, folks. It can't <u>get</u> any simpler than that, and yet humanity has proven we <u>still</u> can't grasp it, we <u>still</u> can't understand it and we want the associated suffering and death that's going to come with refusing to live by that basic rule."

It would even trickle down to the most trivial aspects of human life. Most people don't particularly like having a phone call ignored or being told a lie or an unconvincing excuse, for example. If each of us undertook not to do this to others, therefore, the transformative effect would be profound. Imagine a world where instead of people doing exactly what suits them, in their own individual circumstances, right there and then, their first thought would be 'is there any way in which the action

I'm about to take is likely to impact negatively on others?' Only if the answer is 'no' does the action go ahead.

The 'do no harm' dynamic can be extended by a further four words to: 'Do No Harm, But Take No Shit.' Although apparently a wisecrack, (and probably not a phrase to teach the kids,) this actually contains everything you need to know about how to live life morally and in accordance with eternal truths, in just seven words. This phrase stands as an easily-digestible summing-up of the two central tenets of Natural Law. These are also expressions of the duality of the male and female principles that occur everywhere in nature.

The first is frequently referred to as the Non-Aggression Principle. It is an expression of the sacred feminine, and it represents the 'do no harm' and 'do not treat others in a way you would not wish to be treated yourself' dynamics. It means you respect the right of others to be left alone and to not have coercion brought into their lives against their will, and you yourself can expect the same rights to be afforded to you.

If, however, any individual or institution breaks that principle, then the second key tenet comes into force. This is masculine in nature, and is the Self Defence Principle. This essentially involves any individual doing whatever is necessary to protect themselves, their family and their property against any threat or incursion brought about by a violation of the Non-Aggression Principle. The very embodiment of 'take no shit,' if you prefer. Though I can't help observing that, if everyone were to live life according to the 'do no harm'/ Non-Aggression Principle, there would never actually be any need for the Self Defence/ 'take no shit' Principle to be put to use!

Right and wrong behaviours are absolute, and not open to interpretation, regardless of how repugnant that notion might be to the proud and arrogant human ego. The idea that what constitutes 'truth' is down to the individual, and that one man's take on it is no more or less valuable than the next man's, is known as Solipsism. Truth doesn't do interpretation. It just is.

Personal obligations

Natural Law is the ultimate truth, and it dishes out karmic consequences to humans based on the free-will choices that are made, both on an individual, and a collective basis.

I realise how uncomfortable it will be for many to accept this as being the case. I understand because it was deeply uncomfortable for me when I first came to a realisation of it. But how any individual might feel about it is neither here nor there. Many may choose to reject what I'm putting forward here, in which case, that's their free-will choice and their karma. But everything I've come to discover can be verified and validated with research, and there is a wealth of information available to do just that for anyone with enough of an enquiring mind and a free spirit.

I also do find that an understanding of Natural Law and real truth does tend to answer way more questions than it raises. And with the number of questions my mind has generated over the years, any path that answers a great many of them strikes me as the right one to be on!

Despite how it may at first sound, there's nothing arrogant in stating that you know something to be the truth if it passes all the appropriate filters and methods of discernment. Absolute statements are something that people have a problem with, and some will point to them as being no different to religious dogma, with an adherent of one man-made religion or another defiantly spouting from a lectern that something is the truth because whatever holy book their religion instructs them to believe in tells them so. The *real* truth transcends religious belief systems, and *knowing* something through the gift of intuition with which humans are endowed, is a very different thing to *believing* it to be the case. It is possible to *know* the truth if you choose to align yourself with it.

Another thing that comes with an understanding of truth—and which tends to be equally unpopular with many—is that you also take on a personal responsibility for communicating that knowledge to other people, so they too have the opportunity to come to the same level of awareness. It's necessary for there to be a period of assimilation when an individual first comes across this information, so they can fully collate and process it. But there comes a point where a personal obligation towards helping others to understand what you've learned comes into force, and to absorb and hoard knowledge and spiritual truths for yourself, rather than pass it on to others, is a morally wrong behaviour. With truth comes responsibility. Think about the karmic implications that the elite priest-classes and secret-societies are bringing on themselves through having suppressed information for so many millennia from those they deem unworthy, the 'goyim', and keeping it for the tactical benefit of just the privileged few 'in the know.' The truth is a gift that is intended for everyone. It doesn't come with exclusivity rights.

There are many ways in which truthful information can be communicated, and the most effective method will depend on the skill-sets and personalities of each individual. I'm not much of an in-your-face activist myself, so bellowing through a bullhorn outside some elitist gathering isn't really my thing. It was revelatory and humbling for me to realise that the reason I became a music fan so early in life, and went on to pursue work in DJing, radio and in writing, was to place me right where I needed to be when I came to an eventual understanding of truth.

Someone else may well lack these skills but have others. I'm a hopeless write-off when it comes to technology, but others will be able to use their technical skills to design websites, write software programmes, create graphics or make videos. Others will be brilliant at talking to people on an individual basis and putting forward compelling information in a conversational fashion. The methods aren't important. The fact that you're participating in the process of getting real truth out there in whatever way works best for you, is.

Mark Passio produced a wonderfully on-point podcast addressing this very subject a while back, which I re-posted to my Soundcloud page. As well as the responsibility for communicating truth, he went in acidically on what he calls the AIs, (the appallingly ignorant)–those who avoid personal responsibility for truth despite the wide availability of information–and the SAAQs, (semi-aware armchair quarterbacks.) We all know these. These are individuals who display a degree of understanding of what's really going on in the world, but whose only contribution is to argue with others on chat forums and Facebook threads, concealing their identity with a login name and avatar, and all from the safe comfort of their keyboard. Or they abuse and attack those that *are* communicating helpful information and who have had the balls to do it under their own name. These people are weak cowards, and far worse than those who remain ignorant. One commenter on my page described it as 'the best podcast I've ever heard,' observing that 'nobody could put it better than this.' If I haven't just sold you the idea of taking a listen I don't know what more I can tell you! You'll find it here:

- https://soundcloud.com/mark-devlin/mark-passio-vitriolic-rant

'Ownership' by deception

All humans are born into this 3D reality as free beings, and any claim of ownership over them by any individual or agency is a fiction. Despite this truth, the dark priest-class have indeed duped most of the human population into consenting to their own 'ownership.' This is achieved by way of the so-called 'legal' system that is in place in much of the Western world, and in many other countries such as Australia and New Zealand. Anything that is claimed to be 'legal,' as opposed to 'lawful,' is a fiction. True rights and laws can only be granted by the creative force behind the Universe. Any claim to legality by any man is a fallacy. The system of so-called 'law' in place in most of these countries is derived from the system of Maritime, or Admiralty Law used in England during the seafaring days of Empire. Maritime Law has come to replace Common Law, or the 'law of the land,' which is a system more closely linked to Natural Law and the recognition of the inherent rights to freedom with which all humans are born.

Through clever use of language and the double-meaning of words, the controllers have tricked individuals into having corporate entities created in their name. These corporations remain the wholly-owned property of the Crown Corporation of the City of London, the head of which is the British Monarch. The City of London, (rather like the relationship of the Vatican to Italy and Washington DC to the United States,) is an entirely autonomous State separate from England, with its own Mayor, its own police force, and its own set of 'laws.' When you step into the 'square mile' you are no longer in England. Despite her position as its figurehead, the Queen is required to request permission to enter its territory, and as part of the structure of hierarchy with which the elites seem so obsessed, is considered subservient to the Mayor for as long as she is in the territory. (Readers can make up their own minds as to the symbolic relevance of the dragon statue which marks the entrance to the city's 'square mile,' which is beyond the realms of this particular book!)

This deception, which sees humans signed over as the property of the State and considered akin to seafaring vessels, is achieved ingeniously by way of one particular document . . . the birth certificate. Word-magic is at work here. 'Birth' is phonetically identical to 'berth,' which is what a ship is said to be in when docked, and the meanings are taken to be interchangeable. When a human is born, they are delivered via the 'birth canal,' in the same way that a ship is said to arrive. What well-meaning parents throughout the world have no idea of–because they're not openly told–is that the birth (berth) certificate forms a bonding contract between the parents and the Crown Corporation, whereby the child in question is represented as a corporate entity, separate to the flesh-and-blood sovereign individual. From the moment the contract is signed, that child is considered the property of the State, and bonds are issued and traded on the stock market in his or her name. This is why the individual is then required to apply for documents such as driving licences and passports, and becomes liable to pay taxes. Because within the legal fiction that they have unwittingly been entered into, they are owned property.

This state of affairs can only exist in a fiction, because no individual can truly be owned by any other individual or organisation. An indication of the fact that a corporate entity, rather than the flesh-and-blood being that it represents, is being addressed, is when official Government correspondence spells out the name in capital letters. More double-meaning wordplay here, this style of lettering indicating that the subject is the 'capital,' or property, of the State. This is why communications from the Inland Revenue in particular–along with most other Government departments–always show the recipient's name in capital letters, while their address generally appears in both upper and lower-case.

As far as the system sees it, a contract has been entered into by the parents, through their own free will, stating that their child is now the property of the State. And the use of capital letters is their 'fair warning,' (harking back to the previous concepts of consent,) of what's going on. The fact that you didn't understand is of no consequence to them in their warped mindset. They told you in their own way.

(The issue of ambiguous contracts was the subject of a story which emerged in 2010 when, for an April Fool's Day prank, the retailer Gamestation issued a contract whose Terms & Conditions stated that those signing it undertook to give up their mortal souls. 84 per cent of those receiving the contract duly signed it without noticing what they had just agreed to. There are some clear parallels here with what goes on in the 'real' world on a daily basis.)

Information about this grand method of deception is now freely available on the internet, and has led to huge numbers of individuals seeking to disassociate themselves from their Government 'owners.' It has led to a move towards 'losing the legal name,' in recognition that the identity on a birth certificate is fraudulent and is not truly representative of the individual using it. Those particularly well-informed on how the Maritime Law set-up works, have even started defending themselves in Courts of (fraudulent) Law, arguing that, by renouncing their birth/ berth certificate, they no longer have any contractual ties to the Crown, and are therefore not bound by any of its laws. It remains a fact, however, that very few have been successful in challenging the system on this basis without huge personal cost to themselves and their families. It would be a different story, however, if vast numbers of people were to do so in unison, fully armed with the knowledge of how they have been deceived into a contract that has no legality under Natural Law, the only true and binding law in the Universe. This whole subject area is a complicated minefield, loaded with word=magic, but it *can* be investigated fully on-line by any reader with sufficient curiosity and time to delve into it.

Choices and consequences

For a good couple of years I puzzled, like so many others, over why the 'elites' do some of the seemingly strange things that they do, such as apparently pre-announcing their plans through popular culture, and leaving their symbolic calling-cards everywhere. At all levels of the control system, there are disclaimers such as this, some more blatant than others. We find expressions of it in the small-print at the bottom of financial contracts, in public notices advising you that you're being filmed by CCTV, in the 'side-effects' (so 'effects' then!) documented with pharmaceutical drugs, and with the lists of double-barrelled multi-syllabled chemicals on cans of fizzy drinks. Less obviously, as readers will recall from the chapter on Predictive Programming, we find highly-veiled announcements of the controllers' future false-flag events encoded into Hollywood movies, TV programmes, music videos and record sleeves.

It was only after I came to understand how everything in creation is bound by the workings of Natural Law, that the penny dropped. I realised that when the powers-that-shouldn't-be do such things, it's their sick and twisted way of observing the laws of morality that are built into the construct of the Universe. They feel that by announcing what they plan to do—or what the nature is of something they've already done—they are giving us, the people, the opportunity to raise our objection to it if we so choose. When no such objection is given, the psychopaths feel that they are free, under Natural Law, to go right ahead with what they plan to do, and avoid karmic payback for it. In their diseased, distorted view of things, they take our non-objection to having the Non-Aggression Principle violated, to be our unspoken consent, or tacit approval, for what they've told us they are doing.

There are so many flaws to this way of thinking that it almost defies belief. But, given that we're dealing with a deeply psychopathic mindset, any expectation of true logic, morality of expressions of humanity would be futile.

First of all, to feel the need to cryptically encode any explanation is in direct contravention of the laws of morality. This is duplicity and deliberate obfuscation. With Predictive Programming it would take someone highly skilled in the art of decoding symbols—not to mention with enough time on their hands to constantly study such things—to be able to constantly call the manipulators out on what they feel they've adequately communicated.

Even if their signs and notices were made abundantly clear, they would *still* be in violation of the Non-Aggression Principle, since any form of Government or authority seeking to impose its will on any individual goes right against it. Human beings are born inherently sovereign and free, and have a right bestowed on them by the creative force behind the Universe to live out their lives this way without incursion or coercion. To take someone's lack of disapproval for an action you wish to take–whether you've announced it clearly or not–as a green light for going ahead and violating their right to be left alone–means you've just flown in the face of the moral law of the Universe, and you can now take the karmic consequence for having done so.

It's interesting that, despite their warped interpretation of what Natural Law means for them, and their sheer arrogance in assuming they can cheat its results, the 'elites' still recognise its effects as something to which they at least need to pay lip service. If they didn't, they would steam right ahead and stamp the boot of oppression down on humanity without a thought for needing to cheat the Universe and its methods. It's certainly why these rich old men employ police and military foot-soldiers to do their bidding for them, rather than getting their own hands dirty. While police and military types can often feel superior themselves through the status that their uniform or job title gives them, the truth is that, by following the orders of their superiors unquestioningly–without judging for themselves whether the actions they are about to take are morally right or wrong–*they* are the ones bearing the *personal* karmic consequence for what ensues, not those that gave the orders.

Ever noticed how it's never the sons of politicians and generals that are sent out to die on the frontlines of war zones? We'd be living in a very different world if the police and military would all wake up and understand how they're being cynically manipulated by their superiors, and refuse to do their bidding any longer. There is hope, however, as more and more are leaving the police and military by the week, having come to a difficult understanding of the true nature of what it is they are really a part of.

The reason the controllers have to present apparently acceptable justifications for continually taking our nations to war, is that they know that to blatantly announce that they are going into some foreign nation or other to slaughter and subjugate the population and steal the natural resources, is highly likely to be met with disapproval and resistance from the general public. But portray that foreign nation's leader as a tyrant or despot–particularly one who's 'killing his own people'–to a public whose perceptions of the world are shaped only by what Government ministers and the mainstream media tell them, and the justification for intervention is there. The masses will go along with the 'something must be done' approach, and military action, in which it's clear many thousands will lose their lives, is written off as 'necessary.' Grudging public consent is there, and the manipulators take that as a green light to press ahead with what they'd always planned to do.

The same dynamic can be seen when it comes to paying taxes. The reality is that no-one voluntarily pays tax. We have it extorted from us with the threat of fines or imprisonment if we resist. The very notion of tax is a blatant violation of the Non-Aggression Principle of Natural Law, because it represents the State forcing its will upon individuals. It's made all the more immoral when you understand the true nature of money as debt, too.

But this is another area in which the public gives its consent to an immoral act which goes against human decency and their own common interest. Because the myth that 'taxes are necessary' has been embedded into the public psyche, there's no co-ordinated resistance from people to having their money stolen from them, so again the State takes this as consent and unspoken approval for this act.

Centuries ago, there was a key maxim of Roman Law which stated: "He who would be deceived, let him be deceived." Exactly the same principle is at play here. The statement is saying that anyone ignorant enough not to realise that they are a sovereign spiritual being and an expression of the divine—rather than a corporate entity, and therefore not answerable to any world-based authority—deserves their slavery. They have tacitly consented to their control, because not saying no is taken as having said yes.

The same eternal truths regarding free-will choices and consenting were understood in these past epochs, and were being used by the governmental systems of the day in the same way they are today. Now, as then, so many situations only transpire because the masses are allowing it through their consent. A withdrawing of this consent on a wide, collective basis, is the key to ending slavery and subjugation. When we all learn this lesson and apply it, our shared experiences will change, and not a day before.

501

The numbers game

That such a small number of individuals, when compared to the world population, have been able to successfully control the rest of humanity for so long, seems almost inconceivable. However, there is actually encouragement to be drawn from the fact that they've been able to do it—particularly when you realise that their greatest strength has been their unity of spirit and intent, and their observation of how the nature of reality works.

It's their understanding that everything is made up of resonating light and sound energy that fuels the need to keep their targets—us—in a constant state of low-vibrational fear. And so human society is structured in such a way, with manipulated wars, 'terrorist' events, social conflicts, financial crises, etc, all designed to generate fear and all its negative-energy derivatives—guilt, panic, regret, anxiety, worry, stress, hate, envy, resentment, selfishness, cowardice. And, as we've discovered along the way with this book, the music business plays its part in maintaining this constant low level of consciousness in humanity too. When you factor in the death and suffering that occurs in the non-human world—from the insane bloodbath brought about by the requirements of the food chain that sees millions of living things slaughtered every day, to the *trillions* of animals meeting their terrifying and horrific ends in slaughterhouses—you can imagine the colossal tidal wave of fear-based low vibrations that are going out into the energy field of this reality, 24/7. 'Fear Is The Key', as the title of an Alastair MacLean novel rightly observed.

So it's interesting to muse on what would happen if the elites were to stop performing their Satanic rituals, with all the negativity that they entail. Add that to the concept of a mass humanity awakening to its true nature, and raising its consciousness to a higher level of resonance in its millions, breaking free of the subliminal programming that's been imposed on it, and truly seeing the world for what it is. With this process, we get to see the would-be controllers and their motives for what they really are, and the full potential that we—in our collective numbers—have for shaping the kind of reality that we wish to experience with our positive thought and intent. Then, a very different type of future to the nightmare worldwide concentration camp that's planned for us, starts to come into focus.

A human society awakening in this way, is the route out of our ongoing suffering as a species. If such a small number of 'elites' have been controlling 95-per cent-plus of humanity for so long through pooling their negative intent to influence reality—how few of us would it really take to negate that power, and over-write it with a better version of reality? One that observes the tenets of Natural Law—and specifically the Non-Aggression Principle—and spells a better deal for all humanity? A scenario where 'do no harm' becomes so much of an instinctive norm, that it doesn't even need to be stated? As so many researchers and commentators in this field have observed, and have been trying to tell us for so long, this type of reality is a genuine possibility. It's only a question of whether enough of us make the free-will conscious choice to bring it about, and change our thoughts and behaviours accordingly. This is how reality works—it's a blank canvas waiting to have written on it whatever type of experience is desired by the participants.

This great truth was summed-up brilliantly in an article by John Assaraf on the wakingtimes.com website:

> "All of our interpretations are solely based on the 'internal map' of reality that we have, and not the real truth. Our 'map' is a result of our personal life's collective experiences. Our thoughts are linked to this invisible energy and they determine what the energy forms. Your thoughts literally shift the Universe on a particle-by-particle basis to create your physical life.

> "Look around you. Everything you see in our physical world started as an idea, an idea that grew as it was shared and expressed, until it grew enough into a physical object through a number of steps.

> "You literally become what you think about most. Your life becomes what you have imagined and believed in most. The world is literally your mirror, enabling you to experience in the physical plane what you hold as your truth . . . until you change it."

When you're able to raise your consciousness above the confines of the programming, the old tricks just don't work any more. A Nicki Minaj record can be seen for the toxic piece of mind-controlling garbage that it is, and the cynical lies of a moronic BBC newsreader spouting whatever propaganda their bosses have instructed them to, can be seen for just that. In a society where the majority of the population is perceiving reality in this way–or even just enough of us to reach a critical-mass tipping point–the controllers' version of reality no longer holds its power. This is where we need to be, and *right now* offers the best opportunity humanity has ever had to achieve it. The manipulators recognise this, too. It's no accident that human society has changed so radically in such a short period of time.

A hallmark of the elite class through the generations has been their meticulous planning and their incredible displays of patience. They plan their moves decades, even centuries in advance, knowing in many cases that those of them doing the planning won't be alive by the time their schemes come to fruition. That's the level of focus and dedication towards their cause that these enemies of humanity have displayed. But the rapid reshaping of human society in the past two decades is inconsistent with their calmly-calculated methods. The recent and current unleashing of such a huge arsenal of human-control measures smacks of a desperate attempt to head off humanity's conscious awakening

We have the power, and we can withdraw our consent for their methods any time we choose to. Without our acquiescence and approval, they're finished, and we get the type of future we always should have had in harmony with the moral laws of the Universe. Lenon Honor expressed this sentiment in one of his 'Good Vibrations' interviews in 2013

> *"Now, I recognise that of course there are secret-societies and there are individuals who have agendas. But ultimately, these things would not exist if enough people recognised that there was no need for these things, and so would not participate. In other words, they would not comply. They would not purchase, they would not support these different expressions of these dark, sinister occultic forces. In other words, the power that these forces have is given to them by people. It's not that these forces have power in and of themselves–they have*

no more power than the human species has. But if the human species ultimately <u>gives</u> the power to it, then it will have the power. In other words, it is an aspect of the degree to which this human species has externalised its power. That's where the real problem is.

"All of the degrees of manipulation and mind-control that's going on, you can put it all together, and it still has very little relevance to me in my life in terms of, I am ultimately the power within my life, and ultimately, the creator of my human experience here.

"So with some individuals, you could say, oh, that person is asleep, they don't know what's taking place and they're all caught up in this entertainment industry, externalising power to Jay-Z or Beyonce or Rihanna or whoever. But it can also be applied to the individuals who get so accustomed to analysis as to the dark, sinister occult forces. Because an individual is not focusing on what can <u>they</u> do individually to refine their internal condition so that <u>they</u> can ultimately create something different."

And on a later 'Alchemy Radio' podcast with host John Gibbons, Lenon expanded upon the internalisation-of-power dynamic. This, combined with the example of a life lived in line with truth and morality, is what's needed to arm the next generation with the personal tools that will be necessary to overcome the tyranny that will be attempted against them. The solutions lie in our thoughts, emotions and actions, in balance, on a mass collective scale.

"You should be refining yourself day-by-day as a man or as a woman, working on the thoughts that you keep, the words that you speak and the actions that you take . . . In other words, if you have all these negative thoughts, you're worried about The Illuminati, you're worried about reptilian shapeshifters, you're worried about global bankers, and on and on and on . . . it's going to have an adverse effect on you, because you're always externalising power . . .

"So it's one thing to identify those things, yes, but what's the next step? Well now, you have to <u>internalise</u> to where you begin to take power

of your own destiny. And not only your own destiny, but for future generations, and that's why for positive relationships, that's key . . .

"It should always be about Truth. Speaking Truth. Living Truth. Living an ethically and morally just lifestyle. And in a positive relationship, you have two people doing that. So into that situation, children are being born and raised into this dynamic now."

In my 2014 interview with him, British activist Tony Z mused on the sheer resilience of the human spirit to *still* be able to access higher consciousness in spite of the very best plans that have been laid to keep it locked down.

"Energy, as in the zero-point stuff, is actually consciousness. In other words, if we have access to free energy, we have access to coherence and consciousness, and when we get access to consciousness, nothing can be hidden. So everything becomes revealed. And that's the biggest thing that they're frightened of.

"So what they've needed to do has been to use fluoride, Aspartame, mobile phones, HAARP and all the other frequency-generation systems, to destroy any coherence, to set up a situation whereby the fluoride, for instance, will interfere with your pineal gland to stop it from accessing your higher-self, and expanded consciousness. Because it's in that way that they destroy our ability to understand what's going on. They lie to us, they change all the physics, they come out with false histories, they programme you through television, they give you GMOs, vaccines, all these things to destroy coherence. And what we've actually managed to do is come out the other end <u>still</u> retaining consciousness even after all of their efforts!"

It's sobering to reflect that the adults living in the world today, are the generation that will decide the future course of humanity. It's *our* actions and responses that will determine the type of world our children and all future generations will have to live in. Are we up to the job?

In summing up, and expressing what needs to occur, I can't put it better than the brilliant Matt Hancock, writing for the Check The Evidence blog site, (www.checktheevidence.co.uk):

> *"Collectively, we are inside a burning house, and rather than getting everybody out and safe, we are voting for the next fire-starter. Collectively, we are wasting time and energy on trivia and authorised pastimes, like walking around with our faces in our cellphones, (selfowns,) and Tweeting away like a bird on a wire. While the banksters continue to go unpunished for plundering the public, homelessness, (and increasingly, poverty in general,) is being criminalised. It is madness. Collectively, our toleration of this inhuman control system is insane.*

> *"But the Universe will help those who work according to their life's purpose, so it can and will help many more of us. It is my view that this process can only really be interfered with if we allow somebody else to be the middle-man for us, to provide us with pre-packaged beliefs or world-views, or counterfeit synchronicities in the form of Predictive Programming . . . or any other kind of cunning deceit from the control system in general.*

> *"The authorised controlled opposition (mis)leaders are there to derail us, to interfere with our natural process of realising truth. They have chosen their path, but we are not obliged to give them any attention whatsoever. The individual mind is one of the greatest gifts imaginable, therefore one of the greatest crimes is to steal the ability of that mind to perceive reality. But in a stroke of evil genius, we have been manipulated into giving away our ability to perceive reality. We give it away willingly by listening to liars, believing that they have our best interests at heart simply because, as normal human beings, <u>we</u> would never stoop so low. This is terminally naive and it has to stop.*

> *"We are in a global war right now—an information war, a war on the mind, a spiritual war. Participation in this war is essential, in vast numbers. We need millions upon millions of people to come together and put an end to this insanity, this psychopathic control system, this*

evil. It won't happen overnight—that simply isn't possible—but it can happen over time. The more people there are speaking out, the more likely it is that new people will listen and start to reject the control system they had never previously recognised, and then start to speak out themselves.

"This is a recipe for exponential growth. The hardest part was always going to be getting the immovable object moving. But that has already begun thanks to a multitude of brilliant and selfless human beings, many of whom are no longer with us—at least not here in the realm where spirit meets matter. Thanks to the integrity and the diligence of such people, there is a window of opportunity here, now, like never before. We must take full advantage.

"The alternative is the assisted suicide of the entire human race."

We can have a paradise over a prison-planet, human freedom over slavery and tyranny, any time we collectively choose. One man or woman can't change the world, but they can be an essential component in the process that does. Imagine a person sat alone at home reflecting on how little difference their contribution would make to changing anything. Now imagine 100,000 other people each sitting alone at home thinking the exact same thought. Also, imagine the ripple effect if each person coming to an understanding of great truths imparted this knowledge to just one other person in an 'each one teach one' fashion, then that person imparted it to just one other, and so on . . .

The fork in the road has never been more blatant. In one direction lies a nightmare society ruled by tyranny, oppression and perpetual slavery. In the other, lies a future where humanity finally takes back the reins from the force of evil that's been controlling it for thousands of years. We're hurtling ever closer to this final choice by the day—as a glance at any mainstream news bulletin reminds us—and if the former is allowed to become reality, the future it will bring can be barely be contemplated. How would we explain to our children and grandchildren that we did nothing to prevent it? We still have that opportunity to achieve the latter, however, and it's those of us here today that will decide. No-one else. As Led Zeppelin's 'Stairway To Heaven' puts it: 'There's still time to change the road you're on.'

Only one question remains, therefore: How much do we want it?

Resources:

Mark Passio's hugely detailed website:

- www.whatonearthishappening.com

Max Igan's website:

- www.thecrowhouse.com

Check The Evidence blog site: Everything But The Kitchen Synch:

Part 1:

- http://www.checktheevidence.co.uk/cms//index. php?option=com_content&task=view&id=399&Itemid=76

Part 2:

- http://www.checktheevidence.co.uk/cms/index. php?option=com_content&task=view&id=400&Itemid=76

Part 3:

- http://www.checktheevidence.co.uk/cms/index. php?option=com_content&task=view&id=401&Itemid=76

THE SOUND OF FREEDOM

TSOF is a free, fortnightly showcase of conscious music, old and new, compiled by Mark Devlin. It stands as the inspiring antithesis to the corporate agenda, offering meaningful music by switched-on, awakened artists.

The full archive so far is available at:

- http://soundcloud.com/mark-devlin/sets/ the-sound-of-freedom-the-full

TSOF can also be found on Mixcloud, Podomatic, and iTunes.

GOOD VIBRATIONS

A free, ongoing series of conversation-based podcasts, covering a huge array of topics within the truth/ conspiracy/ consciousness/ spirituality fields.

The entire archive so far is available at:

- http://soundcloud.com/mark-devlin/sets/ good-vibrations-podcast-series

CONTACTING THE AUTHOR

The author welcomes all feedback and communication, (as long as it's polite,) to the following e-mail address, and guarantees a personal reply to all messages received:

- mark@markdevlin.co.uk

- www.markdevlin.co.uk

- www.youtube.com/markdevlintv

- www.musicaltruthbook.com

- www.twitter.com/musical_truth_

Index

Made in the USA
Middletown, DE
17 March 2024

51050505R00298